From the Many to the One

The Society for the Humanities
Cornell University

Studies in the Humanities
Edited by Max Black

FROM THE MANY TO THE ONE

From the Many to the One

*A Study of Personality and Views of Human Nature in
the Context of Ancient Greek Society, Values, and Beliefs*

A. W. H. Adkins

Cornell University Press
ITHACA, NEW YORK

First published 1970 by arrangement with Constable and Company Ltd, 10 Orange Street, London W.C.2.

International Standard Book Number 0–8014–0604–8
Library of Congress Catalog Card Number 76–127774

Printed in Great Britain

ERIC ROBERTSON DODDS

in whose steps must follow all who
wish to understand the ancient Greeks

Contents

Contents

Preface

This book is concerned with Greek views of human nature: it is a study of personality and views of human nature in the context of ancient Greek society, values and beliefs. In writing such a book, I have wished to make its contents available not only to those whose primary interest is in Greek civilisation, and who know Greek, but also to those who, having no Greek, are interested in the kind of questions raised by the discussion of human nature, and who desire to pursue their interest in the context of ancient Greece. For the reasons set out in the first chapter, it seems to me to be necessary, in order to discuss these questions in the ancient Greek context, to study in some detail a restricted number of important Greek words. To enable the Greekless reader to read the book, these words are transliterated. I am, of course, aware that it is more difficult for the Greekless reader to read a book of this nature than one which uses English words throughout; but I would contend, and hope that any Greekless readers will agree with me, that some of the points I am trying to make here could only be made at much greater length, while others – and those some of the most important – could not be made at all, if this method were not used.

Of the making of books on human nature there is no end, and will be no end; for no one book can examine from more than one point of view a landscape which at every step has always some new prospect to offer. Those readers who wish to survey the Greek portion of this landscape further would be well advised to begin by reading, if they have not done so already, E. R. Dodds, *The Greeks and the Irrational* (Berkeley 1951), B. Snell, *The Discovery of the Mind* (translated from the German by T. G. Rosenmeyer, Blackwell 1953), and Alvin W. Gouldner, *Enter Plato* (New York and London 1965). All of these works are accessible to the Greekless. From their authors the reader will obtain penetrating and perceptive surveys of this varied countryside from three different points of vantage, on the basis of which he will be able to construct for himself a more three-dimensional and detailed picture. From all three I have learned much about human nature in the Greek context, by no means all of which, as will be immediately apparent to anyone who reads their works, appears in this book, though this too is a study of human nature in the Greek context: any work which discusses human nature in any context must have its criteria of relevance dictated by the particular viewpoint on which its author elects to take his stand. Any author who endeavoured to say everything on the subject would end by saying nothing.

It will be evident that in this book I am the debtor not only of my own profession, but also of the specialists in semantics, anthropology, sociology, and psychology, from whom I have learned much. The debt remains, even if, as may well be the case, no specialist in any of these fields would countenance the use I have made in this work of what I have learned; and it is gratefully acknowledged.

More specifically, it gives me great pleasure to acknowledge my debt to Professor E. R. Dodds, to whom my thanks are due once again, as on so many occasions in the past. To reading this work in typescript he has generously devoted more of his time than I could have hoped for, and his many searching and illuminating comments have not only enabled me to remove numerous errors, but have also enhanced my understanding of the subject. (On some occasions I have remained obdurate in my heresies: for these, and for all errors of detail which remain, I alone am responsible.) To him I also owe my epigraph, which had not been consciously present to my mind in choosing the title for this work, but whose existence leads me to hope that my observations on Greek personality may not be entirely alien from Greek experience. With great respect and affection this book is dedicated to him, to whom my developing understanding of the Greeks has long owed, and continues to owe, so much.

My thanks are due also to my wife, who read the work in the interests of the general reader and drew my attention to many obscurities of exposition, some of which I have been able to remove; to Mrs. Barbara Anderson, who conjured an elegant typescript from my tangled and maculate longhand; to Mrs. A. G. Conner, for assistance in retyping corrected sheets; and to Mrs. Betty Tamminen and Mrs. Olga Vrana for typing and a variety of other forms of assistance in the later stages of preparation of the typescript.

Preface

This work received its final revisions, the proofs were read and the indexes made, during the academic year 1969–70, which I spent at Cornell University as a Senior Visiting Fellow of the Society for the Humanities. It gives me very great pleasure to be able to thank here Cornell University, the Society for the Humanities and its Director, Professor Max Black, for their warm and friendly welcome, their manifold kindnesses and generosities, and for the leisure accorded to me not only to complete this book but also to pursue many other projects in conditions ideal for research, in a magnificently equipped library, on what must be one of the most beautiful university campuses anywhere.

Note on Transliteration

A few words are needed to explain my transliterations. These are direct: each Greek letter is represented by its equivalent in the Roman alphabet, whether or no the English pronunciation of that letter coincides with that of the Greek. This has resulted in a few apparent anomalies: for example, the word normally spelt 'psyche' in English appears as *psūchē*; but as the Greek word has implications quite different from those of 'psyche', the distinction in spelling seems to me to be an advantage. In general, I have marked long vowels on the first occasion of a word's appearance. Short vowels are not marked at all. except in the case of words like *nŏŏs* (p. 14) and *prŏēgmena* (p. 226), where the Greekless reader might well otherwise pronounce the two vowels together, and to distinguish *ĕthos*, etc., from *ēthos*, etc. (p. 182). Where the spelling of adjective and adverb differs only in the quantity of the final 'o' – e.g. *kakos* and *kakōs* – I have always marked the long 'o' of the adverb. For greater simplicity, nouns and adjectives are usually quoted in the nominative, singular or plural, verbs in the infinitive. However, *phusis* is occasionally quoted in the dative, *phusei*, since the usage in this case is so characteristic of those Greeks who discuss *nomos* and *phusis*.

Pronunciation need present few difficulties, provided that it is remembered that there are no unpronounced vowels in Greek, i.e. that a word like *psūchē* is disyllabic. Apart from this, there is no agreed pronunciation of Greek among scholars in Britain; for example, different scholars pronounce 'ē' as in 'three', as in 'whey', or (roughly) as in 'bear'. In pronouncing Greek words, the Greekless reader will be well advised to adopt a stress accent, as in pronouncing English, and to place it on whatever syllable his knowledge of Latin or Italian leads him to believe plausible. This accent will be wrong, frequently in position, always in kind, for the Greeks of the classical period employed a pitch accent; but as the resulting pronunciation will bear a close resemblance to that of the majority of classical scholars educated in these islands, including the present writer, the Greekless reader may presumably be forgiven for using it.

Foreword

During the period discussed in this work the psyche of the Greek, as revealed in literature, seems to have gradually developed a more stable unity out of what is at first a seething multiplicity; the political units in which he lived, at first a multiplicity of virtually autonomous households, then city-states of moderate size, were amalgamated and absorbed into great empires; and he, from feeling himself a member of a group small enough for his contribution to its activities to be noticeable, came to feel himself alone, face to face with powerful forces over which he had no control. For all these reasons, but particularly the first, this work is entitled *From the Many to the One*; and I take as my epigraph the words of Plato in the fourth book of his *Republic*,

Having become one person instead of many

1. The Concept of Human Nature

A. The Concept in General

We use the phrase 'human nature' in a variety of types of context in modern English; and it is doubtful whether the majority of us could offer a definition of the phrase which would cover all of its usages. The development of such a definition, however, is not a function either of this chapter or of this book: though the book may – and, it is my hope, will – incidentally throw some light on the manner in which we use the phrase in our own culture, if only in virtue of certain differences between our own usage and that of the Greeks, the purpose of this book is to discuss views of human nature among the Greeks. ('Views', not 'view': as will soon become apparent, the Greeks differed widely from one another on the subject.) Nevertheless, the range of our usage of 'human nature' is immediately important; for that range will suggest to the reader the range of topics which he will expect to find discussed in a treatment of the concept in any society. 'Human nature', then, we may say in preamble, may at different times advert to, or light may be thrown on a society's view of it by:

(1) The psychological model of the human being.
(2) The physiological model of the human being.[1]
(3) The view of the relationship of mankind to the animal kingdom.
(4) The basic chemical and physical picture of the organism, in relation to the chemical and physical picture of the cosmos as a whole.
(5) The view of the individual's relationship to society as a whole, and to other groups within the society; the relative importance of different groups; and the values used to maintain the situation, and challenge and reprehend any attempted subversion of, or divergence from, the values.

[1] (1) and (2) may well be linked closely; and in the Homeric poems, as we shall see, they are virtually indistinguishable.

(6) The view of the relationship between man and his gods.

(7) The eschatological view of man's position in the cosmos.

Our use of 'human nature' is implicitly or explicitly linked at different times to our views of *at least* these seven subjects: even those who regard (6) and (7) as meaningless are, in taking such a view, defining their view of human nature thereby; and certainly (6) and (7) are important for the discussion of most known societies at most periods.

Again, whether we are discussing our own society or another, we may use any of these seven categories to throw light on that society's view of human nature in an emotively neutral manner, observing how one belief is linked with another to furnish a view, or views, of human nature, more or less coherent, characteristic of the society in question; and we may further observe how that view or views affects human behaviour in the society. Even the values of the society, mentioned in (5), may be studied as a system of pressures of greater or less strength. However, for anyone holding them within the society they are of course not emotively neutral. They throw much light on a society's view of human nature, for the most powerful word of value used to commend an individual in any society indicates, in a manner which I shall discuss below, the society's highest expectations from him, and hence its views of human nature at its best. But in fact any one of these categories may be employed to furnish persuasive and protreptic arguments: from our view of the characteristics a human being possesses *qua* human being, we readily pass to a view of the manner in which he ought to behave;[1] so that 'human nature' readily becomes a normative and emotionally loaded term.[2] So (1), (2), (3) and perhaps (4) above could be used to commend certain kinds of behaviour as 'natural', and in some circumstances could be set against views of the requirements of human nature expressed in terms of (6) and (7).

B. Language, 'Meanings' and Values

In studying 'human nature' in any culture, then, we should certainly interrogate the material in terms of the categories already mentioned;

[1] Whether or no this is philosophically justifiable, it is a commonplace of thought; and we are concerned here with actual thought-patterns, not only with valid ones.

[2] An extreme example would be 'It's agin human nature to fly. If the Almighty had intended us to fly, He would have given us wings.'

but if we do no more than this, we shall arrive at an unnecessarily external picture of the culture. In the remainder of this chapter I shall endeavour to indicate a method whereby a less external view may be obtained; a method which is employed in the subsequent chapters. This section is prefatory, and contains no theory which will be unfamiliar to any students of even the most rudimentary semantics; but it is a necessary foundation to the rest of the work.

The concern of this book is to discover the Greek view, or rather views, of human nature. Views of human nature, as of anything else, are necessarily carried by language, by words; and if we think seriously about this not very surprising observation, we may be drawn to wonder how we know 'what the Greek words mean', and further, what we mean when we assert that we do know this, or that we 'know Greek'; and, for reasons already apparent, we should ask this question not only in respect of words in general, but also in respect of value-words, which pose their own problems.

However, it will be best to begin with words in general in English, and enquire what it means to 'know English'; or, an even more basic question, what we mean when we say that the word CAT 'has the "meaning" "cat"'. Evidently we do not mean that *anyone* on reading the letters CAT, or hearing the sound produced by pronouncing them, 'perceives the meaning' and thinks of an animal with silky fur, four legs, retractable claws and a long wavy tail. For to 'perceive the meaning' is not at all like perceiving the cat: some knowledge is required. If I say that an acquaintance knows English, and a friend denies it, we should discover which of us is right by going to the acquaintance and finding out whether, for example, on being faced with an animal with silky fur, four legs, retractable claws and a long wavy tail, he used the symbol 'cat', whether in speech or writing, to refer to it. Knowing the meaning of CAT is not knowing some strange thing which CAT has – a meaning – it is knowing how to use the symbol 'cat' when speaking or writing English.

We may now turn to the implications of saying that the Greek word *ailouros* 'means' 'cat'. Having begun with the trivial example of CAT 'meaning' 'cat', we need not now be tempted to say that '*ailouros*' and 'cat' both refer to some strange thing, the 'meaning', to which each is connected. We can now say simply that, on being

3

faced with an animal with silky fur, four legs and so on – in short, with a cat – the ancient Greek said or wrote *ailouros* if he wished to refer to it. If we now imagine an ancient Greek and a modern Englishman, neither knowing the other's language, both looking at the same cat, and the one saying, writing or thinking '*ailouros*', the other saying, writing or thinking 'cat', we see quite clearly that though *ailouros* 'means' 'cat' (I shall discuss this later) there is no 'meaning' in the situation with which both are in contact. The only thing common to the two situations is the cat, and the fact that each is taking notice of it and in the simplest sense thinking about it. The Englishman is using 'cat' to refer to a silky-furred animal with four legs, retractable claws and so on, and to link this experience of such an animal with earlier similar experiences; and if *ailouros* behaves in exactly the same manner in ancient Greek, the situation is exactly the same for the ancient Greek. (As will appear, 'similar' and 'exactly the same' require further discussion; but certainly the Greek too is using his word to refer to the animal and to link this experience with others.)

Considerations of this kind are relevant not only to those philosophising about the nature of language and meaning: due weight should be given to them by anyone who has to translate from one language into another. If one thinks of words as having 'meanings', the fact that 'meaning' is a noun tends to make one think of a meaning as a thing, as though a word were a kind of pin-cushion and the meaning were a pin with a label on it stuck into the pin-cushion. Now as soon as one begins to learn a second language it becomes apparent that a single word may 'have more than one meaning'; and if one has the pin-cushion picture, one thinks rather in terms of selecting the appropriate little label from the foreign pin-cushion which gives the sense required in the English sentence. If we take as an example the Greek word *aretē*, a word which will be important in the subsequent discussion, we shall find in the lexica that in different contexts it 'has the meanings' 'courage', 'skill', 'success', 'prosperity', 'strength'. If we are translating *arete* into English, we can normally use only one of these words to translate it; and if we have the pin-cushion picture, we shall only concern ourselves with the label we select, not with the others: after all, one can remove a single pin from a pin-cushion without disturbing any of the other pins; and we may well not wonder

4

why this pin-cushion should contain precisely these pins and no others. Furthermore, we are likely to assume incautiously that the Greeks were conscious of the pins and labels too, and that each time they used *arete* with what we should consider to be a different meaning, they were conscious of this.

Such an assumption is misleading and confusing, and interposes a barrier between ourselves and the Greeks (or any other people we are studying). Our reason for saying that the word 'has two meanings' is that we find it necessary to use different words in English to render it on different occasions; but the Greeks were under no such necessity, and were unaware that we, in speaking modern English, would experience it. The most reasonable assumption to make is that the Greeks, in using the same word where we use different ones, observed and were concerned to emphasise resemblances in their experience which, for one reason or another, appear less important to us. The point requires careful statement. The Greeks used the one word *kleis* of keys and collar-bones. It should not be inferred, evidently, that the Greeks could discern no difference between keys and collar-bones; though even in the case of such physical objects the choice of words indicates certain resemblances detected by the Greeks between *their* keys and collar-bones. In the case of words of this type, little that is important is likely to be lost in translation from one language to another on most occasions: though even here the interpreter should not neglect this possibility, and should especially have it in mind when studying poets: one of the poet's principal resources is to activate the overtones of words, derived from their range of usage, as fully as possible; and ancient poets were not unaware of this.

However, not all words are of this type. In this study we shall be concerned with such psychological terms as *psūchē* and *thūmos* which, though they have conventional equivalents 'soul' and 'spirit', differ very much in usage from the English words; and indeed different English words are used on different occasions by translators to render them. Similarly, *phusis*, conventionally rendered by 'nature', has a different range of usage from the English word. In the case of such words as these, there is no physical object to which we can readily point to define the term, and to render likely an approximation in 'meaning' between the words used in different languages: the manner in which the word behaves indicates, and goes far to mould, the manner in which its users thought of the phenomenon in question.

In these circumstances, it becomes doubly important not to speak of a word in a foreign language as having a number of 'meanings', but to think of it as a tool which has uses. No-one will suppose that a usage of a word is a thing; attention will be directed on the word as something that persists through its usages, and we may be induced to enquire why the word has precisely these usages, neither more nor less; and the range of usage of a word is a most important clue to the understanding of the people in whose language and culture it appears.

The word 'cat' will serve as a trivial illustration. One might suppose that so simple a word could never lead to misunderstanding. If we show a tabby cat to two of our English-speaking friends, and each says 'That is a cat', they must surely mean the same thing. But suppose one of our friends is an elderly maiden lady, the other a keeper from the London Zoo professionally concerned with lions, tigers and other *felidae*: if we now take them to see a lion or a tiger, the keeper may well reply 'That is a cat', while the elderly maiden lady is unlikely to do so. So when they agree that the tabby cat is a cat, they do not 'mean' the same thing by 'cat' on that occasion either. The reason is clear: the range of instances in which they are accustomed to use the symbol 'cat' is different. The experiences which the symbol calls to mind when they hear it or see it, and to which in using it they wish – or in the case of the maiden lady seeing the lion, do not wish – to link their present experience, are different.

We may now turn to the man who knows both ancient Greek and English, and says '*ailouros* "means" "cat"'. It is now evident that the man, in this situation, has two symbols, one English, the other Greek, to choose from when he has the experience of a silky-furred animal with four legs, retractable claws and a wavy tail and wishes to register it as such; and if he is to be entirely correct in his assertion that '*ailouros* "means" "cat"', the range of usage of the Greek and English symbols must be identical. For, returning to the Zoo keeper and the maiden lady, we observed that the *same* word had a different 'meaning' for them because they applied it to a different though overlapping range of instances. Now it is evident that in translating from one language into another we are frequently placed either in the position of the

Zoo keeper or in that of the maiden lady. That is to say, the English word by which we render a foreign one may have a wider or a narrower range (or a different range but one similar in scope) than the word we are using as an equivalent for it. On every occasion on which this occurs we are losing *something* in translation. In the case of a word like 'cat' or 'collar-bone', this is usually trivial and unimportant; but when we are concerned with words like *psuche*, *thumos* or *phusis*, it is of the utmost importance. The range of these words indicates the nature of the concept in Greek; and there is no one visible or tangible object to act as a control on the usage. *Psuche*, *thumos* and *phusis* correlate together phenomena that we classify differently: there is no English equivalent. Accordingly, we have no concept of *psuche*, *thumos* or *phusis*; and to use English words merely falsifies the situation. In this book, therefore, such key words as are *importantly* untranslatable will not be translated, but transliterated; and the manner of their usage in Greek will become apparent in the course of the discussion. (We shall also see that the range of the terms varies in Greek during the period covered by this book: the concepts *thumos*, *psuche* and *phusis* are not constant.) This is highly significant: if neither *phusis* nor any other Greek word has the same range as 'nature' in English, no Greek can discuss precisely what we mean by human nature, for the terminology is not available; and if he uses *phusis*, his discussion, as will appear, will be influenced by the total range of *phusis* in Greek. The 'meanings' supplied by lexicographers do not advance, and do much to hinder, our understanding of the kind of phenomena discussed in this book: by breaking up into fragments the unity of the Greek word they impose an alien structure on the material, and conceal its true structure.

In saying this, I do not of course wish to deny that one can – or that the Greeks could – analyse words in one's own language, and draw distinctions between one usage and another. Aristotle frequently does this; and in the ancient world there are later Greek lexica of earlier Greek, necessitated by marked changes in the range of usage of words during the development of ancient Greek. But – particularly in the case of psychological and similar terms, where no one physical object is directly denoted, or ethical terms, for reasons to be discussed below – the onus of proof that any Greek of the period treated in this book did clearly distinguish (say) one usage of *psuche* from another, though he does not explicitly do so,[1] rests with those who contend that this is the case; for this is the less plausible view, and seems in conflict with the indications of the study carried out in these pages.

This is one interpretative tool; but it is not the only one necessary in discussing the kind of words relevant to this book. As has been said, religious, ethical and political terms must be considered; and the treatment of these in different languages and cultures raises further problems. For value-words are words of a very special kind. Indeed, it may be felt that what has been said about linking up previous experiences of silky-furred animals with this experience of a silky-furred animal has little relevance to words like 'good' and 'bad', which seem to be applied much more freely than words like 'cat', 'horse' or 'elephant'. However, any such word of general commendation will, in any society – or, in a pluralistic society, in any group whose members share common values – be applied not at random but to persons or events possessing certain definite characteristics. To say this is not to assert that in enunciating the propositions 'that is a good man' and 'that is a good apple' one is implying that there is any characteristic shared by the apple and the man. We are concerned with instances of the same kind: if one says 'Jones is a good man and so is Brown', one is conveying one's judgment that Jones and Brown have some characteristics in common in virtue of which one is prepared to commend them by calling them 'good men'. In saying 'Jones is a good man' one is conveying the judgment 'Jones possesses the qualities a, b, c and so on, and I (or my society) approve of these qualities'; and in saying 'Brown is a good man' one is conveying the same judgment about Brown. (To analyse the situation in this manner does not, as is sometimes assumed, imply that one has not a 'good reason' for approving precisely the qualities that one does approve, as will become apparent in the subsequent chapters.) One will not approve of the same qualities in men and in apples; but in the case of men or apples they must remain the same over a period of time, at all events for oneself, or communication becomes impossible.

[1] Some thinkers draw explicit distinctions, as is to be expected; e.g., Aristotle distinguishes types of *psuche*, pp. 173 ff., and of *phusis*, pp. 172 ff. and 178 ff.; while the Stoics have several uses of *phusis*, pp. 217 ff.

The application of value-words in practice is, of course, somewhat more complex than this. The *full* range of human qualities a, b, c . . . n commended by 'good' will not, in the nature of things, be possessed by many individuals. Two responses to this situation are possible: one may either restrict the application of the word to those few individuals who do possess all the qualities, or employ it to commend those whom the commender deems to merit such commendation on the basis of those qualities, out of the whole range commended by the word, which they do possess. 'Commended by the word' is important, for the possession of a quality not included among those commended by the word evidently does not entitle one to commendation by the word: if one's being good is not affected by one's success in English, then it is pointless to adduce one's success to prove that one is good, and if one's being *agathos* is unaffected by one's justice in early Greek it is pointless to adduce one's justice to prove that one is *agathos*. However, some of the qualities which are commended by 'good' or *agathos* may be deemed to be dispensable in a particular instance by a particular commender provided that other qualities, deemed to be indispensable, are present. Only empirical observation will reveal this; but as a consequence Jones and Brown may not have *identical* commendable characteristics, even though the same person is using the same word of commendation, though they must have qualities drawn from those commended by the word, some of which are likely to be held to be so important that the use of the word virtually guarantees that Jones and Brown each possess them, or that the commender believes this to be the case. This concession to human frailty may evidently affect the application of any value-word in any language. In the present study, however, it is the full range of the value-words, and the qualities included in or excluded from that range at any period, that throw most light on the discussion.

It should now be evident that, when it is maintained that the Greek word *agathos* 'means' 'good', this proposition enunciates something much more complex than '*ailouros* "means" "cat".' To say '*ailourous* "means" "cat"' is to say that, faced with the same silky-furred animal, an ancient Greek will say '*ailouros*', an Englishman 'cat'. But to say that *agathos* 'means' 'good' is to say that, wishing to express high approval of a man, an ancient Greek said '*agathos*', whereas a modern

Englishman says 'good'. It is not to say anything about the qualities in virtue of which the ancient Greek terms his favoured man *agathos*, the Englishman his favoured man 'good'. Accordingly, in the case of a word like *agathos* it is even more important than in the case of words like *psuche* and *thumos* not to speak of 'meanings' but to examine the range of the word and discover the qualities in virtue of which it is applied: only in this manner can one discover what anyone who used the word wished to convey. There is no reason which can be adduced *a priori* why ancient Greek and modern Englishman should approve of men in virtue of their possession of the same qualities, though many writers on the ancient Greeks have tacitly assumed that this is so. The qualities in virtue of which they do apply the words will be determined by the general world view, and the view of mankind, which each possesses; and this is an important indicator of that world-view, and view of mankind. As will be seen, the behaviour of value-terms both reflects the world-view and also helps to mould it.

Again, any language contains a number of different words for approving or disapproving of men in virtue of their possession of different qualities. In different circumstances we might approve of a man by terming him 'good', 'just', 'honourable', 'successful', and so on, or disapprove of him by using the contraries of these words. Now all these words are value-words, applied in virtue of the presence or absence of certain qualities; and approval may be more or less powerful, so that if a man qualifies, in virtue of the characteristics he possesses, for the application of one of these value-terms but not for another, or qualifies for one term of approval, one of disapproval, there may well arise the question which is the more important, and more powerful. Take the phrases 'poor but honest' and 'clever but shifty'. Evidently anyone using these phrases in this form values honesty more highly than wealth, since the inapplicability of 'rich' does not prevent the phrase from conveying, on balance, approval; and honesty more highly than cleverness, since the applicability of 'clever' does not prevent the phrase from conveying, on balance, disapproval. These two examples seem quite obvious to us, since we have a gradu-ated scale of values which most of us never analyse; but we must not forget that other societies, particularly those far removed in space and time, may have other scales of values which they never analyse.

Thirdly, it is necessary to distinguish two broad groups of qualities in virtue of which men may be approved or censured. In any society there are activities in which success is the criterion; in these commendation or the reverse is reserved for those who actually succeed or fail. In the evaluation of such activities, what a man intended to do is of little account: no-one intends to fail. We do not say – not, that is, unless we are being consciously epigrammatic, and using the words to convey a sense different from that which they normally bear – 'X is a good general but he never wins battles' or 'Y is a good tennis player but he always loses'. To be a good general or a good tennis player is to be successful. On the other hand, in any society there are also those activities, such as contracts or partnerships, in which men co-operate with one another for a common end. Since the only basis for co-operation is justice and fairness – however these may be evaluated in the society in question – it is in terms of justice, or some similar word, that the relationships of men who co-operate will be evaluated. If we say 'he was the best player at that Wimbledon', we intend to convey that he defeated or was capable of defeating any other tennis player who was present at Wimbledon in that year. But if we say 'he is a good citizen', we mean that he acts justly towards other citizens. Co-operation, and breaches of co-operative excellences, raise questions different from those of success or failure. 'Did you mean to lose (or win) that game of tennis?' is normally a question not worth asking; but 'Did you intend to shoot him or were you really aiming at a rabbit?' is a perfectly sensible question, even though there may be societies in which the answer makes no difference to the treatment the killer receives. Co-operation and competition, then, entail very different attitudes to intentions.

Now terms of value must of necessity be applied to both groups of activities, competitive and co-operative. The activities are very different in kind, and approval or disapproval is given in terms of very different criteria. In fact, we in English use 'good' and 'bad' in both groups; but it is clearly possible – and, as will appear, it is the case in early Greek – that in a different society there might exist two[1] sets of value-terms, the one confined in use to commending and de-

---

[1] Or more. In Greek at some periods *dikaion*, *kalon* and *agathon* all have different types of criteria. See my *Merit and Responsibility* (Clarendon Press 1960), pp. 225 f.

crying competitive activities (successes and failures), the other to commending and decrying co-operative activities. In such circumstances, it is best to distinguish these groups as competitive values commending competitive excellences (or decrying their absence) and co-operative values similarly related to co-operative excellences.

If we take all these points together, it should become clear that it is of the utmost importance to study the range of usage of value-terms, for only in this way can we discover what is being commended; and that we need to know which of these value-terms are the most powerful, so that we know what qualities are held to be characteristic of the human being at his best. The relevance of the distinction between competitive and co-operative excellences will become clearer as the discussion proceeds: not only does it help to elucidate the value-system of the society, the form which that system takes in Greek society also, as I shall argue, profoundly affects the personality structure found among the ancient Greeks, revealed by the behaviour of *psuche*, *thumos* and similar words. The study of these words along with the key Greek words of value will serve to render less external our study of the Greek views of human nature; and when this is added to discussion of the questions raised in the first part of this chapter the reader will, it is hoped, be offered a discussion at once familiar, in that it raises the kinds of question expected and at the same time faithful to *Greek* views of human nature, in that it raises them in terms appropriate to the Greek pattern of concepts and values.

2. The Homeric World

A. Introductory

The Homeric poems are the product of a long oral tradition of bardic poetry. Their sources are saga and folk-tale; and neither from these, nor from oral epic itself, is a sustained analysis of their authors' view of human nature to be expected. Such bards have different concerns. Their compositions, however, bear witness none the less to a view of human nature whose several aspects are remarkably coherent, as will appear.

In these discussions 'Homeric man' and 'Homeric society' refer to the human beings and society portrayed in the Homeric poems. It is unnecessary to discuss here the extent to which these poems mirror any actual society of ancient Greeks. For later Greeks they portrayed the values and behaviour of the Heroic Age of Greece, and thus undoubtedly represent one of the Greek views of human nature and its possibilities. In the opinion of the present writer, the coherence of the phenomena discussed in this chapter argues powerfully that they, at least, are rooted in historical reality, even if no event described in the poems ever took place.

B. Homeric Psychology and Physiology

Our clue to Homeric psychology and physiology must be the manner in which the poems use certain words. These must be studied without importing preconceptions from other cultures; for, if we suppose that our own everyday presuppositions and use of psychological words are 'common sense', and that the phenomena must always have presented themselves in this manner to the man in the street, we may not take Homeric psychological language seriously. We may insist that the language is merely poetic, particularly as similar expressions occur in a fossil state in certain kinds of English poetry; and we may forget that the reason why a phrase is coined in the first place is likely to be that it expresses better than anything else that has occurred to its author what he is trying to say. All fossils were once alive; and

13

Homeric psychological language finds a suitable habitat in the Homeric world as a whole.

The most important words are *psuche, thumos, kradiē, ētor, kēr, phrenes* and *nŏŏs*. I begin with *psuche*, since it becomes the most important word in later chapters, and 'psychology' is derived from it. In Homer, however, it is less important. It has been said that its *esse* is *superesse*, that its role is simply to survive death, that it has no function in the living human being; and indeed it is the *psuche* which leaves the body at death, through the mouth (*Iliad* IX, 409), through a wound (*Iliad* XIV, 518), or simply from the limbs (*Iliad* XXII, 362). To say that the *psuche* left the body is to say that the human being (*Iliad* V, 696) or the animal (*Odyssey* XIV, 426) died; and no return of the *psuche* is possible (*Iliad* IX, 408).[1] Having left the body, the *psuche* passes, when the appropriate rites have been performed, down to Hades (see below, p. 33). However, though it is inactive in the living individual, the Homeric Greeks are conscious of its presence: Agenor reflects (*Iliad* XXI, 569) that Achilles has only one *psuche*, and that he might be killed; Achilles complains (*Iliad* IX, 322) that he is forever staking his *psuche* in war; and (*Iliad* XXII, 161) Achilles and Hector as they ran round Troy were contending for Hector's *psuche*. Homeric man is aware that he possesses a *psuche* while he is alive.

His *psuche* is not his self, or his personality. (It is, as will appear, in many ways almost devoid of personality.) Achilles says (*Iliad* IX, 401) that all the treasures of Troy are not worth his *psuche* to him; he and his *psuche* are separable in his mind.

We may of course render some of these uses of *psuche* by 'life', others by 'ghost'; but in thus using different words we misrepresent the position, for Homeric man used the same word in all the instances, and the presumption is that all appeared alike to him; whereas the range, and consequently the overtones, of 'life' and 'ghost' are very different in English, and break up in translation what in Homeric Greek is one. The *psuche*, then, is an individual while he lives, and departs at death to continue an existence (to be discussed later) in Hades. Patroclus' *psuche*, before his body is buried, comes to Achilles in a dream (*Iliad* XXIII, 65):

[1] Andromache 'breathes out her *psuche*' in a swoon, *Iliad* XXII, 467; and this is clearly remediable. But this is an unusual usage.

There came to him the *psuche* of wretched Patroclus, like him in every respect, in size and beautiful eyes and voice, dressed in just such clothes as he used to wear.

The *psuche* of Patroclus looks and sounds just like Patroclus in life. The differences are expounded by Odysseus' mother when Odysseus calls her *psuche* up from the dead (*Odyssey* XI, 216 ff.):

My son, most hapless of all mankind, Persephone, daughter of Zeus, is not cheating you. No, this is the way of it for mortals when they are dead: the sinews no longer hold together the flesh and bones. The mighty fire subdues them, when once the *thumos* has left the white bones, while the *psuche* has flown away like a dream.

Since the *psuche* looks and sounds like the living person, Odysseus had expected other characteristics to persist, and had attempted to embrace his mother; but the *psuche* flew off 'like a shadow or a dream'; and Odysseus lamented that Persephone had cheated him with a mere image of his mother.

Neither Homer nor any other early writer has a concept of 'spiritual' as opposed to 'material': the *psuche* is composed of a very tenuous stuff, which resides in the body while the individual is alive, flies away through some orifice at death and goes down to Hades.

From there it may be summoned and, if given blood to drink, may address the living (*Odyssey* XI, 98). Already we may see that the distinction between physiological and psychological is difficult to draw in these poems.

The Homeric *psuche* has no specific mental or emotional functions in life: it is simply that whose presence ensures that the individual is alive. To observe the mental and emotional activity of Homeric man, we must turn to the other words listed above, whose conventional renderings, all of which are somewhat misleading, are: *thumos*, 'spirit'; *kradie*, *etor*, *ker*, 'heart'; *phrenes*, 'mind' or (physiologically) 'diaphragm' or 'lungs'; *noos*, 'mind'. The manner in which these words are used, if we take it seriously, reveals a psychological landscape quite different from our own. We are accustomed to emphasise the 'I' which 'takes decisions', and ideas such as 'will' or 'intention'. In Homer, there is much less emphasis on the 'I' or decisions: the

Greek words just mentioned take the foreground, and enjoy a remarkable amount of democratic freedom. Men frequently act 'as their
kradie and *thumos* bids[1] them': Odysseus (*Odyssey* IX, 302) was wonder-
ing whether to attack the Cyclops when 'another *thumos* restrained
him'; Athena tells Telemachus to give her on some future occasion
(*Odyssey* I, 316) 'whatever gift his *etor* bids him give'; and 'grief
came upon Achilles, and his *etor* debated between two alternatives
in his shaggy chest' (*Iliad* I, 188). Examples could be multiplied:
this is 'ordinary language' in Homer.

The words require separate discussion. *Thumos* differs somewhat
from *kradie*, *etor* and *ker*, since the latter are *prima facie* more physical
and 'organic', while *thumos*, as we have seen (*Odyssey* XI, 216 ff.),
may be said to leave the white bones at death. The difference, however,
should not be overemphasised. True, food and drink cause men to
receive *thumos* in their chests once again (*Odyssey* X, 461); and a stirring
speech may stimulate a man's might and *thumos* (*Iliad* XV, 500).
But a man's might may be not co-ordinate with his *thumos*, but in it:
Achilles filled his *thumos* with might (*Iliad* XXII, 312, cf. *Odyssey* I,
320); and this raises the question whether *thumos* is a psychological
function, an organ with a physical location in the body, or something
physical, but not an organ. That is to say, it raises the question for
the modern reader; but it is doubtful whether it is a relevant one.
Philologists link *thumos* with Latin *fūmus* and Sanskrit *dhūmas*, both of
which mean 'smoke'. Even if the link were treated as certain, it
would not follow that *thumos* necessarily conveyed any idea of 'smoke'
to a Homeric Greek, for it is usage, not etymology, that 'gives words
their meaning'. However, since Homer has no non-material language,
it is worth exploring the possibility that, though the word never
'means' 'smoke' in Greek, some notion connected with smoke is
conveyed by *thumos*. Some scholars seem to find a link in the idea
of breath as it comes visibly from the nostrils in cold weather. I
find this not fully convincing.[2] If we think of smoke in everyday
life as neatly encased in fireplace and chimney, and in literary terms
as the blue smoke from the distant shieling, such a link may appear

[1] Homer uses a singular verb; see below, p. 46.
[2] Nor does E. L. Harrison, 'Notes on Homeric Psychology', *Phoenix* XIV
(1960), pp. 63 ff., q.v.

reasonable; but we have still to account for the usage of *thumos* in Homer and in later writers. The examples already quoted suggest that *thumos* is impulsive; but there seems little reason to correlate impulse with breath emerging from the nostrils. However, early man's fire was not enclosed in fireplace and chimney; he must sometimes have found himself close to it; and in these circumstances the smoke and air immediately warmed by the fire are hot, swirling, choking and apparently very active. If we suppose that the remote Indo-European chose to denote this aspect of fire with the common ancestor of *thumos*, *dhumas* and *fumus*, and that the *thumos* (in the Homeric usage) which one notices first is most likely to be one's own, then what is denoted by *thumos* seems clear: the hot, swirling, surging – and sometimes choking – sensations produced by feelings of anger and other violent impulses. Plato (*Cratylus* 419E) derives *thumos* from 'the raging (*thusis*) and boiling of the *psuche*'. *Thumos* had a more restricted (and *psuche* a wider) usage in Plato's day; but his words convey a similar impression.

Thumos, in fact – and the same is true of *kradie*, *ker* and *etor* – records Homeric man's experiences in the manner in which he experienced them. He had not the conceptual framework with which to distinguish between a psychological function and an organ with a physical location; and though he could doubtless have distinguished between the latter and, for example, a vital fluid in the body, his interests gave him no reason to do so.

He felt a surge within, a hot sensation within the chest, and that was *thumos*. If he felt a backward impulse he might say, with Odysseus (*Odyssey* IX, 302), 'but another *thumos* restrained me'. If he did something without external constraint, but reluctantly, he might say, as Zeus says (*Iliad* IV, 43), that he acted 'willingly, but with unwilling *thumos*'; and he supposed, as we have already seen, that food and drink increased the *thumos*, and that it departed at death, and – unlike the *psuche* – vanished altogether. An insistence on classification and treating English equivalents as real entities might induce us to suppose that in the first case we are concerned with an impulse (since presumably, even if *thumos* is sometimes a psychological function, Odysseus only has one), in the second with a psychological function, in the third with a generalised vital force; but the classification would

be ours, not Homer's. In different circumstances, his experience of
the inner surge induced him to use language in these ways as the most
accurate method of recording it: he has no answer to the question
whether *thumos* is a function or an expression of a function, for he
has never asked the question.

Since the Homeric poems do not distinguish the material and the
spiritual, it follows that *thumos*, *kradie* and all the rest are, like *psuche*,
conceived of as possessing confusedly together qualities which we
should distinguish in this manner. It is not, of course, that Homer
reduces mental and spiritual qualities to material ones: by not distinguishing, he just as much ascribes mental and spiritual qualities
to aspects of the individual to which we should not ascribe them. In
the case of *kradie*, *ker* and *etor*, which are translatable as 'heart' in
most contexts (though *etor* may be part of the heart), it has sometimes
been argued that the usage must have originally been psychological,
since the internal sensations must have been felt long before man was
familiar with his anatomy; and it has been argued in reply that wounds
as well as dissection may furnish anatomical knowledge. Both arguments are unnecessary: the sensations within would be felt unanalysedly,
the distinction between physiological and psychological not being
present to the mind at all; and the physical organ, once discovered,
would not be distinguished from its functions and sensations. *Thumos*,
kradie, *ker* and *etor* are all confusedly physical locations or organs to
which certain emotions are ascribed, and the psychological functions
whereby these emotions find expression. It may not be possible to
find an exact location in the chest for the *thumos*; but when an author
whose psychological language is not markedly metaphorical exhorts
his heroes to put shame in their *thumos*, it seems reasonable to suppose
that he is thinking of some definite location in space.

Again, these aspects of the personality are not merely emotional:
they partake of consciousness. One may feel emotions in them,
but they may themselves feel, and be conscious of, the emotions. I
confine my examples to grief and joy: Aeneas' *thumos* rejoiced in his
chest (*Iliad* XIII, 494); Hera rejoiced in her *thumos* (*Iliad* XIV, 156);
Menelaus' *kradie* and *thumos* was[1] gladdened (*Odyssey* IV, 548);
Telemachus nursed mighty grief in his *kradie* (*Odyssey* XVII, 489);

[1] Once again, Homer uses a singular verb; see below, p. 46.

the suitors try to placate Odysseus with gifts until his *ker* is gladdened (*Odyssey* XXII, 58); Telemachus wished Mentes to be gladdened in respect of his *ker* (*Odyssey* I, 310); Zeus' *etor* laughed for joy when the other gods were embroiled in strife with one another (*Iliad* XXI, 389); and Aphrodite was grieved in respect of her *etor* (*Iliad* V, 364) when wounded by Diomedes. Illustrations could be given for the other emotions: there seems to be no emotion which the *thumos*, *kradie*, *ker* and *etor* cannot feel, and be conscious of feeling, nor which one cannot feel in them.

Consciousness being present, it is not surprising to find them thinking, or people thinking with them: Penelope rebukes her maidservants (*Odyssey* IV, 730) for not rousing her when her son Telemachus departed, though they knew well in their *thumos* when he went on board his ship; Odysseus' *kradie* had many forebodings of destruction (*Odyssey* V, 389) when Odysseus was wrecked and thrown into a rough sea; we have already seen Achilles' *etor* debating; Odysseus' *ker* was making plans for the suitors' downfall (*Odyssey* XVIII, 344); and it is very frequently indeed the *thumos* in which internal debate takes place: examples will be given below.

Accordingly, their functions overlap those of *phrenes* and *noos*, though these are the words usually rendered by 'mind'. The *phrenes* have a physical location – they 'hold the liver' (*Odyssey* IX, 301) – understood by ancient Greek, and most subsequent, scholars to be the diaphragm, though R. B. Onians[1] makes a powerful case for the original location having been the lungs. The *noos* is sited in the chest, as will be shown below. The intellectual usages of these words require little illustration. Hector realised in his *phrenes* that Deiphobus was not near him (*Iliad* XXII, 296); Athena persuaded Pandarus' *phrenes* (*Iliad* IV, 104); Achilles was prudent in his *noos* (*Iliad* XXIV, 377); and Dolon (*Iliad* X, 391) complains that Hector has misled his *noos*. It is unusual for *phrenes* or *noos* to be said to instigate action; though (*Iliad* IX, 119) Agamemnon says that he acted foolishly through having obeyed his baneful *phrenes*.

The use of *phrenes* in contexts concerned with conduct ethically judged is similar. At first Aegisthus was unable to seduce Clytemnestra; for she had 'good' (*agathai*) *phrenes* (*Odyssey* III, 266); and a similar

[1] *The Origins of European Thought* (Cambridge 1951), pp. 23 ff.

reason is given for Eumaeus' remembering to make an offering to the gods (*Odyssey* XIV, 421), and for Penelope's chastity and loyalty to the absent Odysseus (*Odyssey* XXIV, 194). Ethical behaviour is described in intellectual, or apparently intellectual, terms in Homer and later Greek: a situation which will be discussed more fully below. It should be noted that the Homeric *noos* is not, though the word is the same, the pure intellect of later philosophy: Homeric man does not engage in abstract speculation, and is only concerned with practical reason.

Just as *thumos*, *kradie*, *ker* and *etor* are capable of thought, so are *noos* and *phrenes* capable of emotion: the shepherd rejoices in his *phrēn* (the singular is used as well as the plural) as the flock follows him (*Iliad* XIII, 493); while Paris says to Hector (*Iliad* III, 60 ff.):

> Your *kradie* is always as unwearied as an axe which goes through a log, wielded by the hands of a man who is cutting out a ship timber by his skill, and it assists his own strength. Just so is your *noos* fearless in your chest.

Here we pass readily from *kradie* in 60 to *noos* in 63. The functions of the two are clearly the same here, though to ask whether *kradie* and *noos* are considered to be identical by the poet in this context would be pushing the question too far. Certainly *noos* and *phrenes* are as capable of emotion as *thumos*, *kradie*, *ker* and *etor* are of thought. Furthermore, both the *phrenes* (whether in lungs or diaphragm) and, as we see from the last quotation, the *noos* are sited in the chest, as are *thumos*, *kradie*, *ker* and *etor*. This too suggests that in the experience of Homeric man thought usually has a high emotive charge.

Noos and *phrenes* are much more intellectual than emotional, however, and differ from each other in that *noos* is more concerned with noticing present facts or picturing future ones, *phrenes* with reasoning about them. *Thumos* is highly emotional, as we have seen; yet it is in the *thumos* that anxious deliberation – and in an epic poem most deliberation is anxious – characteristically takes place. *Ker*, *kradie* and *etor* are more emotional than intellectual, and seem not to differ significantly from one another. The reason for the existence of the three words may in part be metrical convenience; but to grant this is not to concede the type of idiom as a whole to be mere poetising: the representation of separate springs capable of impulse, emotion and thought, the existence of, so to speak, separate 'little people' within the individual, seems natural in the light of Homeric psychology and, as we shall see, physiology in general.

For Homeric physiology – as we should distinguish it, though the line between physiology and psychology is blurred in Homer – must appear strange to the modern reader. Snell, in the penetrating first chapter of *Die Entdeckung des Geistes*,[1] starts from the ancient critic Aristarchus' observation that in Homer the word *sōma* does not mean 'living body', but always 'corpse', in opposition to the *psuche* which leaves it at death. Aristarchus held that *demas* was the Homeric Greek for 'living body'; but Snell points out that the word only occurs in the accusative of respect: e.g. 'he was small in respect of his *demas*', and that where we would say 'his whole body trembled', Homer would use *guia*, and for our 'sweat poured from his whole body *melea*. Both words are neuter plural, and mean 'limbs': *guia* being the limbs as moved by the joints, *melea* the limbs in their muscular strength. In such phrases as 'he washed his body', or 'the sword pierced his body', Homer uses *chrōs*, which means 'the skin'. There is no word for the body as a whole: *chros* is the bounding limit of the body, *demas* its structure, and the plurals *guia* and *melea* refer to it as an aggregate of units. Snell points out that the drawings of the human figure found in geometric art – on Greek pottery, that is to say, of the eighth century B.C. – have precisely this property; and concludes that there is convincing evidence from Homeric language – and language both mirrors thought and helps to mould it – and from the visual arts that the early Greeks perceived the body as an aggregate, not as a unit.

Physiological and psychological phenomena, then, closely parallel one another in Homer. Another passage will serve to illustrate the completeness of the resemblance. Ajax (*Iliad* XIII, 73 ff.) says:

And my *thumos* in my chest is zealous to fight . . . and my feet below and my hands above are eager.

[1] There is much more in Snell's account than can be mentioned here. The reader may consult T. G. Rosenmeyer's translation of Snell's work, *The Discovery of the Mind* (Blackwell 1953); and, for other discussions of Homeric psychology, J. Böhme, *Die Seele und das Ich im homerischen Epos* (Leipzig and Berlin 1929); Harrison, op. cit.; and the earlier writers there cited.

Here *thumos*, feet and hands instigate the action, and in precisely the same manner. All are felt as springs of action: the blurring of what we should distinguish as psychological and physiological is complete.

It remains to enquire how far Homeric man feels himself to exist as a whole, and what relationship he experiences between himself and his parts. In the first place, a man may yield to his *thumos*, as in *Iliad* IX, 109, where this is given as the reason or cause of Agamemnon's slighting Achilles. Agamemnon might presumably have restrained his *thumos* or any other part of himself; as Achilles, when his wrath comes to an end, proposes that both should do (*Iliad* XIX, 65):

> But let us allow these things to be over and done with, having subdued our *thumos* in our chests.

In such usages it is the whole personality, even if this can be expressed only by the personal pronoun, that inhibits impulses. This, as we have seen, is not the most usual picture in Homer: the parts appear more frequently than the whole, the relation to the whole is not clear, and there is no word for the whole, apart from the implications of the personal pronouns. Nevertheless, where there is to be restraint, the personality as a whole must restrain. In *Iliad* I, 188 ff., Achilles'

> *etor* debated in his shaggy chest whether he (and here the pronoun is masculine, referring to Achilles: *etor* is neuter) should draw his sharp sword . . . and slay Agamemnon, or check his anger and restrain his *thumos*.

The *etor* may have debated, but Achilles himself, not his *etor* or any other part of him, must control his *thumos*.

On the basis of the previous discussion, it seems clear that all these forms of speech constitute a direct record of the manner in which his experience presented itself to Homeric man – or had presented itself during the time when the formulaic epic vocabulary was being formed. The last is a necessary qualification in any Homeric discussion; but in this case the general picture of Homeric psychology and physiology is so homogeneous as to suggest that these expressions to the end of the oral tradition still recorded experiences in the manner in which they were experienced. Indeed, it is as true to say that the psychological vocabulary a society uses moulds the manner in which it experiences as that its experiences mould its psychological vocabulary. The initial usage records the experiences; later generations learn it, and interpret their experiences in its terms. Homeric language, then, would have tended to encourage the fragmentation of Homeric man's psychological experience in any case. This is, however, only a small aspect of the situation; I shall try to show later that Homeric man's psychological experience can readily be understood in terms of the total situation in which he found himself.

For the moment, however, we must examine individual aspects of the situation. It is already clear that in such a psychology as this the idea of 'decision' is unlikely to be important. Snell roundly denies[1] that in Homer anyone is ever represented as taking a decision at all, as saying to himself 'It all depends on me which way I decide, and I decide to do X'. He selects as a crucial example *Iliad* XI, 404 ff., where Odysseus, isolated on the battlefield, laments:

'Woe is me, what is to become of me? It is a great ill if I flee, in terror at the host of enemies. But it is worse if I am caught alone; and Zeus has routed the rest of the Greeks. But why did my *thumos* say these things to me? I know that *kakoi* run away from the war, whereas he who is brave in battle must stand his ground firmly, and either be struck or strike another.' While he was pondering these things in his *phren* and in his *thumos*, the ranks of the Trojans advanced.

Then there follows a simile, and at line 420 Odysseus 'first of all slew blameless Deïopites'. No decision is mentioned; and, Snell insists, if a psychological vocabulary does not mention decisions, then for that society there are no decisions.

To understand the situation, we should examine as wide a range of contexts as possible. In most cases there is no deliberation: the character simply says that his *thumos* bids him to do something; and what his *thumos* bids him to do, that in most cases (circumstances like those in the passage above being the exception) he does. So in *Iliad* XVIII, 90 f., Achilles tells his mother that he will never return home to Greece:

Since my *thumos* does not bid me live or exist among men unless Hector first is struck by my spear and loses his life.

[1]B. Snell, 'Das Bewusstsein von eigenen Entscheidungen in frühen Griechentum', *Philologus* 89 (1930), pp. 141 ff.

Here there is no question of a decision, for of two possibilities the one is not even considered. At 101 we have merely 'But now, since I shall not return to my native land . . .'.

We may add other types of expression. A different psychological model appears at *Iliad* II, 3 ff. The other gods and men are asleep:

> But (Zeus) was considering in his *phren* how to increase the prestige and prosperity of Achilles, and destroy many by the Greek ships. And this appeared to him in his *thumos* to be the best plan, to send a baneful dream to Agamemnon.

Odyssey XI, 230 ff. is slightly different: Odysseus has summoned up the *psuchai* of the dead, and does not wish them to come and drink the blood all at once, since he wishes to question them separately:

> And this appeared to me in my *thumos* to be the best plan. Drawing my sword . . . I did not allow them all to drink the black blood at once.

These differ from one another in that the former passage appends 'what seemed best' in the infinitive, whereas the latter expresses it as a separate statement. The latter leaves a gap between the plan that seemed best and the action. The former bridges it to some extent, but less than does 'I decided', where the personal pronoun makes it easier for the mind to pass from decision to action. For there is a distinct difference in model – which, as has already been said, is most important in psychological matters – between 'I decided' and 'it seemed best to me'. The latter suggests a kind of spectral balance into which the reasons on one side or the other are poured until at length, after due consideration, the balance goes down by itself and action ensues. The model is quite different from one involving the idea of decision. This statement requires very careful wording. E. R. Dodds says[1] 'it seems a little artificial to deny that what is described in passages like *Iliad* XI, 403 ff. . . . is in effect a reasoned decision taken after consideration of possible alternatives'. Artificial, if the denial were meant to imply that Homeric characters were automata, at the mercy of *thumos*, *kradie* and other functions which were sharply distinguished from themselves; for as we have seen, this is not the

---

[1] *The Greeks and the Irrational*, chapter 1, n. 31.

case. Not artificial, if one wishes to emphasise the differences in the 'feel' and implications of this model: anyone with this model of personality as the only one he knows is faced with a very different psychological landscape from that familiar to us; and that the implications are very different will become clear in discussing the philosophers.

Nor have we yet exhausted the differences. Homeric man believes that the gods not infrequently act directly upon him or some part of him, causing him to do what he would not otherwise have done or have an idea which he would not otherwise have had, or to perform an action more effectively than he would otherwise have done. Glaucus, wounded, prayed to Apollo; and he (*Iliad* XVI, 528 ff.) straightway caused his pains to cease and put *menos*, vigour, in his *thumos*; and Glaucus immediately began to take an active part in the fighting again. This is one example of a frequent phenomenon in these poems: sudden access or increase of vigour in a warrior on the battlefield is ascribed to the action of a god putting *menos* into the warrior, often into his *thumos*. (In *Iliad* XVII, 451 Zeus puts *menos* into a hero's 'knees and *thumos*': another example of the close parallelism of function in Homer of what we should distinguish as physiological and psychological organs.) Not only *menos* may be implanted. Odysseus (*Odyssey* XIX, 485) says that Eurycleia has recognised him despite his disguise because a god has put the idea in her *thumos*. Nor need the *thumos* be the recipient. The goddess Strife (*Iliad* XI, 11) put great strength in the *kradie* of each of the Greeks; Telemachus alleges (*Odyssey* XIX, 10), as a pretext for depriving the suitors of weapons, that some supernatural power has put into his *phrenes* an apprehensive thought of possible quarrels among the suitors; and when Agamemnon finally acknowledges his mistake in depriving Achilles of his prize Briseis, he says (*Iliad* XIX, 86 ff.):

> But I am not the cause, *aitios*. No; Zeus and *moira*[1] and the Fury that walks in darkness are the cause, who cast fierce blindness, *ate*, into my *phrenes* on that day when I myself took away Achilles' prize. But what could I do? The goddess brings all things to pass, *Ate*, the eldest daughter of Zeus, who blinds all mankind, baneful one.

[1] For *moira* in Homeric thought, see *Merit and Responsibility*, Ch. II.

25

Sometimes no psychological function is mentioned, as in *Iliad* X, 366, where Athena puts *menos* simply into Diomedes:[1] the divine stimulus, idea, or folly, may be implanted generally in the person concerned.

It seems most unlikely that this usage is mere poetising: it suits the general pattern of Homeric psychology too well. Homeric man was, it appears, unusually aware of the 'given', spontaneous aspect of human personality, and ascribed this to divine intervention. His unusual awareness, I shall argue, is likely to be a result of a prominence unusual in our culture of this aspect of his experience: a prominence entirely suited to the total situation of Homeric man.

Homeric man, then, not only has a psychology and a physiology in which the parts are more in evidence than the whole: he believes that the gods may act directly upon him or some aspect of him to affect his actions for good or ill. If we are to understand the function of this belief for Homeric man, we must consider the manner in which he evaluates such ascriptions of causation.

They clearly do not, and are not intended to, absolve him from responsibility for his bad actions or failures, or deny him credit for his good actions and successes. In *Iliad* XII, 290 ff. we are told that the Trojans would not have got the upper hand at this stage in the battle, had not Zeus stirred on his son (by a mortal woman) Sarpedon against the Greeks. This is followed by a simile comparing him with a lion whose *thumos* urges him against his prey; and in 307 we return to Sarpedon with

So then did his *thumos* urge Sarpedon to rush upon the wall.

The chain of causation is no longer pursued beyond Sarpedon's *thumos*; and for the acts which his *thumos* prompts him to perform Sarpedon is certainly responsible. This kind of instance is a particular case of a general tendency found in Greece and in other societies: a course of action said to be planned, caused, or instigated by a god, or prophesied by an oracle is nonetheless, when the actions are described in detail, and evaluated, attributed to the human beings who perform it; and certainly no warrior society could afford to allow the excuse for cowardice that a god had caused it, or would wish to diminish the credit for successes on these grounds.

[1] And cf. *Iliad* XVII, 118; XXI, 304.

26

The case of Agamemnon, however, is more complex.[1] He says that he is not the cause of his action, but that Zeus, *moira* and the Fury are; and he uses very emphatic language. Nevertheless, he is not attempting to avoid recompensing Achilles. He cannot: he treats the action as a disastrous mistake, but this does not absolve him from the necessity of remedying its consequences and bringing Achilles back into the battle, so that Agamemnon himself may avoid *elencheië*, shame (a term which will be discussed below). This is a necessity even if Agamemnon regards the action, as being the result of *ate*, as 'not his action' at all. But does he? He may indeed say that Zeus, *moira* and the Fury are the cause; but in the very next line he says not merely 'I took away' but 'I myself took away', adding a very strong word for 'myself'. Agamemnon is able to ascribe an action to external causes and to himself in adjacent lines, despite the fact that he has said that he is not responsible in so many words immediately before. This may be illogical, but seems explicable. Agamemnon has committed an error which has led to disaster. Now no-one intends – or, in a calculative psychology, plans – to fail. Agamemnon cannot understand how he came to do such a thing, and feels there was some element in the situation not under his control. Since his society ascribes a wide range of unexpected psychological phenomena to divine instigation, Agamemnon naturally speaks in these terms. Nevertheless, at the same time Agamemnon is aware that he – the unity represented by the personal pronoun – harmed Achilles. The statement that he was not the cause may serve to relieve Agamemnon's internal stresses, but it does nothing else. Agamemnon's different statements are not harmonised with one another.

All these aspects of the Homeric situation reveal Homeric man as a being whose parts are more in evidence than the whole, and one very conscious of sudden unexpected accesses of energy. A study of Homeric man vis-à-vis his fellows and the gods, to which we shall now turn, will necessarily show him functioning more as a unit, but will also furnish the context in which his fragmented psychological condition can be understood.

---

[1] On Agamemnon's apology, see the brilliant and illuminating discussion in E. R. Dodds, *The Greeks and the Irrational*, chapter 1.

C. Homeric Man and his Fellows

Here we shall consider the values of Homeric man in the social context in which they are found, and discuss the standard at which Homeric man had to aim in order to satisfy the demands of society, and the pressures on Homeric man which result from the attempt to behave in the required manner.

Homeric man[1] lived in a society of virtually autonomous small social units termed *oikoi*, noble households under the leadership of a local chieftain, or *agathos*. The *oikos* was the largest effective social, political and economic unit. Its head was responsible for defending its members in war and in what in Homeric society passed for peace – for such a society can never be securely at peace – and for ensuring his own prosperity and theirs, which derived from his own. He had also to defend the interests of any wanderer from outside the *oikos* whom he took under his protection: a defence which might require actual fighting. There was no larger effective group to which he could turn for help in discharging these functions.[2] An assembly of heads of *oikoi* could indeed be held to discuss questions which affected more than one of them; but, as Homer tells the story, no assembly was held in Ithaca between the departure of Odysseus and the occasion, some twenty years later, when Telemachus called one in *Odyssey* II; and that assembly achieved nothing. The head of *oikos* could rely on no-one else; and the other members of the *oikos* needed him to secure their very existence; so that the demand that he should succeed was categoric. The most powerful words of denigration used of actions in Homer are *aischron* – a neuter adjective whose range spans what we distinguish as 'ugly' and 'shameful' – and *elercheie*, the state of mind, or the condition vis-à-vis his fellows, of the hero conscious of having done something *aischron*. We may perhaps not be surprised to discover (*Iliad* II, 298) that Odysseus holds that, for the Greek army besieging Troy,

[1] This is a condensed version of my discussion in *Merit and Responsibility* (Clarendon Press 1960), chapter III. Proof is there offered of a number of statements whose truth is assumed here.

[2] The *Iliad* (e.g. I, 277 ff.; IX, 37 ff.) and the *Odyssey* (e.g. I, 391 ff.) speak of kingship over larger groups than the *oikos*, so that this is in a sense an overstatement; but neither poem shows us kingly power being effectively exercised over a larger group, and the society's values seem to reflect the situation described in the text.

it is *aischron* to remain for a long time and then return empty-handed; for our own values in wartime are not dissimilar. However, when Odysseus disguised as a beggar blunders into Eumaeus' farmyard, and is attacked by his dogs, Eumaeus says (*Odyssey* XIV, 37 f.):

> Old man, the dogs came near to destroying you suddenly; and then you would have caused me *elencheie*.

Again (*Odyssey* XVIII, 223 ff.), Penelope thus rebukes Telemachus for allowing the disguised Odysseus to be maltreated by the suitors:

> How would it be, if our guest while sitting thus in our house should perish as a result of his grievous mishandling? For you there would be *aischos* (a noun closely linked with *aischron* in usage) and shame among mankind.

Eumaeus did not know that Odysseus was coming; while Telemachus wished to protect his guest, but was heavily outnumbered by the suitors. In some societies Eumaeus could plead ignorance, Telemachus *force majeure*; but not in Homeric society. Here the most powerful terms of denigration are applied quite simply to failure to ensure the safety and well-being of the members of the group of which one is the head. It makes no difference to the evaluation of the situation whether the failure results from cowardice, or from mistake or *force majeure*: only the result is taken into account. Homeric society is a 'results-culture'.

Society's highest commendation is naturally reserved for those who can produce the desired results, and for those qualities in them which appear most relevant to their production. *Agathos* is not a title of the head of *oikos*, but the most powerful adjective available to commend a man in Homeric society; for the head of *oikos*, as a warrior-chieftain, is expected to unite in himself all the qualities which this society needs most and values most highly. He must be strong, brave and successful; for no quality has any value unless it leads to success. He has a great advantage over his followers, for he is wealthy and can purchase full armour and a chariot, and the leisure to become proficient in their use. He is, as they can see, a much more effective fighter than they are; and provided that he actually succeeds in preserving the group in war and in what passes for peace in Homeric society, they have every inducement to commend him as *agathos* and his admired qualities as *arete*, together with the success which in such a situation cannot be distinguished from the qualities which are conducive to it. The admired qualities are in fact best characterised as 'strength-and-bravery-and-wealth-leading-to-or-preserving-success', the hyphens indicating the unitary and unanalysed nature of *arete* for Homeric man. High birth is included in *arete*, since in Homeric society, a society without coined money, wealth consists of land, flocks, house and slaves; and these are possessed by the *agathoi* and inherited.

Other qualities, such as justice and self-control, are less highly valued by this society. A wronged individual sets a high value on obtaining redress for himself; but society in general sees so much more need for the success-producing qualities of the *agathos* than for his justice and self-control that the latter are no part of his *arete*. It follows that so long as the *agathos* is successful in protecting the group he remains *agathos*, no matter how unjust he may be, and cannot be effectively censured, since he retains his *arete*, on which he sets most store. Both Agamemnon in the *Iliad* and the suitors in the *Odyssey* retain their *arete* no matter how much wrong they do to Achilles and to Odysseus: it is the latter whose position is *aischron*, and who are showing themselves *kakoi* (the opposite of *agathoi*), in so far as they are failing to protect their own interests. As a result, when (*Iliad* XIX, 85 ff.) Agamemnon acknowledges that he was in some sense 'wrong' to deprive Achilles of his prize, the slave-girl Briseis – the action which occasioned the whole Wrath – he does not mean that he has now realised that it was morally wrong to take Briseis. He concludes that he was 'wrong' from the fact that Hector has carried his victorious attack right up to the Greek ships, as – it is implied – he would have been unable to do had Achilles not been sulking in his tent. Now though it was not *aischron* for Agamemnon to deprive Achilles of his prize, it is certainly *aischron* for Agamemnon, as leader of the expedition, if the Greeks fail to capture Troy. Agamemnon thought he could take Briseis from Achilles and capture Troy; and had he done so his *arete* would have been unsmirched. Discovering this to be not the case, he relinquishes Briseis to Achilles, and acknowledges that he has made a mistake. It is in this sense that he holds that he was wrong.

The behaviour of *agathos*, *kakos* and the other words which commend or decry most powerfully in Homer indicates quite clearly the kind of qualities expected of a man, the characteristics of – male – human nature at its highest. (Woman have their own *arete*: they are expected to be chaste and skilled in household tasks.) Qualities of character, physical attributes, intellect, social position and 'external goods' – as we should distinguish them – are all confusedly commended together. All distinguish the *agathos* from the *kakos*, who is ineffective in war (since, whatever other characteristics he may have, he is inadequately armed) and of low social position. Since *agathos* and *kakos* serve in all their usages to commend and decry what is good and bad of its kind, the *agathos* represents the human being at his most admired, the *kakos* the reverse. In such a society, the *kakos* has little chance of becoming *agathos* – for he cannot save in exceptional circumstances[1] acquire land, the foundation of wealth – but, in a society of small and insecure units, the *agathos* may well fail and become *kakos*. There is little temptation to regard the *agathoi* and the *kakoi* as distinct species in these circumstances; though there are some signs of this in later writers.

The status of the competitive excellences, the paramount importance of success and failure, and the irrelevance of intentions in evaluating the successes and failures of the *agathos*, must be at least in part responsible for the characteristic Greek psychological 'model', which is intellectual and calculative, not volitional; but this will require further discussion later.

Not only is the Homeric *agathos* always capable of falling from his *arete* by failure or mistake; he is also subject to the sanction of his society, which equally disregards intentions. In *Iliad* VIII, 139 ff., Nestor advises Diomedes to retreat before Hector, since Zeus is clearly favouring Hector. Diomedes acknowledges that Nestor's advice is reasonable, but adds, 147 ff.:

Yet this terrible grief comes upon my *kradie* and *thumos*: Hector one day will say as he speaks among the Trojans 'The son of Tydeus (Diomedes) fled before me and went to the ships':

[1] As Phoenix acquired land from Peleus (*Iliad* IX, 480 ff.), where the language seems to show the exceptional nature of the favour. (Phoenix was, furthermore, an *agathos* by birth, driven away from his own *oikos* for offending his father.)

On that day, says Diomedes, may the earth swallow me up. Nestor replies, 153 ff.:

> If Hector calls you *kakos* and lacking in valour, the Trojans . . . and their wives . . . whose sturdy husbands you have slain, will never believe it.

Nestor cannot say 'Don't worry. It isn't true.' If the Trojans believed, and spread it abroad, that Diomedes was *kakos* and lacking in valour, this would cause terrible *elencheie* for him. And naturally so: he lives in a society without writing, without permanent records which can be consulted later. What matters is what is said of him by his contemporaries, and remembered by future generations; and if that is false, there is no alternative source of information from which he could be rehabilitated. This is both a results-culture and a shame-culture: even where the result is not disastrous to the individual and his group, if the behaviour can be represented as being unworthy of an *agathos* by common report, this is *aischron* and entails *elencheie*. (We shall see below the effect this has on the psychology of Homeric man.) One's self, in the last resort, only has the value that others put on it: one cannot fall back, in Homer or for long afterwards, either on one's own opinion of oneself, or on the knowledge that one has done one's best.

D. Homeric Man and his Gods

In societies which believe in gods, the view of human nature is likely to be affected by the attitudes which the gods are believed to hold towards mankind, and which mankind should have towards its gods, and also by the characteristics which the divine nature is believed to possess.

In Homer, we must seek first the differences between the nature of his all-too-human deities and that of men. They are immortal, *athanatoi*: they do not die. They are not eternal: myth records their births and their parentage, as we see already in Hesiod's *Theogony*. They have *īchōr* in their veins, not blood (*Iliad* V, 339 ff.). When Aphrodite was wounded by Diomedes:

> Then flowed the immortal blood of the goddess, *ichor*, such as flows for the blessed gods; for they do not eat corn nor drink wine, and so they are without blood and are called *athanatoi*.

This, however, and 416 of the same book, are the only occasions on which we hear of this substance in Homer; and it may well be an *ad hoc* explanation, in this book of the epic where the gods not only come down and fight on the field of battle like humans, but are – in some cases – very much less effective fighters than Diomedes, to account for the fact that though Diomedes can wound Aphrodite, he cannot kill her, since gods and goddesses are different from men in some way.

A more important statement occurs at *Iliad* IX, 496 ff., a passage in which a Greek embassy is trying to induce Achilles to give up his wrath and return to the fighting:

> But, Achilles, subdue your mighty *thumos*. It is not necessary that you should have an implacable *etor*. Even the gods themselves can be turned by prayer from their purposes; and their *arete, tīmē* (status and possessions)[1] and strength are much greater than a man's.

The gods have much more *arete, time* and strength than a man; and apart from the fact that they do not die, this is the only important difference between men and gods of which Homer tells us.

That men die, and the gods do not, is of course an important difference. In *Iliad* VI, 145 ff., Glaucus, on being asked his parentage by Diomedes, replies:

> Great-hearted son of Tydeus, why do you ask about my lineage? The race of men is like that of leaves. Of leaves, some the wind strews on the ground, and the forest as it flourishes produces more when the season of spring comes on. So one generation of men comes to being, as another passes away.

When its members do pass away, they go to Hades, where no hope awaits them. In *Odyssey* XI, as we have seen, Odysseus raises the *psuchai* of the dead. His primary purpose (*Odyssey* X, 493 ff.) is to consult the shade of Teiresias,

> The blind prophet, whose *phrenes* remain with him. Persephone granted to him his *noos* after death, to him alone of all the dead to have his senses. The rest flit about like shadows.

---

[1] See my ' "Honour "and "Punishment" in the Homeric Poems', *B.I.C.S.* vii (1960), pp. 23 ff.

The *psuche* in Homer, as we have seen, is a mere shadowy double of the living man which, inactive in life, leaves him at death, through his mouth or through a wound, and departs to Hades. There it passes an existence not quite so witless as the words quoted above might suggest: though the *psuchai* can speak to Odysseus only when they have drunk the blood of the victims he sacrificed for them, *Odyssey* XXIV shows us the heroes in Hades reminiscing interminably with one another on the triumphs and failures of their earthly lives; and in *Odyssey* XI, 568 ff., Minos is portrayed settling disputes among the dead.

Again, though the *psuche* experiences no emotions in life, the *psuche* when separated from the body may feel emotions; for example, the *psuche* of Agamemnon still grieves in Hades (*Odyssey* XI, 387); the *psuche* of Achilles pities Odysseus, and rejoices at the successes of Neoptolemus (*Odyssey* XI, 471 and 540); and the *psuche* of Ajax remains angry at his defeat in life by Odysseus (*Odyssey* XI, 544).

The disputes of the dead with one another are settled by Minos; but there is no Last Judgment, no punishment for wrongs committed against one's fellow-men in this life. (Tityus, Tantalus and Sisyphus had consorted with the gods, and had wronged them, not their fellow-men, in a manner not given to the ordinary run of mankind.) Nor is there any reward for good deeds either: the only exception to the common lot is Menelaus for whom, as Proteus says in *Odyssey* IV, 561 ff.:

> It is not decreed by the gods . . . that you shall die. . . . No; the immortals will send you to the Elysian plain and the ends of the earth, where yellow-haired Rhadamanthys is, where life is easiest for men. There is no snow, nor great storms nor rain. No, Oceanus ever sends forth the breezes of shrilly-blowing Zephyrus to cool men. For you have Helen as your wife and are the son-in-law of Zeus.

This is neither reward for good deeds, nor does it occur after death; Menelaus is not to die. For the rest of mankind, who do die, there remains Hades, gloomy, dank and neutral, of which Achilles could say (*Odyssey* XI, 489 ff.) that he would rather be a labourer for a poor landless man on earth than rule among the dead. To say this, of course, is not to say that, being dead, it is not better to have been a man of position and repute while on earth, and to have died an honourable death. (Achilles has power and position among the dead, *Odyssey* XI, 485 f.) Agamemnon contrasts his own death with that of Achilles, who died bravely in battle and received a sumptuous funeral (*Odyssey* XXIV, 93 ff.):

> Thus you have not lost your name, even though you have died. No; for ever there will be fair fame for you throughout all mankind, Achilles. But what pleasure is there for me, though I brought the war to an end? For Zeus contrived a miserable destruction for me on my return, at the hands of Aegisthus and my baneful wife.

It is *aischron* for Agamemnon to have died as he did; and in the shame-culture of the dead this is the most important aspect of his position. (Nor is this Homeric only: we shall see that in fifth-century Athens the same evaluations occur.[1]) On the other hand, the greatest consolation of the dead is that they still enjoy fair fame on earth, and that their families are flourishing: Achilles enquires about his father Peleus and his son Neoptolemus (*Odyssey* XI, 492 ff.), and, as we have seen, rejoices greatly at Neoptolemus' successes.

It is presumably such considerations as these that render Glaucus' sentiments quoted above so unusual. Mankind may be like leaves, or like the grass that is cut down and withers; but while they live their *arete* may leave a mark that will be remembered when they are down in Hades. And there is perhaps in the background, though it would be rash to dogmatise, a hope of something more: Apollo may say to Poseidon, who has challenged him to fight (*Iliad* XXI, 462 ff.):

> Earth-shaker, you would not say that I am sane if I am to fight with you for the sake of wretched mortals, who like leaves at one time are full of vigorous life, eating the fruit of the earth, and at another time perish lifeless.

Yet Poseidon laments on another occasion (*Iliad* VII, 446 ff.):[2]

---

[1] See below, pp. 66 ff.

[2] And cp. *Odyssey* XIII, 128 ff., where the Phaeacians have flouted Poseidon's wishes by bringing Odyueus home safely. All passages which mention the wall have long been suspected as later additions to the *Iliad* (cp. most recently D. L. Page, *History and the Homeric Iliad*, Berkeley, 1959, pp. 315 ff.); but the thought and belief of both passages seem entirely appropriate to the far-from-omnipotent deities found in all parts of the Homeric poems.

Father Zeus, is there any mortal over the boundless earth who will any more tell his intention and plan to the immortals? Do you not see that the long-haired Achaeans have built a wall for the ships and have driven a trench around it, without giving hecatombs to the gods? Surely its fame shall exist as far as the light of dawn is spread; and they will forget the wall which I and Phoebus Apollo toiled to make for the hero Laomedon.

These self-same leaflike creatures can achieve ends of their own without consulting or sacrificing to the gods. This is true, even though Zeus consoles Poseidon, by saying that he can easily destroy the Greek wall afterwards: the Greeks have nevertheless built it without offering hecatombs; and Zeus does acknowledge that it might be reasonable for a lesser god than Poseidon to have such fears, 456 f. We have seen that, immortality apart, it is an excess of *arete*, *time* and strength that divides the gods from mankind. It seems a reasonable conclusion that, since *arete* is not *qualitatively* different in god and man, if a man were to manifest enough *arete* he would become a god. The conclusion was sometimes drawn, its most notable appearance being in the *Nicomachean Ethics* (1145a22) of Aristotle, where it is recorded as a common belief. (The response of the gods to this possibility will be discussed in later chapters, where it becomes more important.) Even if this goal is rarely to be achieved,[1] there is fame to be sought to prevent one's memory from being extinguished among men; and this the *agathoi* pursue, for the most part without thoughts such as those of Glaucus: after all, their very existence may depend on the successful performance of the activities commended by *arete*, not merely the fame which is also to be won.

[1] Aristotle treats this as the limiting case of 'heroic and divine *arete*' which is 'beyond us' – the *arete* of a Heracles or Asclepius; and it is true both that Aristotle did not regard this as possible for ordinary mankind, and that those who had achieved such apotheosis in the past had in at least some accounts of their lives one divine parent. However, Aristotle says that 'what people say' is 'by excess of *arete* men come to be gods': the popular belief need not have been qualified in the manner of Aristotle's discussion, and well suits the remainder of Homer's picture of gods and men. After all, in the *Odyssey* at all events, Calypso (V, 135 f.) says that she would have made Odysseus, who had no divine blood (or *ichor*) in his veins, immortal and ageless: possibly not divine, but a step in that direction, taken not through *arete*, but as the result of a favour conferred; and if *ichor* is set on one side, it is difficult to discern any definite qualities other than immortality and agelessness that distinguish Homeric god from Homeric mortal, save their excess of *arete* and *time*.

E. Emotional Responses

One more facet of the picture remains to be added. Homeric Greek has not only a wide range of psychological functions, but a rich emotional vocabulary, included in which are *ochthein*, *chōesthai*, *meneainein* and two verbs of emotional speech, *apeilein* and *neikeiein*. (I cite verbs in the infinitive.) These words in the lexica are each given a wide range of 'meanings': *ochthein*, 'be sorely angered, vexed in spirit'; *chōesthai*, 'be angry, be distressed, be grieved at heart'; *meneainein*, 'desire earnestly, be angry'; *apeilein*, 'promise, boast, threaten'; *neikeiein*, 'quarrel, wrangle with, chide, upbraid'.[1]

These 'meanings' inevitably prevent the reader from understanding the psychological phenomena which the Greek words present: to promise, to boast and to threaten are not the same activity, nor are being angry and being grieved at heart; and if one word expressing anger also expresses grief, while another also expresses earnest desire, it seems clear that the anger expressed by the two words is dissimilar; for the Homeric Greek, having Greek as his only language, and not thinking in terms of any other, presumably used each of these words over the range of instances in which he did use them because he discerned resemblances between the situations more important than the differences which we – mistakenly – emphasise when we use different words on different occasions to translate them. The range of usage of each should, accordingly, throw light on Homeric psychology.

Neikeiein is used to characterise Nestor's statement (*Iliad* VII, 161) that not even the chieftains of the Greeks are willing to face Hector; Euryalus' remark that Odysseus does not look like an athlete, but a merchant (*Odyssey* VIII, 158); and a message sent from Zeus to Poseidon by Iris (*Iliad* XV, 210). Now the message Zeus gave to Iris was (160 ff.) 'Tell him to stop fighting and rejoin the other gods on Olympus, or go into the sea. If not,' (163 ff.)

> Let him take thought then in his *phren* and in his *thumos* lest, strong though he is, he be not able to endure to await my onset, since I say that I am much mightier than he, and older; yet his *etor* recks nothing of declaring himself equal with me, whom even the other gods fear.

[1] This is a condensed version of my article 'Threatening, Abusing and Feeling Angry in the Homeric Poems', *J.H.S.* (1969), vol. LXXXIX, pp. 7 ff.

Of these examples, the first appears to be a rebuke, the second an insult, and the third a sharp command combined with a threat. Yet all are *neikeiein*.

Apeilein is used (*Iliad* XXI, 452) by Poseidon in recalling how Laomedon defrauded them and

> *Apeilein* that he would bind together our feet and hands above, and sell us into far away islands.

It is used (*Iliad* XXI, 161) of a speech made by Pelegonus, in which he declares his lineage and his native land; and (*Iliad* VIII) when Diomedes is counselled by Nestor to flee before Hector, since Zeus is manifestly helping Hector. Diomedes replies (146 ff.) in a speech already discussed in another connection:

> Yes, indeed, all these things, old man, have you said as is right. But this terrible grief comes upon my *kradie* and *thumos*: Hector one day will say as he speaks among the Trojans 'The son of Tydeus fled before me and went to the ships'. Thus one day will he *apeilein*; and then may the broad earth yawn beneath me.

Again, *Iliad* XXIII, 863, *apeilein* is used of vowing a sacrifice to a god.

Laomedon seems to be uttering a threat; Pelegonus, in saying that his grandfather was the river Axius and his father the spearman Pelegon, is not; but he is not boasting either, if 'boast' implies, as it does, either exaggeration or a manner of speech disapproved by society. Pelegonus is telling the truth, and the truth he is telling, and the mode of his telling it, are not disapproved by Homeric society. Hector will not be threatening to harm Diomedes, for Diomedes will not be there and the event will be in the past. Nor will he be uttering words that are exaggerated, untrue or disapproved by those who hear them; and Diomedes has no right to disapprove of them as a boast, even if he supposes that Zeus is helping Hector, since such help, as we have seen, is not held to diminish a man's credit for what he does. Accordingly, neither supposed future hearers nor Diomedes should use the word 'boast'. 'Speak proudly' seems adequate, if we only consider this passage; but why did the Homeric Greek classify speaking proudly with threatening? It is possible to speak proudly without threatening to harm another; and why should these be classified with vowing a sacrifice?

Ochthein is ascribed to Menelaus when Panthus threatens him across the corpse of Patroclus (*Iliad* XVII, 18); to Zeus (*Iliad* I, 517) when Thetis asks him to help the Trojan cause until the Greeks have to compensate Achilles, and Zeus reflects that he will have to quarrel with Hera; to Zeus again (*Iliad* IV, 30) when Hera does complain of his behaviour; to Odysseus when he is debating whether to fight or flee (*Iliad* XI, 401 ff.), when he fears he will drown (*Odyssey* V, 298), when he thinks Leucothea is trying to trick him to his death (*Odyssey* V, 355); and to Eurymachus (*Odyssey* XXI, 248) when he cannot string the Bow of Odysseus.

The Loeb translator renders some of these by 'anger' and some 'grief'; and different translators disagree about the correct rendering of individual passages. We need not argue the claims of one against another: all are, and must be, inadequate, for these words express phenomena characteristic of a society very different from our own.

In *Iliad* I, 80, Calchas is afraid to reveal Apollo's demands to Agamemnon, 'for a king is mightier when he *choesthai* with a man of lower estate'; in *Iliad* XXI, the gods are watching the battle and according to their several sympathies (519) some *choesthai*, others exult greatly; and in *Iliad* XXII, 289 ff., when Hector is fighting with Achilles:

He spoke, and poised his long-shadowed spear, and hurled it, and struck the middle of the shield of Peleus' son, and did not miss; but the spear sprang back far away from the shield, and Hector *choesthai* because his swift weapon had flown from his hand in vain; and he stood downcast, for he had no other ashen spear.

Finally, in *Odyssey* II, Telemachus has just made a speech full of emotion to the people, complaining that the Ithacans are not protecting him against the depredations of the suitors, and ending (79):

'. . . But as it is you are implanting incurable grief in my *thumos*.' So he spoke and *choesthai*, and hurled the staff on the ground, bursting into tears; and pity seized upon the whole people.

We might hold that Agamemnon would be simply angry with Calchas, if we took this passage in isolation; but none of the other passages seems to refer to 'anger' or 'wrath' simply, though they are frequently so translated; and if we use words such as 'distress' or 'grief' (both of which are lexicographers' 'meanings' for *choesthai*) in such passages, we conceal the fact that the same word is used in each case in the Greek – a fact which we have still to explain.

Lastly, *meneainein*. All the gods pitied Odysseus (*Odyssey* I, 20) except Poseidon 'who *meneainein* continually against him until he reached his native land'; and (*Odyssey* XXI, 125) Telemachus 'struggled three times and *meneainein* to draw the bow, and thrice he relaxed his strength'. If we translate these passages, we shall presumably have to render the former as 'was angry', the latter as 'was eager'; but Homer uses the same word.

Here we have five words, expressing aspects of the psychology of Homeric man, each of whose range of usage corresponds with the range of usage of no English word; and the list of such words could easily be extended. Homeric man also lives in a society whose structure and organisation differs from that to which we are accustomed, and – a closely linked phenomenon – in a society which evaluates human behaviour in a quite different way. The usage of these words which express emotion is also linked to the structure and evaluations of Homeric society. I have already[1] quoted Odysseus' reflections (*Iliad* XI, 404 ff.) when isolated on the battlefield, and his conclusion that *agathoi* must not flee, whatever the odds. That passage begins (403) 'Having *ochthein* he addressed his great-hearted *thumos*'. In the passage as a whole Odysseus is passing before his mind the stark realities of Homeric *arete*. The *agathos'* justification for being termed *agathos* is that he is *successful* in defending his group; and this is interpreted as entailing, among other things, that one must never retreat: there is no question of discretion being the better part of valour. Not good intentions, but results, are demanded of the Homeric *agathos*, in all his activities: he is constantly faced, or threatened, with a demand that he should succeed in doing what he cannot do; and a psychological response of frustration, distress and anger, all confused together, seems not inappropriate to his situation. This response is *ochthein*.

[1] Above, p. 23.

Choesthai, too, may be felt when a project is frustrated, as Hector in *Iliad* XXII *choesthai* when he misses his aim; but Calchas' fear of Agamemnon's *choesthai* indicates that a man in this mood will take action if he can, and will still be held to *choesthai*; whereas *ochthein* suggests at least anxious deliberation, and that when action takes place (if this is possible) *ochthein* has come to an end. Telemachus in *Odyssey* II, though he can do nothing himself, is quite sure what he wants the Ithacans to do for him; and Hector, having thrown his spear, does not say 'What shall I do?': he may be downcast but he is not baffled, for he believes – erroneously – that Deiphobus is nearby with another spear. *Choesthai* seems to denote the emotional state of a man who has received an unpleasant stimulus from his environment (and so far resembles *ochthein*); but whereas the man who *ochthein* says 'What am I to do?' in frustrated and angry distress and bafflement, the man who *choesthai* is taking a much more positive attitude to the obstacle in his path: while the emotions of the man who *ochthein* are swirling and eddying, those of the man who *choesthai* are flowing in one direction, though the use of the word implies that there is at least for the moment an impediment to his reaching his goal, or that the goal has not yet been reached: the emotions are confusedly grief and anger at once.

Meneainein is different again. The psychological phenomenon which links the usages is a powerful forward drive. (*Meneainein* is from the same root as *menos*, a word mentioned above.) Poseidon manifests this to Odysseus' disadvantage, Telemachus in an effort to string the bow. (We may contrast the *meneainein* of Telemachus who believes he can string it with the *ochthein* of Eurymachus who – to the detriment of his *arete* – realises that he cannot.)

From our own experience we can distinguish these psychological states; yet we have not a psychological vocabulary which classifies them in this manner, while Homer has a very rich one. (The words discussed do not exhaust the possibilities.) The reason for the existence of this vocabulary lies in the total situation of Homeric man. His most important terms of value evaluate not his intentions nor his efforts, but their results. He is always 'up against it', judged in terms of his successes and failures; further the sanction is overtly 'what people will say', and over this he has no control, and he cannot set his own consciousness of his self and its value against the estimation of his fellows, since his self has only the value which they put upon it. In these circumstances he can and does have intentions, form plans, make choices, but these are not the most important aspect of the situation in his eyes (or anyone else's). Externally, what is important is the result: internally, what is important to him is his psychological response to the situations in which he finds himself, partly because these are directly relevant to his success or failure, partly because, his choices and plans being less important, his psychological conditions gain added importance for him. These linguistic usages, in fact, give an accurate report of the psychological pressures of living in a shame- or (a phrase which expresses a more fundamental fact about Homeric society) a results-culture.

Apeilein and *neikeiein* are similarly affected by the nature of Homeric society and its values. *Apeilein* occurs in situations which we should distinguish as threatening, giving one's lineage, speaking magniloquently, or vowing, situations which may be considered both from the point of view of the person who *apeilein* and from that of the person affected, both of whom are living in the highly competitive Homeric world, in an environment indifferent and actively or potentially hostile, in the precarious condition I have already described. The pull of *arete* leads the person who *apeilein* to try to 'make his presence felt'; and all his efforts to do so are likely to be classified together by him, since this resemblance is more important to him than the differences emphasised by our translations. *Apeilein* fulfils this function in Homer. When Laomedon threatened Poseidon and Apollo, when Pelegonus narrated his lineage, both were asserting themselves; and if Hector were to have told of the flight of Diomedes, or Teucer had vowed a sacrifice to Apollo, they would have been manifesting themselves. The other *agathoi* in this competitive society are as precariously situated as those who are 'making their presence felt'; and in such circumstances to hear another speaking magniloquently, magnifying himself, is to hear oneself by implication depreciated, at least relatively. The depreciation may be direct and intentional, as in the case of Hector and Diomedes; if Hector is believed, Diomedes' reputation will fall and he will incur *elencheie*. Hector is not threatening to do something to Diomedes; but he is threatening his status and reputation. However, in such a society it is unnecessary for another man to be mentioned by name, or even for the man who *apeilein* to have any particular person in mind. If he magnifies himself, or someone with whom he is associated, he is claiming a larger share of the attention of men for himself or the other person; and since it is on the attention of men that one's fame depends – and fame is of paramount importance – anyone who hears such magniloquent words may feel himself 'threatened' to some extent. In so far as a man, or a society, can only pay attention to the deeds of a certain number of persons (and on that attention, in a non-literate society, depends any knowledge of oneself in future generations), if one person receives more of the attention there is less for the others. Similarly Apollo, who, like the rest of the Greek gods, has to be induced to cause himself trouble on a mortal's behalf, would feel himself impinged upon by Teucer's vow of a hecatomb, though he would welcome the sacrifice in itself.

Neikeiein too is closely linked to the situation of Homeric man: if only results count, it is not worthwhile to distinguish a moral error from a mistake, where both lead to disaster, whether one is reprehending or being reprehended: a disastrous result is *aischron*, and will meet with disapproval, the same kind of disapproval, whatever the cause; and the man disapproved of will feel the same kind of shame, whatever the cause of the disaster. On two occasions (*Iliad* VI, 442 ff., XXII, 104 ff.) Hector says 'I feel shame, *aideomai*, before the Trojans, both men and women': on one occasion the shame would be caused if he skulked away from the war like a coward, on the other it is caused by a mistake in strategy which has led to a disaster. To reprove either a moral error or a mistake is *neikeiein*, as is Euryalus' terming Odysseus a merchant, and hence deficient in *arete*: all the situations are *aischron*, and show the person reprehended to be *kakos*.

All five words, then, classify psychological experiences and overt behaviour in a manner significant to Homeric society, a manner which is unfamiliar to us. The man who *ochthein*, *choesthai* or *meneainein*, and both the man who *apeilein* or *neikeiein* and the man who is affected by his doing so, are responding in a manner systematically different from ourselves. Once the barrier interposed by the lexicographers' 'equivalents' is removed, we can appreciate the subtlety and sensitivity of the Homeric poems as literature of action, emotion and response, and realise that we have in them documents of great anthropological and psychological interest; for here we have a language which records clearly and with precision what it is like to live in a shame- or results-culture.

F. Conclusion

In a sense, it is not the fragmentation of the Homeric personality, but the development in other cultures of the ego-centred personality, that requires explanation. However, it is desirable to recapitulate the several aspects of the Homeric personality, and to endeavour to indicate the extent to which Homeric society favours this personality pattern, and discourages others.

We have seen that success is of paramount importance, good intentions of no importance, in this society: a situation which renders it impossible to distinguish between moral error and mistake, where the success and failure of the *agathos* are in the balance. Further, the sanction of the society is overtly 'what people will say of one's actions', over which one has oneself no control. If one's good intentions have no value unless crowned with success – which is not the agent's to command, and depends on more than good intentions – and one only has the value that other people put upon one, then one's actions are evaluated in terms of matters external to one's self; and there seems little likelihood of the development of a unitary self or of those aspects of 'will' which are manifested in deciding. (Bearing up bravely against adversity, being self-controlled or strong-willed in this sense, is demanded of Homeric man: this is *tolmān* or *tlēnai*, an adjective formed from the root of the latter word being used to describe the storm-tossed Odysseus.) And, as we have seen, a unitary self is little in evidence in the Homeric poems. The Homeric hero's *thumos*, his *kradie* or some other aspect of him suggests or prompts action, though he acts. His *thumos*, *kradie* or some other aspect of him feels an emotion, or he feels an emotion in it. There is no automatism, for his consciousness is diffused through all the 'parts' as well as residing in the unity represented by the personal pronoun. Even if, as in *Iliad* XI, 403 ff. (where 403 'He addressed his great-hearted *thumos*' becomes at 407, with reference to the same speech 'But why

44

did my *thumos* say this to me?') we find formal contradictions in the language, we should not simply reflect that these are formulaic[1] utterances (as they are) and dismiss them from consideration. Formulae are metrically convenient units; but they do not, in a system so flexible and artistic as that found in Homeric epic, control in the first instance the *content* of what is said, though they may demand that when the content is the same the form should not vary. Here we can discern a reason for the existence of both forms of expression in the same context. Neither the *thumos* nor any other individual 'part' is ever said to speak as a means of introducing direct speech in Homer: though one's *thumos* may bid one to do something, as we have seen, it is not credited with quoted sequences of words, whether the dialogue is internal, as here, or external; and this presumably reflects Homeric psychological experience. Accordingly, Odysseus addresses his *thumos* in 403. Having done so, however, he rejects what he has said, and accordingly distances it from himself by ascribing it to his *thumos*. The unitary self may not be important, but the unity represented by the personal pronoun exists: it can check the *thumos* and the other 'parts' or, as here, distance itself from one of them.

Where there is no conflict, however, this unity is so lightly experienced that, as we have seen, not merely *thumos*, *kradie* and similar aspects of the individual, but also hands and feet, may be felt as springs of action. The great overlapping of function displayed by *thumos*, *kradie* and the rest may be thus explained: when the *thumos*, *kradie* or any other aspect is felt as prompting action or supplying ideas, it is, where there is no conflict, the whole active aspect of the personality that is manifesting itself in this particular 'organ', the whole having, so to speak, flowed into whatever organ is mentioned. Similarly, when the 'I' represented by the unity of the personal pronoun is addressing some 'organ', that 'organ' is for the moment imbued with the receptive aspects of the whole personality. Even when allowance has been made for metrical convenience, the number of words available indicates the low degree of unity and cohesion felt by Homeric man in his psychological experience: one 'little man' (so to

[1] The Homeric epics, being oral poetry, contain many 'formulae', expressions of convenient metrical form and length to suit the dactylic hexameter in which they are composed, which appear repeatedly in the course of the poems.

speak) within him after another addresses and prompts him, or is addressed and prompted by him. Experience furnishes all the 'little men' with consciousness and emotions; and there is as yet no analysis to furnish a *conceptual* distinction between thought and emotion in general, which in practice occur together: Homeric language records the experience of Homeric man. A further indication that we have here not a mere use of language, but the experience of the active personality for the moment behaving in the manner suggested, may perhaps be sought in the language itself: even when Homeric language ascribes the prompting to *two* sources, the *thumos* and *kradie* together standing as subject, the verb remains singular even where the plural would be metrically possible.

Where such a structure, or absence of structure, prevails, it seems not unreasonable to suppose that sudden psychological surges, or equally sudden cessations of drive, will occur; and that these will be both more prevalent, and also more noticeable, features of a psychological landscape of this nature, as will the 'given' nature of a suddenly occurring idea. We may suppose that the Homeric Greek misascribed these in attributing their source to Apollo, Athena and the rest, and yet acknowledge that the phenomena for which he was attempting to account were real and present to his experience. The language may, of course, overstate the case. Any psychological model may overemphasise some aspects of experience at the expense of others. More recent 'ordinary language' psychological models have sometimes underestimated the 'given' and spontaneous elements in our own psychological and physical behaviour and experience. However, it is so appropriate that the Homeric situation should have encouraged the formation of precisely the type of personality structure that we find in the poems that it seems difficult to deny that the language furnishes a broadly accurate record of the psychological experience of Homeric man. This impression is confirmed by the vocabulary of emotion to be found in the poems which, as we have seen, does not correspond to our own, but well expresses fitting responses to the stresses and strains of living in a results-culture.

The Homeric situation also favours, as a model for what we characterise as 'deciding', the picture of a psychological balance inclined by the relative weight of the advantages poured into the scale-pans.

Since the goal of action is to maximise one's own *agatha* ('advantages'), a desirable end, a positive drive towards that end, once discovered, will be present. The agent may feel the utmost doubt and anxiety over the identity of the more advantageous course of action in a crisis; but so soon as an answer to the problem presents itself, the identification of the course of action as the most *agathon* available in the circumstances carries with it a desire for its fulfilment, and bridges the gap between thought and action. For a variety of reasons, as we have seen, the personality has little core: it is not surprising that the emphasis should be on the 'balance' during the period before action; and the nature of the goal, in addition to the psychological structure, does not encourage the idea of decision at the moment of action.

Lastly, we may consider one manner in which Homeric society describes the behaviour of others from without. We have already seen[1] that the possession of good (*agathai*) *phrenes* is the basis of sound behaviour in tune with the values of society. Similarly, *eidenai*, a Greek word usually rendered 'to know', is used in many phrases where we should use expressions to denote character. For example, Achilles (*Iliad* XXIV, 41) '*eidenai* fierce things', while Eumaeus (*Odyssey* XIV, 433) '*eidenai* in his *phrenes* things that were right'. We should say that Achilles had a fierce disposition, Eumaeus a righteous one. There is here a great distinction between the Greek manner of experiencing and representing this type of situation and our own, a distinction which, in one form or another, is present throughout the whole period discussed in this book. The Greeks emphasise intellect and calculation in their accounts of behaviour. However, in each period discussed we must attempt to evaluate this situation in its wider context. Here (*Iliad* XXIV, 40 ff.) Apollo says of Achilles that

> His *phrenes* are not righteous, nor his *nŏēma* (similar to *noos* here) bendable in his chest, but he *eidenai* fierce things, like a lion which, yielding to its great might and proud *thumos*, goes against men's herds to find its food.

If we render *eidenai* here as 'know', and then mentally transfer it to contexts in which we use the word 'know', we shall regard the

[1] Above, pp. 19. f.

47

phrase as extremely intellectual; for we use 'knowledge' of what we regard as certain, opposed to the subjective, the doubtful and the emotional. But Homeric man has no such concept or experience of knowledge. We have seen that his *phrenes* and *noos* may feel emotion; and he has no knowledge which is not practical, capable of leading to action, and none which he has divorced from emotion: Homer can pass with no difficulty from '*eidenai* fierce things' to a simile of a raging lion. We should consider the whole range of *eidenai*, which is used in 'emotional' contexts, and so is linked with emotion, desire and impulse; and in using the word 'calculative' to describe the Homeric model – and it is difficult to find a less unsatisfactory term – we should beware of correlating this with dispassionate calculation. The situations are instinct with emotion: all the resources of personality, not merely the intellect (which is not sharply distinguished in Homer), are involved.

The picture presented by the description and evaluation of Homeric man and his behaviour is remarkably coherent: the elements of which it is composed discharge functions entirely appropriate to the situation as a whole. Many of these elements persist into later Greek society, and affect the descriptions, analyses and solutions of later periods. We may not, however, assume that their functions remain entirely unaltered: this must be considered on each occasion in the light of the evidence as a whole.

3. Other Traditional Views

A. Introductory

The arrangement of the material in a discussion of this kind poses inevitable problems. The Homeric world has a unity of its own; but from Hesiod onwards we are concerned with anarchic and piecemeal development. Some problems arise from the nature of our sources: much is lost, and links have to be inferred. But even if we had an abundance of material, it would be difficult to present a clear line of exposition. New developments affect only a few thinkers at first. Nothing has the status of dogma, and old attitudes persist long after the appearance of new ones. I shall endeavour to present in this chapter Greek beliefs and attitudes which are traditional in the sense of being independent of the scientific and philosophical thought which will be the subject of later chapters. However, certainty is not always possible: early science and philosophy inevitably have their roots in the attitudes and beliefs of the society in which they emerge, and some passages in authors not classed as scientists or philosophers may be dependent either on traditional or on scientific thought. Indeed, classification of authors, though broadly useful and meaningful, should not conceal from us the fact that, in the early history of thought in particular, a non-'scientist' might produce a 'scientific' idea for himself; and whether 'scientist' or no, he may well be unable to harmonise all his ideas with one another. Scholars have sometimes attempted to equip ancient Greek writers with a theology and set of beliefs which, they insist, must furnish a coherent and consistent dogma. This misrepresents ancient Greek religion, which is confused, anarchic and undogmatic. Examples of this will appear in this chapter. We should also be cautious in assuming complete coherence in early philosophical and scientific theories: here the fragmentary nature of the sources permits wide divergencies of interpretation in an attempt to produce a coherent theory for the writer, whose works may, in their complete form, have contained unresolved inconsistencies.

This chapter, then, will contain some material later in date than the next chapter, which will be devoted to the beginnings of medicine and philosophy; and in both we shall be concerned not so much with 'traditional' and 'new' authors, as with 'traditional' and 'new' ideas, with the *caveat* already expressed.

The views to be discussed in this chapter are not homogeneous nor monolithic. If they are termed 'traditional', it is easy to give the impression that no Greek during these centuries ever thought for himself, made a discovery or hit on a new idea. This is untrue, as will soon be apparent. Hesiod already, particularly in the *Theogony*, shows clearly the results of systematising thought; and at all times and on all topics the dominant characteristic of the Greek intellectual landscape is variety. Nevertheless, there is a distinct difference in ethos and approach between the views to be discussed in this chapter and those in the following chapters; though, for reasons already given, the traditional views set out here persist long after those of the scientists and philosophers – always a minority – had been developed.

B. The Origin and Development of Man

The Homeric poems make no mention of the creation of mankind, which appears first in a famous passage of Hesiod's *Works and Days* (109 ff.). One need not assume from this that there was a 'Homeric audience' which knew nothing of such things, a 'Hesiodic audience' which was better informed. The subject matter of epic is different from that of didactic poetry; and there are indications that certain other myths, first met in Hesiod, were in fact known to the Homeric tradition, but suppressed by it. One could never guess from Homer's portrayal of the Olympian gods the dark and bloody myths of the earlier generations of gods which appear in Hesiod's *Theogony*. Yet for Homer too Zeus is 'son of Cronos'; and this implies much of Hesiod's account.

In Hesiod we find not one creation of mankind, but five. First, while Cronos was still ruling in heaven, the Olympian gods made a golden *genos* (race, generation) of men, who 'lived like gods, with a heart free from care, without toil or woe'. They did not suffer from old age, but were always 'alike as to (the strength of) their hands and feet'. They had a life of pleasant feasting on the good things which the earth provided of its own accord; and death for them was like falling asleep. When this race was covered by the earth, they became beneficial *daimones* (lesser supernatural powers) who are kindly and watch over men. (The manuscripts add that they keep watch invisibly over judgments and cruel deeds; but some scholars doubt whether these lines are rightly located here.) After the earth had covered them, the Olympians made a second, silver, *genos*, very different from the first. Its children took a hundred years to become adult; and once adult they lived only a short time, for they kept wronging one another, and would not serve, nor sacrifice to, the gods. Accordingly, Zeus – who had by this time ousted his father Cronos from the throne of heaven – was angry and 'hid them away'. They, having vanished beneath the earth, became blessed spirits of the underworld. Thereupon Zeus made a third, bronze, *genos*, of men who had great strength and loved war. They had bronze armour, bronze houses, and bronze tools: there was no iron. The members of this *genos* destroyed each other by their own hands and went down to Hades, and left no name behind them.

A pattern seems to be developing; but Hesiod next relates that when the earth had covered the bronze *genos* Zeus made a fourth, which was more just and better than its immediate predecessors, 'a godlike *genos* of "heroes", who are called demigods', the *genos* which dwelt in the boundless earth immediately before our own. Some of these were killed in the war against Thebes, some in the Siege of Troy; but (167)

> To the others father Zeus, son of Cronos, vouchsafed a livelihood and a place to dwell apart from men, and established them at the ends of the earth. And they dwell with their *thumos* free from care in the Islands of the Blest by the deep-eddying Ocean, blessed 'heroes', for whom the grain-giving earth three times a year bears honey-sweet fruit.

A *genos* better than its predecessor; but then Zeus made another, iron, *genos*, whose characteristics provoke an outburst from Hesiod (174):

> Would that I were not among the fifth (*genos* of) men, but either had died before or had been born afterwards. For now indeed there is a *genos* of iron, and men never cease from toil and woe by day, and from destruction

by night; and the gods will bring harsh troubles on them. Yet even these
will have some good things mixed with their woes. And Zeus will destroy
this *genos* of mortal men, when they have grey hair on their temples at
the time of their birth.

Hesiod continues with a picture of a society in which every social
relationship, every loyalty, will have broken down and vanished (197):

Then *Aidōs* (shame at doing wrong) and *Nemesis* (anger at seeing another
commit wrong and prosper), with their beautiful bodies wrapped in white
robes, will go from the broad-wayed earth to the company of the immortal
gods, and leave mankind; and grievous sorrows will be left for mortal men,
and there will be no resource against evil.

The basis of this account is a schematic myth. Schemes of successive
ages occur in oriental texts, though not in the form of sequences
of metal-races in any extant version. Such schemes are mythical,
not historical; but the historical element in Hesiod's account should
not be overlooked. The part of the narrative concerned with more
recent events has at least one foot in history. Hesiod knew that the
men of the Bronze Age (in the archaeologist's, not the mythographer's,
sense) used bronze tools; and he and his audience knew, so that it is
unnecessary for him to mention it, that in their own day iron tools
were usual. The more remote ages are purely mythical: there is
nothing to suggest that Hesiod believed that their members used gold
and silver tools; and the qualitative, ethical values given to the metals
also betoken mythological, not historical, modes of thought.

The scheme of four metal-ages may be a Greek variant of schemes
of ages found elsewhere; but it seems unlikely to be Hesiod's own, for
there is little inducement to develop a new schematic myth if one
proposes immediately to disrupt it by introducing a non-mythical
element, as Hesiod does here. The myth requires continuous degeneration; but Hesiod knew that the age immediately before his own had
been the Heroic Age of Greece, generally regarded as a good time to
have been alive. Writers in other places and at other periods would
have suppressed this historical fact in the interest of mythological
neatness. Hesiod yields to history; and in so doing manifests an early
indication of a temper of mind which was to play a large part in Greece.

Much, however, remains schematic; and the scheme portrays continuous degeneration as a fact, related without ethical intent. Justice
is praised where it occurs; and it renders life more tolerable where
it does occur; but it does not and cannot halt the steady progress to
the horrors of the last stage of Hesiod's account. The silver and bronze
races deserved their ends; the golden and 'heroic' did not. No reason
is given why the gods should create successively worse races: the
myth simply expresses the belief that they do so.

If, however, we state that Hesiod believed that human nature
inevitably tended towards the worse[1] with the passage of time, we are
using more systematic terminology than Hesiod can command. His
five *genē* are five separate creations, with very different characteristics.[2] It is clear that Hesiod regards them all as being human; but he
has not asked, and it would be pointless for us to enquire, what
renders them all human. Mythological thought does not raise such
questions.

Once the scheme was accepted, myth could locate other events
relevant to the origin and development of Man within it. Pindar, in
his *Ninth Olympian Ode* (42 ff.), refers to the Greek myth of the Flood,
and narrates how Deucalion and Pyrrha (the Greek Mr. and Mrs.
Noah), on coming down from Mount Parnassus, on the top of which
they had survived the flood, first made a house, and then 'without
wedlock made a stone progeny to be of one people (with each other)'.
These were called *lāoi* ('people', here derived from *lāas*, 'a stone').
Deucalion and Pyrrha themselves procreated, in the usual manner,
the brazen-shielded ancestors of the rulers of the Locrians (in whose
honour the *Ninth Olympian Ode* is composed), young men 'sprung
from the daughters of the race of Iapetus and the mighty sons of

---

[1] Hesiod's source (cp. *Works and Days* 174 f.) may well have treated this as
part of a cycle which, taken as a whole, returned by some means, either directly
or gradually, to the golden *genos*. Plato's myth in the *Politicus* 269C ff. may well
be derived from the same source (e.g. *Works and Days* 181 may be compared
with *Politicus* 270D/E), though Plato, in his usual manner, has imbued the
material with his own thought. Hesiod himself has little interest in the possibility
that life might be less unpleasant for future generations of mankind.

[2] In our manuscripts the text is very fragmentary at the point of the creation
of the Iron *genos*, and it is not clearly stated that Zeus created it. However,
given the schematic nature of the account, it would be necessary for Hesiod
to state very explicitly that Zeus – or the gods in general – had *not* created it.

Cronos'. Pindar treats the story of the Flood allusively, as a well-known story. His account is filled out by that of Apollodorus, a writer probably of the first century A.D., but one drawing on earlier mythographers. In his version (I, vii, 2) Deucalion, son of Prometheus and grandson of Iapetus, married Pyrrha, daughter of Epimetheus and Pandora, the first woman, made by the gods. When Zeus wished to destroy the bronze *genos*, Deucalion on Prometheus' advice made a chest, and set sail in it with Pyrrha. They floated for nine days and nights, during which time the greater part of Greece was flooded and all men except a few who fled to the high mountains were drowned. After nine days and nights the chest drifted to Mount Parnassus, where Deucalion and Pyrrha landed. Zeus allowed Deucalion to choose any gift he wanted, and he chose to make men. On Zeus' instructions he and Pyrrha took stones and threw them over their heads; and the stones which Deucalion threw became men, while those that Pyrrha threw became women. Hence people were called *laos*, from *laas* a stone. Deucalion and Pyrrha also procreated children in the usual manner, among whom was Hellen, whose sons were Dorus, Xouthus and Aeolus; and Xouthus' sons were Achaeus and Ion. Hellen was the eponymous ancestor of the Hellenes in general, Dorus, Aeolus, Achaeus and Ion of the Dorians, Aeolians, Achaeans and Ionians respectively.

This myth is set in the Hesiodic pattern of the five ages or *gene*, at the point where the bronze *genos* perished, though the account of its perishing differs from that given in the *Works and Days*. The thought is, however, more historical, and is concerned to demonstrate – not without an ulterior motive – continuity of descent at least from the bronze *genos* onwards, at all events at the highest levels of society. Pindar too is starting from the end of the bronze *genos*: the 'heroes' of the 'heroic' *genos* also used bronze weapons, and the 'brazen-shielded' ancestors of the Locrian kings, born after the Flood but procreated by Deucalion and Pyrrha, who belong to the bronze *genos*, are 'heroic'. Pindar only mentions the ancestors of the Locrian kings, for it is to a Locrian audience that his ode is addressed; but Apollodorus makes it clear that members of all the main branches of the Hellenic stock claimed descent from Pyrrha and Deucalion, and hence a direct connection with the bronze *genos*. If we combine the two versions, and take into account the link between *laos*, people, and *laas*, stone, it is clear that it is the nobility that traces its ancestry from the bronze *genos*, while the common people are sprung from stones.

It is impossible – and pointless to try – to harmonise this account completely with Hesiod's Five Ages. If one made the attempt, the stone-people would be the common people of the 'heroic' age, who, in the discontinuities of that myth, ceased to exist (as did also the nobles) at the end of that age. This much more historical account has a different purpose. The 'Five Ages' myth emphasises the inevitable degeneration of the human race, though its mode of doing so posits five separate races. The Deucalion story sharply distinguishes the provenance of nobles and common people, gives intellectual respectability to the claim of many Greek noble families to derive their lineage from a 'hero', and could well be used as a 'justification' for the rule of the noble families, clearly made of 'better stuff' than the commons.

That Greek thought of the period held it possible that some of the human race were procreated by Deucalion and Pyrrha, some sprung from stones, renders it meaningless to look for any concept of human nature founded on the unity of the human race. Here as elsewhere, however, the point should not be overstated. The myth has the precise purpose of justifying class-division, and might be employed as an argument that individuals of different classes should not marry; we should not infer, however, that the Greeks had an idea of biologically different species here, whose union would be unproductive. The idea is much too sophisticated for the period, and the purpose of the myth is different.

We should note that Pandora is treated as being 'the first woman' in Apollodorus. The same account occurs in Hesiod, *Works and Days*, 54 ff. In this passage of Hesiod, Pandora is made by Hephaestus out of earth and water. It is difficult to relate this to the scheme of the Five Ages. In Apollodorus' account, however, she is Pyrrha's mother; and in Hesiod's *Catalogue of Women* Deucalion's daughter, which places her at the end of the bronze *genos* or the beginning of the 'heroic' *genos*. Now Hesiod was something of a misogynist; but even he did not suggest that the greater bliss of the golden and silver *gene* lay in the absence of women: indeed, mothers are mentioned in the account of the silver *genos* (*Works and Days*, 130). We should not conclude that Hesiod supposes that 'the human race' only begins with the bronze *genos*, so that the first female of that species is the 'first woman'. The myth of Pandora is a separate one, not constructed to fit into the Five Ages; though it remains true, as we have seen, that the last three *gene* are much more 'historical' than the earlier ones.

This is not the only kind of discrepancy: there is an alternative belief in the nature of the origin and development of Man, associated with the name of Prometheus. This belief receives its fullest treatment of the kind with which we are concerned in this chapter in Aeschylus' *Prometheus Bound*. In this play, Aeschylus acknowledges the existence of the 'Five Ages' belief, and rejects it. When Zeus had just come to the throne after the deposition of Cronos, 231 ff.,

> He took no account of wretched mortals, but wished to destroy the whole *genos* and beget a new one. . . . But I rescued mortals from being rent in pieces and going to the house of Hades.

In Hesiod's myth, Zeus' assumption of power marks the end of the golden *genos*, the beginning of the silver. Zeus, says Prometheus, wished to destroy one *genos* and create a new one; but Prometheus prevented him. There is continuity from the beginning of the human race. Such a view is evidently in this respect much more historical, less mythological, as is the condition of these men, who, if a correlation were possible, would correspond with Hesiod's silver *genos*. In Hesiod's account they had a hundred-year childhood and a short adult life, marked by wrongs committed against gods and their fellow-men; nevertheless they had a higher status than the subsequent *gene*, and became blessed spirits of the underworld after death. In Aeschylus the whole account is fuller and more realistic. They did not know how to construct houses, but lived underground in sunless recesses like ants. They could not tell summer from winter until Prometheus taught them to tell the seasons by the stars. He also taught them to count (459), to write (460 f.), to domesticate animals (462 ff.), and to sail the seas (467 ff.). In addition, he taught them medicine (478 ff.), prophecy of various kinds (484 ff.), and (500 ff.)

Who would say that he had discovered the benefits of mankind hidden within the earth, bronze, iron gold and silver, before I did? No one, I am sure, unless he wished to talk nonsense.

The emphasis on real, not mythological, gold and silver, bronze and iron may again be an implied reference to the Hesiodic version, as may Prometheus' insistence that he, and not any steady progression of ages or *gene*, brought these metals into the hands of men.

References or no, there is a profound difference between the two versions. Degeneration from a golden age is opposed by a progress from helplessness and barbarism to civilisation. Pessimism is opposed by a qualified optimism – qualified in so far as Prometheus had to give these blessings to mankind in the teeth of Zeus' opposition, an opposition which at the period portrayed in the play has chained Prometheus, for punishment, to a rock in the Caucasus; and Zeus is still in power. We have, unfortunately, only one play of Aeschylus' Prometheus trilogy, and we do not know Aeschylus' ending. It used to be assumed that Zeus mended his ways and became a benevolent ruler of mankind in the last play; but this is mere supposition, and much in fifth-century Attic belief portrayed a Zeus far from benevolent. However, this myth portrays mankind, with or without Zeus' approval, as having made progress. Not necessarily as being on an upward path whose end is not yet in sight: the Greeks, when optimistic, were in general inclined to be complacent, and to assume that the goal of mankind's development had been reached, or at least that it could be described (as Plato did) and aimed at.

After Aeschylus had written the Prometheus trilogy, then, a Greek acquainted with the work of both Hesiod and Aeschylus, or the wider current of thought and belief in which they wrote, could certainly choose between these two world-pictures, pessimistic and optimistic, of the origin and development of mankind. (I do not mean to imply that such Greeks in the first half of the fifth century B.C. – or the majority of Greeks for long afterwards – could be divided into those who consistently held the optimistic, and those who consistently held the pessimistic view. Surviving literature indicates that early Greeks, and even Aeschylus himself, readily held at the same time conflicting views on matters of myth and religion; in different moods, the same person might well hold each of these views in turn.)

The extent to which an optimistic view was current before the time of Aeschylus is a matter of inference. Prometheus occurs in Hesiod too: there, in an evident aetiological myth, to explain the Greeks' practice in sacrificing to the Olympians, he is portrayed as tricking Zeus into accepting the bones and fat as the gods' portion of a sacrifice, leaving the bulk of the meat to the human worshippers (*Theogony* 548 ff.). Zeus (*Works and Days* 50 ff.) in anger

> Hid fire, but the noble son of Iapetus (Prometheus) stole it again for men from Zeus the counsellor in a hollow fennel-stalk, and escaped the notice of Zeus who delights in thunder.

Zeus' punishment of mankind, on discovering Prometheus' theft, consisted in the creation of Pandora, which, as we have seen, took place in Hesiod's account after the period of the golden and silver *gene*, who presumably enjoyed the benefits of fire before Zeus hid it.

Here Prometheus confers one benefit on mankind by securing for them the best part of sacrificial offerings; and both he and mankind are punished, mankind by being deprived of the benefits of fire. Prometheus confers a further benefit by stealing fire back again; and mortals are again punished. In Hesiod he appears as a clever meddler, whom Zeus punished, as in Aeschylus, by binding him to a rock in the Caucasus, and assigning an eagle to devour his liver; though he is thus punished for his deceit over the sacrifices, not for his theft of fire. All his actions, as Hesiod tells the story, end disastrously; and his woes, and those of mankind, suit Hesiod's worldview; but why was such a bungler, who succeeds in benefiting neither mankind nor himself, ever named Prometheus (which transparently signifies Forethinker), if Hesiod's version of the story is the only one current in early Greece? Furthermore, it is difficult to understand the religious motive for composing a myth of the hiding of fire already possessed by mortals, and its subsequent recovery by Prometheus. The myth of the theft of fire not already possessed is much easier to account for as a belief of early craftsmen who believe that their powers have to be won from a jealous heaven; and craftsmen worshipped Prometheus before the time of Aeschylus. Craftsmen naturally set a high value on their craft, are likely to contrast the present situation with the less happy lot of mankind if the craft were not known, and so might well have a – moderately – optimistic view of development and progress. By the time Prometheus had become associated with craftsmen – and he was doubtless originally, as H. J. Rose maintains, merely a clever trickster – he might well be associated with optimism. If this has any foundation in fact – and it is frankly speculative – Hesiod's rather odd account of the hiding from mankind of a fire already possessed by them and its subsequent recovery by Prometheus may result from an attempt to fit Prometheus, whose theft, from a craftsman's point of view, benefited mankind, if not Prometheus himself, into Hesiod's own overall pessimism: mankind originally had all blessings, so that the golden age cannot have lacked something so beneficial as fire; yet Prometheus stole fire, as myth relates; accordingly the theft must constitute the recovery of fire originally possessed by mortals, but taken from them in punishment; and the theft must result in yet more woes for mortals.

Here we should observe the difficulty, already noted at the beginning of the chapter, of classifying the material. Exception may well be taken to my setting Aeschylus' account in this chapter at all. His version of the development of mankind is in a real sense clearly more 'modern' than Hesiod's; and the tone of Prometheus' utterances in the play, in critically rejecting the other model of human development, doubtless owes much to contemporary thought. Thus far Aeschylus' version is forward-looking, and points onward to the more radical thinking of the later years of the fifth century. However, Aeschylus' picture is still ahistorical: the idea of the culture-hero and Titan himself conferring benefits on mankind all at once is pure myth; and though the development from helplessness to civilisation is historical as the decline from a golden age is not, the historical sequence from bronze age to iron age, present in Hesiod's account, is absent from Aeschylus' version. Aeschylus' thought points both backwards and forwards: he is much less 'traditional' than Hesiod, but I find it quite appropriate to discuss his Prometheus-myth in this chapter.[1]

---

[1] In Plato's *Protagoras*, on the other hand, Protagoras is portrayed by Plato (320C ff.) as teaching a less 'traditional' version. The gods created man and the animal species and gave them to Prometheus (Forethinker) and Epimetheus (Afterthinker) to equip with the qualities which would enable them to survive. Some have speed, some claws, some prickles, and whereas predators have few young, their prey have many. There is scientific observation here; but when

C. Psychology

The psychological structure which is characteristic of Homeric man does not persist in its entirety after the Homeric poems. Certain aspects continue: the calculative model – though 'calculative' is, as already noted, somewhat misleading[1] – or the picture of the spectral balance, the absence of a concept of will, are endemic in the ancient Greek view of man, and will appear in different guises at different periods. But the extreme democracy of Homeric psychology does not persist, though some early writers draw freely on Homeric vocabulary for their own compositions: a central core of self is beginning to develop, despite the tensions of a shame- and results-culture, many of which still remain, as will be seen. There is no analysis of the situation in the writers of the seventh, sixth and fifth centuries, of course: they have neither the interests nor the conceptual equipment required; but the change from Homeric phraseology gives one indication of the development.

Parallel with this is the emergence of historical individuals with well-defined personalities. This is most apparent in the case of authors. In the bardic tradition the majority of the material handled by the bard was inherited from earlier bards. The society being non-literate, the transmission was oral, and the poem existed only in performance, in which the inherited and the bard's own intended or accidental variations were inextricably intertwined. To perform a long poem in this manner necessitates the 'spontaneous' occurrence to the mind of the formulaic material acquired by the bard in the course of his

Epimetheus exhausts all the qualities before equipping man, Prometheus steals fire and the skill in arts and crafts from Athena and Hephaestus and gives them to mankind: the whole is still set in the framework of myth. However, Protagoras also observes that mankind originally had not the political skill; and so either lived in isolation, when they fell prey to wild beasts, or assembled into cities, and, for want of political skill, were forever wronging each other, so that their associations broke up. Zeus accordingly sent Hermes to grant justice and reverence to mankind, so that human associations might be possible. The whole is a blend of traditional and new. It is more optimistic than Aeschylus' version: the gods want men and animals to be equipped for survival; and when the survival of the human race appears doubtful, Zeus himself – not Prometheus – sends them another, additional skill even, though the theft-motif can apparently not be discarded from the earlier part of the myth.

[1] Above, p. 48.

training: when performing, the bard necessarily feels himself under the sway of forces not altogether under his own control. Such spontaneous surges are attributed to deities, in this case usually the Muses, who are – significantly – the daughters of Memory. It is their function, so far as the oral bard is concerned, to supply his material, which exists nowhere 'on paper', when he needs it, *not* to supply inspiration for poetry more sublime than the poet could otherwise compose: the most heartfelt invocation of the Muse occurs at the beginning of the Catalogue of the Ships in *Iliad* II, a versified Army List, distinguished by its being difficult to remember and the greater necessity, since the facts and figures were held to be historical, of remembering it correctly. The bards are, accordingly, in a state of some tension: it is clear from the Homeric poems themselves that a good bard was valued, and naturally any bard would desire to win what renown he could; yet he was, in performing as a bard, heavily in the debt both of his profession and the Muse. Phemius the minstrel, praising himself to Odysseus, says (*Odyssey* XXII, 347):

I am self-taught, and the god caused all manner of lays to spring up in my *phrenes*.

'Self-taught', unless the author is asserting the impossible for this bard of the heroic age, must be understood in terms of a bardic tradition: Phemius has developed new poems from the formulaic stock he has inherited. More important here is the conjunction of 'self-taught' and 'the god': even in striving to accord himself the maximum of credit, he has to acknowledge the spontaneous, 'given' element in his life and work. Phemius is not referring directly to the moment of performance; but the performer must have felt this tension acutely. One must not extrapolate without due care from the case of the oral bard, who is in a very special situation; but the Homeric hero too is striving for fame, and at the same time possessed of a highly spontaneous and fragmented personality, some of whose promptings he attributes to divine agency.

Without necessarily asserting any more than an interesting parallelism, we may note the emergence of literate authors with highly individual, and in some cases craggy, personalities, and also a greater centralisation of the personality structure in general. It is possible to

illustrate this by linguistic development. In later chapters it will
again be necessary to survey a wide range of psychological functions.
Here the discussion may be confined to the development of *psuche*;
for it was *psuche*, the least significant in life of the psychological
functions in Homer, that was to become the core or carrier of the
personality in the more reflective and analytic systems of psychology,
so that the different functions in such systems became functions of
the *psuche*.

Development begins at a time when scientific and philosophical
thought can have no part to play. The old Homeric use indeed continues. Tyrtaeus (10, 14)[1] can exhort the Spartans to fight without
sparing their *psuchai*: elsewhere (15, 5) he uses *zōē*, the ordinary
Greek word for biological life, in the same phrase. Hyperbolically
(11, 5) he can even exhort the soldier to treat his *psuche* as an enemy,
death as a friend; and late in the fifth century Euripides can use 'to
be fond of one's *psuche*' in the sense of 'clinging to life' (*Iphigenia at
Aulis* 1385). We find the usage which we render 'ghost' employed
by Aeschylus of the dead Agamemnon (*Agamemnon* 1545) and Darius
(*Persae* 630); and by Sophocles of the shade of Laius (*Oedipus at Colonus*
999).

Furthermore, we observed in Homer that *psuche* was a tenuous
physical stuff, for Homer has no concept of the non-material; and we
shall discover that the early doctors and philosophers hold a similar
view. In this light, some expressions which we read as metaphors
should probably be differently interpreted. In Sophocles' *Electra*
(775) Clytemnestra speaks of Orestes as 'born from her *psuche*', and a
few lines later of Electra as 'draining the blood of her [Clytemnestra's]
psuche'; while in Euripides' *Ion* (1168) a servant reports a feast thus:

> When the hall was full, adorned with garlands they filled their *psuche*
> with rich food.

Now Electra was only metaphorically draining the blood of Clytemnestra's *psuche*; but it does not follow that the blood of her *psuche*
is itself a metaphor; and when we recall that the Athenians of the fifth
century still offered food and drink to the *psuche* of the dead, which

---

[1] The references, in the case of elegiac poets, and lyric poets other than Pindar,
are to Bergk's edition.

was nourished thereby, we may reasonably conclude that the *psuche* is, in life and in death, a tenuous physical stuff in the fifth century too. The question will be treated more fully below.[1]

The *psuche* has acquired new characteristics since Homer. It now experiences sensation and emotion in life. Not in the earlier writers discussed in this chapter; but in the sixth century Hipponax (43 Bergk) has a 'much-groaning *psuche*' and Anacreon (4 Bergk) a *psuche* under the influence of love; while in Simonides, who lived in the late sixth and early fifth centuries, we find the injunction (85, 14) to 'gratify one's *psuche* with good things' and (140, 2) to 'obey the courageous temper of one's *psuche*'. A *psuche* which experiences sensation and emotion is new: earlier poets like Sappho, Alcaeus and Archilochus are highly emotional, but they do not mention *psuche* in this connection. In the fifth century, the usage appears in Aeschylus: the ghost (*psuche*, *Persae* 630) of the dead Darius (840) exhorts the Persian elders to 'give their *psuche* some pleasure every day, since wealth is of no avail to the dead'. The *psuche* has some gratifications which do not endure beyond the grave. *Psuchai* in Aeschylus are also enduring (*Persae* 28), brave (442), or cowardly (*Agamemnon* 1643); and may experience woes or pains (*Seven against Thebes* 1033, *Prometheus Bound* 693). The emotional *psuche* has evidently arrived by the beginning of the fifth century. (Sophocles, Euripides and other later writers produce copious examples.)

The *psuche* can also think in the fifth century. It shows little sign of active intelligence in Aeschylus, though it can be addressed, like Homer's *thumos*, and must therefore have consciousness: Antigone apostrophises her *psuche* (*Seven against Thebes* 1034). In Sophocles, the *psuche* once addresses its possessor (*Antigone* 227): the guard, explaining why he has not come more quickly, says 'my *psuche* said many things to me (to dissuade me)'. The expression, however, is quaint and unusual, and may be humorously intended: there is humour in the passage. Already in Sophocles, however, the *psuche* displays active intelligence.[2] Philoctetes (*Philoctetes* 1013) accuses Odysseus of corrupting Neoptolemus:

[1] See chapter 4, pp. 107 ff.
[2] This use of *psuche* in the *Philoctetes* may be a result of the New Thought, which influenced the play in other respects: see *Merit and Responsibility*, p. 189.

Your *psuche*, ever looking out from an ambush, had well instructed him . . .
to be cunning in working harm.

The harm is to deceive Philoctetes' *psuche* (54). In Euripides, Orestes
tells his sister that he knows that there is intelligence in her *psuche*
(*Orestes* 1180); and examples could readily be multiplied.

The *psuche*, in fact, can now manifest every aspect of the personality;
and it is quite naturally used in fifth-century authors in contexts
where it could be replaced either by 'person' or by the personal
pronoun. So Aeschylus in a fragment speaks of the *psuche* adrift on
the waves; the Chorus in Sophocles' *Ajax* (154) says that anyone who
aimed criticism at great *psuchai* could not miss; Oedipus (*Oedipus at
Colonus* 1207), when sought by Creon, asks Theseus to reassure him
that no-one will get control over his *psuche*, clearly referring to his
person as a whole;[1] while in Thucydides, who uses *psuche* very rarely,
we find (I, 136, 4)

> Themistocles also argued that he had opposed Admetus in some business
> matter, and not when his *soma* was at stake; but that, if Admetus handed him
> over to his enemies, he would be depriving him of the safety of his *psuche*.

Here in two balanced clauses *soma*, body, and *psuche* are each used of
the person to make precisely the same point. (Thucydides does not
contrast *soma* and *psuche*: he contrasts both *psuche*, III, 39, 8 and *soma*
as in VIII, 45, 4, denoting persons, with inanimate resources, *chrēmata*;
and this is interesting, in view of the influence which medical thought
is held to have had upon Thucydides, for doctors, as will be seen in
the next chapter, freely contrast *psuche* with *soma*.)

Two points must be made in summing up the 'ordinary' usage
of *psuche* at this period. In the first place, we are not concerned here

---

[1] This, at all events, is what Oepidus is saying, in the immediate dramatic
context. Sophocles may well intend the audience, knowing that Oedipus is
soon to be heroised, also to have the 'spirit of the dead' aspect of *psuche* in their
minds: the *psuche* of the heroised Oedipus will be a powerful ally when he is
dead. (Jebb's contention that *psuche* never refers to the spirit of the dead in
tragedy, *Oedipus at Colonus* 997 ff., is unsound: see Aeschylus, *Persae* 630, *Agamemnon* 1545.) Of course, in order to get possession of the *psuche* of the dead
and heroised Oedipus Creon would have to remove Oedipus' body, too, to The-
ban territory (see p. 70 below).

with a theory of the *psuche*. No ancient Greek of the fifth century analysed, as I have just done, the usage of *psuche*, and came to the conclusion that he and his fellows ascribed these characteristics to the *psuche*. On the other hand, here as always we must beware of ascribing separate 'meanings' to the word, which are simply the different English words we are compelled to use in rendering the one Greek word into English. What we have discovered is the range of attributes which a Greek of the period found it natural to ascribe to his *psuche*; and in the increase of range, particularly in the fifth century, we see the development of the *psuche* as the core or carrier of the personality in Greek thought.

There remains a use of *psuche* attested for the first time in this period which does betoken a deliberately adopted, and unusual, viewpoint. Xenophanes (6, 4) says that Pythagoras once saw a puppy being beaten, and asked the man who was beating it to stop 'for it is the *psuche* of a friend, which I recognise by its voice'; and Pindar (*Olympian* II, 68 ff.) says:

> All men who have had the courage three times . . . to keep their *psuche* utterly free from injustice, have accomplished the road of Zeus to the tower of Cronos: in the islands of the blest sea breezes waft about them and golden flowers blaze.

Here we have an unusual belief, and an unusual usage of *psuche*: Xenophanes is deriding the belief as bizarre, and Pindar only rarely exhibits it, when it was held by the particular patron for whom he was writing. It is associated with the names of Pythagoreanism, Orphism, and with mystery-cults in general. There is no need to attempt to distinguish these cults for the present purpose: all are agreed in according to the *psuche*, once separated from the body, a much more real personality and existence than did the usual Greek belief of the period. Some, like Pythagoras, believed that the *psuche* would be reincarnated in another body, human, animal or plant: Pythagoras (A8)[1] claimed that he could remember the whole sequence of his incarnations. Pindar here expresses the belief that three just lives would release one from the cycle of reincarnations. Others held

[1] The reference is to the edition of Diels/Kranz, for which see chapter 4, note I.

that after one existence the *psuche* went to a better or worse lot after death, as a result of certain things that it had done or left undone in this life.

Where justice is the criterion, belief in a Last Judgment is possible;[1] but the evidence suggests that in all its forms this is a belief of a minority in Greece,[2] and one whose use of *psuche* does not clearly antedate the appearance of an increased range of the word in 'ordinary language'. Indeed, Aeschylus and Aristophanes make use of the belief without using *psuche* in this sense (*Suppliants* 228 ff.; *Eumenides* 269 ff.; *Frogs*, 145 ff. and 354 ff.). This belief and the developments in 'ordinary language' each give greater emphasis to the *psuche* as the core and carrier of personality, and reflect an increased consciousness of individuality; but they are parallel phenomena; neither is the cause of the other.

D. Life and Death

The characteristic view of life and death in the Homeric poems is that this life is all, the next dank and shadowy. At its most insubstantial the *psuche* merely flutters and twitters witlessly in (the house of) Hades; at best the *psuchai* are cheered or saddened there by their surviving fame, good or ill; and the success and good fame, or failure and ill-fame, of their descendants, similarly affect them; but they are themselves too far away to be able to exert any influence on events in this life; and their existence is too insubstantial and 'unreal' to offer any hope of reward, or fear of punishment, for the deeds and misdeeds of this life.

---

[1] See *Merit and Responsibility*, pp. 140 ff.

[2] The question is difficult. The belief is certainly rare in extant literature; but we have only the recorded thoughts of a small minority of Greeks, mostly drawn from Athens, and from one social class of Athenians. Democritus (B199 and B297 Diels/Kranz) speaks of it as a belief which blights the life of many; and this may have been true in cities of which we know nothing. (*Kakopragmosunē*, 'evil-doing', in B297 indicates that Democritus is speaking of a Last Judgment for those who have committed misdeeds in this life, not the unpleasantness of the dank but neutral Homeric Hades.) In Athens, the problem remains: the State sponsored the Eleusinian Mysteries, which were deeply reverenced by the Athenians, and propagated belief in salvation through initiation, yet in funeral orations over men dead in war the 'Homeric' view of the next life is characteristic (see, for example, Demosthenes 60, 34, Lysias 2, *passim*); and here the audience must be a large one, drawn from much of the citizen-body.

That the dead are in a neutral Hades, far away, is not the only belief held in the centuries after Homer; but it continues to be prevalent. 'To go to [the house of] Hades' is a commonplace for 'to die'[1]. The prospect, once there, is no more pleasing: Theognis says (973 ff.):

> No-one of mankind, whom the earth covers and who goes down to Erebus, the abode of Persephone, takes pleasure in hearing the lyre or the flute-player, or in raising to his lips the gift of Dionysus.

This remains the most usual – or best attested – view of Hades throughout the period under discussion, and beyond. However, the dead, as in Homer, have some consolations, or woes. In the course of the great lament in Aeschylus' *Choephori*, Orestes thus apostrophises his father, the murdered Agamemnon, 345 ff.:

> For if you had been wounded by the spear and slain under Ilium by one of the Lycians, father, you would have left fair fame in your palace, and would have established an admired life for your children as they went their ways; and you would have had a high-heaped tomb in a land across the sea, a death bearable for the palace.

The Chorus adds, 345 ff.:

> You would have been welcomed by your comrades there who died gloriously (*kalōs*), a ruler, august, of high status, conspicuous beneath the earth, and would have been the minister of the mightiest rulers there (Pluto and Persephone). For you were a king, while you were alive.[2] . . .

An honourable death incurred while fighting bravely in battle would have earned Agamemnon fair reputation on this earth, and a position of high status and esteem in the shame-culture of the dead. Nothing more is to be hoped for than this even by one who was a king on earth; and nothing to be feared other than the scorn of one's fellow-dead. Such scorn is imagined as Agamemnon's lot now; and nothing worse than rebukes and insults is the lot of Clytemnestra, Agamemnon's

---

[1] See, at the beginning of the period covered by this chapter, Tyrtaeus 12, 38, Mimnermus 2, 14; at the end, Sophocles, *Trachiniae* 4, *Philoctetes* 1349, *Oedipus Tyrannus* 1372.

[2] For a similar idea, cf. Demosthenes 60, 34.

wife and murderess, when she too goes to Hades (*Eumenides* 96 f.). One of Antigone's motives for burying Polyneices, though the penalty is death, is that she wishes to be on good terms with him after death (*Antigone* 73 ff.); and Oedipus (*Oedipus Tyrannus* 1371 ff.) says that he does not know how he will be able to look his parents in the face in Hades. Some of these situations are terrible enough; but there is no Last Judgment in addition to be feared.

Another belief locates the dead much nearer to the living. Since the corpse or the bones after cremation has been placed in the earth, and the living have seen it placed there, there is always the inducement to suppose that not merely the visible and tangible remains of the dead are there, but his personality, doubtless dimmed and dulled in some respects, as well. If the dead man is there, and conscious, even to a reduced extent, of his surroundings, powers to help or harm are likely to be assigned to him; and the living will prudently try to assure his good will by appropriate offerings. Certain archaeological evidence suggests that the practice of feeding the dead by pouring liquids into their graves was known in the eighth century B.C.; and the dead risen, from their graves nearby, were held to frequent the city during the spring festival of the Anthesteria. Again, Plato, *Laws* 865D3 ff., records as 'an ancient myth' that

> The man who has died a violent death, and has lived as a free man with a free man's passions, is angry with his killer while he is still newly dead and, being himself filled with fear and terror because of the violence he has suffered and seeing his killer going about his daily life as and where he had been wont to do, is afraid and, being himself in a state of alarm, does all he can to alarm the man who did the deed.

The dead man is nearby, sentient, capable of emotion and of affecting the living. The same belief occurs in tragedy. We have seen that in the great lament of the *Choephori* the Chorus refers to Agamemnon as in Hades (354 ff.). Yet we find in the same play (479 ff.) the following lines in which Orestes and Electra invoke their father Agamemnon:

> *Orestes*: Father, who died in no kingly manner, grant me lordship over your palace when I ask it. . . . For thus would mortals' customary feasts be established in your honour. Otherwise, at the sumptuous and steaming

banquets of burnt offerings made to those beneath the earth you will be
without a share, *atīmos.*
Electra: And I will bring libations to you out of my inheritance from our
ancestral palace when I marry; and I will hold this tomb in highest honour
of all.
Orestes: O Earth, send up my father to watch over the battle!
Electra: O Persephassa,[1] grant us goodly victory!

They remind Agamemnon of the shameful circumstances of his
death, and add, 495 f.:

Orestes: Are you stirred up by these hurtful words, father?
Electra: Do you raise up your most dear head?

Orestes and Electra are here addressing Agamemnon as a powerful
free-lance spirit lurking in his tomb, who can give them help if he
will. They offer to him the same kind of threats and inducements
which the Greeks of the period offer to the Olympian gods; for
though the murdered Agamemnon should be eager to avenge himself
(as they indeed remind him, 491 ff.), spirits and deities are always
liable to be capricious in Greece, and the dead's wits are dulled: in
pouring the libation to Agamemnon, the Chorus calls upon him to
listen 'from his dimmed mind' (157), and Orestes, who has just been
calling on Agamemnon's help, refers to him (517) as 'dead and not
thinking'. (The text has been doubted in the second case, not in the
first.) Yet if his help can be secured, it is powerful.

We have already seen that the ordinary dead, in this strand of
belief, are held to have some power to affect the living. The men
and women who are the principal characters in tragedy are far from
ordinary; and they, in death, sometimes are, or approximate to,
'heroes', in the sense which that word comes to bear after Homer
and Hesiod. For Homer, describing an age gone by, 'heroes' are the
prominent living warriors who fight in the foremost ranks of the
Greeks and Trojans. Some have one divine parent and might be termed
'demigods'; but when killed they go down to Hades and flutter with
the rest. For Hesiod, the 'heroes' belong to the age before his own.
Those who were killed in battle, as we have seen, are in Hades, while

[1] Peresphone.

69

the remainder are not dead but alive in the Islands of the Blest; a reward promised to Menelaus in Homer on the grounds that he is Zeus' son-in-law.

In this belief, the 'heroes' are, by the time of composition of the poems, either dead and in Hades or living and in the Islands of the Blest, in either case too far away to help or harm, and in the former too powerless in addition. The belief which ascribed some power to any dead person, however, could ascribe superabundant power for good or ill to those who had given signs of such power in life. It is this power that is ascribed to Agamemnon here; to Achilles in Euripides' *Hecuba* (107 ff.); and to Oedipus in Sophocles' *Oedipus at Colonus* (385 ff.). What is acknowledged, and worshipped, in these dead men, is power: Oedipus is not heroised in *Oedipus at Colonus* because he has been morally rehabilitated, or because his character has in some sense improved – his character remains what it was – but because the strange power which men feel to inhere in this terrible blind old man is to continue beyond his death.

These examples are drawn from literature, but the belief is not confined to literature, myth and legend. (The tragic poets in fact seem disinclined to use the word 'hero', but the belief is the same.) The power of a 'hero' was exercised locally, in the land where his bones were buried.[1] Hence Creon in the *Oedipus at Colonus* wishes to carry off Oedipus from Attica, where he has taken refuge, back to Thebes. In life, the Delphic Oracle seems to have encouraged the belief: Herodotus (I, 67) tells how the Spartans, urged by Delphi to do so, searched for and discovered the bones of Orestes at Tegea, and carried them back to Sparta. Having done so, they were able to defeat the Tegeans, which they had previously been unable to do; for they now had the aid of Orestes. Similarly the Athenians in 475 B.C. transferred the bones of *their* 'hero' Theseus from Scyros to Athens.

Some worshipped as 'heroes' in this sense, like Theseus, Heracles and Oedipus, belong to the age of 'heroes' in the sense of Homer and Hesiod; and some have one human, one divine parent. Neither qualifi-

---

[1] Professor Dodds has suggested to me that the hero-cult grew up round local beehive-tombs in the post-Mycenean period of fragmentation: the hero, so to speak, embodies for wishful-thinking peasants the protective power of a vanished *oikos*. This seems to me very likely indeed.

cation was essential: heroisation might be accorded to anyone whose superabundant powers in life were supposed likely to survive his death. If the Spartan lawgiver Lycurgus was ever a living man – for many worshipped as 'heroes' never existed at all – he furnishes the first *historical* example of heroisation of which we know. Not, however, the last: in the full light of history (Thucydides V, 11) the inhabitants of Amphipolis heroised the dead Spartan general Brasidas who had fought so vigorously on their behalf while alive.

Beside the belief that the dead were remote and strengthless, there was then a belief that they were nearby in their tombs and had some power – and that some had a great deal. This is not an area of belief in which one expects rigid compartmentalisation, a state of affairs in which every believer has to make a firm choice of one belief rather than the other. Aeschylus shows how they are entwined together: in the *Choephori* lament, as we have seen, Agamemnon is referred to as both in an 'Homeric' Hades and able to help from his tomb. This is the kind of illogicality to be expected in this area of belief.

The dead, accordingly, all have the power, in one belief, to affect human life to some extent, and some possess a power and a status half-way between average men and gods. Indeed, it was held that sufficient *arete* could render a man divine (Aristotle, *Nicomachean Ethics* 1145a22).[1] Nevertheless, the 'hero', whether in his tomb or in some confused way also in Hades with high status, existed in an abode of gloom with a dulled mind. There was, however, a third strand of belief, first attested for us in the 'Homeric' *Hymn to Demeter*, which can hardly be later than the sixth century B.C. This describes the establishing of the mysteries at Eleusis, and states, 480 ff.:

> Blessed is he among men upon earth who has seen these things; but he who is not initiated and has no part in them never has a share of such good things when he is dead in the gloomy darkness.

To those who are initiated a better lot is offered after death. We may compare one of Pindar's *Laments for the Dead* (frag. 121):

> Blessed is he who has seen these things before descending beneath the earth: he knows the end of life, and its principle, given by Zeus.

[1] See above, note on p. 36, for the sense in which this is to be understood.

'He who has seen these things' is the initiate: we are once again concerned with a mystery-cult. Other fragments set out the initiates' advantages: they are perpetually to enjoy the light of their own sun, to ride, wrestle, throw dice, and in general live as gentlemen of leisure, in flowery meadows amid shady trees with golden fruits. To some, this future existence may have appeared overmaterialistic – similar beliefs were castigated by Plato (*Republic* 363D) as offering an everlasting drinking-party – but it is undoubtedly more attractive, and implies a more 'real' future existence for the *psuche*, than that offered by the other strands of belief.

How this belief was conceptually linked with others is suggested by the gold tablets found in the graves of adherents of a mystery-cult in the Greek-inhabited part of South Italy, in Crete, and in Thessaly. The tablets belong to the fourth and third centuries B.C., but the general tenor of belief is similar, and such beliefs long persisted. (The Eleusinian Mysteries, for example, persisted until the end of the fourth century A.D., when they were suppressed as a result of the influence of the early Christians.) The reason for the existence of these tablets is significant: the *psuche*, it seems, needs to have topographical information and appropriate forms of words to use on its journey to Bliss below. Mistakes would have serious consequences: the *psuche* is warned not to drink from a spring on the left of the palace of Hades, but to seek another cool spring which flows from the Lake of Memory. It is instructed thus to address those who guard the spring: 'I am the child of earth and starry heaven, but my birth is heavenly. This you know yourselves. I am parched and perishing with thirst. Give me straightway water from the Lake of Memory.' The guardians will give water to the *psuche*, which will subsequently 'reign among the other heroes'. Another stage on the journey is a meeting with Persephone and the other infernal gods. The *psuche* is to say: 'I come pure from pure. I claim to be of your blessed race, having paid the penalty for unjust acts committed. . . . But now I have come as a suppliant before the Lady Persephone, that she may graciously send me to the abodes of the pure.' Persephone is then to reply: 'Blessed and fortunate being, you shall be a god instead of a mortal. You have fallen as a kid into milk': and the *psuche*, it is to be supposed, joins the other heroes.

The mystery-cults, unlike other aspects of Greek religion, had something specific to impart to their adherents which marked them off from those who were not members of the cult. There were many cults; and sometimes what linked the members together was participation in secret ritual actions; but there was clearly opportunity here for the propagation of dogma about gods and men. In the case of the gold tablets (whose contents may well have been secret) there is evidently such a dogma; and it is possible to discern how this is linked with other streams of Greek belief. We have seen that, for Hesiod, those 'heroes' of the 'heroic' age who did not die are in the Islands of the Blest, where they enjoy a pleasant life. The initiate of this cult is to 'reign among the other heroes'. His initiation is to render him a hero after death. He is not to be in the Islands of the Blest, for he is dead, but in Hades. He is to reign among the heroes as Agamemnon might have reigned among the dead had he died honourably, or as Darius does in the *Persae* (691 f.). Now *they* seem to be 'heroes' in the sense of the second strand of belief discussed: powerful but dull-witted earthbound spirits lurking in their tombs, confusedly believed to be in some sense also in Hades. These initiated, however, are not to be such: they are to drink of the spring flowing out from the Lake of Memory; and it is to be supposed that they are as a result fully to keep their memory and wits. (The other stream presumably contains water of forgetfulness.) They are to have a much more 'real' future life than Agamemnon or Darius. Again, Menelaus' favoured treatment in Homer was accorded to him because he was Zeus' son-in-law: all these initiates claim to be of heavenly birth so far as their *psuche* is concerned (the body being 'child of earth'), and so with a claim to favoured treatment. Logically, of course, their *psuche* was heavenly, divine, whether they had been initiated or not; but clearly it is the *knowledge* of this fact and the ritual words that are supposed to guarantee the better lot in Hades; an illogicality entirely natural in the context of a closed mystery-cult.

The mystery-cults varied in many respects, but seem to have shared the characteristics of offering a better existence after death to their adherents, on the basis of a more 'real' existence of the *psuche*. This is a quite different belief from that, associated with the official religion, which held that the dead were nearby and must be fed and propitiated; but the idea that the *psuche* had some power, and that some *psuchai* had a great deal, must have helped to render the view of human nature held by the mystery-cults less unfamiliar than it might otherwise have been.

E. Values: Human Nature at its Best

In Homer, *arete*, *agathos* and similar words commended competitive striving for success, prosperity and stability as the highest goal of human nature in this life. This, in general, remains true in traditional Greek values. In the seventh and sixth centuries there was indeed much argument about the nature of *arete*.[1] The Homeric poems portray heroes idealised in terms of the most valued qualities in an environment which is a blend of tradition and imagination. Later poets, faced with harsher realities, attempt to redefine *arete*, usually taking part of the Homeric whole and emphasising it to the exclusion of other aspects.

For Hesiod, a small farmer, *arete* (*Works and Days* 289) commends success *per se*, the kind of success attainable by a small farmer if he works hard; for Tyrtaeus, the war-poet of Sparta, faced with the rigours of the Messenian wars, *arete* commends simply valour (12, 1):

> I would not reckon a man as being of any account because of the *arete* of his feet or for wrestling. . . . (not even) if he had every ground for fame but fierce valour; for a man does not become *agathos* in war if he should not hold firm when he sees bloody carnage, and thrust at the enemy from close at hand. This is *arete*.

Xenophanes likewise pours scorn on some qualities agreed to be *aretai* in his day. He says that a victorious athlete would be awarded a front seat at the games, meals at the public expense, and a prize (2, 11):

> Though he is not worth it, as I am. For better than the strength of men and horses is my wisdom, *sophiā*.

No amount of athletic success would bring sound government, stability and fair-dealing to a city; whereas Xenophanes' *sophia*

---

[1] See also *Merit and Responsibility*, pp. 70 ff.

would have this effect. His *sophia* is evidently practical wisdom exercised in a political context. Practical wisdom is not unvalued in Homer, and is part of *arete* in so far as it is an activity leading to success and prosperity; but Xenophanes is attempting to give it new emphasis and isolation. It is perhaps worth noting that Xenophanes avoids asserting that his *sophia* is *arete*. As will be seen in the later discussion, it was very difficult to deprive the successful soldier of his claim to *arete*: *sophia* might be enrolled as an *arete*, but the need for successful valour in a *polis* was too evident to be ignored.[1]

These Greeks are clearly now concerned with the problems of living in a *polis*. Theognis – or the poems of the Theognid corpus – reflects another aspect of the problems involved in the change from Homeric to later forms of social organisation. One Theognid poem has (185 ff.):

A man who is *esthlos* does not hesitate to marry a woman of low birth, *kakē*, if she furnishes him with much money; nor does a woman of high birth refuse a husband of low birth, but wants a wealthy husband rather than an *agathos*. They honour wealth. The *agathos* has married from the house of the *kakos*, the *kakos* from the household of the *agathos*. Wealth has thrown lineage, *genos*, into confusion. So do not be surprised that the *genos* of the citizens is deteriorating, Polypaides; for good things, *esthla*, are being mingled with bad, *kaka*.

Clearly something has happened. To honour wealth in Homeric society – and everyone did – would lead the *agathos* to marry from the household of the *agathos* – as all *agathoi* did – for the *kakoi* had no wealth. What has happened since Homer is the invention of coined money, which has important differences from wealth in land and flocks. Land is restricted in quantity: in small Greek states, very restricted. A group of families possesses it. It is likely to be inalienable in early times. Indeed, if it were not, with what else could one purchase it? Accordingly, that group of families will continue to possess it, wealth will be allied to membership of that group, and the way of life of that group as a whole will be socially most admired – and socially most necessary since, as has been seen, they form the most effective force for attack and defence possessed by the society.

[1] See below, p. 150.

Coined money, however, is not restricted in quantity to the same extent as is land; and it can be gained in different ways, such as trading, which it greatly facilitates.[1] The old *agathos* may despise such methods: the life of a merchant was always despised by the Athenian gentleman, for whom farming was the only reputable alternative to complete leisure, or a life of political activity, in peacetime. Since land is restricted and money less so, the old *agathoi* may find themselves relatively less prosperous in comparison with a new trading class. If they inter-marry with that class, they lay themselves open to the gibe expressed in the lines quoted above. What is thrown into confusion is *genos*, the same word as that used by Hesiod of the Five Races. I do not assert that either this, or the Deucalion story which ascribes creation at different times and from different materials to nobles and people, is in Theognis' mind. However, *genos* alludes to the practice, which had doubtless lasted for generations, of intermarriage among a small group of families: for an *agathos* to marry outside the group is to throw *genos* into confusion. There is no word for human nature as yet in the sixth century B.C.: there is only *arete*, which is the mark of the *agathoi*, *kakotēs*, possessed by the *kakoi*. There is powerful inducement here to treat the nature of the two groups as very different; and to say that *genos* has been thrown into confusion since good things are being mingled with bad is to think in precisely these terms. This is not necessarily mere invective.

If he takes the inherent aspects of Homeric *arete* – birth, prowess, military skill and practical intelligence – as the essential ones, the Greek in this situation may say, as the author of another Theognid poem (315 ff.) says:

> Many *kakoi* are rich and many *agathoi* are poor; but we will not take wealth in exchange for our *arete*; for the one remains with a man always, but possessions pass from one man to another.

This *arete* is presumably birth and warlike qualities. We may compare 865 ff.:

> To many useless men the god gives good, *esthlos*, prosperity, which is of

[1] For an argument linking the invention of coinage with the rise of the Greek tyrants, see P. N. Ure, *The Origin of Tyranny* (Cambridge University Press, 1922).

no benefit to the man himself or his friends; but the great fame of *arete* shall never die, for a spearman preserves his native land and his city.

Such thought is at least emphasising an *inherent arete* and *kakotes* – one which, unlike Homeric *arete*, is not utterly dependent on circumstance. In this direction might lie a view of human nature as such. It is, however, only one possible attitude to the separation of birth and wealth. We have another in Theognis 53 ff.:

> Cyrnus, this city is still a city, but its people are different; those who formerly knew nothing of legal decisions or laws, but wrapped goatskins about their sides, and grazed like deer outside the city, now they are *agathoi*, Polypaides; and those who were *esthloi* before are now *deiloi*.[1] Who could endure the sight of this?

Here *arete* is simply the possession of that wandering prosperity, and apparently the political power that has accompanied it. In a similar strain, but without the bitterness, Simonides the lyric poet, at the turn of the sixth and fifth centuries B.C., observes (5, 12):

> Every man is *agathos* when he fares well, *kakos* when he fares badly.

This is neither bitterness nor cynicism, merely a statement of values as they are. These values direct attention to externals, and make a view of human nature as such less likely to develop.

Also in Theognid poems, however (147 f.), we find the couplet

> The whole of *arete* is summed up in justice, *dikaiosunē*; every man, Cyrnus, is *agathos* if he is *dikaios*.

This couplet has been argued to be of later date, but on inconclusive grounds. In the sixth century B.C. its content is astonishing, assigning, as it does, all the glittering associations of *arete* to the *dikaios qua dikaios*. Even to include *dikaiosune* in *arete* would have been a great change; and this goes much further. Such an insight – that justice is of all qualities most conducive to social stability – might well be reached at a time of great social instability, only to be lost once the

---

[1] The word here functions, as in Homer, as the opposite of *esthlos*. In Attic Greek it is restricted to decrying cowardice.

crisis passed; and it is indeed over a century before a similar judgment is again passed in extant literature.

These attempted redefinitions of *arete* – which belong to the seventh and sixth centuries and to areas of Greece other than Athens – inevitably affect the idea of human nature, even if this is not yet consciously formulated. To redefine *arete*, to use *arete* at all, is to be normative, to assert that a human being at his best has certain qualities. Such normative utterances do not always result from a preliminary survey of human nature as it is; but they may provoke a subsequent examination.

All these definitions have in common one presupposition: whatever is commended, it is commended as giving stability and prosperity to the *polis* more than does any other quality; and to give more stability and prosperity to the *polis* and household is treated as the unquestioned end.[1] The attitude is not surprising, where both *polis* and household have to rely very much on their own resources, and both are insecure. The attitude, and its accompanying values, persisted through the period discussed in this chapter – and beyond, though, as we shall see, other interpretations of the qualities necessary to achieve the end begin to appear in the later fifth century. In the context of traditional values, however, *arete* continues to commend pre-eminently courage leading to success in battle, wealth and social position: the state continues to need most the richer citizens as purchasers of their own armour, and hence the most effective fighting force, and also as contributors to the public finances. Alcaeus (49) attributes to Aristodemus the saying *chremat' aner*, 'money (property) is the man', a view which, in such a situation, is natural both to the state and to individuals. The view, here epigrammatically expressed, does indeed draw attention away from human nature: 'it isn't what a man is, but what he has that matters'. But the need for success in war and in peace does ensure that certain aspects of a man are commended very powerfully in addition. This necessarily entails that these are the

[1] Archilochus' nonchalant attitude (frag. 6) to running away and abandoning his shield, which shocked the Spartans of his own day when he visited them (Plutarch, *Spartan Institutions* 239B), though shared by Alcaeus (frag. 121) is unusual. However, both poets emphasise losing the shield, not losing the battle: to the latter no citizen-soldier could be indifferent; and both poets are said to have been brave fighters.

most important aspects, that a man so commended is manifesting human nature at its best; and to say this is to imply something about human nature as such.

F. Human Nature

In the fifth century, the Greek – or some Greeks – could indeed begin to discuss human nature as such, or rather human *phusis*, the word usually translated by 'nature'. The word is an abstract noun linked with the root of the verb *phuein*, whose passive voice is used for 'to grow'. Etymologically, then, its 'meaning' would be 'growth, manner of growth'. This is not necessarily important, since it is usage that 'gives words their meaning'; but the Greeks seem to have been conscious of the link with the idea of growth in their use of *phusis*.

The word occurs once in Homer (though the related word *phŭē*, 'growth, stature', used especially of outstanding physical appearance, is more frequent): there it is used (*Odyssey* X, 303) of the qualities of the magical plant *mōlu*. It does not occur in the extant writings of the seventh and sixth centuries, but it becomes frequent in the fifth, and will be important in the discussion of human nature from now on.

We are, however, in this chapter still concerned with writers whose interests and aptitudes do not for the most part lead them to analyse and systematise. We must observe how they use words: they will not tell us.

The idea of 'growth, result of growth' is very apparent in some passages. A result of one's growth is one's appearance: Aeschylus' Danaus (*Supplices* 496) observes that the *phusis* of the shape of Egyptians differs from that of Greeks; Deianira (Sophocles, *Trachiniae* 308) judges from the *phusis* of Iole (who has not yet spoken) that she is an innocent maiden: she is presumably judging by appearances; the maid (Euripides, *Alcestis* 174) says that the approaching doom has not changed the *phusis* of Alcestis' skin; and Aristophanes' wasp-chorus (*Wasps* 1071) realise that the spectators in seeing their *phusis* may be surprised. (It should by this time be evident that I am not arguing for an exclusive 'meaning' of 'appearance' for *phusis* in these passages, merely that *phusis* here in part draws attention to physical appearance.)

The word may also refer to the parentage from which an individual has sprung: Chrysothemis (Sophocles, *Electra* 325) is by *phusis* from the same father as Electra; and the speaker in a fragment of Euripides (Nauck[2] 360, 38)[1] refers to a girl as not his daughter save *phusei*, by reason of *phusis*, of having begotten her. Since birth confers a position in society, high or low, *phusis* may appear where social position is relevant. Agamemnon (Sophocles, *Ajax* 1259) brusquely tells Teucer to remember who he is by *phusis*, the illegitimate son of a Greek nobleman and a foreigner; to which he replies (1301) that his mother may have been a foreigner, but that she was *phusei* a queen. The word draws attention primarily to birth here; but we must remember that *phusis* is also used in contexts where we translate it by 'nature', and that, for the Greek, it is the same word through all its occurrences. In Euripides (Nauck[2] 75), Alcmaeon concludes that it is true that from *esthlos* fathers *esthlos* children spring, and from *kakos* fathers children who are like the *phusis* of their father.[2] Elsewhere (*Iphigenia at Aulis* 448) we find *gennaios phusin*, 'noble in respect of your *phusis*'. *Gennaios*, *esthlos* and *kakos* all allude to, and commend or decry, some kind of behaviour here; but all are also terms which denote and commend or decry social class; and *gennaios*, like *genos*, is linked with the root meaning 'birth, to be born'. One's *phusis* may be associated with one's social class. Indeed (Nauck[2] 617), a speaker in another fragment says:

> There is no darkness so intense, no secret abode in the earth, where a man of low birth could hide his *phusis*, even if he is clever.

The context is lost; but some form of reprehended condition is evidently being linked both with low birth and with *phusis*. *Phusis* may, accordingly, reinforce the attitudes instilled and encouraged by the use of the most powerful terms of value. This is not universal: elsewhere (Nauck[2] 377) a speaker says that if a bastard shows himself to have good qualities, the name of bastard will not destroy his *phusis*. Here inborn qualities are opposed to social status: an attitude doubtless deriving from the New Thought of the sophists, which

---

[1] Tragic fragments are quoted from Nauck, *Tragicorum Graecorum Fragmenta*, 2nd edition (Leipzig 1889).

[2] Cf. Plato below, pp. 151 ff.

will be discussed in a later chapter. Other qualities may be connected with the circumstances of one's birth: in Thucydides (VI, 79, 2) Hermocrates, a Syracusan general, exhorts the inhabitants of Camarina, another Sicilian city, to assist the Syracusans rather than the invading Athenians, and not to help those who are their enemies *phusei*, by *phusis*, and destroy those who are their kin *phusei*. Here the idea of birth is prominent: Camarina was founded from Syracuse, and both cities are Dorian, whereas Athens was Ionian; and friendships and enmities between states are or, according to Hermocrates, should be, determined by *phusis*, a word which – to repeat – we render in other contexts by 'nature', though it is the same word in Greek on each occasion.

As we shall see below, *phusis* in its association with the New Thought is used to contrast what is real and basic with what is merely conventional. In the contexts discussed here too the effect of using the word is to convey that certain qualities are inherent; but the presuppositions, prejudices and attitudes of society very much influence society's view of the nature of those qualities. (We shall see that the New Thought is not free from this.)

Phusis is also used with reference to time of life: to one's prime in respect of *phusis* (Aeschylus, *Persae* 441); to youth in respect of *phusis* (Sophocles, *Antigone* 727, *Oedipus at Colonus* 1295, Aristophanes, *Clouds* 515). The link with birth, and qualities resulting from it, seems clear; but such a usage imports into *phusis* the idea of change.

In the New Thought, the most memorable statements concerning human *phusis* portray it as something whose characteristics and demands are the same in all individuals. The word, however, has a variety of usages, and in the kind of passages under discussion here is readily used of distinguishing characteristics and aptitudes. So some birds are good omens by *phusis* (Aeschylus, *Prometheus Bound* 489); an individual may be cowardly by *phusis* (Sophocles, *Ajax* 472); a barbarian has a barbarian *phusis* (Euripides, Nauck[2] 139 ≡ Aristophanes, *Thesmophoriazusae* 1129); and the generalisation that human beings differ in their *phusis* is expressed (Euripides, Nauck[2] 759).

Phusis may determine one's intellectual aptitudes: Themistocles' *phusis* rendered him the best man at improvising what the situation required (Thucydides I, 138, 3); but also and much more frequently one's ethical characteristics: in Euripides' *Bacchae* (314 ff.) Teiresias maintains that the behaviour of Bacchantes under the influence of Dionysus will depend on the *phusis* of each; Achilles (Euripides, *Iphigenia at Aulis* 930) says that since he has a free *phusis* he will fight bravely; and Nicias, writing of the Athenians, says (Thucydides VII, 14, 2) that their *phuseis* are difficult to rule. The effect of competitive excellences is evident in the last two examples. *Arete*, 'human nature at its best', is the mark of a free individual who can defend himself and his own, and rule others, but submits to the rule of others only reluctantly. To have a free *phusis* is to have been born as a free individual, and carries certain implications about one's nature: one will aspire to display *arete*, though the social implications of the term will debar many free citizens from actually doing so. We may thus analyse the effect of the usage; but the Greek experiences the phenomenon as an unanalysed whole: *phusis* possesses all these aspects.

In some societies and intellectual contexts to ascribe something to *phusis* in the sense now seen to be developing would be to treat it as unchangeable, an inescapable influence on behaviour; and hence outside the scope of praise and blame. Here, however, we find Neoptolemus saying that all things are distasteful when one abandons one's own *phusis* (Sophocles, *Philoctetes* 902) and does what is not fitting for oneself; while in Euripides (*Helen* 998) Theonoe says:

> I am so constituted (*pephūkenai*, a verb from the same root as *phusis*) as to be righteous and I wish to be, and . . . there is a great temple of justice in my *phusis*. I have received this from Nereus and I shall try to preserve it.

Theonoe has her sense of justice as an inheritance from her maternal grandfather, apparently in the same manner as she received her prophetic powers from him (*Helen* 15). She could fall short of her *phusis*, but she will not; unlike Polyneices who says (Euripides, *Phoenissae* 395) that, exile as he is, he must play the slave, against his *phusis*,[1] for gain. In Thucydides (III, 64, 4) the Thebans say of the Plataeans

---

[1] In a number of these examples the idea of status derived from birth is apparent; but for the Greek the *word* is the same as in contexts in which we render it by 'nature' without a second thought.

that their past good behaviour was not appropriate to them; but that it has now been demonstrated 'what their *phusis* always wished'. *Phusis* may be good or bad, so that to depart from it may be good or bad, in the eyes of the fifth-century 'ordinary Greek', who does not believe that it completely controls his behaviour, whether for good or ill. Indeed, it may be moulded or trained: Ajax (*Ajax* 545 ff.) says of his infant son, brought in to what Ajax still believes to be the scene of his triumph over his enemies:

> Lift him into my arms. He will not be afraid if he is in truth my son. No; but he must straightway be trained in his father's rough ways and moulded like me in respect of his *phusis*.[1]

His birth will guarantee that he shows no fear; but training will improve his *phusis*.

Phusis, then, in these writers has not the usage which the phrase 'human nature' would lead us to expect. It is none the less relevant to discuss it. It is the only word available to convey the idea of human nature: it denotes the 'given' in an individual resulting from his birth, and in more analytic writers might have a different usage, in which nature is distinguished from nurture and surroundings. There are examples of such distinctions in some of the later writers we have been discussing in this chapter; but these seem dependent on the New Thought, and will be considered below. Traditionally in the fifth century – and we should remember that only in the fifth century does the word gain any currency, and that it is not very frequent even in Aeschylus – *phusis*, in denoting birth, denotes also all the additional qualities which a status-ridden society ascribes to an individual's being born in a particular stratum of that society. It does not serve to distinguish the natural from the conventional. The qualities concerned are for the most part social and ethical, the ethical qualities concerned being those commended by *arete* and decried by *kakiā* in men, and so status-linked.[2] Intellectual qualities are rarely

[1] Cf. the views of Plato in the *Republic*, 424A, below pp. 155 f. 'Ways' is *nomoi*; but there seems to be no reference to the *nomos/phusis* debate.

[2] Neoptolemus' distaste for lying in the *Philoctetes* may be new. The play has many novelties in values, cf. *Merit and Responsibility*, p 189. Women's *arete* is different (*Merit and Responsibility*, pp. 36, 83 f. (28), 161 f.), and so different qualities are singled out as theirs by *phusis*.

concerned: the ascription of Themistocles' intellect to his *phusis* may be a sign of New Thought. (The reason is not that earlier Greeks did not regard intelligence as innate, merely that they were more interested in other qualities.) *Phusis*, then, in writers such as these, has very much the same overtones as 'birth and breeding', good or bad. There is of course no fully worked-out theory behind this usage, only a general attitude to life.[1]

These human values draw men on to strive, to compete, to reach upwards; and we have seen in Homer that the gods are nervous about the possible results. The gods are now more powerful, more remote, and – from Hesiod onwards – are expected to take an interest in human morals, reward the just and punish the unjust. Since most Greeks still believe in a neutral existence after death, such reward and punishment must still occur in this life.

Some early writers – for example, Hesiod (*Works and Days* 267–85) – seem to believe that such punishment always occurs; but in the civic turbulence of the seventh and sixth centuries, sometimes culminating in the rule of a tyrant, who had either succeeded by unjust means or at all events was held to have done so by those he had worsted, the belief was difficult to sustain: if the tyrant prospered and died in his bed, injustice had not been and could not now be punished. Not, at all events, in the person of the tyrant himself; but in early Greece, as in many other societies, the family unit was evidently regarded as more important, and in some sense as more real, than the individual. We should remember that, in a society which, like that of early Greece, contains a high proportion of small farmers, the plot of land cultivated by the family furnishes the family's livelihood;

---

[1] The *word*, however, may be borrowed from the early philosophers, who supply the first post-Homeric usages. If Thales' 'the blessed man is he who is healthy in body, resourceful in *psuche* and well-educated in his *phusis*' is genuine (and the language has characteristics of a later period), this would be earliest (c. 600 B.C.); and Bias' 'If you are ugly, repair what is lacking in your *phusis* by human excellence in your behaviour (*kalokāgathiā*)' probably next (c. 550 B.C.). We are dealing with small and scattered fragments; but it is perhaps significant that these concern human *phusis*, the result of growth. (Thales and many other early philosophers are alleged to have entitled their cosmologies 'On *phusis*', but there is no *quotation* recording such a usage in their own words before Heraclitus, c. 500 B.C.) Or it may simply be an Ionic word: these philosophers write in the Ionian dialect.

and that the plot is in early Greece not only inherited but inalienable, and no alternative means of making a satisfactory living exists; so that the plot of land persists and is of vital importance, while those who work it change. These circumstances furnish powerful reasons for the low importance of the individual in comparison with the continuing plot of land and its continuing family. In this context, it is possible to believe that, should the individual himself escape punishment for his misdeeds, the penalty may be incurred by his children (or by his more remote descendants: Herodotus (I, 91) records that the fall of Croesus was the punishment for the misdeeds of his ancestor Gyges five generations earlier).

Now so long as a society acquiesces in such a belief, it furnishes an explanation for the good or bad fortune of any individual, whatever his character: if he is just and prospers, or unjust and meets with disaster, it is what he deserves; if he is unjust and prospers, a descendant will suffer; and if he is just and meets with disaster, he is paying for the misdeeds of some ancestor. This explanation covers all the possibilities; and the third possibility, that one's own injustice should harm a descendant, might well act as a restraint in itself, not only out of family feeling, but out of the need for a prospering progeny to offer rites to oneself when dead. However, the fourth possibility, that one should be just oneself and suffer for the misdeeds of an ancestor, presses hard, and the harder the more the individual feels his own importance. By the time the belief is attested in extant Greek literature, the individual is already complaining: Theognis, or one of the writers of the Theognid corpus, says (735 ff.) that the gods should see to it that the wrongdoer

> Should straightway pay for the harm, *kaka*, he has done, that the wrongful deeds of the father should not be harmful, *kakon*, to his children, and that the children of an unjust father who are themselves just . . . should not pay for the transgression of their father. . . . As it is, the man who does wrong escapes, and another man endures the harm, *kakon*, thereafter.

In these circumstances, if we remember that human nature at its best is manifested in the possession of the maximum of prosperity, there is the most powerful of inducements to pursue that prosperity by whatever means, and chance the vagaries of divine retribution:

one might well be brought to disaster if one were just, to pay for the misdeeds of some ancestor.[1] It should be noted that the idea of *hubris* does not make the solution any easier: in this same short Theognid poem the misdeeds are referred to as *hubris* (732), and the problem remains. To use the word may increase the threat of divine retribution; *hubris* may be invoked as an explanation of disaster; the pattern of *hubris*, excess and infatuation, punished by disaster, *ate*, may be traced by an Aeschylus treating of the myths and legends of Greece; and undoubtedly the Greeks of the archaic and pre-sophistic periods were wont to look at the world in terms of these concepts. Nevertheless, *in life*, as this poem shows, to term an action *hubris* is not to treat divine retribution on the wrongdoer himself for that action as inevitable.

The gods are sometimes just, sometimes jealous. We have seen[2] that, by a superabundance of *arete*, a man may become a god; and *arete* draws a man on to compete as vigorously as possible for whatever he may achieve. The gods do not wish to share their privileges with mankind; and where the line between human and divine can be crossed in this manner, are not surprisingly alert to prevent anyone from doing so by an excess of prowess and prosperity. The story of Polycrates' ring illustrates the belief. Amasis (Herodotus III, 40 ff.) was disturbed by his ally Polycrates' success, since he knew 'that the powers above are of a jealous disposition'. He accordingly advised Polycrates to throw away his most valuable possession. Polycrates threw a ring into the sea; and when this was returned to him from the belly of a fish, Amasis renounced his alliance with Polycrates: 'for Polycrates will not come to a good end when he is fortunate in everything and finds even what he throws away'. The jealousy of heaven will crush

---

[1] This renders the *successful* commendation of *dikaiosune* to anyone who thinks he will fare better by not being *dikaios* very difficult. There was, from Hesiod and Solon onwards, no lack of Greeks to urge *dikaiosune* upon their fellows; but the goal is, and remains, success, one's own and that of the unit with which one identifies oneself; and unless it can be shown that *dikaiosune* leads to success, or at all events that *adikiā* leads to certain disaster, *dikaiosune* will not be pursued when *adikia* appears more profitable. The society's own values commend the pursuit of success above all else. For the difficulties involved in commending *dikaiosune* successfully, see *Merit and Responsibility*, chapters VII, VIII, IX.

[2] Above, p. 71.

him in the end. The motivation is quite unhistorical;[1] but it shows the popular modes of thought of the period.

If the gods are jealous, the more reflective and cautious may advise circumspection. One method of doing so, and the one which casts most light on views of human nature, is to say 'Bethink you you are mortal'; and a number of extant Greek writers offer this advice, which is relevant to a variety of contexts.[2] Pindar (*Isthmian* V, 14 ff.), having spoken of fame and glory, adds

> Do not seek to become Zeus. You have all things, if a share of these fine things should come to you. Mortal things befit mortal men.

In other words, pursue glory in moderation. Sophocles (Nauck[2] 531) has

> Our mortal *phusis* should think mortal thoughts: we should recognise that there is no-one except Zeus who is the dispenser of what is to be.

Zeus has more power than we have; it behoves a mortal to know his place.[3]

The reflection may be used to console. Pindar's *Third Pythian Ode* is addressed to Hiero of Syracuse, who is ill. He reminds Hiero that Asclepius, who sought to restore Hippolytus to life, was slain by a thunderbolt from Zeus; so that (59)

> We should seek from the gods what befits mortal minds, discerning our nearest business and of what estate we are. Do not, dear *psuche*, strive after immortal life, but make use to the full of all *practicable* resources.

Death bounds our mortal span; we should tailor our thoughts accordingly. (Pindar is here speaking in terms of the Olympian religion, not that of the mystery-cults.) It is the common lot, and even a Hiero must accept it.

The thought may also be used to commend or advise moderation

---

[1] See How and Wells, *A Commentary on Herodotus* (Oxford, 1912), vol. I, pp. 266 f.

[2] We may contrast Aristotle, *Nicomachean Ethics* X, 1177b31 ff. Aristotle's position is very different: see below, pp. 203 f.

[3] Pindar, however, knows and accepts myths relating that the gods rendered some mortals immortal, *Nemean* X, 12 ff.

in emotions. In Sophocles' *Trachiniae* (472 ff.) Lichas says to Deianira, the wife of Heracles:

> But, dear mistress, since I observe that you are thinking as mortals should think . . ., I will tell you the whole truth and will not hide it.

Lichas has brought Iole with him, sent on ahead by Heracles, as a rival to Deianira; but the latter's immediate response is apparently self-controlled.

Similarly a character in Euripides (Nauck² 799) reflects:

> Just as our body is by nature mortal, so anyone who is moderate should not have his anger undying.

Again, in Euripides' *Bacchae* we find (395 ff.):

> Cleverness (*to sophon*) is not wisdom (*sophia*), nor is thinking thoughts that are not mortal.

Here Pentheus is being censured for his false wisdom or cleverness in refusing to accept the Dionysiac religion: acceptance would be true wisdom. To think thoughts that are not mortal is in the immediate context of the play to question the authenticity of Dionysus. However, in the wider context of late fifth-century Athens to prefer human cleverness to belief in the gods had far wider reference.

To think mortal thoughts, then, or to acknowledge one's mortal nature is in these traditional writers to be moderate and recognise that the gods are over mankind and have more power. In quoting such passages, or Greek reflections on moderation, some modern writers paint a picture of the Greeks of the period as naturally prudent and self-controlled, with no proud aspirations: a picture which should hardly survive the reading of a single page of an author of this date. *Arete* is ever drawing men of spirit on and upward to success and excess. The authors quoted may urge the thinking of mortal thoughts, and interpret this as being moderate and circumspect; but *arete* is human nature at its best, and *arete* is immoderate, competitive and never satisfied.[1] There is here a perpetual tension between the limita-

---

[1] For a paean to the capabilities of man, see Sophocles, *Antigone* 332 ff.; and generally, *Merit and Responsibility*, chapter VIII.

tions of human nature – death, disease, and lack of capacity in individuals – and the stimulus of Greek values, with the belief that the most *agathos* of men have joined the ranks of the gods. The gods themselves hold the tension in some kind of equilibrium: what happens when they cease to do so will be seen later.

G. The Development of the Personality

We have observed in this chapter indications of the development of a more stable core, associated with the words *psuche* and *phusis*, in the Greek personality structure; a development which is more pronounced in the fifth century than in earlier writers. Nevertheless, the stresses and strains of living in a results-culture remain: a moral error, in which choice and personality are involved, can still not be distinguished from a mistake, where failure and disaster, and hence loss of *arete*, are concerned. A moral error, such as Creon's in forbidding the burial of Polyneices, which led to the tragic outcome of the drama, is an *hamartiā*[1] (Sophocles, *Antigone* 1261 ff.); as is a mistake, such as Deianira's giving Heracles a deadly object in the belief that it was a love-charm (Sophocles, *Trachiniae* 1136). Furthermore, Prometheus (Aeschylus, *Prometheus Bound* 266 f.) says:

> I committed an *hamartia* of my own free will, I will not deny it: by benefiting mortals I have brought woes upon myself.

Arete commends upon a man (or a god) that he should succeed. Prometheus has not done so; and an *hamartia* has occurred. But *Prometheus* does not consider his action to have been a moral error, though he agrees that it was an *hamartia*; nor does he regard it as a mistake, subjectively reckoned – an action, that is, whose unpleasant results for himself he did not foresee (though, 268, he admits that he had not expected Zeus' revenge to take such an extreme form); nor is Prometheus' action an accident. His action is an *hamartia* because he has – quite deliberately – performed an action which was not in his own interest, which diminished his prosperity and success.

In the range of *hamartia* we see the tensions on personality imposed

[1] For a fuller discussion of this question, see my 'Aristotle and the Best Kind of Tragedy', *C.Q.* N.S. XVI (1966).

by the results-culture values of traditional *arete*. If any fall to disaster entails loss of *arete*, than which nothing is more important, and some of these are inevitably beyond the control of the agent, then the idea of such control, of choice, of will is unimportant ethically, and unlikely to develop psychologically: a situation here reflected in the usage of *hamartia*. It has often been observed that there is no word for 'will' in ancient Greek; and here we see much of the reason for this, and for the development in its place of a psychological model usually termed 'calculative'.[1]

As a result, though some kind of a stable personality-structure has now made an appearance, it is as yet not very far developed; and this may be associated with other phenomena in ancient Greece. For Aristotle (*Poetics* 1450a38) character is less important than plot in tragedy; and here he agrees with the practice of the extant tragedians, in whose works sharply realised character has a comparatively small part to play. This may answer to some extent to the actual consciousness of the fifth-century Greeks, even if by Aristotle's own day some further development had taken place. Again, in some extant tragedies there are, or appear to be, quite sharp discontinuities of character and behaviour.[2] These have been reprehended by modern critics;[3] but it is possible that they may indicate not merely a low degree of consciousness of character in the tragedians, but actual real-life behaviour of individuals living under the stresses of such a society as this.

[1] But see above, p. 48, and below, pp. 196 ff.

[2] The most striking example is the sudden madness of Heracles (Euripides, *Heracles* 875 ff.), totally unprepared for by any of Heracles' previous behaviour. In the tragedy the cause is direct divine intervention; but such sudden complete breakdown, or the lesser discontinuities observable elsewhere, might well be commoner in this type of society than in others, whatever causes the society itself might have ascribed to its more distressing manifestations. Cp. Aristotle, *Problems* 953a10 ff., discussed below, pp. 205 f., on Heracles, Plato, Socrates and *melancholikoi* in general.

[3] Aristotle too reprehends inconsistency of characterisation, *Poetics* 1454a26 ff.; and adds 'even if the original is inconsistent and furnishes to the poet such a character for representation, still he must be consistently inconsistent'. It is not certain that Aristotle would have reprehended the same instances as modern critics. Any society will regard *some* degree of inconsistency as abnormal. My point is that a higher degree of inconsistency and discontinuity may well have been normal among the Greeks.

4. 'Presocratics' and Doctors

A. Introductory

In this chapter I shall discuss the views of human nature of the Presocratic philosophers and the early Greek doctors whose works are to be found in the Hippocratic corpus. Each group requires definition. In Diels/Kranz, *Fragmente der Vorsokratiker*,[1] are to be found writers whose primary concern is with cosmology, with the rudiments of physical science and with the physical composition of man and the rest of animate nature; and also writers whose primary concern is with ethics, politics and rhetoric. It is customary to distinguish these groups as Presocratics and sophists, and this will be my practice here; except that, since the distinction is one of subject matter and some writers in fact treat of both types of subject, the division will be by content, not by author. 'Presocratic' material will be discussed in this chapter, 'sophistic' in the next.

The physical constitution of man naturally also interested the early doctors. In the Hippocratic corpus we possess writings certainly not all by Hippocrates. Indeed, it seems possible that none is, for their content does not harmonise very well with the admittedly very brief and allusive reference to Hippocrates' doctrines in Plato (*Phaedrus* 270C–D). The writings we possess are in a variety of styles and present a variety of medical theories, and seem to be an assemblage of the best Greek medical writing of the fifth and fourth centuries B.C.

The doctrines to be discussed in this chapter are merely a selection of the more important views: both halves of the chapter reflect periods of intense thought and discussion, comprehensive treatment of which would require a book longer than this one.

---

[1] Citations and quotations are from the sixth edition. References preceded by 'A' are to reports by later writers of a philosopher's doctrines, those preceded by 'B' to fragments of the doctrines preserved in the philosopher's own words by later writers.

B. 'Presocratics'

(i) *Phusis*

As we have seen, early Greek thought readily accepted myths of five separately created human races, or of a creation of the majority of the human race from stones. In the early sixth century B.C. however there began to appear in the prosperous Ionian cities of the Greek-colonised seaboard of Asia Minor and the adjacent islands thinkers who may be regarded as philosophers and cosmologists; and some of these attempted different kinds of explanation of the nature of mankind in the light of their general theories. Some general discussions offered by these writers will be relevant; but it will also be useful to pursue the question in terms of *psuche* and *phusis*. It will soon become apparent that, though these Greek words furnish us with 'psychology' and 'physiology' in English, they do not serve to draw this distinction in Greek.

The philosophers of this period were attempting to give an all-embracing account of the cosmos. Anyone who engages in this must, unless he is simply to list phenomena, treat some things as more 'basic' or perhaps – a type of usage found in many philosophers at many periods – more 'real' than others. The Presocratic philosophers, from Thales onwards, do not list, but seek a unifying principle or principles in terms of which an explanation of observed phenomena can be attempted. In the first instance the existence of the principle seems to have been more important than its function as an explanation: Thales' assertion that all things are water, however it is to be interpreted, may be intellectually satisfying in that it gives the impression of introducing order into chaos, but its explanatory function is minimal. However, we are informed – the word occurs in no *quotation* from a Presocratic philosopher prior to the fifth century – that from Thales onwards these philosophers used *phusis* to denote the subject-matter of their enquiries, and entitled their works 'Concerning *Phusis*'. *Phusis* in this usage refers to the cosmos, but particularly to that aspect of it which underlies appearances: as Heraclitus (B123) said, '*phusis* is wont to hide itself'. Diogenes of Apollonia (B2) makes the implications clearer:

It seems to me . . . that all existing things come into being from alterations to the same thing, and are the same thing. This is evident. For if any of the things which now exist in this cosmos (earth, water, air, fire and all the rest that are seen to exist in this world) were different from another – different, that is, in its own basic *phusis* – and were not the same thing transformed in many ways and changed, things could not mingle with one another in any way, nor could there be any benefit or damage from one thing to another, nor could any plant grow from the earth nor any animal nor anything else come to be. . . .

We are not concerned here with the details of the argument. For the present purpose, what is important is the use of *phusis* to denote the real, even if unperceived and unacknowledged, in opposition to what appears to the senses or is thought to be the case. This *phusis* has its own requirements; it governs the growth and change of human beings (Epicharmus B4); and condemns us to death (Gorgias B11a, 1) at the end of our allotted span, in addition to causing changes in the inanimate world. The idea of necessary change, of necessary sequences of *events*, is present; but the conclusion that one must *act* as *phusis* demands is not usually drawn. The atomists Leucippus, Democritus, and later Epicurus and the Roman Lucretius held that the cosmos was governed by irrational *phusis*, the chance interplay of the atoms; but even they, albeit with some difficulty, found place for free will in their systems, as well as for the regularities of nature. (The atomists will be discussed more fully in a later chapter.)

This remains true in contexts where, in translating, we are likely to render *phusis* by 'instinct', though here, as always, we should remember that we are concerned with the same word throughout in Greek. Democritus (B278) says:

> For human beings it seems to be a necessity to have children, arising from *phusis* and the state of affairs established from of old. We can see this in other animals too: they all have offspring as a result of *phusis*, not from any benefit that accrues to them.

Yet elsewhere (B276) Democritus recommends that one should not have children: 'necessity' evidently does not remove the possibility of choice. We may also observe that Democritus here can ascribe the situation to *phusis* and environment ('the state of affairs established from of old') together, without feeling any apparent need for further analysis. Elsewhere he, and the thinkers of this type, are more careful. In these writers, as in those discussed in the last chapter, *phusis* may refer more generally to the endowments one was born with, including one's social position and its advantages. Being more analytic thinkers, however, they are sometimes concerned to distinguish nature from nurture. Epicharmus (B40) indeed says that it is best to have *phusis*, but second to learn. ('To learn' is a supplement to fill a lacuna; but it is a very plausible one.) The idea of innate skills which do not require training is deep-seated; but he acknowledges elsewhere that practice gives more than good *phusis* (B33). Democritus (B242) maintains that more have become *agathoi* from training than from *phusis*; and a similar view appears in Critias (B9).

We must examine all these passages in the light of the usage of *phusis* and *agathos*. To be *agathos* is to have certain skills and qualities, but also to belong to a particular stratum of Greek society; and we have seen that *phusis* in other fifth-century writers serves precisely to link the possession of the skills and qualities denoted and commended by *arete* with birth into a high position in society. In B40, Epicharmus indeed acknowledges the primacy of *phusis*, in what context we do not know, and allots second place to learning. Democritus and Critias are specifically concerned with becoming *agathos*: they do not deny that one may become *agathos* from *phusis*, but claim that more do so from training. The claim fits well, with all its implications, into the situation in which the sophistic movement found itself, as will appear in the next chapter. In the fifth century, any Greek hearing these words would almost inevitably be aware of the overtones of 'birth' in *phusis*; but when Protagoras (B3) maintains that 'teaching requires both *phusis* and training', the word may possibly be devoid of social overtones. (The remark might, of course, be addressed to the *agathoi*, to insist that their high birth, and consequent *arete*, untrained does not suffice.) At all events, 'nature' and 'nurture' are here not alternative routes to *arete*, but necessary concomitants. It is not clear whether Protagoras means that both *phusis* and training are necessary in order to teach or in order to be taught; but this does not affect the point made here.

We find yet another attitude in Eucnus of Paros (Bergk frag. 9), who maintains that long practice in the end becomes *phusis*. Similarly

Democritus (B33): *phusis* and teaching are much the same; for teaching too moulds the individual, and in doing so it imparts *phusis* to him. These writers agree with Ajax in the last chapter[1] that *phusis* can, in a sense, be imparted.[2] Aristotle later quotes the Euenus passage (*Nicomachean Ethics* 1152a32), and comments that custom is like *phusis* in that it is difficult to change.

Euenus and Democritus may have written without ulterior motive: but the social overtones of *phusis* in fifth-century Greek are powerful, and a fifth-century Greek of lower status might well have been attracted by the thought of having new, improved, *phusis* imparted to him by training. The next chapter will show the importance of the acquisition of political skills in the educational programme of the sophists. Such acquisition increased the pupil's *arete*; and *arete* too is traditionally linked with birth and social position. There are other attractions: the reliability of *phusis* is important, Democritus B176:

Chance gives great gifts, but is unstable, whereas *phusis* is self-sufficient; and so with a quantity less but reliable it gets the better of the greater offered by hope.

Reliable self-sufficiency is a key idea in Greek thought about the human condition.[3]

However, the loss of social overtones in the use of *phusis*, insofar as it occurs,[4] or at all events its separation from the once-for-all circumstances of birth, is perhaps more important at this period, for it upsets the prejudices and presuppositions of traditional society; as, in a different way, does Democritus' 'there is intelligence to be found in the young, folly in the old; for time does not teach one to think: seasonable nurture and *phusis* do that' (B183). We saw in the last chapter that *phusis* was associated with time of life; and traditionally the elders – those who are 'of such an age in respect to their *phusis*'[5]

[1] *Ajax* 545 ff. Above, p. 83. I do not contend that the *Ajax* passage is necessarily moulded by the New Thought.

[2] And cp. Plato, *Republic* 424A, discussed below, p. 155.

[3] See *Merit and Responsibility*, pp. 34 ff., 53 f., 158, 223, 230 ff., 241 (13), 348, 354 (24). As a mark of philosophy, p. 354 (21).

[4] We shall see that the sophists' contrast of *nomos* and *phusis* has implications connected with *arete* (pp. 118, 125 f.).

[5] Above, p. 81.

– are the repositories of wisdom. The New Thought is changing all that; and the disturbing new doctrine is accompanied by a new usage of *phusis*, or by the loss of certain aspects of the old one.

The effects of the idea of *phusis* in ethical contexts will be pursued further in the next chapter. We may now consider the constituents which thinkers of this type believed human *phusis* to possess. The word *phusis* is not always used in the quotations I shall discuss below; but the writers concerned (and I give only a small selection) wrote, or are said to have written, books about *phusis*, and sometimes separate works on human *phusis*; and the manner in which these quotations fit into the whole picture will soon become apparent.

Had Thales or Anaximenes been asked what they believed to be the basic constituent of a human being, they would presumably have answered 'water' and 'air' respectively, since they held these to be the basic constituents of everything. With Xenophanes, however, we reach a more complex situation: he held (B33, and compare 29) that 'we all come to be from earth and water'; while Empedocles (B96, 98) derives bones, blood and 'the rest of flesh' from earth, air, fire and water; and (B105) 'the blood round the heart (*kardiā*) is men's thought'. On the other hand, Empedocles also says (B107):

> From earth, air, fire and water all things are compounded and fitted together, and *with them* men think and feel pleasure and pain.

The distinction between 'blood is thought' and 'we think with our blood' has not yet been clearly drawn. Perception too poses its problems. A common solution in ancient Greece was that we perceive objects in the outside world with similar material in ourselves.[1] So Empedocles (B109):

> We perceive earth with earth, water with water, the divine aether with aether, and destructive fire with fire, love with Love and strife with baneful Strife.

Aether is here used as a synonym for air; and Love and Strife are the two active principles in Empedocles' cosmology, which cause the

[1] But contrast Anaxagoras and Heraclitus, Theophrastus *de sensu* 1 ff. (Empedocles, A86, 1.).

combination of the basic elements into the existents of the sensible world, and their subsequent dissolution (B20):

> This process can be clearly observed throughout the mass of mortals' limbs: at one time all the limbs which are allotted to the body come together into one, under the influence of Love, (when the individual is) in the prime of flourishing life; at another time separated by baneful Strife they wander separately on the shore of life. The same is true for shrubs, for fishes that live in the dark waters, for beasts that live in the mountains and for birds that fly on wings.

When the elements are assembled and compounded by Love, the organism flourishes; when Strife begins to separate them again, it ceases to exist. The elements do not perish (B8):

> I shall tell you another thing: there is no coming-to-be[1] of any mortal thing, nor is there any end in baneful death, only mixing and separation of what was mixed, and this (i.e. the mixing) is termed 'coming to be' by mankind.

Space does not permit the discussion of the theories of a large number of these philosophers. Nor is this necessary for my present purpose, which is to demonstrate how they treat human nature in terms of their overall theories of the cosmos: earth, air, fire and water, and the principles of Love and Strife are the principles of Empedocles' entire cosmology.

It is open to these thinkers to explain particular human conditions in terms of their theory of *phusis* in general; but this is better discussed in the context of medical thought.

(ii) *Psuche*

On meeting the translation 'soul' for *psuche* in the Presocratic and other philosophers, the modern reader may wonder why no thinker seems to have disputed the existence of *psuche*; for many would be classified – not entirely correctly – as materialists. *Psuche*, however, for these thinkers is that element of a living creature which distin-

---

[1] He uses the word *phusis*: a usage observed in the last chapter. It is unusual in these writers. Empedocles' philosophy is in verse, however, and metre may sometimes guide the choice of words.

guishes it from a dead one:[1] a linguistic usage which, as we have seen, could be exemplified from non-philosophical writers. None of these thinkers denied that there was a difference between living and dead substances: there are substances which grow, reproduce themselves and (in some cases) move; and these have *psuche*. Thales indeed blurred the usual distinction (A3) by ascribing *psuche* to at least some inanimate things: he spoke of the *psuche* of the magnet, precisely because it is capable of causing movement in iron (A22). According to Aëtius, Thales (A22a) was the first to define *psuche* as 'what is always moved or self-moved'; and in this he was followed by almost all thinkers.[2]

These thinkers, then, had to explain *psuche*, life, in terms of their theories of the cosmos; and they were of course influenced by empirical considerations to some extent. In the first instance, their observations were presumably confined to man and possibly domestic animals. In these, one clear difference between a living and a dead specimen, or a living specimen and a pebble, is that the living one breathes; and Xenophanes (A1) concluded that *psuche* was breath, Anaximenes (B2) that it was air, as did Diogenes of Apollonia (A20), or 'air-like', as did Anaximander, Anaxagoras and Archelaus. Another characteristic of the living mammal is that it is warm (as is its breath); and Parmenides, Hippasus, and Heraclitus held that *psuche* was fiery. Heraclitus (Hippon, A10) is said to have derived 'to live' (*zēn*) from 'to boil' (*zein*), which calls *thumos* to mind,[3] and suggests that introspection may have supplied some of the data; though Heraclitus' belief that fire was the first principle of the cosmos must have played its part. The genesis of some of these ideas is far too complex to discuss in the space available here. Others concluded that it was water, Hippon apparently (A10) because *psuche* resembles *psūchros*, cold, and he identified 'the cold' with water. Other theories were more complex: Zeno of Elea (A1) is said to have held that it was a mixture of the hot, the cold, the dry and the wet, with one having the upper hand; Empedocles that it was a resultant of the appropriate mixture of earth, air, fire and water. B109, quoted above, may point to this.

All these theories would now be regarded as materialist; and this

---

[1] For an explicit statement, see Diels/Kranz, Anonymus Iamblichi 4, 2.
[2] But contrast Diels/Kranz, Anonyme Pythagoreer B, 1a (I, 449, 24).
[3] Above, pp. 16 ff.

is a general characteristic of the Presocratics. That Anaxagoras' Nous or Mind, which he invoked as the ordering principle in his cosmos, was merely a very fine material (B12), is notorious. To say 'materialist', however, implies the existence of an opposed 'immaterialist'; and there is no indication that anyone at this period, philosopher or no, had a concept of the immaterial. For we may not say that Anaxagoras, in terming mind 'the finest and purest of all things', was, with the inadequate concepts available, 'really' asserting that mind is immaterial. What is important is the use that he can make of his view of mind; and the implications of the two statements are very different. The *psuche* of ordinary language is material; and the philosophers take the same view. Where the *psuche* is composed of one element it can naturally exist outside the body: air, for example, is all about us. One may then speculate whether the air, fire or other substance when functioning as *psuche* is the same as air or fire in general; and where an affirmative answer is given this is one of the roots of the belief in a cosmic *psuche*. However, the air, fire or other substance, when not enclosed in a body, appears not to have sensation or other qualities characteristic of *psuche*; and some thinkers argued that *psuche* consists of the substance with a different temperature or humidity: Diogenes of Apollonia held that the *psuche* of all animals is the same (B5), air much warmer than air about us, but much cooler than that near the sun. When the *psuche*-substance leaves the body, one might expect it to lose its individuality; yet it would be possible for such thinkers to hold that a simple *psuche* retained its individuality, since it was apparently possible to hold that a compound *psuche* did so. Empedocles, as we have seen, derived all things from his four elements, Love and Strife, and held that the *psuche* was a blend, or the resultant of a blend, of all four. Yet he believed in transmigration (B115) of something which preserved its individuality throughout a cycle of incarnations, though it might be incarnated in very different bodies. The retained individuality is a necessary part of Empedocles' world-view: presence in the cycle is a punishment for wrong-doing, and the punishment is sustained throughout the incarnations. Empedocles terms what transmigrates and is successively reincarnated not *psuche*, but *daimōn*; and many scholars hold that *daimon* is in Empedocles to be distinguished from *psuche*. (As so frequently in the case of

Presocratic philosophers, the fragments do not permit the point to be decisively settled.) This may be so: the fact that subsequent Greek writers use *psuche* with reference to this aspect of Empedocles' thought is irrelevant, for their own linguistic usage rendered it natural for them to do so; but inasmuch as Empedocles' universe consists of the four elements, Love and Strife, and the *daimon* is not identified with any one of these, it must be a compound of more than one; so that he must have held it to be possible that a compound of elements could survive outside the body.

In these writers neither the distinction nor the separability of *psuche* from body implies that the *psuche* is held to be immaterial. We are not concerned here with the logicality of the views of any writer, but with the picture of human nature conveyed by his views as a whole.

The atomists find themselves in a somewhat different position. Democritus is reported (A102) to have said that *psuche* was *soma*, body. Earlier thinkers took it for granted that *psuche* was material, as we have seen: when they distinguished *psuche* from *soma*, they were not distinguishing immaterial from material. Later atomists had an immaterialist view of *psuche* to oppose; but in 420 B.C. (Democritus' *floruit*) such a view seems unlikely: Socrates himself (as opposed to Plato's portrait of him) cannot be shown conclusively to have held such a view. The atomists' fundamental position is that nothing exists but atoms and void; and one might state that *psuche* was *soma* simply to indicate that it consisted of atoms, with no polemical intent whatever. The polemical assertion of the atomists at this time may concern merely the necessary dispersion of the atoms of the *psuche*, previously held in by respiration (Democritus A106), at death.

Psuche was variously located in the body by different thinkers: Hippon (A3) is said to have sited it – rather unusually – in the head; Philolaus, a Pythagorean, held (B13) that the heart (*kardia*) was the principle of *psuche* and of perception; while Protagoras and Apollodorus, we are told (Protagoras A18), placed it in the chest. Democritus (A104a) is said to have distributed it throughout 'the whole perceiving body'; and in this was followed by the later atomists, the Epicureans.

Psuche being so material, it is affected in a material way by different states of affairs. When one is drunk, one's *psuche* becomes damp

(Heraclitus B117); and since for Heraclitus *psuche* is fire, it is death to the *psuche* for it to become entirely water (B36); so that (B77) it is either delight or death for the *psuche* to become damp. This presumably depends on the degree of dampness. To bring moisture near to the *psuche* is not in moderation harmful: '*psuchai* (B12) are vaporised from the things that are damp'. (In all respects, Heraclitus' philosophy is a tension between opposites.)

In 'ordinary Greek', as we have seen, *psuche* was becoming the core and carrier of personality. In these philosophers, sometimes *nous* (mind) is separated from *psuche*. Philolaus (B13) not only said that the heart (*kardia*) was the principle of *psuche* and perceptions, but that the head was the principle of *nous*. On the other hand, it is reported (Parmenides A45) that Parmenides, Empedocles and Democritus identified *psuche* and *nous*. The answers of later, and less fragmentary, writers will be discussed in subsequent chapters.

A sharper distinction between body and *psuche* is developing. This is an inevitable result of isolating *psuche*, however material one's conception of it, as the vital principle, in an analytic writer; for isolating one pole of the opposed pair, in such a writer, will lead to consideration of the other. Even the atomists, though they naturally insist that *psuche* is body, distinguish between *psuche* and body (in the normal sense of the word). The distinction is, as is to be expected, most sharp in the case of the Pythagoreans and others who believe that the *psuche* survives the death of the body and lives a life in which pleasure and pain are possible when separated from the body: Philolaus (B14) holds that the soul is yoked to the body and as it were buried in it as in a tomb; while Empedocles (B126) says that a divine power 'enfolds the *psuchai* in a tunic of flesh'. Such beliefs, whose effects we shall observe in Plato, not only oppose *psuche* to body, but render *psuche* the more real of the two. They are, however, the views of a minority of Greeks.[1]

C. Doctors

(i) *Phusis*

Before attempting to draw any conclusions from the foregoing discussion, we may examine some early medical views. As in the case

[1] See above, p. 66.

of the Presocratics, only a sample of this rich and complex tradition can be discussed, and many questions must be left on one side.

The practising doctor is faced with particular problems from which the speculative cosmologist is free. He has a patient, an individual who is ill: he must try to find out what is the matter, and what he can do about it; and the patient will either recover, or not. But the doctor, and more particularly the early doctor, is not fully in control of the situation; there is something in the patient that will help to determine the result of the treatment.

This is the *phusis* of the patient, however interpreted; and we shall see that doctors disagree on the interpretation. All doctors, however, might agree with the apologia for medicine expressed in *On The Art* 11:

> It is not doctors who are to blame for anything that the patients suffer as a result of a tardy diagnosis, but the *phusis* of the patient and the *phusis* of the disease.

The *phusis* of the patient, whether as an individual or as a human being, also limits what medicine can do (8); and to seek to do more than skill or *phusis* permits is nearer to madness than to ignorance. Nevertheless, provided this is borne in mind, the *phusis* of the patient can be compelled to disclose her secrets, even against her will, by one who knows the art of medicine. The work is a vivid portrayal of the difficulties of diagnosis, treatment and prognosis presented by human *phusis* as the doctor sees it: the baffling complexities of the changes in the physical well-being of the patient, together with their unseen causes. The doctor's preoccupations necessarily strip *phusis* of its social overtones.

But what causes, and how much of *phusis* in general, as treated by the philosophers, are relevant to the doctor? Here the answers differ. The author of *On Regimen* holds (I, 2) that the doctor must understand the whole of human *phusis*; but (I, 3) discourses also on the *phusis* of all animals, as well as that of mankind, all of which, he contends, consist of fire and water: fire is able to move everything, water to nourish everything. These two are for ever in conflict, now one, now the other, gaining the upper hand. Neither can completely vanquish the other, however; for when the fire uses up all the water, it lacks nourishment; and when the water uses up all the fire, it lacks movement, comes to a halt, loses power and becomes nourishment for the fire again. Again (I, 4) there is really no birth or death, merely mingling and separation. To speak of birth and death is to use the language of *nomos* (custom), to speak of mingling and separation is to speak in accordance with *phusis*[1]. He attempts to explain (I, 9) the development of the foetus in terms of fire and water, and (I, 10) the configuration of the body in general in a similar manner. He also recommends (I, 2) that the doctor should observe the rising and setting of the stars, so that he may know 'how to guard against the changes and excessive conditions of foods, beverages, winds and the entire cosmos, all of which cause diseases'.

This doctor wishes to begin in everything from the first principles of the natural philosophy of his day, the most prominent influence on this aspect of his thought being Heraclitus. Very different is the pronouncement of the author of *On Ancient Medicine*. His contention is that medicine is a long-established art, which was flourishing long before the arrival of the new natural philosophy. He says (20):

> Some doctors and learned men say that one cannot know medicine unless one knows what man is: anyone who is to treat men correctly must learn this. Their argument leads in the direction of natural philosophy, in the manner in which Empedocles and others who have written about *phusis* have written about man from first principles, how he came to be and from what elements he is composed. But I think that whatever any learned man or doctor has written about *phusis* has less to do with medicine than with painting; and I think that one cannot learn anything clear about *phusis* from any other source than medicine. It is possible to acquire this, when one has a proper grasp of medicine, but until then it is far from possible. I mean the knowledge which consists in knowing accurately what man is, the causes which bring him into being, and the rest. For this at least I think a doctor must know about *phusis*, and take much trouble to find out: what man is in relation to foods and beverages, and in relation to different activities, and what will be the effect of each on each individual. We must not say simply that cheese is a bad food, since it causes a pain to anyone who eats it. We must specify the nature of the pain, the reasons for it, and the constituent of man that is discommoded by it. For there are many other harmful

[1] For *nomos* and *phusis*, see below, pp. 112 ff.

foods and beverages, which affect a man in different ways. I would therefore put the matter in this way: 'Wine undiluted with water has such-and-such an effect on a man.' Then all who knew this would know that this is the effect of wine, and the wine itself is the cause; and we know on which of the parts of a man it most of all has this effect. I should like the truth to be expressed in this manner in all other cases too. For cheese – since I used that as an example – does not harm all men in the same way: there are some who suffer no ill-effects from eating it, but rather, if it suits them, are wonderfully strengthened by it; while others have great difficulty in digesting it. The *phusis* of these types of people differs; and it differs in respect of the constituent of the body that is hostile to cheese and is stirred up and put in movement by it. Those in whom such a humour is present in greater quantity and with greater power naturally suffer more severely. If it were bad for human *phusis* as a whole, it would harm everyone.

The author, then, disdains the *a priori*; and he will not accept from another branch of knowledge broad generalisations which he must apply to his medicine. He insists that *phusis* differs from one man to another; though the last sentence of the quotation seems to imply that he ascribes some sense to the phrase 'human *phusis* as a whole'. But knowledge of the *phusis*, whether of the individual or of mankind as a whole, can only come from medicine itself. This is, he insists, the old way of practising medicine; and he pours scorn on the new method with its philosophical postulates. Suppose (13) a man eats raw meat and wheat straight from the threshing-floor, and drinks only water: he will become ill. What should be done for him? A 'new doctor' strictly speaking ought to prescribe heat or cold, dryness or moistness; for if the injury was caused by one of the opposites, it should be cured by the other. But the most obvious means of cure, as well as the most reliable, would be to give him bread instead of wheat, boiled meat instead of raw, and some wine to drink. But is it the heat of the wheat, or the cold, or the dryness, or the moistness, that the baker took away from it? The wheat has been mixed with water, baked with fire, and many other things have happened to it, and it has lost some of its qualities and has acquired others as a result of mixture and combination. Again (15) the adherents of the other school of medicine cannot practise their theory. There is no absolute hot or cold, dry or moist, which is nothing else. They have to use the same foods and beverages as anyone else, and anything which is hot will also be astringent or insipid or possess some others out of a whole range of possible qualities.

In practice, doctors of the two schools, or points of view, might well not differ very much from each other. The author of *On Regimen* may ascribe everything ultimately to the interaction of hot and cold; but being a doctor who has to cure individual patients he must, as the author of *On Ancient Medicine* points out, use materials as they are found in the world about us; and indeed the author of *On Regimen* insists (I, 2) on the importance of different kinds of food and exercise, and the relationship of one with the other. He even says:

> When all this (including the knowledge of the cosmos mentioned above) is known, the discovery is not yet complete; for if it were possible to discover for each individual *phusis* an amount of food and a quantity of exercise without excess or deficiency, one could maintain the individual's health with certainty.

The author holds that this is impossible to achieve in the individual case; but this is his goal, for even a slight excess or deficiency gradually builds up a condition of disease; and he claims to be more adept at this than other doctors. On the other hand, the author of *On Ancient Medicine* is not concerned with mere rule-of-thumb: he does wish to attain to a knowledge of human *phusis*, and he makes his empirical observations, and asks his questions, within a conceptual framework. His conceptual model is founded on the humours, and he explains what he sees in terms of these.

The difference in practice may have rested largely on the manner in which the doctors explained what they did; but the difference should not be underestimated. To us, the medicine of the Hot and the Cold and the medicine of the humours may be equally exploded theories; yet, though the explanation in terms of the humours may have been no less erroneous, it was an explanation in terms of what was empirically present, even if its function was misunderstood. The *phusis* with which the author of *On Ancient Medicine* is concerned is visibly present; that of the author of *On Regimen* is the reality that underlies appearances, and such a doctor's attention was not primarily directed to 'mere' appearances. The treatment might be very similar where a remedy already existed; but the former, empirical, attitude was more likely to lead to new discoveries.

The increasingly systematic study – for though the author of *On Ancient Medicine* claims that his is the traditional method, it must have shared in the new surge of intellectual activity – by doctors of both views must have led to a new consciousness of human nature in its physiological and psychological aspects as something which, differing as it did from individual to individual, nevertheless behaved broadly in accordance with certain rules. Indeed, the doctor could not be unaware of his dependence on the *phusis* of his patient. We have seen the author of *On The Art* arguing that what the doctor can do is limited by the *phusis* of the patient; but within those limits, *phusis*, says the author of *Epidemics* (VI 5, 1), is the true doctor which without education or learning supplies what is needed, tears, moisture in the nostrils, sneezing, discharge from the ears, and so on. No doctor, particularly in the infancy of medicine, could be unaware of his dependence on the patient's natural resources. The wider implications of this will be discussed after consideration of the doctor's use of *psuche*.

(ii) *Psuche*

We shall not now be surprised to discover that the *psuche* of the doctors is material. It is, according to the author of the *Epidemics* (VI, 5, 2), continually being produced up to the time of death; and if the *psuche* too is burned up by the disease at the same time (as the body), it causes the body to waste away. The author of *On Human Nature* (6) notes that those who maintain that man is essentially blood argue thus: seeing the blood flowing from a wound (and the subsequent death, if enough flows) they suppose that the blood is the *psuche* of the man. (He opposes the view, but in the interests of a more complex material account.) The author of *On Regimen* has most to say on the subject. Under the influence of Heraclitus, among others, he holds (1, 7), that

> *Psuche* enters into a man, having a mixture of fire and water, a portion of the body of the individual. These (bodies), whether male or female, . . . are nourished by the diet.

All that he consumes must have 'all the parts'; for if there were any element of body or *psuche* lacking in the diet, that part of body or *psuche* would receive no nourishment. (This recalls the homoeomeries of Anaxagoras, B1 and B5: this author is an eclectic and draws on others besides Heraclitus.)

There is no sign of an immaterialist *psuche* in the doctors: we are concerned with a vital principle which requires sustenance throughout life, and ebbs or is consumed when the body is diseased. Medical preoccupations also concentrate the attention on human nature in its physiological and psychological aspects as something which is very much affected by the individual's way of life. We find awareness of this in writers whose primary interests are not medical: Democritus (B234) says:

> In their prayers men ask for health from the gods, and do not know that they have the ability to attain this within themselves; and by doing the opposite of what they should through lack of self-control, they become betrayers of their own health to (or as a result of) their desires.

Again, Antiphon the Sophist (B2) says that for all men their mind leads their body to health and disease and everything else. There must have been a period when causal links between regimen and health were understood for the first time; and the idea appears fresh to Democritus: his point is that men do not know this, not that they fail to act on their knowledge.

There are passages in the dramatists which may owe something to medical theory and language. This is quite likely: Aeschylus' dénouement of the problem of the *Oresteia*, whether Orestes can be justified for having killed his mother Clytemnestra, depends in part on a current medical theory: the father is the true parent of the child (*Eumenides* 658), while the mother merely nurses the seed in her womb. Accordingly, when we read in Sophocles (*Electra* 785) Clytemnestra's complaint that Electra was sucking out the blood of her *psuche*, we should not conclude, though the sucking was metaphorical, that the whole phrase is a metaphor. Sophocles thought of *psuche* materially, and it seems most likely that he associated blood quite literally with it. (After all, blood might be poured as an offering to the *psuche* of the dead.) Similarly, when Clytemnestra later (775) says that Electra was born from her *psuche*; when Euripides' Menelaus (*Andromache* 541) says that he expended a large part of his *psuche* in the capture of Troy; when the Cyclops (Euripides, *Cyclops* 340) says that he will not cease to benefit his *psuche* by devouring Odysseus; when a servant in Euripides' *Ion* (1169) says that the guests were filling their *psuche* with food; and when Strepsiades (Aristophanes, *Clouds* 712) says that the 'Corinthians' (bugs) are drinking up his *psuche*; we need not suppose that the original writers of these lines, and their audience, did not take them in a literal sense, as their material view of *psuche* would readily enable them to do.

One cannot state dogmatically that the doctors and philosophers must have influenced such expressions as these, or that there is any cause-and-effect relationship here: the link between blood and *psuche* is primitive as well as philosophical and medical, and all the Greeks of the period supposed the *psuche* to be material (or rather had not entertained the possibility that anything could be immaterial). However, it is only in the fifth century that such expressions begin to appear; and there are indications that certain aspects of the doctors' and philosophers' use of *psuche* appeared strange and comic. Aristophanes in the *Clouds*, a comedy devoted to mockery and attack upon the New Thought, makes much play with the word *psuche*. We have just observed Strepsiades howling that the bugs were drinking up his *psuche*. This is literal; and it is also a joke. The ordinary Greek might well assume the *psuche* to be material – as he did – and yet find the detailed conclusions of philosophers and doctors from a similar view of the *psuche* to be bizarre and comic; and Aristophanes' expression suggests a simple exaggeration of the medical language we have already discussed. Earlier in the play (94) Strepsiades points out Socrates' school to his son Phidippides with the words 'This is the thinking-shop of clever *psuchai*', referring to Socrates and his pupils, who are portrayed on the stage as wraithlike pale creatures. It is evident that 'ghosts' is still very much called to mind by *psuche* in ordinary Greek; and ghosts are witless. The thinking *psuche* in ordinary language, a manifestation of the later fifth century, may well be a result of 'New Thought': certainly the fact that these thinkers speak much about both *psuche* and learning appears droll and unfamiliar to Aristophanes, or at all events to his audience. Such thought may well in general have assisted the *psuche* to gain new status as the core and carrier of the personality; though the development, as we have seen, had made progress before the New Thought.

On the other hand, we see that in a real sense traditional writers, philosophers and doctors live in the same world of thought, so far as concerns human personality. The philosophers and doctors draw out detailed implications of traditional attitudes; they systematise; and doctors make discoveries. Nevertheless, they live in the same material world; and distinctions are not drawn: blood may just as readily be 'thought' as 'that with which we think'; and the two views are equally materialistic. The real distinction lies between those doctors who interpret what they see, and those who treat reality, to the detriment of 'mere' appearances, as what lies behind appearances – a distinction which will be pursued in the next chapter.

5. Human Nature and Ethics in Early Thinkers: 'Sophists', *Nomos* and *Phusis*

We have observed in earlier chapters that the ethical goal of the Greeks, the goal which was commended to them by the most powerful values of their society, was the prosperity, stability and self-sufficiency of the basic unit; and it is evident that good health is a desirable. The writers of the last chapter have made clearer the connection between certain types of human behaviour and good or bad conditions of body and *psuche*; and this mode of thought could readily be employed in ethical contexts. Democritus' own ethical position sets no high value on great wealth: those for whom he is writing seem unlikely to achieve it; but in other respects he shows how such connections may be used in ethics. His own goal is a state of contentment, *euthūmiā* or *euthūmeisthai*, of which the word 'pleasure' is sometimes used; but, like later atomists, he does not recommend the indiscriminate pursuit of pleasures (B3):

> He who wishes to *euthumeisthai* should not engage in many activities, whether private or public, nor choose activities which are beyond his *phusis* or capacity. No, he should so guard against this that when fortunate chance strikes him and leads him on to excess by the appearance which it presents, he will set it aside and not grasp at more than his abilities permit. An appropriate quantity is better than a great quantity.

Again, B191:

> *Euthumia* comes to men as a result of moderation in enjoyment and due balance in life. Defects and excesses are wont to change and cause great movements in the *psuche*. Those *psuchai* which are stirred up by great changes of state are neither stable nor do they enjoy *euthumia*. One should accordingly direct one's mind to what is possible, and be content with what one has, having little thought for things that are envied and admired ...

but rather directing one's attention to the lives of those in distress, and considering their great sufferings, so that your own possessions and condition may appear to you great and enviable, and that you may cease to desire more than you have, and so cease to suffer in your *psuche*. For he who admires those who have great possessions and are accounted fortunate by other men, and who is at all hours brooding on them, is always compelled to attempt something new and to run the risk, as a result of his desires, of doing something that cannot be set right, of the things that the laws (*nomoi*) forbid.

He also (B187) contrasts the value of body and *psuche*:

It is appropriate that men should esteem the *psuche* rather than the body; for perfection of the *psuche* sets right the inferior condition of its 'hut', whereas strength of the 'hut' without intelligence makes the *psuche* no better.

Democritus, and the atomists generally, do not represent the ethic of the more articulate and prominent members of Greek society, whose views are, for the most part, what we possess;[1] for they wrote most of the surviving literature, and it is only from written documents that knowledge of values can be obtained. However, Democritus represents one ethic that can be developed from the new thought on human *phusis*. For Democritus, *phusis* is not sharply opposed to *nomos* (law, custom) to the detriment of the latter, as in the thinkers we shall consider below. He says (B248, and cf. B245):

The *nomos* wishes to benefit the life of men; and it can do so, when they themselves are willing to be benefited; for the law shows its own excellence, *arete*, to those who obey.

In Democritus' eyes, *phusis* is not something unlimited, on a basis of which one should strive, or which leads one almost irresistibly to strive, for excess of all kinds. The individual's *phusis* sets bounds beyond which he passes at his peril, or at least at the peril of his *euthumia*, at which in Democritus' view he should be for ever aiming. That *phusis* differs from individual to individual is a view shared

[1] Democritus may sometimes agree *verbally* with those who draw extreme conclusions from the dominant ethic, e.g. B267 'by *phusis* ruling is appropriate for the *kressōn*, better or stronger'. However, the implications are unlikely to be those of Thrasymachus' position (below, pp. 117 ff.): Democritus' ethic has a quite different tenor.

by ordinary men and doctors in the fifth century, as we have seen; but B191 suggests the thought of the doctors and some other philosophers, rather than the reflections of the ordinary man. The first three sentences are particularly 'medical'. Among other writers of the period Parmenides (A46) is said to have supposed that the intelligence was affected by the supremacy of hot or cold in the individual, the better and purer intellect being that resulting from the supremacy of heat; and good and bad memory were similarly linked with the predominance of heat or cold. It is not clear whether Parmenides thought it was possible to vary one's degree of heat or cold by one's actions; but Heraclitus (B117) on the basis of a different theory held that the *psuche* becomes wet – and harmed – when one is drunk; and doctors (e.g. *Humours* I, 7) speak of the bad effects of excesses of all kinds on the *psuche*. The presuppositions of Democritus' B191 are linked with this type of thought.[1]

The most notorious use of *phusis* in the sophists, however, is one in which it is sharply opposed to *nomos* with very different intentions. *Nomos* spans both law and custom. In a conformist age or individual the usage might endow unwritten custom with the same overtones and ethical (if not legal) sanction as written law; but in an age of doubt, questioning and revolt it might equally (as it did in the latter part of the fifth century in Athens) reduce law to the status of custom: a very low status in an age of revolt and change.

However, to understand the matter we need to observe the use of *nomos* and *phusis* in non-ethical as well as ethical contexts. Democritus himself is said to have maintained that perceptible qualities existed only by *nomos* (A1, 44); and in an authenticated fragment (B9) he says that qualities like sweet and bitter exist only by *nomos*, and that in reality there are only atoms and void.[2] We find Philolaus,

[1] It should be noted that Democritus, despite his atomism and his contention that *psuche* is body and that it is irretrievably dissipated at death, nevertheless values the *psuche* much higher than the body. The *psuche* is now the carrier of intelligence; and Democritus is part of an intellectual movement.

[2] Our late source insists that other thinkers of the period believed that perceptible qualities existed by *phusis*, but anyone searching for the reality behind appearances, and holding that all visible things are 'really' earth, air, fire and water, or some similar theory, would be unlikely to express this by saying that appearances existed by *phusis*: it seems more likely that most thinkers of the period did not ask themselves the question in these terms.

a Pythagorean, insisting that a proof in geometry works by *phusis* and not *nomos* (B9); and we have seen doctors under the influence of philosophy similarly distinguishing *phusis* from *nomos* as basic reality from appearances. The link with ethics may be closer than is at first apparent.

The most extensive surviving ethical quotation from a thinker of this period on the subject of *nomos* and *phusis* occurs in Antiphon the Sophist (B44); and seems to be part of his work 'On Truth':

Justice (*dikaiosune*), then, is not to transgress what is laid down by *nomos* in the city in which one lives. A man would accordingly make use of justice in a manner most advantageous to himself if he were to treat the *nomoi* as important when witnesses are present, but the edicts of *phusis* as important when he is alone; for the edicts of the *nomoi* are adventitious, whereas those of *phusis* are necessary. Those of the *nomoi* arise out of compacts between men, not as a result of natural growth (*phūnai*, a verb from the same root as *phusis*), whereas those of *phusis* are a result of natural growth and do not arise out of compacts between men. Supposing, then, that a man transgresses what is laid down by *nomos*, if he escapes the notice of those who made the compact, he is free from both shame (*aischūnē*, linked with *aischron*) and actual damage, while if he does not escape notice, he does not escape these penalties; but supposing, against possibility, a man violates one of the requirements implanted (*xumphuta*, from the same root as *phusis* and *phunai*) by *phusis*, if he escapes the notice of all mankind, the damage to him is no less, and if all see, no more; for he is not damaged on account of an opinion, but on account of truth. The purpose of the present enquiry is to consider these matters, because the majority of things which are just in terms of *nomos* are laid down in a manner which is hostile to the requirements of *phusis;* for *nomoi* are laid down concerning the eyes and what they must or must not see; about the ears and what they must or must not hear; . . . Now none of the things which the *nomoi* prohibit to mankind is more friendly or akin to *phusis* than the things which they enjoin upon it. But living and dying depend on *phusis*, and living results from what is advantageous, dying from what is not advantageous. And the advantages laid down by the *nomoi* are chains upon the *phusis*, whereas those laid down by *phusis* are free.[1] It is not the things that cause pain that benefit the *phusis*, when the matter is properly considered, rather than those which cause pleasure: accordingly the things which cause pain could not be advantageous; for those which are really advantageous must not harm, but benefit. . . . [Under the terms of the *nomoi* those people act correctly] who defend

[1] The 'immoralists' are portrayed by Plato as valuing freedom so highly that they treat self-control as being enslaved to oneself, *Gorgias* 491E5.

themselves when they are attacked and do not themselves begin action; and those who benefit their parents even when the parents behave badly towards them; . . . and of these requirements one could find many that are hostile to *phusis*; and in them resides the likelihood of suffering more pain when one could suffer less, and experiencing less pleasure, when one could have more, and being badly treated when it would be possible not to be badly treated.

Now if those who submitted to these provisions received help, and those who did not, but opposed them, received damage, obeying the laws would not be without benefit; but as it is, justice based on *nomos* is not strong enough to help those who submit to such provisions; for first of all it allows the sufferer to suffer and the agent to act; and it did not (at the time) prevent the sufferer from suffering, nor the agent from acting; and if the case comes up for punishment, there is no special advantage for the sufferer which the agent does not enjoy also; for the sufferer must persuade those who are to punish that he has suffered, and he asks to be allowed to exact punishment; but it is just as much possible for the agent to deny. . . .

We revere and honour those born from noble houses, but those who are not, we neither revere nor honour. In this we behave in a barbarian manner, since we are by *phusis* all born (*phunai*) the same in every respect, both Greeks and barbarians. One may consider the requirements of *phusis*, which are compulsory for all mankind . . . and in none of these matters is any one of us separated off as barbarian or Greek. We all breathe into the air through mouth and nostrils and . . .

This is an important document. (It is fragmentary, and some words depend on the restoration of the text, but the general sense is quite clear.) *Nomos* and *phusis* are the cornerstones of the doctrine; and various aspects of the usage of *phusis* buttress it. *Phusis* stands for truth and reality against mere opinion and appearance; and here we see the *nomos/phusis* opposition of the philosophers quoted above, in the different context of human nature, it is true; but the source of this overtone for *phusis* is clear. Next, *phusis* denotes the manner in which an organism has grown and so now is, with its inherent qualities and needs: this overtone is drawn from both 'ordinary Greek' and from the doctors, but the emphasis on specific needs, and the insistence that living and dying depend on *phusis*, not convention, suggest the latter. The dogma that *nomos* and *phusis* must be opposed to each other is not explained: we cannot determine whether this is an effect of thinking in terms of appearance and reality, where, for example, sensible qualities and atoms-and-void are necessarily quite different, or whether Antiphon merely observed that the legal systems that he knew did their best to suppress the requirements of *phusis*, as understood here, and tacitly assumed that this must be a requirement of legal systems.

At all events, the requirements of *phusis*, the real, the 'ingrown', are clear: to maximise pleasure and satisfaction of desires, and to minimise pain and frustration. We appear to be remote from Democritus. However, another passage of Antiphon (B58) runs as follows:

> The man who, on going against his neighbour to harm him, fears that he may fail to achieve what he wishes and as a result get what he does not wish, is more prudent (*sōphrōn*). For while he is fearing, he delays; and while he is delaying, the lapse of time frequently diverts his mind from his previous wishes. Now when a thing has happened it is not possible for it not to happen; but while it is still about to happen, it is possible that it should not happen. Whoever thinks he will harm his neighbours and not suffer himself is not prudent (*sophron*). Hopes are not always a good thing; for such hopes have cast many people into irretrievable disasters, and they themselves have been found to suffer the harm they were expecting to do to their neighbours. No-one could better judge of the prudence (*sōphrosunē*) of another man than he who fortifies himself against the immediate pleasures of his *thumos* and can conquer himself. The man who wishes to gratify his *thumos* forthwith is desiring the worse (more *kakon*, harmful to himself) in place of the better (more *agathon*, more beneficial to himself).

This sounds like Democritus; and almost gives the impression of being the answer of another speaker in a dialogue opposing the earlier passage quoted. Two points, however, should be noted. In B44 the complaint against justice is not only that it is contrary to *phusis*, but that it is disadvantageous: if it were advantageous, it would be pursued. In B58, justice is more advantageous for the type of person there mentioned, who is presumably the ordinary man in normal circumstances who, in most societies at most periods, is unlikely to be able to get away with being unjust; and the pursuit of justice is commended upon such people. However, neither in B58 nor in that part of B44 in which there is a discussion of the possible desirability of pursuing justice, rejected in the light of the hazards of the courts, is there any mention of *phusis*. All Greeks are commended by their own ethical system to maximise their own self-interest, prosperity and stability; and both groups mentioned here are attempting to do so. However, it appears that for Antiphon in these passages, unlike Democritus, it is only the person who has the power to do this on a large scale, in virtue of his own natural resources, who is expressing his *phusis*: the *phusis* of lesser individuals has the same needs, desires and drives, but such individuals would not be able successfully to give their *phusis* satisfaction, and would only meet with disaster if they tried to do so. They have to do the best they can, pursue self-interest within the limits of their resources, and give their desires what crumbs of comfort they may.

The injunction to live according to *phusis*, then, appears to be addressed here to the outstanding individual. For Antiphon, 'outstanding' is to be reckoned in real terms: the last paragraph of B44 sets aside the claims of mere noble birth, claims which, as we have seen, were buttressed by the use of *phusis* in ordinary fifth-century Greek. Indeed, Antiphon might appear to go further, and to be using *phusis* to commend absolute equality: 'we all, barbarian and Greek, breathe the same air'. The fragment unfortunately breaks off at this point, but Antiphon presumably listed other physiological resemblances. Here we touch on another aspect of human nature important in fifth-century thought: the distinction between Greek and 'barbarian' (which is simply the Greek word for 'foreigner, of alien speech'). The Persian Wars at the beginning of the fifth century B.C. endowed the Greeks, faced with a common foe, at least retrospectively, when the victory had been won, with a sense of unity, of a common Greekness, which they had not previously possessed. This set them off as Greeks from the barbarians who inhabited the rest of the world: a difference which, as we shall see, was treated as real even by Aristotle. So to divide the world renders even more unlikely the development of a concept of human nature as such. The march of the Persians into Greek lands, however, also brought to the notice of the Greeks the wide variety in customs and practices existing in the world;[1] and this in itself must have devalued *nomos*. If one only knows of one's own *nomoi*, one will accord them a higher status than if one knows that one's neighbours manage the matter quite differently. One may then enquire, on a basis of cosmologically or medically

[1] Cf. e.g. Herodotus III, 16, on burial customs.

based physiology, what all mankind has in common; and these are the characteristics which exist on a basis of *phusis*.

All these characteristics, and the desires resulting from them, are in all mankind; and so far *phusis* is a leveller and universaliser; but, in the view of Antiphon and some of the writers we shall discuss below, only the outstanding individual can give his *phusis* full satisfaction, and make it the touchstone of his conduct; and here we are moving back towards the stratified view of society traditional in Greece, and the code of values that supports it.

In Antiphon B44 we have little mention of values; but the 'immoralists' Callicles and Thrasymachus, as represented by Plato's portrait of them, fill this lack. So in the *Gorgias* (483A7 ff.) Callicles[1] says:

> According to *phusis*, everything is more *aischron*, shameful, which is also more *kakon*, harmful to oneself – as, for example, suffering injustice; but according to *nomos* committing injustice is more *aischron*. For to suffer injustice is not an experience which befits a man, but one fit only for a slave for whom death is preferable to life; a man who when he is wronged or insulted is incapable of helping either himself or anyone else for whom he cares,

while in the *Republic* (344C) Thrasymachus declares that injustice is stronger, more 'liberal' and more befitting a master than justice.

Here we come to the nub; and we can see that, as might indeed be expected, the ethical doctrine of *phusis*, though it is derived in part from cosmology, nature philosophy, and medicine, has other sources in addition. It may be possible to prescribe a way of life on the basis of even the first steps in medicine; and Democritus' prescriptions indeed appear to be an attempt to do this, and to relate it to the medicine concerned. But the counsel of Antiphon and Callicles is not explicitly linked to medical discoveries; and it is difficult to imagine how it could be so linked. None of the extant doctors – not surprisingly – deduces from the fact that all men by *phusis* possess a stomach that *phusis* demands that the stomach's gratification must be at all times maximised (as Callicles does, in effect, Plato, *Gorgias* 494A6 ff.) and that it is better for the individual to do so. However, when we include traditional values of 'human nature at its best',

---

[1] For Thrasymachus, see *Republic* I, 336B ff.

arete, the picture becomes clearer. It is the mark of the *agathos*, the human being at his best, to succeed in his enterprises and maximise his own well-being; and if he performs those services that the group requires of him successfully, the group has never been able effectively to pass moral censure upon his breaches of co-operative excellences. *Arete* has always expressed what is essential, in the Greek view, to 'human nature at its best'; and justice, self-restraint and similar qualities have not been part of this. As a result, *arete*, not surprisingly, colours the usage of *phusis*; and *phusis*, by emphasising the needs and desires common to all mankind, furnishes an additional intellectual framework to justify the *agathos* in behaving in the manner in which, as an *agathos*, he was already behaving, without effective censure, in Homer.[1]

In a sense, this use of *phusis* should have discouraged one of the 'ordinary language' fifth-century overtones of the word: that relating to high birth. For *agathos* too, at the end of the century, in commending, as it had always done, the successful soldier and politician, was beginning to commend the pupils of the sophists who, having learned from them rhetoric and such statecraft as there was, might expect to be the most successful politicians. Whoever proved capable of profiting from such instruction clearly possessed the *phusis* to do so, and, in a usage also current at the period,[2] could be said to be acquiring new, improved *phusis* as a result of his instruction. This might be expected to benefit the intelligent who were not of high birth. However, sophists were expensive; and those who had the money and leisure to take long courses of instruction from them were naturally the wealthy, the 'better families' of Athens, who thus acquired a new claim to be termed *agathos*, a word already applied to them. Their *phusis* in the ordinary language sense already gave them status and privileges: they were already *agathoi* by *phusis*. Told by some sophists, with supporting arguments, that *phusis* made certain demands on them – a point of view they were unlikely to resist – the whole range

---

[1] For 'immoralists' is a misleading, though customary, label for such thinkers as Antiphon, Callicles and Thrasymachus. They are not rejecting the values of their society, merely drawing from them their logical conclusions. See *Merit and Responsibility*, pp. 232 ff.

[2] Above, p. 95.

of *phusis* with all its overtones (high birth – in the case of the *agathoi* – against low, reality against appearance, general and universal against arbitrary and particular, inevitable against adventitious) would draw them on to do what *arete* already commended, or failed to decry. We must always remember that *phusis* is one word throughout its whole range of usages, and that the Greeks have no other language in terms of which to think of *phusis*.

The opposition of *nomos* to *phusis* appears in non-philosophical writers, but in a manner which makes it clear that the usage is drawn consciously from philosophy and the sophistic; a view reinforced by the fact that the principal non-philosophical writers who exemplify the usage are Euripides, Aristophanes and Thucydides, all of whom in different ways – Aristophanes in part by portraying views to which he is hostile – reflect philosophical and sophistic usage in their work. It is worth quoting some of these, both to indicate the manner and extent of the influence of the doctrine, and also to round it out: here, as always, sophistic writings are tantalisingly fragmentary.

Euripides, in fact, shows (*Ion* 642 ff.) that the usage need not decry justice. At all events, Ion says:[1]

> And – a thing which is to be prayed for by men, even if they are unwilling to do so – *nomos* and *phusis* alike have rendered me just, *dikaios*.

This usage of *phusis* resembles other, 'ordinary-language' uses in tragedy in which, as we have seen, the characteristics of *phusis* differ widely from individual to individual; and it is contrary in sentiment to the usual opposition of *nomos* and *phusis*; but the form of language suggests that it is so expressed in conscious rejection (whether Euripides' or another philosopher's) of the usual doctrine. More normal is a one-line fragment (Nauck[2] 920) of Euripides:

> *Phusis* desires it, which cares nothing at all for *nomos*.

This raises a question implicit in this usage of *phusis*: to what extent is it inevitable that one should follow *phusis*? *Prima facie* the answer cannot be 'altogether', or there would be no laws or customs

---

[1] And cf. *Bacchae* 893, and Anonymus Iamblichi, D/K 6, 1, fin.

in opposition to *phusis*; but the extent to which *phusis* must, as opposed to ought to, be followed, requires further determination.

Thucydides, in the Third Book of his history, portrays an important debate arising out of the revolt of Mytilene, one of the states in Athens' empire. The revolt having been crushed, the Athenians decided to kill all the adult males and enslave all the women and children, and indeed despatched an officer to carry their orders to Mytilene. The next day they relented somewhat, and a second Assembly took place, at which Cleon counselled that the Athenians should not revoke their order, while Diodotus argued for leniency, each on a basis of the self-interest of the Athenians. Cleon argued (III, 37, 4) that the Athenians should recognise that those who want to be cleverer than the *nomoi* for the most part bring cities to destruction, whereas those who distrust their own cleverness and rate themselves as more ignorant than the *nomoi* . . . for the most part are successful; and he maintained (III, 37, 3) that ignorance combined with prudence and self-control (*sophrosune*) is more beneficial than cleverness combined with licence. The point of view suggests Democritus; and, since the argument as a whole does not fit the particular situation very well, is doubtless a reflection derived by Thucydides from some sophist or philosopher. It is to be noted that Thucydides unlike Democritus (but like Antiphon) does not use *phusis* in this situation. A little later (III, 39, 5) he uses *phunai*, the verb from the same root: 'men are is so constituted, *phunai*, as to despise those who do them services, and admire those who do not yield.' Here the *phusis*-standard seems to be affected by the requirements of *arete* once again: the simple pursuit of one's own basic desire would, it might be supposed, induce a man to regard help as merely convenient; but any enemy who helped and yielded would, in Greek eyes, be showing himself *kakos*, deficient in *arete*, and so to be despised.

Thus Cleon commends a harsher course. Diodotus argues that lenient treatment for the Mytileneans will make it easier for the Athenians to rule their empire as a whole; and he adds (III, 45, 3):

All men are by *phusis* (*phunai*) both in private and in public life liable to err (*harmartanein*), and no *nomos* will deter them from this; for mankind has already run through all possible penalties in an effort to suffer less injustice from wrongdoers.

He adds that this is true unless they can find a more terrible penalty than death; for this is no deterrent (III, 45, 4):

No; poverty by its constraint engenders boldness, and affluence through pride (*hubris*) and insolence instils greed; and the other conditions of human life, as a result of other passions, lead men into dangers, according as each condition is mastered by some irresistible and mightier impulse. And hope and desire are ever-present, the one leading, the other following; the one thinking out the plan, the other suggesting the facility of fortune; and these cause the most damage, and being invisible overmaster the dangers that can be seen. In addition to these, fortune contributes no less to urge men on; for sometimes she manifests herself unexpectedly and draws men on to run risks even when their resources are insufficient; and this is true of states not less than of men, for they are fighting for the greatest prizes, freedom or rule over others, and each individual, when he looks at himself with all the rest, unreasonably rates his strength as greater than it is. In a word, it is impossible and a mark of great folly for anyone to suppose that when human *phusis* is zealously set on doing something, there is any means of diverting it by the power of *nomoi* or any other terror.

In the first part of this passage Diodotus appears to be arguing that *phusis* furnishes the motivation for each and every human action; for *each* condition of human life is supposed to be accompanied by its own basic drive. However, the last sentence suggests merely that *when* the drives of human *phusis* are aroused, neither *nomoi* nor anything else can withstand them. It is probably best to interpret the beginning of the passage in the light of the end: reasoned philosophical discourse on such topics is still in its early stages, and the language of the beginning could be interpreted to mean no more than that there are drives appropriate to each human situation, not that they must always be active as motives. There is ambiguity in the language; and Diodotus is arguing a case, not analysing the human condition.

This may be compared with a passage from the sophist Gorgias' *Defence of Helen* (B11). The author states (6) that Helen must have acted either as a result of the wishes of fortune and the plans of the gods and the decrees of necessity, or because she was abducted by force, or persuaded by words, or seized by love; and he undertakes to prove Helen guiltless no matter which of these causes is appropriate to her situation. If the causation was supernatural, the weaker is so constituted, *phunai*, as to be overcome by the stronger (6): Helen is weaker than fortune, gods or necessity, and should be acquitted. The sophist then deals quickly with physical *force majeure*, a valid defence in the Greek courts; but then (13) assimilates persuasion to *force majeure* as something that comes from outside and affects the *psuche* as it wishes; and (15) treats love similarly: 'for what we see has not the *phusis* we wish it to have, but what it chances to have; and through sight the *psuche* is moulded in its behaviour too.' He takes extreme cases of persons having been frightened out of their wits by what they have seen; and concludes that Helen ought to be acquitted.

This argument is offered as a defence of Helen merely; but it would serve to acquit anyone of anything. Gorgias may not realise this: he is using the thought of doctors and philosophers for a particular purpose, and may not be aware of the wider consequences; and he too is arguing a case. He is not concerned with the opposition of *phusis* and *nomos* here; but the passage serves to show the extremes to which a thesis may be taken at this period by an author engaged in pursuing the implications of ideas.

Only, however, by such authors: a Gorgias writing a sophistic set-piece may produce what would entail the closing of the law-courts, but Thucydides' Diodotus, despite his sophistic borrowings, is arguing for no such thing. He is not claiming that all the Mytileneans should be absolved since *phusis* controls everything, so that we are not responsible beings: he is arguing – rather confusedly – that if the Athenians are lenient their subjects will be easier to govern; and concludes (III, 48) that, on a basis of calculation, not pity, they should try the guilty Mytileneans and allow the rest to inhabit their island in peace. This conclusion does not follow from his sophistic premises: being able to live in peace, like all other conditions, should spur the Mytileneans on to resist the Athenians in their own interest at any opportunity; but in general no Greek of the period concerned with a practical decision is so swayed by theory as to conclude that ethical judgment, reward and punishment are irrelevant in human activity. Diodotus draws on an empirical generalisation, 'no matter how severe penalties are, crimes are still committed' and a philosophical theory of human behaviour which rather more than explains it; but his conclusion is a strictly practical one.

In fact, no Greek of the period states that human beings are always subject to *phusis*, and cannot be affected by anything else. Even Aristophanes, who is hostile to the current of thought of which the *nomos/phusis* analysis is a part, does not attribute this belief to the sophists and their followers. It is true that the Unjust Argument (*Clouds* 1075) says:

> Well; I pass on to the necessities of *phusis*. You have erred; you have fallen in love; you have committed adultery; and you have been caught.

'Necessities' might appear to allow no choice; but the speech immediately continues:

> You are lost; for you don't know how to speak. But if you consort with me, use your *phusis*, be wanton, laugh, and consider nothing shameful, *aischron*.

Despite 'necessities', 'use your *phusis*' seems to imply the possibility of choice,[1] of not using it. The position may be that of the last sentence of Diodotus quoted: all are sometimes so under the constraint of *phusis* that they must act at its behests. (It should be noted that Diodotus does not say that these people should be absolved for what they have done: we cannot suppose that the innocent Mytileneans acted at the behest of *phusis*, the guilty ones from some other motive; and the Unjust Argument clearly supposes that being caught submitting to the necessities of *phusis* will land one in court.) On the other hand Antiphon in B44 seems to suppose that self-control is always possible, that one can choose when to act in terms of *nomos*, when in terms of *phusis*, though B58 has a rather confused doctrine of how this is to be done. At the beginning Antiphon suggests fear as the dissuader, and hopes that the individual's mind may be diverted to other goals before the fear subsides; at the end, he speaks of the individual 'conquering himself': the personality can inhibit the drives of *phusis*. The analysis in terms of hopes and fears recalls Thucydides' Diodotus, though Antiphon is not convinced that hope must triumph. (If there is any direct link, Thucydides is echoing the sophist, not vice versa.) Both views should be contrasted with that of Democritus (B191), who

[1] Cf. Democritus B276 and 278 above, chapter 4, p. 93.

rates highly the possibility of individual choice, on a basis of which serenity (*euthumia*) can be achieved, and counsels directing the mind to particular subjects rather than, with Antiphon, hoping that some deterrent may prevent action long enough to enable the mind to be diverted to some other goal by the passage of time. Again, Cleon evidently regards self-control as possible.

Now the average Athenian was shocked by the new *nomos/phusis* doctrine: Aristophanes expresses that shock in the *Clouds*, and the effect of his comedy, Plato believed, was still powerful enough, almost a quarter of a century later, to have contributed to bringing about the condemnation of Socrates, accused in the *Clouds* of teaching the Unjust Argument (which in the play propounds the *nomos/phusis* doctrine). Lines such as '*phusis* desired it, which cares nothing at all for *nomoi*', quoted above, and Medea's '*Thumos* is more powerful than my reasoned plans' (Euripides, *Medea* 1079) were notorious. Most Athenians, like most members of any society at any time, had to pursue self-control, *sophrosune*, for most of the time. The word spans self-control and prudence: the Athenian termed *sophrosune* the kind of behaviour that he held prudent for him, in his own best interests. *Sophrosune* was not an *arete*, a human excellence, during most of the fifth century,[1] though a few usages of this kind appear towards the end; but it was the best ordinary man could do. *Arete* was not for most Athenians, anyway, and they clearly believed that self-control was possible. So, too, in most circumstances, did not only Democritus and Antiphon,[2] but Diodotus, the Unjust Argument, Callicles and Thrasymachus. One need not act according to *phusis*; but anyone who had the chance would do so, as Glaucon maintains in Plato's *Republic* (359C). If the just and unjust man had power to do whatever they pleased, desire would lead each along the same path:

[1] Many scholars deny this and cite Aeschylus, *Septem* 568–9 and 610, where Amphiaraus is spoken of as 'most *sophron* and most *agathos* in valour' and 'a man *sophron*, just, *agathos* and pious'. These lines seem to me to indicate that *sophrosune* is not an *arete*. The adjective corresponding to *arete* is *agathos*; and *agathos* in both passages is distinguished from *sophron*.

[2] This is clear from Antiphon's position as a whole, despite 'supposing, *against possibility*, a man violates one of the requirements implanted by *phusis* . . .' in B44.

We should catch the just man going in the same direction as the unjust man as a result of his desire to have more, which every *phusis* is so constituted (*phunai*) to pursue as an *agathon*, though it is constrained to honour equality by *nomos*.

Space does not permit a long discussion here of Greek values in the later fifth century B.C.[1] It must suffice to say that the traditional values, in which the goal is prosperity and stability, *eudaimoniā*, and the *agathos*, the man whose characteristics are commended by *arete*, is the prosperous, brave and successful man, are still dominant. Competition, not co-operation, is enjoined on the *agathos*. In the light of this situation, it is clear that *phusis* here is related to the idea of 'human nature at its best'. The paradigm of human *phusis* is the *agathos*.

Here perhaps we may disentangle some of the strands in the *nomos/phusis* doctrine. There are some desires – food, drink, sex – which any school of medicine or biology will isolate as existing in the organism by *phusis*, 'naturally'; but Greek doctors are far from counselling maximum gratification of these desires. Callicles' and Thrasymachus' claim that *phusis* demands such maximum gratification is drawn from another source. There are also desires for advancement, security, political power; and these are commended by *arete* as *agatha*, goods, to be pursued at all times with all the resources at one's command: the successful pursuit of these is commended as the mark of the human being at his best. Such desires too, as we have seen, are treated as arising from *phusis*: it is not surprising that the behaviour of the human being at his best should be treated as being a manifestation of human *phusis*; and the 'ordinary language' use of *phusis*[2] must have had its part to play here. Desires for self-aggrandisement could not be effectively censured in the fifth century B.C., any more than in Homer:[3] the *agathos* might pursue them to the limit of his powers, provided the necessary success and prosperity were secured for his group. Again, the *agathos* might gratify his appetites to the utmost without ceasing to be *agathos*; and where both these desires and those for self-aggrandisement are treated as arising equally from *phusis*, the conclusion that maximum gratification of such desires

[1] For this, see *Merit and Responsibility*, chapters VIII–XII.
[2] Above, pp. 79 ff.
[3] Even in the law-courts. See *Merit and Responsibility*, chapter X.

and appetites is a demand of *phusis* readily follows. We shall discover, however, that – even if they would have little realised it themselves – the pursuit of such gratification is not the most important goal that the adherents of this *phusis*-doctrine set themselves.[1]

There remains the question of development of personality structure. We observed in chapter 3 a tendency for *psuche* to become, in 'ordinary Greek', the core and carrier of the personality during the course of the fifth century. This is paralleled in the use of *psuche* in the philosophers; but the analyses of human motivation and behaviour discussed in this chapter require comment.

On the one hand, the psychology of action remains calculative, for the ethical goal is still prosperity and stability, a desired condition requiring calculation of the means for its attainment: with the proviso that 'calculation' does not imply, any more than it did in Homer, that emotion is not present, and abundantly present, in the transaction. Such a psychology has no room for 'the will': as we have seen, it is still the whole person, represented by the unity of the personal pronoun, that inhibits the desires where an analysis of this kind is given.

However, there is, as we have seen, another analysis, in which hope contends with fear, desire with repulsion, as in Antiphon B58, and in Diodotus' speech. In this analysis the ebb and flow of emotion, the spectral balance, is in the foreground, while the core of the personality is little emphasised. It is true that in the same passage of Antiphon the importance of self-control is urged, and that Diodotus and Gorgias are each pleading a case. Yet the resemblance of their analysis suggests that the unity of the personality is not yet very strongly felt; and this is not surprising, for all the tensions of the *arete*-standard, the requirement of the *agathos* that he shall succeed in doing what it is impossible for him to do, are still present. This seems likely to be an accurate report of Greek psychological experience at this period: *psuche* denotes such core as the personality possesses, but the personality is subject to powerful conflicting internal stresses, linked closely with the organisation and values of the society, which impose great strains on the individual; and these internal stresses remain much more in evidence than is any unifying or harmonising principle.

[1] Below, pp. 146 f., 161 f.

6. Plato

A. Introductory

Hitherto we have discussed for the most part either writers whose view of human nature has to be inferred from their poetry, drama or history or writers who, while they may have set out a coherent view of human nature in their complete works, survive in fragments too short to permit of an entirely confident restoration. Plato, however, sets out at length his observations on the human situation, even if no one view clearly emerges; and his circulated works, if not his lectures, seem to have survived almost complete. Problems remain: Plato's early and middle dialogues profess to set forth the views of his master Socrates, who left no written works; and the doctrines of these dialogues vary. The attempt to determine which views are Socrates', which Plato's own, is unlikely ever to reach a definitive solution; but the problem will require some mention in this chapter.

B. *Psuche*

Plato's fully developed view, or views, of the *psuche* is indissolubly bound up with his eschatology; but Socrates may not have held such a position. In the *Apology*, indeed, probably Plato's earliest written work and hence likely to reflect Socrates' own views, Socrates represents himself as agnostic about life after death (42), and without anything at all resembling the elaborate eschatology found in the later Platonic dialogues. Some hold that Socrates was tailoring his words to suit the jury; but so much of the speech is calculated to offend Athenian susceptibilities that this seems an inadequate explanation. The use of *psuche* itself in the dialogues is not without problems; for in the *Crito*, an early work, Socrates does not use *psuche* of 'the more valuable element in us, which is damaged by injustice', that he is there describing (47E). To employ such an elaborate periphrasis might suggest that he was unaccustomed to use the word *psuche*. This is surprising, for Xenophon in the *Memorabilia*, his account of Socrates' conversations, freely opposes *psuche* to *soma* (as in I, ii. 23,

I, iii. 5); and it seems natural to suppose that the unphilosophical Xenophon acquired this linguistic usage from Socrates. But whatever be the explanation of its absence from the *Crito*, in the majority of the dialogues *psuche* is a key word. Plato's basic usage is best illustrated by a passage in the *Phaedrus* (245E):

> Every *soma* (body, here in the sense of 'object') whose motion[1] is imparted to it from without is devoid of *psuche*, whereas that whose motion comes from within itself has *psuche*, since that is the *phusis* of *psuche*.

Self-motion, then, betokens the presence of *psuche*. Earlier in the same passage (245C) Plato also maintains

> Every *psuche* is immortal. For that which always moves is immortal. That which moves something else and is moved by something else, when it has a cessation from motion, has cessation from life. Only what moves itself, inasmuch as it does not desert itself, never ceases from motion, and this is the spring and principle of movement for everything else that is moved.

Plato has added to the Presocratic nature-philosophers' view of the *psuche* as the source of self-motion (which raises no question of its ontological status, and is compatible with a wide variety of philosophies) the belief, drawn from 'Pythagoreans' and mystery-cults, that the *psuche* is immortal. I repeat the reasons for not rendering *psuche* by 'soul'. First, 'soul' implies a particular view, or one of a range of views, with eschatological implications, whereas *psuche* is in itself a neutral word shared with doctors, nature-philosophers and ordinary Greeks. In English, the debate would concern the existence of the soul. In Greek, to debate its existence in mankind and animals would be absurd: one can distinguish a living from a dead specimen of these, and the difference results from the presence or absence of

---

[1] The word here rendered 'motion' (*kineisthai*) is used later by Aristotle of change in a wider sense, including growth and development; and he discusses at some length *psuche* in plants. He was not the first thinker to ascribe *psuche* to plants: Empedocles (B117) claimed to have been a plant, as well as a boy, a girl, a bird and a fish during the course of his transmigrations; but the implications, and his method of discussion, are quite different. Other early thinkers who did not take Empedocles' 'Pythagorean' view of *psuche* might have concluded that plant growth implied the presence of *psuche* in plants; but their extant fragments indicate little interest in the subject.

psuche, be one Pythagorean, atomist or man in the street. The Greek debate concerns the nature of that *psuche* in life and its lot after death, whether dissipation, neutral Hades or reward and punishment. Secondly, 'soul' in English does not immediately call to mind thought, emotion or desire, even if further reflection would add these; while for Plato, as had become the case in ordinary Greek as the fifth century developed, the *psuche* thinks, has aptitudes, and – sometimes – desires and emotions.

The last point requires further discussion: Plato's position shows at least striking changes of emphasis in different dialogues. In the *Phaedo*, a major dialogue from the beginning of Plato's middle period, Socrates insists that the true philosopher would turn away from the *soma* so far as he could, and devote himself to his *psuche* (64E); for the philosopher's aim in life is to separate his *psuche* from his *soma*, which is 'practice of death' (67E), since death consists in separation of *soma* from *psuche* (64C). Such a man cares nothing for the pleasures of the *soma*, and devotes himself to acquiring pure knowledge, in which the senses are a positive hindrance: 'when the *psuche* tries to consider anything in company with the *soma* it is evidently deceived by it'; so that the *psuche* of the philosopher will not only shun bodily pleasures, but also sense-experience from the *soma*, as an inferior source of information.

Plato had several reasons for distrusting empirical data: his ethical preoccupations led him to search for perfect examples of justice and the other excellences, not to be found in the sensible world: his geometrical interests made him aware that geometers' figures are not the real objects of geometry; and certain logical puzzles linked with the existential and predicative functions of the verb to be, combined with a consciousness, derived from Heraclitus, that the sensible world is a world of continuous change, occasioned a doubt of the reality of the world revealed to us by the senses. Accordingly, the philosopher, the lover of truth, will turn from this world and pursue reality, the reality of the world of unchanging Forms,[1] with his *psuche* alone (66E).

The injunction to pursue reality with the *psuche* persists in Plato's doctrine: the immortal *psuche* with its power to grasp ultimate reality is naturally more valuable, real, and divine than the body, a thing

[1] See below, p. 135.

of change and decay.[1] However, the relation of the *psuche* to desire varies. Here, in the *Phaedo*, we find (65C) that the *psuche* 'thinks best when neither hearing nor sight, pain nor pleasure, troubles it'; and (66C) 'the *soma* fills us with passions, desires and fears, and all sorts of phantasms and follies, so that, as they say, it really prevents us from thinking at all'.

These quotations suggest that pleasure and pain can upset the *psuche*, but arise in the *soma*, to which they belong, so that the *psuche* itself does not experience pleasure or pain, merely distraction; and on several occasions in the dialogue[2] pleasures are equated with bodily pleasures. Yet (83C) Socrates says that

> The most serious harm is that the *psuche* of every man is compelled, at the same time as it is greatly pleased or pained by anything, to believe that the object which occasioned the violent emotion is particularly distinct and true; whereas it is not.

The *psuche* here experiences the pleasure or pain; and this puts it into bondage to the body, for each pleasure or pain rivets it to the body and makes it body-like, so that it imagines that those things are true that the body says are true.

The *psuche* can experience pleasure, but it should not (83D); for all pleasures are assumed to be bodily, and these contaminate the *psuche*. Yet elsewhere in the dialogue (67E ff.) the philosopher is said to long all his life for wisdom, and to be in love with it; and one might have supposed that he might experience some pleasure on attaining his desire. The *Symposium*, a dialogue of about the same period as the *Phaedo*, amplifies the theme of the love, *erōs*, of the philosopher for wisdom, which plays only a small part in the *Phaedo*.

---

[1] Plato clearly held the *psuche* to be incorporeal (see Simmias' summing-up of the position, and analogy with the *harmoniā* of a lyre in opposition to its material parts, *Phaedo* 85E; and cf. *Timaeus* 34B ff.). He still speaks of the *psuche* sometimes, however, in a manner which implies materiality, e.g. *Phaedo* 81C, cf. p. 219 below. The implications of his philosophy as a whole indicate that *psuche*, in his eyes, is immaterial; but it is surprising that he does not devote more time to making the point, a new and startling point in the Greece of his day.

[2] E.g. 83B. The language of 64D, where 'the so-called pleasures' is used of bodily pleasures, may imply the existence of other pleasures; but Plato's emphases in the *Phaedo* give no opportunity for discussing them.

The speaker here is not Socrates, but the priestess Diotima, whose words Socrates reports. The *Symposium* as a whole is concerned with *eros*, love in the sense of passionate desire; and Diotima urges (210A ff.) that everyone who wishes to follow the path of *eros* aright should begin by feeling *eros* for an individual *kalon*[1] body, in which he should beget *kalon* discourse; then he should observe the kinship of the *kallos* (the noun answering to the adjective *kalon*) in one beautiful body with that in another, and regard as one and the same the *kallos* which is possessed by all beautiful bodies; then he is to set a higher value on the *kallos* he finds in *psuchai* than that which he finds in bodies; then to pass to the *kalon* in customs and laws, and thence to the *kallos* in branches of knowledge. After all this (210E)

> When anyone has been educated to this stage in the concerns of *eros*, viewing the *kala* rightly and in order, he will suddenly see, as he comes towards the goal of his dealings with *eros*, something wonderful and *kalon* in its *phusis*, the very thing which is the reason for all the previous toils. First, it always exists and does not come to be or pass away, nor increase nor decrease, nor is it partly *kalon* and partly *aischron*, nor *kalon* at one time, *aischron* at another, nor *kalon* in one respect, *aischron* in another. . . .

Eros, accordingly, is the driving force that leads a man on from the love of a beautiful body ultimately to the contemplation of the *kalon* in itself. Evidently, at least from the stage where the kinship of the *kalon* in *kalon* bodies is to be recognised, the *psuche* is involved in this *eros*, for the body is incapable of such recognition; and the *eros* for *kalon* laws, customs and branches of learning must be felt entirely in the *psuche*, as must that for the *kalon* in itself. The use of the one word *eros*, however, and the account of the progress from one stage to the next, treats as identical the drives for these very different objects.

Here we have *prima facie* a very different doctrine from that of the *Phaedo*. However, we should not treat the *Phaedo* as though it were a dispassionate treatise on the *psuche*: it is a dialogue instinct

---

[1] In order to understand the *Symposium*, it is necessary to understand the range of *kalon*, which is untranslatable. It spans 'beautiful', 'fitted for its purpose' (a good harbour would be *kalos*), and is also the most powerful word available to give ethical commendation of an action. (It is, in writers after Homer, the opposite of *aischron* in every respect.) In following Plato's argument it is of the utmost importance to recollect the ethical overtones of the word.

with emotion, with a puritanical revulsion from the body and all its works as something impure, contrasted with the purity of the *psuche* that has properly shunned it (67C). Only devotion to philosophy can separate the *psuche* from the body in life, and ensure that it departs to a place of bliss at death (81A): those who are just and temperate merely from conditioning and habit become ants or bees in their next existence (82A). The revulsion from bodily desire and pleasure is so profound that desire and pleasure can only be seen in these terms, though intellectual desire and pleasure are implied by other statements in this very dialogue. This is combined with the wish to defend philosophy as a way of life: philosophers were regarded as very queer fish by the 'Greek in the street' at this period; and possibly with the desire to represent Socrates as an ascetic in all things, for the manner in which his enemies claimed that he had corrupted the young was not entirely intellectual. This combination of motives seems to have led Plato to the extreme statement of the *Phaedo*. The *Phaedo* is an apologia: the *Symposium* is protreptic, and a protreptic work must base itself on the values and desires of those one wishes to persuade.

Pederasty was common in the circles at Athens in which Plato moved: accordingly, Plato begins from *eros* for boys, and represents it as the first step on a ladder which leads to the contemplation of the *kalon* in itself. He must start from something which his audience will grant to be desirable; and his use of *eros* throughout has great protreptic value. To say this is not to deny that Plato himself may have felt the *amor intellectualis* of the mystic for the objects of his philosophy (nor yet that Plato was almost certainly himself homosexual); but an acknowledgment of Plato's protreptic purpose may help to resolve some contradictions in his dialogues. In his *Protagoras* (351B ff.) Socrates is made to put forward the view that pleasure is the *agathon*, pain the *kakon*: a view sharply contrasted not only with the *Phaedo* but with the majority of the dialogues. But the outcome of the discussion is the demonstration that, to maximise one's pleasures, a hedonistic calculus is needed: one must balance immediate pains against future pleasures, immediate pleasures against future pains; and only the intellect can perform the calculations. The prime importance of the intellect is thus demonstrated. In both *Symposium* and *Protagoras* Plato begins from something acknowledged by his readers to be desirable, to lead them in the direction in which he wishes them to go: in the *Phaedo* he is defending a way of life. Where persuasion is so important, and emotions run high, some contradictions are perhaps to be expected.

Nevertheless, a coherent view of the nature, and proper goals, of the *psuche* can be constructed from these dialogues, if due allowance is made for their purpose; and the later dialogues make this explicit. The *psuche* is divided into three in the *Republic*: Plato distinguishes the *logistikon*, 'that in the *psuche* by means of which it calculates and reasons' from the *epithūmētikon*, 'that with which it loves, hungers, thirsts and is stirred by other desires' (439D) and the *thūmoeides*, the spirited aspect which feels anger at injustice and strives to right wrongs (440E). The *thumoeides*, unless corrupted, obeys the orders of the *logistikon*, whereas the *epithumetikon* is unruly. The analysis of the *Republic* is reinforced by the brilliant picture, in the *Phaedrus* myth (246B ff.), of the disembodied *psuchai*, portrayed as charioteers with two horses each, following the gods in their circuit of the cosmos. At the uppermost point of the circuit, outside the vault of heaven, is 'the colourless, formless and intangible truly existing essence', which is visible only to the mind, 'the pilot of the *psuche*' (247C). The intellect of the gods is nurtured on this, and what they see, while drawn by their teams of obedient horses, on each revolution suffices them until the next circuit (247D). The other *psuchai* stand just as much in need of the nutriment to be derived from the contemplation of these essences, but (246B) the pair of horses that the charioteer of the human *psuche* drives are ill-matched, 'one noble and *agathos* and sprung from similar stock, the other quite the opposite': clearly a mythological portrayal of *logistikon* (the charioteer), *thumoeides* and *epithumetikon*. As a result (248A) when even the best of the other *psuchai* reaches the top of the circuit, the charioteer – the intellect – is so troubled by his horses – spirit and desire – that he hardly glimpses the realities; and many in the scuffling and confusion fail to see them at all. Any *psuche* that sees any of them is safe until the next circuit; but any that fails to see them on a particular circuit grows heavy, loses its wings and falls to earth. Then, it is the law (248C) that such a *psuche*, provided that it has seen the realities at all, should not pass into an animal at its first birth:

The *psuche* that has seen most shall be born into a man who is to become a philosopher or a lover of beauty (*kalon*) or one of a cultured and 'erotic' nature, the second (that which has not seen quite so much) into a man who is to be a king ruling lawfully or a warlike ruler, the third into a politician or a man of business or finance, the fourth into an energetic gymnast or someone connected with the cure of the body; the fifth will have the life of a prophet or one who conducts mysteries; a poet or some other imitative artist will be united with the sixth, a craftsman or farmer with the seventh, a sophist or demagogue with the eighth, and a tyrant with the ninth.

The order is interesting, though there is no room to discuss it in detail here. In Plato's ranking of any kind, the philosopher always appears at the top, the tyrant at the bottom, with the sophist and demagogue somewhere near. The reason for the presence of the philosopher's companions in the top grade is doubtless that the *Phaedrus*, like the *Symposium*, is concerned with *eros* felt for the *kalon*, to which is again ascribed the power of leading towards reality (250C ff.). In the *Republic*, the philosopher is supreme and this method of suasion is abandoned, though erotic language is used of the love of philosophy, *Republic* 490B, 521B; and at a different level erotic rewards are offered to the brave soldier, 468B. Taking the *Phaedrus* list as a whole, we have a gradation of types of person and life based on the amount of ultimate reality that the *psuche* has perceived before coming into a body. Any *psuche* that has never perceived ultimate reality at all cannot enter into a human being; for (249B)

A human being must understand a general conception, which arises from the collecting into a unity by means of reason many perceptions of the senses; and this is a recollection of the things which the *psuche* saw once when it journeyed with a god and, turning its eyes above what we now say exists (the sensible world), raised its head into the realm of real being.

The *psuchai* in general do not return to the great circuit in the train of the gods for ten thousand years, but remain in a cycle of lives on earth: at the end of each life they undergo a judgment on the basis of the justice or injustice of that life, and are rewarded or punished accordingly, returning in a thousand years to draw lots and choose another life, each choosing whatever it wishes. Only the *psuche* of one who has been a philosopher without guile or a philosophical lover for three successive lives can escape, for its wings are restored to it in the three thousandth year.

Many strands of earlier thought and belief appear in this myth: the belief in transmigration of souls, in a judgment after death, the belief that presence in this world at all is the result of some failing in another existence, but that three 'good lives' will set one free from the cycle: all these have been observed in the minority view of human existence already discussed.[1] Plato, however, has infused the whole with his own philosophy: for Empedocles (B115), some terrible crime precipitated us into this life; for Plato, the reason is failure to perceive ultimate truths; and Plato has added the requirement that the three lives should be philosophical to the belief, attested by Pindar (*Olympian* II, 68 ff.), that three just lives would suffice to free one from the cycle of being. (Plato's belief demands justice too; but he believes, *Republic* X, 619C–E, 621C–D, that only philosophy will guarantee justice.) Plato's assertion of the need to have perceived these ultimate truths, the Forms, is here stated in a myth; but it is an integral part of Platonic philosophy. In the *Phaedo* (74 ff.) Socrates is so certain that our knowledge of, for example, absolute mathematical equality cannot have been derived from sense-experience that he bases on this an argument for the existence of the *psuche* before it came into the body; and in the *Parmenides*, though the Theory of Forms is logically battered by Parmenides to the point where it appears utterly untenable, Parmenides himself is nevertheless depicted (135B) by Plato as holding that absolute essences must exist, however difficult it may be to state the theory properly; and Plato at least did not explicitly deny (though he may have given the view much less emphasis in his later dialogues) that human knowledge of these essences must be obtained outside this life.

These essences, the Forms, are concrete universals with an existence separate from that of all particulars; and only acquaintance with these, more or less dimly remembered, will enable us to form concepts when reminded of them by the confused and confusing data of sense-experience. Animals cannot do this; hence those *psuchai* which have never seen the Forms at all cannot enter human bodies – a Platonic modification of the Pythagorean doctrine – though souls which have

[1] Above, chapter 3, pp. 65 ff.

seen the Forms may enter animal bodies. (In the myth of Er in the
Republic (620A ff.) the *psuche* of Orpheus chooses the life of a swan,
the *psuche* of Ajax that of a lion, on a basis of their experiences in their
previous life.) It is knowledge of the Forms which gives human beings
their characteristic humanity. This is, however, not the only function
of the gradation from philosopher to tyrant: tyrants are not necessarily
the least efficient of mankind at forming concepts and, though there is
evidently a case for ascribing to the philosopher the greatest power
of abstract thought (since, in Plato's terms, he is always, so far as
possible, in communion through recollection with the Forms), the
list as a whole is not arranged on this basis: the primary result of
having seen the Forms is an ability to use words at all, and word-
using ability does not steadily decline through the grades Plato offers
here. The list has another purpose, an ethical one: the types of life
are arranged according to the degree of approval or disapproval
that Plato accords to them. The approval or disapproval is partly
moral, partly social; but, though Plato could not have closely linked
this to the degrees of conceptualising ability of the people concerned,[1]
he, like Socrates, did hold that *arete* is knowledge; and this tenet
serves as some kind of a link.[2]

Those *psuchai* that come into this life for the first time, then, have
great differences in their nature, depending on the extent to which
they have viewed the Forms; and this endows them not merely with intellectual, but with moral differences. Their first life is assigned to them,
they do not choose it; and those on the lower grades of Plato's scale
would have little chance of living a life of justice. The just tyrant is a
contradiction in terms for Plato. However, after a life of injustice,
duly punished after death, such persons – unless their injustice is so
flagrant that they are retained in Hades for ever as examples (*Republic*
X, 615D) – have another choice of life, and may choose a life in which
justice is possible (*Republic* X, 619D); though they may not – in the

[1] Another gradation appears at the end of the *Timaeus*, 90E ff. There the
degree of irrationality and immorality of those incarnated originally as men
resulted in a variety of inferior second incarnations, the worst men being
reincarnated as shellfish. This is imposed upon the *psuche* in the *Timaeus*; it
does not result from a choice. (Yet another different account appears in the
Phaedo, 81D ff.)

[2] For '*arete* is knowledge', see below, pp. 158 ff.

doctrine of the *Phaedrus*, at all events[1] – choose a philosophic existence, since they have not seen sufficient of the Forms. Their justice, accordingly, as we shall see, must depend on habituation and right opinion; but discussion of this must be reserved until later.

C. *Soma* and *Psuche* in Ethics

Eschatologically, then, justice is of primary importance to the *psuche*. Plato has taken strands of earlier belief and turned them to his own purposes. A very different opposition between *soma* and *psuche* was used by Greek doctors, as we have seen; and Plato was able to draw on this also, in his own way. The idea that a particular regimen would serve to maintain health, that indiscriminate eating would damage it, that the brief discomfort and pain of medicine and surgery could bring much greater, and long-lasting, relief, was by this time familiar; and since medicine was the best organised field of intellectual activity at the time, its methods enjoyed prestige generally, even if Plato himself had a low regard for the use that was made of medical skills in his own day.[2] He was nevertheless willing to draw parallels between the good condition of the *soma* and that of the *psuche*, and the appropriate methods of achieving them.

In the *Protagoras*, for example, Socrates (313C ff.) rebukes the youthful Hippocrates – not the doctor, but a young Athenian – for being so eager to learn from the sophist Protagoras, of whom he knows nothing accurate. The *psuche* is nourished by learning as the body is by food. Many merchants and hucksters of food praise their wares, though no-one but a doctor or a trainer knows which foods are really beneficial. Similarly the sophists, hucksters of knowledge, go round the cities peddling intellectual pabulum, and praising all their wares, though (313D7) 'perhaps some even of them may not know which of the things they sell is good or bad for the *psuche*'; and their customers certainly do not, 'unless one of them chances to have a doctor's skills with regard to the *psuche*'. And the danger to the *psuche* is much

---

[1] In the Myth of Er in *Republic* X, it would appear that anyone could choose a philosophic existence if there were one left when it was his turn to choose; but Plato must have believed that there were few philosophic lives among those available for choice.

[2] *Republic* III, 405A ff.

greater (314A): one can carry food and drink home in a parcel, and consult about it; whereas one has to carry the piece of learning home with one in one's own *psuche*, and the damage (or benefit) is already done.

The parallel is close: a *psuche*-doctor is needed to advise on intellectual regimen, as a *soma*-doctor is required to advise on diet. That the individual, having acquired his new piece of knowledge in his *psuche*, might adopt a critical attitude to it, and reject it, is not considered. Plato's experience of the behaviour of young Athenians in this situation may have justified pessimism as regards the likelihood of this:[1] here it is not even treated as a possibility; and this, as will be seen, is linked with Plato's whole view of human nature.

In the *Gorgias* (464B ff.) the implications are more fully drawn out. *Technē*, skill which really understands what is *agathon*, good for the person or thing to which it is applied, is contrasted with *empeiriā*, knack which is concerned only with giving pleasure. The *technai* concerned with body and *psuche*, the medical and the political, are compared, and each is subdivided into two: the medical into medicine and gymnastics, the political analogously into legislative science and corrective justice. Each of these has an accompanying *empeiria*, knack: medicine has (luxurious) cookery, gymnastics, the art of cosmetics; while legislative science has the knack of the sophist, and corrective justice, rhetoric. All these *empeiriai* were termed *technai* in the ordinary Greek of the day: Plato is deliberately devaluing them; and he asserts (464C) not merely that they act without knowledge but that they 'toady to' their clients; and by associating sophistic and rhetoric with cookery and the art of cosmetics Plato is enlisting powerful social prejudices against the former.

The Greek, like anyone else, desired physical health; and his doctors

[1] New and intellectually exciting doctrines are apt to be accepted uncritically anywhere by some people; and in Greece at this period intellectual movements are a new phenomenon. Again, Plato's Athens is still essentially a shame-culture: questioning of doctrines fashionable among one's coevals – here the intellectual young – might well occasion mockery; and no-one in a shame-culture will court the mockery of the group to which he belongs. Once a view has become intellectually fashionable, it is always difficult to challenge it: in a shame-culture, the difficulty is greatly increased. (And of course the political and ethical doctrines of some of the sophists were, for reasons already discussed, certain to attract many Athenians who regarded themselves as *agathoi*.)

were prepared to advise him on how to obtain it. Having a *psuche*, he naturally wished to have this in the best condition possible, however he interpreted 'best condition': a question which will be discussed below. In both cases he could be persuaded that he ought to choose what was really good for him, rather than what was merely pleasant; for he desired the *arete*, the best condition, of both *psuche* and *soma*, and this could only be obtained if each had its appropriate *agatha*, good things. Now one need not learn medicine in order to be healthy: it suffices that society contains medical experts. The parallel between *psuche* and *soma* might not in itself have induced Plato to conclude that it sufficed that a few in society should be experts on the *psuche*, while the rest were content with the 'right opinion' these instilled; but in the light of Plato's whole position the conclusion was, as we shall see, inevitable.

D. *Soma* and *Psuche* in Physiology

In the *Phaedo* (97B ff.) Socrates expresses the disappointment he experienced on reading the works of Anaxagoras. That philosopher posited *nous* (mind) as the cause and organiser of the cosmos and all its contents; and Socrates had hoped for a teleological explanation (97C4):

> And I thought that if this is so, *nous* at all events in arranging all things arranges and orders them in the best manner possible; accordingly, if anyone wished to know how each thing comes to be or perishes or exists, he ought to find out the manner in which it is best for it to exist or suffer or do anything else whatsoever. . . .

Anaxagoras attempted no such thing; but Plato in the *Timaeus* (44D ff.) offers an explanation of the structure of the human being in these terms.[1] The head is spherical, in imitation of the cosmos as a whole,

---

[1] He discusses the genesis of the cosmos in these terms, *Timaeus* 29D ff.; and the status of the Form of the Good in his cosmos, *Republic* 509B, on which the other Forms, and so ultimately the sensible world, depend, entails that the sensible world is as good as it can be, given its unsatisfactory ontological status and (cf. *Politicus* 269D ff.) the fact that the cosmos, which is a living creature, has its own 'cussedness' when, as Plato believed was true of the epoch in which he was living, 'the god' took his hand from the tiller of the universe.

for it is the most divine part of us and rules over the rest. Indeed, Plato finds it necessary to explain why the head has a body (44E):

> In order, accordingly, that it should not roll about on the ground, which has all kinds of hills and hollows, and be puzzled to know how to climb over the one and out of the other, they (the gods) gave it the body as a carriage and means of movement.

So the body acquired length, and shot out four limbs, to transport the head, the container of our most divine and holy part.

This is one aspect of Plato's explanation, the teleological. He asserts that such causation is primary (46D): only what has reason and thought, and hence can form purposes, can be primary; and only *psuche*, whether of a god or a man, can have reason and thought. It is *psuche* that initiates motion, whether in the cosmos or in the individual human being.

However, the whole explanation is by no means so simple as this statement might suggest. Plato does not reject the earth, air, fire and water, nor the 'cooling and heating, solidifying and dissolving' of earlier philosophers (46C ff.): they are the auxiliary causes which the god uses as his servants in perfecting, so far as may be, the cosmos; but they are made of the kind of stuff that can only transmit motion, not initiate it. Plato does not, however, imagine the cosmos to be without laws save those imposed by *psuche* as moving cause (48A):

> The origin of this cosmos came about from the combination of necessity and reason; and since reason was controlling necessity by persuading her to bring to the most *agathon* goal most of the things that were coming into existence, in this manner and thus, through necessity yielding to intelligent persuasion, this universe came to exist in the beginning.

This is a naïve attempt to harmonise teleology and mechanistic explanation: if necessity is merely a blind causal sequence, how can it be persuaded by reason? Plato can offer no answer; but his picture is not yet complete. Earlier thought had for the most part accepted earth, air, fire and water as the primary constituents of the universe; and later thought under the influence of Aristotle was long to take the same view. Plato, however, seeks a mathematical basis for the universe, which both accords well with his own regard for mathematics and suits the speaker: all this account is expressed through the mouth not of Socrates but of Timaeus, a philosopher from Italian Locris, an area of the Greek world much influenced by Pythagoreans. He derives everything (53C ff.) ultimately from triangles, a shape from which every plane figure and thence every solid may be constructed; and he allocates different geometrical shapes as the basis for the differences between earth, air, fire and water. The 'necessary' aspect of the cosmos thus is mathematical in character, even though Plato also speaks of reason 'persuading' it.

The explanation of human physiology, and of the interaction of *psuche* and body, has now to be offered in these terms. *Psuche* was bound into the human marrow by the god, human marrow (73B) being formed from primary triangles of the highest quality, fitted to produce earth, air, fire and water of the best kind; and the god also divided the marrow to be the receptacle of the different kinds of *psuche*: a perfect globe for the head, the receptacle of the divine seed of reason, a column (the spinal column) as receptacle for the other parts of the *psuche*, which are stated to be mortal in this dialogue; and pleasures are sited there (69D), though discussion of other dialogues has shown[1] that Plato's eschatology does not portray the *psuche* that survives death as impassible reason.

Thus linked to the body, the *psuche* of the *Timaeus* may be affected by it, even to the point, it would seem, of being utterly under the control of it. There are diseases of the *psuche* which are due to the condition of the body (86B); and the greatest of these are pleasures and pains in excess. Sexual incontinence is attributed to the abundant flow of one substance resulting from the open texture of the bones, bad temper, rashness, cowardice, forgetfulness and stupidity to acid and salty phlegms and bitter and bilious humours, wandering through the body (86E), which

> find no exit but are pent within the body and blend their vapour with the movement of the *psuche* and cause all manner of diseases to the *psuche*.

An individual in any of these conditions is wrongly reproached as

[1] E.g. p. 133 (the *Phaedrus*-myth).

'being voluntarily *kakos*', for no-one is voluntarily *kakos* (86D): the *kakos* becomes *kakos* as a result of a bad *hexis*, condition, and unskilled nurture of his body, and such experiences are hateful to everyone, and occur against one's will.

This doctrine is evidently dependent on medical thought, and gives a new dimension to 'no-one is voluntarily *kakos*': nowhere else in Plato do we find an explanation in such mechanistic terms. The *psuche* seems to be entangled in a nexus of causes over which it has no control; and one might perhaps expect an explanation of *arete* in similar terms to follow, depriving mankind of responsibility altogether.[1] However, the analogy with physical disease is close: no-one is voluntarily ill, physically, but the question whether one is voluntarily healthy is a nonsensical one; and Plato's view of *psuche* as superior to the body, and the only true cause of motion, however difficult it might be to harmonise with the mechanistic theory given above, ensures that he treats the phlegms and humours as malign influences that can be removed by appropriate means, leaving the *psuche* free to pursue *arete*[2] (87B):

> Furthermore, when men are in such an evil condition (*kakōs*), and the political constitutions are *kakai* and speech in the cities, both in private and in public, is *kakos*, and when lessons which would cure these conditions are nowhere learnt from childhood, as a result of this all of us who are *kakoi* become *kakoi* on account of two altogether involuntary causes. Of these we must always accuse the parents rather than the children and the nurses rather than those in their care; yet each of us must endeavour, so far as in him lies, to flee *kakia* and pursue the opposite by means of his nurture, practices and studies.

The non-physiological aspects of this belong to another branch of study (87B). Physiologically, Plato recommends gymnastic exercise as best; then horse-riding or journeys by boat; and, least satisfactory of all, purging by drugs (89A). One should exercise body and *psuche* together, so that both may be in harmony and equally healthy. These views are found elsewhere in Plato: a proper balance of body and

[1] Aristotle, *Nicomachean Ethics* 1111a25 ff., treats it as nonsense to suppose that good actions are voluntary, bad actions involuntary.

[2] Compare Democritus' views, also medically based, above pp. 110 ff.; and Heraclitus and the doctors, p. 112.

psuche is commended in *Republic* 410B ff., while horse-riding is mentioned along with other forms of exercise in *Laws* 789C ff.: the distinctive feature of the *Timaeus* account is the emphasis on the mechanistic causation of bad moral conditions, which differs at least in degree from later Platonic statements, and quite radically from earlier ones.[1] However, the *Timaeus* is fundamentally optimistic: *if* appropriate measures are taken, we recover from our involuntary *kakia* and can lead a good life. Throughout this account, it should be remembered that *kakos* decries a bad specimen of its kind: if anyone concedes that breaches of co-operative excellences render him *kakos*, he must wish to be rid of them, and so must, one would suppose, be in possession of them involuntarily.[2]

E. Values[3]

We have seen that the sophistic advocates of *phusis*, and their pupils, valued the competitive excellences most highly, as most conducive to the prosperity, stability and well-being of the individual and the group with which he at any time identified himself. This might at different times, depending on circumstances, be his family, his family and friends, his political group or faction, or the *polis* as a whole; though even in war it could not be assumed that the *polis* took first place. Justice should be pursued only so far as it was in one's own interest; and the more extreme proponents of the doctrine seem to have assumed that injustice would always be more profitable. Thrasymachus (*Republic* 348C) terms injustice an *arete*; as he had every right to do, in terms of Greek values, if he held that injustice produced the kind of life most valued by the Greeks. The general attitude is not confined to the advocates of *phusis*. *Arete* had always commended those qualities deemed best to promote prosperity, stability and well-

---

[1] Cf. earlier *Protagoras* 352B, and later *Laws* 645A, both discussed below, pp. 156, 160 f.; and also *Sophist* 227D ff., where *stasis*, internal strife, in the *psuche* is spoken of as the characteristic disease of the *psuche*, but no physiological causation is assigned. The implications of the *Timaeus* doctrine, so far as concerns anyone brought up in a city with bad institutions, are more pessimistic than those of this passage of the *Laws*.

[2] It should be noted that the account of the *Timaeus* is presented as being merely 'probable', e.g. 29C (D), 59C.

[3] Platonic Values are discussed at length in *Merit and Responsibility*, chapters XII, XIII, XIV.

being in the group. The ordinary man may disagree with Thrasy-machus about the point at which injustice becomes more profitable;[1] but if it does so, society's values enjoin that it should be pursued. Plato devotes a short early dialogue to a conversation in prison between the condemned Socrates and his close friend Crito, portrayed by Plato as an ordinary decent Athenian. Crito's opinion (*Crito* 45C5 ff.) of Socrates' refusal to escape from prison when he has the chance is quite clear: he thinks Socrates is betraying himself. Socrates claims to have practised *arete* all his life. Crito maintains that a man who is *agathos* and brave (a prominent aspect of *arete*) will choose to live, so that he may protect his children, rather than let them suffer the unhappy fate of orphans. Crito is uneasy about his own position too: he fears that, if Socrates does not escape, others may believe that this was the result of some cowardice and unmanliness, *kakia* and *anandriā*, on the part of Crito and Socrates' other friends.

The ordinary Athenian, in a city allegedly governed by law, still adheres to a system of values little different from that of Homer. The prosperity and stability of the *agathos* and his friends is still of paramount importance; and if the laws must be disobeyed to achieve this, so much the worse for the laws. That Socrates was unjustly condemned is irrelevant: Meno in the dialogue of the same name (71E ff.) makes it quite clear that he will value justice and the other co-operative excellences as a means to the end of *arete*, success and prosperity; but it is the end that is valued, and if other means proved better, they would be chosen.

In terms of these values, Socrates' refusal to escape was not merely an act of folly, it was condemned by the most powerful standards of the day. He had been poor, and so a *kakos*, all his life; he had failed to defend himself successfully in court, which was *aischron* and showed his *kakia*, as did his refusal to escape and aid his family. Yet this was the man whom, in the closing words of the *Phaedo*, Plato chose to term the most *agathos*, prudent and just man of his day. The ordinary Greek would have granted 'just', on which he himself set less value; but *arete* was the quality which led the most *agathos* to become tyrants, not to die a squalid criminal's death in prison. Becoming a tyrant seems to have been a Greek pipe-dream, a natural result of their

[1] See Antiphon above, chapter 5, pp. 113 ff.

value-system: Glaucon's story of Gyges' ring (*Republic* 359B ff.) testifies to this, and Plato devotes much effort to opposing it. We may note the selection of Ardiaeus and other tyrants as the incurable examples tormented for ever in Hades (*Republic* 615C ff.); and Plato's purging of earlier literature in *Republic* II and III is in large part devoted to sweeping away the values of that literature, which commended the way of life of which tyranny was the logical goal. The first *psuche* to choose its new life in the myth of Er (*Republic* 619B) seized on the greatest tyranny it could find. Only *agathoi* will have seriously hoped to gain tyrannical power, as the Thirty Tyrants, who included some of Plato's relatives, had gained it for a period in Athens at the close of the Peloponnesian War; but it remained an ideal, human life and human nature at its best.

To replace the ideal of the tyrant by the ideal of the just man – not, as it turned out, by the ideal of Socrates, for Plato's intellectual journey was to lead him far from the position of his master – was a difficult task. Yet Plato, and Socrates before him, had some resources.

In the first place, in the later part of the fifth century B.C. in Athens, there began to appear usages of *agathos*, *arete* and *kalon* to commend co-operative excellences, and (rather earlier, indeed from Aeschylus onwards) usages of *kakos* to decry breaches of these excellences, followed by similar usages of *kakia* and *aischron*. (Socrates was not the first to hold that justice was an *arete*: his distinction was that he was prepared to die for the belief.) None of the traditional *aretai* cease to be *aretai*, however; and this poses a problem. Traditional competitive and new co-operative *aretai* desiderate very different kinds of action in general, and indeed commend very different kinds of individual; and in a crisis traditional *arete* may commend on an individual, who must now choose, an action or course of action diametrically opposed to that commended by co-operative *arete*. Much hard thought was needed to harmonise the demands of the two; and the solution was not apparent in the later years of the fifth century. In a crisis, traditional *arete*, as being more deep-rooted and more evidently related to the success and prosperity of the unit, would be most likely to take precedence for anyone who was not a Socrates. Crito, a friend and pupil of Socrates, would doubtless be willing to concede that justice

L   145

was an *arete* when not in a crisis; but we have seen his response under pressure. Nevertheless, anyone who acknowledges that the co-operative excellences are *aretai* is open to certain kinds of argument. He knows that the traditional *aretai* are *aretai* because they are 'good for' their possessor and his group; and he may be persuaded to believe that, inasmuch as he is using *arete* of co-operative excellences, they too must be 'good for' him. If he acknowledges that co-operative excellences are *aretai*, but denies that they are good for him, he is then using language in a confused manner, and may fall victim to the Socratic *elenchus*. Polus in the *Gorgias*[1] adopts this position: he grants that committing injustice is more *aischron*, shameful, but insists that suffering injustice is more *kakon*, harmful. He intends to commit injustice, and treat *aischron* as a word of little value. Now *aischron* and *kalon* may have little emotive power when commending co-operative activities, but they are the same words through their entire range of usage, and are for the most part still used to commend and decry competitive successes and failures; in which usage they are very powerful indeed. Accordingly, when Socrates asks Polus to agree that there is a reason why men term *kalon* what they do term *kalon*, namely that it exceeds either in pleasantness or in benefit what they term *aischron*, he does so, for this is true of the traditional usage. But what is *aischron* must then exceed in painfulness or harm what is *kalon*; committing injustice is agreed to be more *aischron* than suffering it; it is certainly not more painful to commit injustice; therefore it must be more harmful to oneself. Polus, confused, has granted to the new *aretai* the same characteristics as the old; and once he has done this, he may be refuted at once.

Clearly Polus should not have conceded that *kalon* and *aischron* are always used of excess and deficit of pleasantness or benefit; for Socrates should *prove* that the new usages of *aischron* and *kalon* are justified in that they have the same characteristics as the traditional ones. Men like Callicles and Thrasymachus were more clear-headed than Polus: demanding that any *arete* must be profitable to its possessor as traditional *arete* was, and finding justice less profitable than injustice, they naturally denied that justice was an *arete*. Socrates and Plato must prove that justice is more profitable to its possessor than injustice,

[1] See *Merit and Responsibility*, pp. 266–7.

and so an *arete*, and choiceworthy; for only then will any Greek, 'immoralist' or ordinary man, choose it. Even in the case of the 'immoralists' – who should not be so termed, for they are not denying Greek values, merely taking them to their logical conclusion – proof can be attempted, for they are not nihilists, and have very definite standards. They and the ordinary man desire *eudaimonia*, a fully satisfactory life with no regrets, which they interpret in terms of political power, wealth and self-gratification. Socrates and Plato agree with them in desiring a fully satisfactory life with no regrets, and in terming it *eudaimonia*; but disagree in their interpretation of its necessary constituents. Thrasymachus, the ordinary man, Socrates and Plato likewise all term *aretai* the qualities they believe necessary to achieve *eudaimonia*; but here too there is naturally disagreement about the nature of those qualities. Thrasymachus and Callicles, however, as sophist and sophist's pupil, regard the political skill, *arete*, which they believe themselves outstandingly to possess, as the necessary means, when combined with the *arete* of courage, to achieve their *eudaimonia* of prosperous political domination; and the exercise of skills demands additional qualities. In the earlier dialogues, up to and including the first book of the *Republic*, Plato employs arguments of differing degrees of cogency[1] to endeavour to prove that justice and the co-operative excellences are among the other qualities needed for the satisfactory exercise of political skills; but such arguments, even when logically cogent, have not the psychological cogency required; and in the remainder of the *Republic* Plato tries a different method, that of constructing an Ideal State.

This method is open to him for reasons given in the last paragraph. All the Greeks of the day used *arete* to commend a skill or skills, as it had always done, and *eudaimonia* to commend a stable, smooth-running and fully-satisfying life. To say this, however, does not *describe* either the skills or the way of life. If Plato can delineate a way of life which his fellows, 'immoralist' or no, will grant to be more fully satisfying, and a skill or skills which will *more efficiently* secure that end, then he has fulfilled the general expectations of the Greek system of values in a manner which, like it or not, they must admit to be more satisfactory than their own.

[1] Discussed in *Merit and Responsibility*, chapter XIII.

In the *Republic*, the *psuche* and the *polis* have important roles to play. With the aid of a tripartite division of each, Plato sketches in a condition of *psuche* and *polis* which he holds to be *eudaimōn*, and then endeavours to prove that justice and self-control are qualities without which the *eudaimonia* of this *polis* and *psuche* could not exist. The attempt contains many fallacies,[1] and is unsuccessful; but here we are concerned with what Plato constructs upon his supposed success, and the implications for his view of human nature. The *eudaimonia* of the *polis* is demonstrated to depend on the wisdom and skill of its philosopher-kings, a very small group; on the bravery of its soldiers, a younger group from whom philosopher-kings will be recruited; and on the acquiescence of the other members of the society. No-one may belong to more than one of these groups. (Some of the soldiers will later become philosopher-kings, but will then cease to be soldiers; and the third group must meddle neither with fighting nor with government.) Plato believe these groups to correspond with real differences in human nature: he narrates a myth (415A ff.) distinguishing the rulers as having gold in their composition, the soldiers (those who will not become rulers later, presumably) as having silver, and the farmers and other craftsmen as having iron and brass. This is a myth; but (435B) Plato states, when not speaking mythologically, that the ideal *polis* is just when each of these natural kinds (types of *phusis*) in it performs its proper function; and the whole well-being of the *polis* depends on the ability of the rulers to distinguish these natural kinds. When the Ideal State begins to deteriorate (546D)

> They will not be very skilled at testing Hesiod's and our *gene*, races, of gold, silver, bronze and iron. And when iron is mixed with silver and bronze with gold, there will arise unlikeness and ill-matching unevenness; and these, wherever they arise, always produce war and enmity.

We have noted in the *Phaedrus*-myth distinctions in human nature based on the extent to which the *psuche* has glimpsed the Forms: here we have another method of distinction into real, natural kinds, equally propounded in a myth at its first appearance, but equally a part of Plato's working presuppositions.

---

[1] Discussed in *Merit and Responsibility*, chapter XIV, pp. 283 ff.

The skill necessary to discern these distinctions is possessed by the philosopher-kings: for these alone can contemplate the Forms, the objective truths of value on which the *eudaimonia* of the state depends. It follows, as the mythological use of gold, silver, bronze and iron would suggest, that the *philosopher* is now pre-eminently the *agathos*. True, in the *Republic* the philosopher-kings possess all other excellences as well: they have been exhaustively tested during the course of their long training, as we shall see; and Plato believes that anyone who has both passed successfully through his moral testing[1] and can truly perceive the Forms will both know what he should do in ethical matters (as opposed to merely having the correct opinion) and will also do it. Nevertheless, in the *Republic* intellectual *arete* takes precedence as the ideal. Plato, in fact, values *sophia*, intellectual *arete*, so highly that he is unable to demonstrate why the philosopher-kings should 'go back into the cave' (*Republic* 514A ff., 519D) and govern the *polis*, as he requires them to do for part of the time. Thrasymachus and the 'ordinary Greek', represented by Glaucon and Adeimantus in the *Republic*, demand of Socrates that he shall show to them that justice furnishes more *eudaimonia* than any other course of action before they will be willing to pursue it in preference to the alternative; for *eudaimonia* is the end. Yet Socrates has to concede (*Republic* 519D ff.) that the philosopher-kings would be more *eudaimon* if they merely philosophised and did not engage in politics; and it would certainly not upset the harmony in their *psuche* in any undesirable manner, for Plato does not hold that one can overdevelop one's intellect as one can overdevelop the other aspects of the *psuche*; so that he is unable to give any adequate reason why the philosopher-kings should govern the *polis*.

However, when, late in life, Plato wrote the *Laws*, he had ceased to believe in the possibility of a philosopher-king; and anyone else placed in a position of absolute power comparable to that of the philosopher-kings would, without knowledge of the Forms, neither understand what needed to be done nor have sufficient self-restraint to refrain from exploiting his subjects (*Laws* 874E ff.). In the state constructed in the *Laws*, accordingly, all are to be subject to a comprehensive and detailed legal code – for otherwise men would differ not

[1] See below, pp. 154 and 163 f.

at all from the fiercest of beasts – and values are adjusted. The education of the state is to be designed to produce a man (*Laws* 666E)

> Who would be not only *agathos* in war, but also capable of administering his city; the type of man who, as we said at the beginning, is really more skilled in war than the warriors of Tyrtaeus; the man who honours courage as the fourth grade of *arete*, not the first, whether it is manifested in individuals or in the city as a whole.

Courage is to be ranked fourth among the *aretai*; and 'capable of administering his city' must be understood in terms of Plato's position as a whole: the sentence taken by itself would command Thrasymachus' approval. For Plato, however, successful administration necessarily requires justice and self-control. It should be noted, however, that the product of this education, who ranks courage fourth of the *aretai*, is 'really more skilled in war than the warriors of Tyrtaeus'. Plato must insist on this, for the citizens of the *Laws*-state are to live in a fairly small *polis*: the end of the *polis* was soon to come, and the day of the Hellenistic monarchies was at hand, but neither Plato nor Aristotle considers the possibility that 'the good life' could be lived in any other form of social and political organisation than the *polis*. A *polis* must always be on its guard against military incursions from its neighbours; and unless the crops can be effectively defended, the inhabitants may starve before the next harvest: Plato must insist on the effectiveness of the citizens of the *Laws*-state as soldiers. Yet brave deeds in war are not to be ranked most important (922A):

> So touching this matter let there be laid down this law coupled with laud-ation, a law which counsels the people to honour to a lesser extent those *agathoi* who preserve the city whether by acts of courage or by stratagems of war; for the greatest honour is to be given to those who are able to observe to an outstanding degree the written pronouncements of their good legis-lators.

The law-abiding citizen is now the ideal: an ideal commended by suasion rather than rigorous proof, for 'right opinion' is the utmost that these citizens can achieve. They are to know 'both how to govern and to be governed'. The ideal seems to approximate to a modern 'democratic' one: its real implications will be discussed below.

F. *Phusis*

Plato, as we have already seen, was opposed to the 'immoralists'' *phusis*-doctrine, which contended both that human nature has certain characteristics, and also that these should be given free rein. Plato's mode of opposition, which might have been based on the rejection of either of these contentions, will be one of the topics discussed in this section.[1]

First, however, certain other aspects of his usage must be considered; for Plato, like the sophists, does not confine his usage of *phusis* to the context of this doctrine. Indeed, more than any earlier writer he emphasises the difference between one human *phusis* and another. Socrates states (*Republic* 370A) that

> Each of us is constituted (*phuesthai*) not altogether like his fellow men, but differing in *phusis*, one better adapted for the performance of one task, another for another.

Here the concern is with aptitudes: one *psuche* may have more aptitude for the cithara than another, or for archery, playing the pipe or any other skill (*Hippias Minor* 375B). The important differences in the *Republic* are those between the philosophers, soldiers and the rest, as we have already seen; but in the passage quoted above, this is one reason for specialisation among the artisans; and (443C) it is right for the man who is a shoemaker by *phusis*[2] to cobble and occupy himself with nothing else, the carpenter to practise carpentry, and

---

[1] As a believer in gods, he also rejects the nature-philosophers' tenet that *phusis*, rather than divine providence, has produced the world as we know it, *Sophist* 265C.

[2] Plato may well have been encouraged to think in these terms by the customs, presuppositions and linguistic habits of his society. *Phusis* in 'ordinary Greek' (above, pp. 79 ff.) spans 'birth', 'social consequences of birth' and 'natural endowments', all confusedly unanalysed. In Athens, as in many societies, craft-skills must for the most part have been handed down in families, so that one's *phusis* might well render one a shoemaker, a blacksmith or a carpenter. Plato is, or believes himself to be, using *phusis* in a more 'internal' manner here; but this may nevertheless be his reason for supposing that some individuals are, for example, shoemakers by *phusis*.

similarly all others. It is to be expected that the philosopher-king will require a very special *phusis*: he must (*Republic* 487A) have a good memory, be quick to learn, gracious, friendly and akin to truth, justice, courage and self-control, by *phusis*. Some of these qualities, one might suppose, are as much the fruit of nurture as of nature; and Plato, as will appear below, acknowledged the importance of right education. Nevertheless, he ascribed to *phusis* much more than aptitudes for skills, intellectual or manual. One may be 'good' (*epieikēs*) by *phusis* (*Republic* 538C), money-loving (*Republic* 549B), free and liberal (*Republic* 562C), illiberal (*Republic* 486B), or tyrannical (*Republic* 573C, *Laws* 710B4). Qualities with which one is endowed by *phusis* may be possessed by either men or women (*Republic* 455D):

> There is no pursuit, among those appropriate to the administrators of a state, that belongs to a woman because she is a woman, or to a man because he is a man. No; the *phueis* are distributed alike in both sexes, and women by *phusis* share in all pursuits and men in all – though a woman is weaker than a man in respect of all of them.[1]

This is not restricted by Plato to administrative skills; a conclusion is (455E) that some women are skilled at medicine and music, others not: all the talents are found distributed in both sexes.

If *phusis* determines one's ethical qualities, it might appear that it is as impossible to render an evil man good as to render a stupid man clever. Indeed, occasionally Plato writes as though one's *phusis* provided a standard response whenever a stimulus was applied. In *Republic* II he has postulated that the soldiers should be like fierce watch-dogs against the foes of the *polis*; and (375B) enquires

> How can they fail to be fierce to one another and the other citizens, when they have such a *phusis* as this? . . . And yet they must be gentle to their friends and harsh to their enemies. . . . Where shall we discover a disposition which is at once gentle and of great *thumos*? For the gentle *phusis* is opposed to the *thūmoeidēs*[2] *phusis*.

[1] *Phusis* in this usage is concerned especially with differences of *psuche*: in *Republic* V, 453C, Plato rebuts an imagined opponent who argues that men and women have physical differences, and so cannot have the same *phusis*.

[2] For *thumoeides*, see above, p. 133.

Plato solves his problem by pointing out that a good watch-dog, with which the guardians have been compared, is both gentle and fierce in this manner; but the manner in which the problem presents itself in the dialogue suggests a simple stimulus-response picture, in which judgment and the mind have no role at all to play.

Nevertheless, Plato is a moral philosopher who hopes to affect human behaviour; and even the 'immoralists' did not contend that one must follow *phusis*, merely that one ought to. In fact, Plato never consciously worked out a doctrine of human *phusis* in all its details; and it is not surprising to find some variation in the implications of his position. We have observed in fifth-century writers that *phusis* has strong overtones of 'birth'. These occur in certain Platonic contexts, appropriately modified. In the *Cratylus* we find on adjacent pages (393B, 394D) the statement that it is portentous if the offspring of a horse is anything but a horse, and the statement that it is portentous and against *phusis* if an impious man is born from a man who is good and holy:[1] he writes almost as if the pious and the impious were distinct species. Again, in the *Republic*, though he mentions the possibility of 'bronze' parents having a 'golden' offspring, or vice versa (415B), he clearly expects that on the whole the various *gene*, 'kinds',[2] in the state will 'breed true' (415A), as indeed the use of different metals in the myth might lead one to expect.[3] Plato is not a naïve

---

[1] We have seen in chapter 3, pp. 79 ff., that in 'ordinary language' in the fifth century, one's *phusis* included the position in society into which one had been born, and hence one's *arete* or *kakia*, which were also socially reckoned in considerable part. *Arete* and *kakia* also commend and decry certain kinds of behaviour, which might also, as a result, be attributed to one's *phusis*. Plato has changed the qualities denoted and commended by *arete*; but he too sometimes treats his *arete* as inheritable by *phusis*, possibly under the influence of these presuppositions of his society.

[2] Plato uses the word *gene* of the silver, golden and other 'kinds' or 'races' in his state, *Republic* 546E, with explicit reference to Hesiod, who used it of his *succession* of *gene* (above, pp. 50 ff.). However, Plato uses it there in a passage in which failure to 'breed true' is emphasised; and in the earlier passage (415A), even while insisting that for the most part the golden, silver and other inhabitants of the state will 'breed true', he also states that all are *sungeneis*, an adjective which implies that all are of the same stock or *genos*. All are human beings. Plato does not wish to deny this and, unlike Hesiod, finds it impossible to overlook the question.

[3] He seems to expect rather more variation in *Timaeus* 19A.

aristocrat: he does not identify members of 'good families' in any existing society with the best members of society in his sense. But he is an aristocrat, from one of the oldest and most famous families in Athens; and he shares their interests thus far in family, and in breeding, of animals as well as human beings. The breeding of animals indeed furnishes him with part of the programme for the *Republic*-state: just as in breeding hunting-dogs and fighting-cocks (459A) one chooses out the best from which to produce the next generation, so even among the rulers of the Ideal State there will be 'better' and 'worse' specimens; and only the better must be allowed to breed: if the worse produce offspring, they must be destroyed. It need hardly be said that the *aristoi*, the carefully selected rulers of the Ideal State, are not permitted to mate with the remainder of the citizens. In terminology, at least, Theognis would have agreed;[1] and though Plato's *aristoi* are very different from the *agathoi* of Theognis, the modes of thought, which are aristocratic, are basically the same.

However, Plato also gives due place to the effects of training. Not only the effects of good training on a good *phusis*, which is of great importance, and forms the subject of much of the *Republic*; he also discusses the effects of bad training and nurture on a good, even a philosophical *phusis* (*Republic* 495A):

> The very constituents of the philosophical *phusis*, when exposed to bad nurture, are in some way the cause, along with the so-called *agatha*, 'good things', riches and all such paraphernalia, of its departing from the practice of philosophy. . . . Such . . . so far as concerns the best pursuit, is the destruction and corruption of the best, *beltistē*, *phusis*, which is rare enough in any case. . . . And it is from these men that are drawn those who do the greatest harm to communities and individuals, and those that do the greatest good, too, if they chance to be swept in that direction; whereas a small *phusis* never does anything great to a man or a city.

Here the *phusis* is an aptitude, a capacity for opposites, like Aristotle's *dunamis tōn enantiōn*, ethically neutral until it has received training and been exposed to influences. This is far from the view that it is a portent if a pious parent has an impious child; for impiety and piety can only be shown in impious and pious acts, so that it makes no

[1] Above, p. 75.

sense to speak of a pious *phusis* that has nevertheless only committed impieties. In such a view, one's *phusis* has a particular ethical quality which must issue in actions which have that quality; whereas the *phusis* that might have led a man to become a philosopher is manifested in the magnitude of his actions, whether for good or ill. Such a man, presumably, might even become a tyrannical man, who results (*Republic* 573C) 'whenever a man either from *phusis* or from habits or from both becomes drunken, erotic and mad'. Some are born tyrannical, others achieve it through their way of life.

One might suppose, from Plato's mythological statements, that the ceiling of one's capabilities was fixed before the *psuche* came into the body, as a result either of the extent of one's acquaintance with the Forms or of the ante-natal choice of life made immediately before one's birth. Yet (*Republic* 424A) he says

> And indeed the state, if once it starts well, goes along as it were in a cycle of growth. For good nurture and education, if carefully adhered to, creates good *phuseis*; and again good *phuseis*, if they receive an education of this kind, develop into better individuals than their predecessors, both for other purposes and also for producing offspring, just as in other animals.

An individual's *phusis*, accordingly, may not only be improved by good upbringing and education: in this passage, at least, the improved condition is also the individual's *phusis*, and, like the *phusis* with which he was born, may be transmitted to future generations. Here again an explicit parallel is drawn with breeding other animals.

Can one elicit from this a doctrine of human *phusis*? Plato ranges from a view, mythologically expressed but important to his philosophy of differing types of individual, whether based on the presence, as it were, of different metals in their nature or the extent of their acquaintance with ultimate truths to a view of the 'improvability' of *phusis* in the lifetime of an individual, combined with a belief in the heritability of such acquired improvements. The statement refers to the rulers of his state, and one might attempt to introduce coherence by postulating the possibility of improvement of one's *phusis* within the category to which it belonged; though it seems more likely that the two views are drawn from two different sources of Plato's presuppositions, the mythological and metaphysical and the social, aristocratic, and eugenic, and that he had not tried to reconcile them. Certainly, as we have seen, he had not, in the ethical field, decided what was the fruit of nature, what of nurture.

Plato's view of the highest possibilities of human nature became more pessimistic towards the end of his life. He always held the philosophical *phusis* to be very rare; and by the time he wrote the *Laws*, he had abandoned all hope of the occurrence of a philosopher-king, and says (918C):

> Only a small class of men, and one few by *phusis* and reared with the best nurture, can hold out for moderation when it falls into needs and desires, and when it is possible to obtain much wealth, remains sober and chooses the moderate in preference to the great sum;[1] the majority of mankind behaves in quite the opposite manner. . . .

In the *Laws*, he can be even more pessimistic than this. No scientific ruler is possible: human comprehension and human good will are both insufficient (875A):

> The reason for this is that no man's *phusis* is capable of knowing what is beneficial for mankind with respect to a state. . . . And secondly, even if a man fully grasps the truth of this as a principle of *techne*, art or skill, should he afterwards gain control of the state, he would never be able to abide by this view and continue always fostering the public interest in the state as the object of the first importance, to which the private interest is secondary; rather his mortal *phusis* will always be urging him on to grasping and self-interested action. . . .

Yet he says that *if* a man should be capable by *phusis*, having been born by some dispensation of heaven (875C), he would rule by his knowledge, and have no need of laws. His hope that this will happen, however, is now minimal.

In his later, pessimistic, mood, Plato holds human *phusis* to be bad, and to require restraint by means that will be described in the next section. Earlier, however, Plato sometimes believes that some human *phusis* is reliably good, or that some is potentially good, and with good nurture would become reliably good. Accordingly, at different times Plato adopts both methods of rebutting the 'immora-

[1] He seems more pessimistic than Democritus (above, p. 110), who appears to hope that his advice will be followed.

lists'' position: some human *phusis* is not at all like that delineated by the 'immoralists', and this either will inevitably render its possessor good, or should be encouraged by nurture to do so; much has 'immoralist' tendencies, and these should be discouraged, in the interests of its possessor.

We have yet to discuss the relationship between human *phusis* and *phusis* in general in Plato's thought. What exists by *phusis* in general is what 'really' exists;[1] which for Plato is what exists in the eternal, invisible, intangible world of the Forms. Only the Form of justice is just by *phusis* (*Republic* 501B). Again, the painter, unlike the carpenter, merely paints what he sees in this world, whereas the carpenter has in mind the paradigm existing in the realm of *phusis* when he makes the objects of his craft (*Republic* 597B). The world of Forms is the world of *phusis*; and these Forms are, or render possible the enunciation of, objective truths of both fact and value: what is just by *phusis* is as objective, and as much part of the ultimate value of things, as what is equal by *phusis*. In Plato's system, then, value and fact are equally objective, and the virtues are 'good for' an individual in this world, just as is the glimpsing of the Forms in the next world. In the words of the *Phaedrus*-myth, 246E:

> The divine is *kalon*, wise, *agathon* (beneficial), and everything of this nature: by these qualities the wings of the soul are nourished and grow, but by the opposite qualities, such as what is *aischron* and *kakon* (hurtful), they waste away and perish.

The divine intelligence, borne round in the revolution by obedient horses, calmly sees and is nourished by the eternal truths (247D); and it is by communing with these that the god is divine (249C). Even the philosopher on this earth has only memory of these things; but (249C)

> a man who makes proper use of such memories is for ever being initiated into perfect mysteries, and he alone becomes truly perfect.[2]

[1] An overtone derived from the usage of the Presocratics, doctors and sophists. See chapters 4 and 5.
[2] The full force of the Greek, in which 'perfect', 'initiate' and 'mysteries' are all expressed by words from the same root, cannot be expressed in English.

The vision of the true *phusis*, the eternal verities, renders the gods divine; the partial vision, gained while controlling their unruly horses, renders human beings human; and the memory of the true *phusis*, which is only fully effective in the philosopher, leads to human perfection on earth. But Plato does not usually[1] maintain that the true *phusis* of a human being, what exists by *phusis* in a human being, is that part of him which perceives what exists by *phusis* in the cosmos as a whole. The *psuche* may, being immortal, 'exist' in a sense in which the *soma*, which comes to be and passes away, does not; but man's mortal *phusis* (*Laws* 875A–B) is precisely what prevents him from being a good ruler.[2] In mankind, for Plato, *phusis* is in most contexts highly variable, and serves to distinguish one individual (or type) from another. Plato, indeed, hardly gives an answer to the question of what all human beings have in common, save the mythological one that all have seen the eternal Forms, which might be rendered philosophically by saying that all are capable of using words, and forming concepts from their experience of sense-data; and his use of *phusis* has little link with this. It is nevertheless important to discuss Plato's usage of *phusis*. In translation, *phusis* is – inevitably – rendered 'nature' in many contexts, for it comes closer than any other Greek word to our 'nature'; but the implications and overtones of the word reflect and affect Plato's presuppositions, helping to ensure that his concept of human *phusis* differs significantly from our concept of human nature.

G. Training and Education

The goal of the new education which began in the latter part of the fifth century B.C. was not surprisingly to produce *arete*, the most valued quality, in its students. The sophists, Plato and Socrates, even

---

[1] In *Laws* 892C he does assert the primacy by *phusis* of *psuche* over e.g. fire or air, precisely because *psuche* 'came to be' earlier. This is a means of maintaining that *psuche* is more important than *soma*, which is composed of elements which 'came to be' later.

[2] 'Mortal *phusis*' implies, as Professor Dodds has pointed out to me, that man has also an 'immortal *phusis*'. Plato never says so in as many words; but Dodds compares 'the mortal kind of *psuche*', *Timaeus* 69C; and the step to splitting human *phusis* into two quite separate *phuseis* would have been a very easy one for Plato to take, on the basis of what he actually writes elsewhere.

if the last named denied that he knew or taught anything, all wished to make their pupils more *agathos*. In Greek, however, one might doubt whether *arete* is teachable; for traditionally *arete*, as we have seen, commended high birth, wealth, and courage and skill, military or other, leading to success; and some of these are evidently not teachable. From Homer onwards, political aptitude leading to non-military success plays a gradually larger part; but politicians were traditionally drawn from a restricted range of families, and political skill was presumably handed down by rule-of-thumb within these families, so that this too might well appear to be inherited. All these qualities taken together are confusedly *arete*; and a Greek of the period might well doubt whether human excellence can be taught, since some aspects are manifestly unteachable and some are apparently not taught. In early Plato, the use of *arete* has the vagueness and confusion of ordinary usage, still further confused as it was from the later fifth century by the inclusion of co-operative excellences are *aretai*; and this seems to prevent him from analysing the content of *arete* and demonstrating that such qualities must be teachable: in the *Protagoras* (319E) Socrates merely contends that since the sons of Pericles are not so *agathos* as their father, *arete* must be unteachable,[1] since otherwise Pericles would have taught them, or had them taught. The 'proof' of course can demonstrate no more than that *arete* is not being taught in the Athens known to Socrates.

Socrates himself, like Plato and the sophists, believed that *arete* could in principle be taught; for *arete* is knowledge. The pupils of the sophists naturally agreed; and here the traditional usage of *arete* is relevant again. The competitive excellences have success as their goal; the end is desirable, and the qualities needed to achieve it are naturally thought of as skills. It is not a question of having good intentions, but of producing certain results. Now in the *Apology* (20A) Socrates compares the training of young men with the training of colts and bulls; and there is no straining of language here: in both cases the endeavour is to train an individual which will function in the approved manner. One mode of thought, however, need not exclude another: in the *Euthydemus* (292B) the function of the political

[1] The argument is ad hominem, and represents neither Socrates' nor Plato's own view.

techne is said to be to make men wise, *sophoi*, and to give them a share of knowledge, if indeed this *techne* is to benefit them and make them *eudaimones*. In this early dialogue, *sophos* denotes political skill in the sense in which any reasonably intelligent individual can hope to attain it. There may be an analogy with training animals; but the teacher, so far, is giving his pupil a skill which he is then himself to exercise intelligently.

However, when the function of *arete* in the city is in question, results must take precedence; for it is by results that the city succeeds or fails, runs smoothly or falls into faction. Already in the *Gorgias* (516A, 517B) Plato is evaluating statesmen in terms of the manner in which the governed treat them at first with the manner in which they treat them after the statesmen have had them in hand for some time. The trained animal should be more docile than the untrained. It is not that Plato believes that human beings are incapable of directing their own lives: after all, no *psuche* can enter a human being unless it has seen something of the Forms, and so is capable of conceptualising and using words. No human being is an automaton: when Plato says (*Laws* 644D) that man is 'the puppet of the gods' he does not mean, even in this most pessimistic of his dialogues, that the gods pull the strings and men dance willy-nilly on the end of them. (Plato, indeed, would probably have preferred such a situation.) The gods have implanted the strings in us, and we can do nothing about their presence; but the resultant behaviour is not controlled by heaven. Human beings have a golden string, called calculation or reason (*logismos*), and a number of other iron ones, passions and desires. (Note the reappearance of metal-symbolism.) The golden string is softer than the iron ones, and 'since calculation is good, rather than forceful, its leading string needs helpers to ensure that the golden element in us may vanquish the other kinds'. *We* must co-operate with the golden string, whose characteristics receive public expression as law: there is a 'we' over against the strings, just as in Homer there is an 'I' over against the various psychological functions, even if in each case it is unexplained, and represented merely by the unity of the personal pronoun.

Each of us is capable of directing his own life by the use of his own reason; and in the earlier dialogues the point is very vigorously made. Socrates (*Protagoras* 352B) says:

The majority of mankind[1] hold some such opinion as this about knowledge, that it is not powerful nor capable of leadership or rule . . . and that often when knowledge is present in a man, it is not knowledge that rules him but something else, sometimes anger (*thumos*), sometimes pleasure, sometimes pain, sometimes sexual passion, sometimes fear. They think of knowledge just as if it were a slave, dragged round by all the rest. Do you hold this kind of view, Protagoras, or do you think that knowledge is something fine (*kalon*) and the kind of thing to rule the man, and that if anyone knows what is good for him and bad for him, *agatha* and *kaka*, he would not be overcome by anything so as to do anything other than the behests of knowledge, but his practical wisdom would be able to help the man?

A powerful statement of Socrates' view that *oudeis hekōn hamartanei*, that no-one errs on purpose; and that *oudeis hekon kakos*, no-one is *kakos* on purpose. Socrates uses *hamartanei* and *kakos* to decry breaches of *co-operative* as well as competitive excellences; but his justification for so using *kakos* is his proof, or assumption, that it must be 'worse for' the individual to be *kakos* in the new usage, as it was in the traditional one; and he asserts that, despite all the buffeting of passion and desire, knowledge of what is best for the individual will inevitably lead him to do it. Protagoras' reply is interesting:

I agree with you, Socrates; and at the same time it is *aischron* for me, if

---

[1] 'The many', 'the majority of mankind' (*hoi polloi*) who are said not to believe in the primacy of intellect may well not be the mass of Greeks. It seems to me unlikely that these at this period had clearly formulated views on the subject: such passages as Euripides, *Hippolytus* 377 ff. seem to me from their language to be derived from the New Thought, rather than 'ordinary Greek'; while Medea, *Medea* 1078 f., is an extraordinary woman in an extreme situation, whose words are intended to signify this. I think it more likely that the reference is to thinkers like Antiphon, Diodotus as portrayed by Thucydides (above, pp. 120 ff.), and some nature-philosophers, who did express such views. As the whole argument of this book is designed to show, it seems probable that the Greeks in general did find great difficulty in controlling their turbulent emotions: my point here is that 'the many' are unlikely to have reflected upon the situation and expressed it in this way. Similarly, *Phaedo* 77B, 'the many' are said to believe in complete annihilation after death – a view not ascertainably held by the mass of Greeks (who are likely to have believed confusedly that the dead were in an Homeric Hades and nearby in their graves), but certainly held by the atomists. The aristocratic Plato thus dismisses his opponents. (Compare also *Sophist* 265C5, where one of the nature-philosophers' tenets concerning *phusis* is said to be 'the belief of the many'; a contention which is very unlikely to be true.) For a different interpretation of the evidence, see Dodds, *The Greeks and the Irrational*, pp. 185–7.

for anyone, not to say that wisdom and knowledge are the most powerful of human attributes.

It would be shameful for Protagoras not to take this view – presumably whether he thought it were true or no. The thinkers of this period, whether moralists like Protagoras or bandits like Thrasymachus and Callicles, are intellectuals first and moralists or bandits afterwards: the intellectual *arete* of Thrasymachus and Callicles, as well as their courage, constitutes the basis of their claim to dominate; and even when they maintain a hedonistic position, Socrates is able to drive them from it by appealing to their intellectual bias. Accordingly, there would be some agreement on the *ability* of the intellect to control the desires and passions, even among those who held that the intellect should merely subserve the gratification of those desires and passions.

However, we have seen that in a civic context good results are more important than good intentions: better to drill one's citizens to succeed rather than risk failure by allowing them to think for themselves; and when the Platonic metaphysic is added, even the ability to think for themselves is devalued, so far as concerns the majority of mankind. In the *Republic* only the philosopher-kings have true knowledge of the Forms, absolute truths of value and of fact: even the soldiers have to be content with 'right opinion'. The latter are to be properly conditioned, by the philosopher-king, when he is introduced into the argument; he is to be compelled to 'practise stamping into human behaviour, in public and in private, the things that he sees there (in the realm of Forms), and not only to mould himself'; and Socrates contends that such a man would be a craftsman good at producing self-control, justice, and all kinds of ordinary civic *arete* in the citizen body (*Republic* 500D). The majority of human beings, to achieve *arete* in the secondary sense which is all that is within their power (for they cannot discern the Forms), need to be properly conditioned. Plato's belief in the ability of knowledge to rule the passions and desires is now less clear. On the one hand, he holds in the Myth of Er, as we have seen, that a life spent in philosophy will ensure that after death and the rewards of the next life we will again make a prudent choice of life on earth; and he apparently holds that the philosopher-kings will certainly behave justly in their rule over the city, for they will have knowledge of absolute truths of fact. Yet the potential rulers will have undergone an extensive testing of their moral responses before they reach that part of their education which fits them for rule: it is not sufficient to test their intellectual qualities. We have seen (*Republic* 495A) that a philosophical *phusis*, exposed to bad nurture, can be corrupted: Plato's programme in *Republic* II–V would imply that even with good nurture an individual with sufficient intellectual potential might be morally inadequate for the role of philosopher-king (e.g. 412C ff.); for though the philosopher-king is only introduced at the end of Book V (473C), the earlier training is devoted to developing just such a ruler. It is not that Plato has only now, in the *Republic*, discovered the passions and desires – he was fully aware of them in the *Protagoras* – but that he has changed his estimate of the ability of the intellect to control them.

In the *Laws*, as we have already seen,[1] he is even more pessimistic: both knowledge and moral fibre are lacking in mankind. Accordingly, all the citizens of his *Laws*-state are to be conditioned; for a human being cannot long resist the buffets of passion, and if the conflict is seen as one between rational desire of the *agathon*, what is good for him, and irrational desire for the pleasant, which may or may not be good for him, the obvious solution is to ensure, if possible, that rational and irrational desire pull in the same direction, that of the 'golden cord'. To that end Plato's conditioning in the *Laws* is directed. From earliest youth the child will be taught the nature of 'true' pleasures and 'true' *agatha*; he will be informed that what is 'truly' noble (*kalon*) is also 'truly' beneficial (*agathon*); and as a result, or so Plato believes, his irrational desires will coincide with his rational ones, and he will pursue what is truly beneficial for him. He will not be an automaton: he will know what he is doing; and, since his laws contain explanations of their provisions (721A ff.), why he is doing it; but he never should have to make a moral choice. He will rationally desire what is *agathon*, and this will be the goal of his actions; and he will have been conditioned to believe that certain things are *agatha*. He will rarely have to choose between means to secure his end: the laws are comprehensive, and will inform him of the necessary means. Plato does not believe that human beings are automata; he does

[1] Above, p. 149.

believe that few of them – by the time he wrote the *Laws*, none of them, failing a miracle – have the necessary intellectual or moral qualities to conduct their lives in the manner most beneficial to themselves or their city, the manner most productive of *eudaimonia*. *Eudaimonia* is the acknowledged goal; and Plato calls on the citizens of his *Laws*-state to abrogate their free will in the interests of their *eudaimonia*, of maximising their possession of 'true' *agatha*. Few Greeks would have admired, or enjoyed living in, the *Laws*-state; but unless he could find flaws in the argument, a Greek would have been compelled to admit that Plato had satisfied the requirements of the Greek value-system. If the ideal of human existence is efficient and successful functioning in an environment in such a way as to maximise one's possession of desirables, and these desirables are prosperity and stability externally, a fully satisfactory existence with no regrets internally (and most Greeks naturally assumed that the external *agatha* guaranteed the internal ones), then the exercise of choice or free will is not of primary importance; and Plato in his desire to secure good things for the cosmos (903C), the state, and the individual – strictly in that order of priority – need pay little attention to choice or free will. Both of Plato's ideal states result from drawing out certain implications of the notion of human nature and the human condition at its best held by the Greeks in general; and his view of training and education is entirely suited to this system of ideas.

H. Conclusion

Many streams of thought and belief unite in Plato's view of human nature; and it is not surprising that not all are fully blended with one another. Nevertheless, a general picture can be drawn. In the first place, some aspects of his view are affected by his birth and upbringing as a member of one of the oldest aristocratic families in Athens. That his use of *arete* should be socially stratificatory – in the *Republic* in particular – is not surprising nor exclusively the attitude of an aristocrat: the *agathoi* had always had a claim, in Greek values, to govern and be socially superior to the *kakoi*; and, as we have seen, in the fifth century the use of *phusis* tended to reinforce this attitude. However, Plato's emphasis on eugenics and careful cleansing of the 'flock' in the *Republic* may well have been encouraged by an aristocratic sense of family coupled with an interest in the aristocratic pursuit of breeding pedigree stock. Plato clearly did not suppose that the self-styled 'best families' in any existing Greek state necessarily contained the potential philosopher-kings, where any were to be found; but he did suppose that, once they were found, they would for the most part 'breed true'. The content of his thought is not taken over from the aristocrats of his day, but the framework may well be influenced by aristocratic modes of thought and presuppositions.

Secondly, there is influence from the mystery-cults and Pythagoreanism. Plato frequently uses technical terms drawn from the mystery-cults. This is in itself not necessarily important; but this manner of thinking of the Forms, in myths at all events, shows that the influence goes much deeper. The adherent of a mystery-cult was shown certain secret objects which ensured his salvation: our earliest document from such a source, the pseudo-Homeric *Hymn to Demeter*, says 'Blessed is he who has seen these things' (480 ff.); and many subsequent documents, drawn from a variety of cults, are similar in this respect. Having seen certain sacred objects gave one a ticket to Bliss, having failed to do so plunged one in Everlasting Mud, in the next world. For Plato in the *Phaedrus*-myth, the extent to which one has glimpsed the Forms, divine objects, in the next world determines one's lot in this world; and the extent to which one has done so depends on one's success in the scrimmage (248B) not on one's desire to do so, for all *psuchai*, or at all events their 'charioteers', desire to see the Forms. Only those who have seen most can become philosophers; and in the *Phaedrus*-myth only three lives of philosophy can free one from the cycle of lives before the ten thousand years are up; while in the *Republic* (619D) only a life of philosophy will guarantee that one will make a sensible choice of the next life in the cycle. Plato's philosophy, his belief in the necessary existence of Forms, and their epistemological function, are in no sense derived from mystery-cults; but the framework of his thought seems to owe something to this source. The belief in a 'real' future existence had been turned by some moralists to moral ends, by postulating a Last Judgment; and this may have appeared in some mystery-cults too. For Plato, it is justice that is rewarded after death, not one's philosophical attainments (*Phaedrus* 248E, *Republic* 614B ff.); but only a life of philosophy will certainly lead the *psuche*, after its thousand years of reward in heaven, to make a sensible choice of its next life on earth (*Republic* 619D): those who have been just out of habit, not philosophy, are precisely those who, in Plato's view, are likely to make disastrously bad choices of their next life on earth (*Republic* 619C). In any one sojourn in the next life, justice is rewarded; but in the cycle as a whole, only philosophy guarantees salvation; and of philosophy only a few individuals are capable, for reasons beyond their control.

Platonic myths are infused with Platonic philosophy; but in the mystery-cults too there is a tension between reward for justice and reward for 'having seen these things'. The mystery-cults did not *cause* Plato's thought to take this turn; but they may have provided a climate of thought, and a framework in which this aspect of his thought seemed natural. (That only a few are capable of *arete* in the fullest sense is also not surprising to a Greek, for whom *arete* has always been the prerogative of a few, from which the majority of mankind were excluded, again for reasons beyond their control.)

A third strand, as we have seen, is furnished by the medical view of the human being, and the analogy between a good regimen for the body and a good regimen, identified with justice, for the *psuche*. This too gives objective value to justice, for no-one can deny that certain types of regimen are bad, others good, for the body; but again encourages stratification, between experts, whether body-doctors or *psuche*-doctors, who *know* what is good for body or *psuche*, and laymen, the great majority, who have only opinion based on what the experts tell them, and must do what they are told.

Fourthly, Plato's view of the human being, after an initial period of optimism concerning the ability of knowledge, when present, to rule, is pessimistic, even in the *Republic*, in respect of the desires and passions. Now no-one can fail to recognise the picture, in the *Phaedrus*-myth, of the charioteer with his two horses, or the non-mythical presentations of conflict in the human *psuche* scattered over the dialogues. We may feel, however, that the picture is overdrawn, that the fragmentation of the *psuche* is over-emphasised. It would be unwise to conclude that Plato's experiences were precisely the same as our own, but that either he is mis-describing them or we are. We have seen the tendency of the shame- (or results-) culture to discourage the development of a unified personality. The essentials of that culture remain in the Athens of Plato's own day, even if Plato himself was endeavouring to change them. Plato's view of the personality, founded on his own experience of himself and his contemporaries, is less fragmented than Homer's, but it is still fragmented; and the reason may be the same.

The contents of Plato's own philosophy are likely to impose complex tensions on personality structure. On the one hand, Plato asserted the unity of the *aretai*, or of *arete*. In the *Protagoras* (329C ff.) the position is argued at length; and in the *Republic* the philosopher-kings cannot possess any *arete* in the full sense of the word unless they possess all the *aretai*. Furthermore, we have seen that Plato in the *Protagoras* maintains the supremacy of reason and its ability to control the passions and desires; and his philosophy is concerned to demonstrate that *dikaiosune* and *sophrosune* are the most important *agatha*; and these, being 'internal' and dependent on the individual's intentions in a manner in which success and failure are not, appear *prima facie* to mitigate the stresses of a results-culture.

However, there is another side. Plato demonstrates that the co-operative excellences are *aretai*; but the demonstration must be the same as that for the traditional *aretai*, and show that they are *agatha*, good for the individual. As a result, anyone who fails to be *dikaios* or *sophron* is acting against his own best interest, which he cannot 'really and truly' wish to do: 'no-one is willingly *kakos*',[1] and 'no-one willingly *hamartanei*, errs'. Anyone who is told that he did not 'really' wish to perform an action which he has voluntarily performed, that he has 'made a mistake', and that every time he acts immorally he has made a mistake, is in a situation as hostile to the development of a well-defined personality structure as Homeric man in his competitive world. The co-operative excellences, for Plato, have taken on the behaviour of the competitive excellences; and the competitive demands of a *polis* competing with other *poleis* remain: the *Laws-*

---

[1] The statement has epigrammatic and protreptic value; and Plato adheres to it even in the *Laws* (860D ff.), though he has long been capable of analyses of human action which render a more complex statement possible, in terms of rational and irrational desire. His insistence on his protreptic epigram leads him to a highly complicated theory of punishment (*Laws* 861E ff.), which there is no space to consider here. (But see *Merit and Responsibility*, pp. 304 ff.)

state is as dependent as other Greek states on the successful valour of its soldiers. If we consider the role of the co-operative excellences in Plato's *Laws*-state, not merely in the individual, we find a similar situation. Plato holds that there are two kinds of atheists: the one has an *ēthos dikaion*, hates unjust men and injustice, and has a great affection for justice and just men, the other, in addition to his atheism, is licentious and self-seeking (*Laws* 908B ff.). We should expect the latter to be punished, as he is (909B), the former, given Plato's desire that all should 'think correctly', to be educated; as is done. But if the treatment is unsuccessful, he is to be executed in precisely the same manner as the criminal, the *adikos* who deliberately commits crimes, whom the legislator perceives to be incurable, is to be executed, as an example to others and in his own best interests (*Laws* 862D ff.). In the last resort, intentions are irrelevant: what matters is 'true' *agathon* or *kakon* conferred upon the *polis* or the individual, which is an 'objective' matter and has no necessary connection with the individual's intentions. Once again, Plato's own views give little encouragement to the formation of a strong personality structure: his solution in the *Laws*, to condition the individual so that rational and irrational desire coincide, is merely an attempt to impose a coherent pattern on a confused tangle of drives.

Fifthly, Plato's view of human nature is entirely bound to the city-state, the only form of political organisation in which he supposed human life at its best to be possible. His problems of values, and their solution, are all seen in the context of the city-state.

Sixthly, in the *Timaeus* Plato puts forward, through the mouth of Timaeus, a mechanistic type of explanation for *kakia* which is not fully harmonised with his other views.

In sum, it is difficult to state that Plato had *a* view of human nature. He emphasises the differences between individuals, and types of individual, and has little to say of any common substrate. Indeed, mythologically speaking only a glimpse of the Forms separates human *psuche* from animal *psuche*. At all events, he has a low view of human nature as exemplified in most – in the *Laws*, in all – individuals. This may well be derived from his own and Athens' experiences. As a prosperous and well-born citizen of Athens, a career in politics would have been a traditional outlet for his energies; but the Thirty Tyrants, who had seized power at the end of the Peloponnesian War and conducted a Reign of Terror, had disgusted him with the extreme oligarchs of Athens; and the fact that their number had contained several who were close relatives of Plato, and pupils of Socrates, was unlikely to render the democrats eager to welcome Plato as one of themselves. Again, the restored democracy had tried and executed Socrates, whom Plato held to have been the wisest and best man he had ever met. Even had they not done so, Plato was too fastidious, intellectually and in other ways, to have become a popular politician; as it was, each of the groups with which he might have identified himself in politics had earned his distrust. Later, he endeavoured to influence the tyrant of Syracuse politically, but this too met with failure. Plato never abandoned hope of influencing practical affairs: no-one who, at the age of eighty, composed the twelve books of the *Laws*, a detailed constitution for a state, could be supposed to have no interest in politics;[1] yet his lack of success in practice may have contributed to his low view of human nature: human beings really need gods to govern them, for no man is capable of it.

Plato's view as a whole is aristocratic and stratified; but Plato's personal aristocratic attitudes should not be overemphasised here. In extant authors, the characteristic value-structure of Greece up to this time is 'aristocratic' and stratified. Plato wishes to replace an aristocracy of the *de facto* 'best families' by those who really possess what he held to be the most important and valuable human qualities.

---

[1] Yet he seems to have felt uneasy that his role was not more practical. The defence put into the mouth of Socrates of the philosopher's inactive role in states as they are (*Republic* 496D) may well be Socrates' own, for it occurs in the *Apology* (31D); but Socrates presumably here speaks also for Plato.

7. Aristotle

A. Introductory

Aristotle, compared with Plato, is cooler, more detached and analytic; he is a natural denizen of the lecture room, while Plato, despite his protestations, would rather have been able to affect immediately the life of his own times. Like Plato, Aristotle is a developing thinker throughout his work: any attempt to present the writings of either as a monolithic system, in which each statement must cohere with all others, can only lead to confusion. Aristotle's interests were spread over the whole field of knowledge, and indeed went far to define the boundaries of the field of knowledge for centuries afterwards. Consequently, he studies human nature from many angles; and in the space available it will only be possible to deal briefly with the most important.

B. Man in the Animal Kingdom

Aristotle, a systematic biologist, uses his method of classification by genera and species, itself developed from the classificatory interests of the later Plato, to place man among the other animals. He is an animal with blood, along with those quadrupeds that bring forth young alive, and also those quadrupeds that lay eggs, and birds, fishes and the whale, as opposed to the bloodless creatures (*Historia Animalium* 505b28);[1] he belongs to the land animals that breathe air (*Hist. Anim.* 487a28); he is sometimes gregarious, sometimes solitary (*Hist. Anim.* 488a2) – for Aristotle's classification is not Procrustean, and a species may have characteristics of more than one genus; and among gregarious animals belongs to the sub-class of 'political' animals, those whose groups are not mere agglomerations but subserve a common end. Man shares this characteristic with bees, wasps, ants and cranes. Again (*Hist. Anim.* 488a27) man is classified

---

[1] Since the titles of Aristotle's works are rather cumbrous, I give them in full only on their first appearance.

with the mule among animals that are always tame,[1] in opposition to those that are always wild, like the leopard and wolf, and those that can be tamed, such as the elephant. This last classification poses problems, as Aristotle realises here and elsewhere (*De Partibus Animalium* 643b5, *Problems* 895b23); for men, horses and dogs are wild in some parts of the earth, and the young of these everywhere. The appropriate distinction is between animals that can be tamed and those that cannot, as Aristotle sees in these passages. In the *Problems* passage he thus explains why men, horses and dogs may be wild, but lions and leopards cannot be tamed:

Is it because it is easier for what is inferior to occur at the beginning, and for a creature to revert to it? For *phusis* – not the first, basic *phusis* but the perfect *phusis* of the creature – is difficult to attain at once. Accordingly, even tame creatures are all wild at first, as for example a child. . . .

The classification must be based on the final development of the creature; and when (*Topics* 130a26) Aristotle defines man as the animal that is tame by *phusis*, he is presumably to be interpreted in this light; for Aristotle's view of *phusis* is teleological, the true *phusis* of a creature being the perfect state to which it tends.[2]

Man is thus given his place in the animal kingdom, as an animal among others. However, the distinctive characteristics of man are equally important: he is the animal that can receive knowledge (*Top.* 132a19), and his *phusis* (*Part. Anim.* 656a4) 'partakes not only of living but of living well' (*eu zen*, a phrase equivalent to *eudaimonia*):

for of all the creatures known to us he is either the only one to partake of the divine, or does so most of all.

Man, rooted in the animal kingdom, and with his position there carefully charted, nevertheless has his divine spark; a statement whose implications will become clearer in the course of this chapter.

---

[1] Plato, *Laws* 766A, holds that man is the most tame of creatures if he has 'right nurture and is fortunate in his *phusis*'; otherwise, the wildest.

[2] See the discussion of *phusis* in Aristotle, below, pp. 178 ff.

C. Physiology

Despite the existence of the *Timaeus*, Plato appears not very interested in human physiology.[1] Aristotle, however, was a biologist, and in his physiological works shows much more interest in the workings of animate bodies; and here he combines analysis in terms of elements familiar from the writings of Presocratics and doctors with his own kind of teleology, in which *phusis* sets the goal towards which the organism should develop, and disposes and organises its parts. A detailed account of Aristotle's physiology would require more space than is available for this chapter: I merely quote a few examples.

Aristotle thus explains the upright stance of human beings (*Part. Anim.* 669b3):

> The warm (element) causes growth, and abundance of blood is an indication of the presence of the warm; and then again it causes bodies to be more erect; and so man is the most erect of animals, and mammals more so than other animals.

No mention of teleological *phusis* here; but (*Part. Anim.* 686a25)

> Man has arms and . . . hands in place of legs and forefeet. For he is the only animal with an upright stance, because his *phusis* and essence are divine. Now the function of the most divine element is intuitive and discursive thought; and this is not easy, when there is much body resting on top of it, for the weight makes the intellect difficult to move. . . .

An interesting combination of teleology and naïve 'Presocratic' physiology. The teleology is, save for the *Timaeus* account, a new factor, as Aristotle realises (*Part. Anim.* 687a5):[2]

> Since he is upright as regards his *phusis* he has no need of front legs, but *phusis* has given him arms and hands instead. Anaxagoras says that man is the most practically skilled of animals because he has hands; but it is reasonable to suppose that he acquired hands because he is the most practically skilled. For hands are a tool, and *phusis* always allots, like a practically wise human being, each thing to the individual that can use it.

[1] All such can only be a 'probable account' (*Timaeus* 29C–D, 59C): and Plato's real interests lie in fields where knowledge in his sense can be obtained.

[2] Though the account of the curative activities of *phusis* in some medical writers (e.g. *Epidemics* VI) implies purposiveness by its language.

The selection of Anaxagoras has point if we remember his use of *nous* and Socrates' disappointment (Plato, *Phaedo* 97B);[1] for Anaxagoras appeared the most likely of the Presocratics to have offered teleological explanations. Now Aristotle is attempting this kind of explanation of physiological phenomena – a different type of explanation from that of the *Timaeus*, for Aristotle's teleology is immanent, the expression of the *phusis* of the creature, whereas Plato's is imposed from without by divine intelligence on refractory and mechanistic matter.

D. *Psuche*

Plato, as we have seen, took the real, separately-existing *psuche* of the mystery-cults, with the 'Pythagorean' belief in its transmigration, and modified the belief in the complete transferability of *psuche* between human beings, animals and plants by insisting that only a *psuche* which had glimpsed the Forms could ever enter a human being, though such a *psuche* might elect to enter an animal. Aristotle has a far more complex view of *psuche*. Everything that has the power of initiating change within itself – not only movement, but reproduction, growth and decay – has *psuche* (*Top.* 140b3); but not all have the same kind. For Aristotle, as for Plato and earlier thinkers in general, the *psuche* remains more important than the body: all natural bodies (*De Anima* 415b18) are tools of the *psuche*, in the case of animals and plants alike, since they exist for the sake of the *psuche*; but Aristotle considers the relationship in more detail than Plato. He spends some time at different places in his works on refuting earlier thinkers: for example, *psuche* cannot be linked with respiration, since creatures which do not breathe – some animals, and plants – have *psuche* (since they move, or at all events change and reproduce themselves) nonetheless (*De Respiratione* 471b30 ff., *De Anima* 410b27 ff.); and he rejects the idea that the *psuche* could consist of one or a combination of the elements earth, air, fire and water (*De Anima* 409b23 ff.), showing that the theory raises more problems than it solves. One of the arguments advanced in its favour had been that only like can perceive like: there are four elements in the cosmos; therefore each must be present in the *psuche*, if the *psuche* is to perceive them. Aristotle, however, argues that 'like perceiving like' requires the *psuche* to

[1] Above, p. 139.

possess more than merely the elements: it will not perceive a bone or a man unless the appropriate proportions of the elements are present, unless, that is, the *psuche* contains elements so combined as to be a bone or a man. This, and the other arguments offered, are intended as a *reductio ad absurdum* to clear the ground for a quite different theory. For Aristotle, *psuche* (*De Anima* 414a12) is

> That by which we live and perceive and think . . ., so that it would be ratio (*logos*) and form, and not matter (*hulē*) and substrate. Now 'substance' is used in three senses . . . of which the one is form, another matter, and the third composed of both; of these matter is potentiality, and form, actuality (*entelecheia*). Since that which is composed of both is the being with *psuche*, it is not the body which is the actuality of the *psuche*, but the *psuche* which is the actuality of some body. So those who take the view that the *psuche* cannot exist without a body, but is not a body of any kind, are correct in their suppositions; for it is not body, but something which appertains to a body; and for this reason it exists in a body, and in a particular body.

Elsewhere (*De Anima* 412b18) he says that if the eye were a living creature, the power of sight would be its *psuche*, whose matter is the eye itself. If the power of sight is removed, the eye is no longer an eye, save in an equivocal sense, as a sculptured or painted eye might be said to be an eye.

It will be remembered that *psuche* is that which is possessed by living creatures, and lacked by dead ones; and that all Greeks are agreed on this, the dispute concerning not the existence in life, but the ontological status, of *psuche*. In Aristotle's philosophy, all the contents of the sublunary world are composed of matter (*hule*) and form (*eidos*), which can be logically distinguished but cannot exist separately from each other. The *psuche*, and its relation to the body, are naturally seen in terms of this philosophy; and clearly the *psuche* must be the form: the living creature is organised and functioning, the newly dead creature alike in all respects, except that it has ceased to function. (Further, since Aristotle is a teleological philosopher, it has ceased to be what it was: a blind eye is not an eye, an amputated hand is not a hand, a dead man not a man, save in some equivocal and punning sense.) Such a form cannot exist away from its body, and it only 'fits' its own body, of which it is the organising principle:

hence the immortality of the *psuche* is ruled out;[1] and even if it were immortal, transmigration of human *psuchai* into animals or plants, which the Pythagoreans – and Plato with modifications – held to be possible, and indeed common,[2] becomes impossible.

Types of *psuche*, then, differ: the *psuche* of one animal differs from that of another animal, the *psuche* of one plant from that of another plant. The most striking differences, however, are between plants, animals and human beings; and here too Aristotle carefully analyses the situation. More than one analysis is possible: where Aristotle is concerned with biological functions, he divides these (*De Anima* 414a31) into nutritive, perceptive, appetitive, locomotor and cognitive. Of these, plants have only the nutritive, which enables them to grow and reproduce themselves, while all animals, even the lowest, have the sense of touch. Animals differ in the number and range of their senses, desires and passions, and many have the power of locomotion; but none, save man 'and any other similar or superior being, if such exist', has the power of thought and intellect. A broad classification in terms of plant (nutritive), animal (sensitive) and human (intelligent, cognitive) *psuchai* is then possible, though, for example, there are gradations of animal *psuchai* with different powers. Of these, the higher presumes and subsumes the lower, 'as the quadrilateral contains the triangle' (*De Anima* 414b31): any creature that possesses animal *psuche* must also possess plant *psuche*, the latter taking care of such functions as growth, the digestive processes, breathing and reproduction.

Human *psuche*, accordingly, subsumes within itself animal and plant *psuche*; for the human being possesses, in addition to distinctive human capabilities, all the functions of the animal and plant. Once again, Aristotle sets man in the total context of the world as he sees it. Ethics requires a somewhat different analysis. In the *Nicomachean Ethics* (1144a9) the nutritive is the *fourth* part of the *psuche*: for ethics, it is sometimes necessary to divide the appetitive aspect into the spirited (*thumos*) and desire. Aristotle is at all times, within the structure of his philosophy as a whole, empirical: noting (*De Anima* 432a22) that some have divided the *psuche* into the cognitive, the spirited and

[1] Of the *psuche* as a whole, that is; but see below.
[2] Above, p. 135 f.

desire, others into the rational and irrational (both divisions being found in Aristotle's own works), he states that in a sense the 'parts' are infinite in number, answering to the functions that the *psuche* is able to discharge; and he is willing to conduct his enquiry in the terms which, for any discussion, seem most illuminating. Further, as we have seen, his most careful statement of the position accords to the *psuche* no 'parts' at all, for human *psuche* is one: it is not human plus animal plus plant, but contains the animal and the plant potentially within itself.

There remains the question of the 'active intellect'. We have seen that *psuche* in general, and the human *psuche* as a whole in particular, cannot exist in separation from its body; but in the *De Anima* (430a10) Aristotle also introduces the distinction between the active and the passive intellect. The distinction between matter and that which works on it, which runs throughout the cosmos, is found in the *psuche* too. Matter is capable of becoming everything; and there is an intellect which is capable of becoming everything, and an intellect which makes everything 'as light does; for in a sense light causes colours which exist potentially to be realised in actuality'. He adds (430a17):

> And this intellect is separable, unmixed and impassible, and essentially an actuality. For the active always has higher value than the passive, and the originative principle than the matter on which it exercises its function. Now knowledge when actualised is the same as its object; and potential knowledge is prior in time [to actual] so far as the individual is concerned, but in general not even in time; but the active intellect does not think at one time and not at another. When this intellect is separated, it is truly what it is, and this alone is immortal and eternal. We do not remember [its experiences outside our body] because this intellect is impassible, and the intellect that receives impressions is perishable; and without this nothing thinks.

This passage has baffled interpretation almost since it was written; and there is no space here for adequate discussion. However, it is clear that a passive, receptive element in thought (compared to matter) is contrasted with an active element (compared to *techne*, art or craft); and absence of the former deprives one of memory. Now human beings, from childhood onwards, are stocking their minds with information, which may function as the data both of memory and of thought. These data must be present in one aspect of the mind, and those that the mind has already received are not always present in actuality to it; one is not constantly remembering all the contents of one's memory. Again, the mind is capable of receiving data which it has not yet received: it is potentially capable of receiving any such data. In both senses, this passive intellect might to said to be potentially able to become all things. On the other hand, these data, once received, do not drift vaguely about in the mind: the intellect is capable of engaging in purposive activities with this material, of thinking rather than merely receiving the data of thought; and this may be the function of the active intellect, which thus acts like a carpenter or any craftsman on his material. This interpretation at least preserves the analogy which Aristotle introduces.

It is not entirely clear why Aristotle insisted on the immortality of the active intellect. It may in part be an inheritance of Platonism; but Aristotle himself emphasises the godlike nature of human reason (*Nicomachean Ethics* 1177a15),[1] and seems to have felt that the kinship was so strong that the (active) reason must be immortal. Certainly Aristotle's conception of the immortal intellect, a part of the *psuche*, has little resemblance to Plato's conception of the immortal *psuche*. It is true that in the *Timaeus* only the rational part of the *psuche* is immortal (and see the discussion of the *Phaedo*, above pp. 129 ff.); but in other dialogues the disembodied *psuche* must be capable of feeling and desire, for it can be punished; and it certainly retains its memory and individuality until its next incarnation.

Aristotle also disagrees with Plato's definition of the *psuche* as a self-moving entity (*De Anima* 408a30 ff.). For him the *psuche* causes motion, but neither moves itself nor is moved.

We say that the *psuche* grieves, rejoices, feels confidence or fear, and again that it is angry, perceives and thinks; and all these seem to be movements (changes). From this one might conclude that the *psuche* itself is moved, or rejoices or thinks. But this is unnecessary. For even if we . . . admit that pain or pleasure or thought are movements . . . and that the movement is produced by the *psuche* – as if for example anger or fear consisted in the heart being moved in a particular manner . . . and of these 'movements' some are spatial, some qualitative changes – nevertheless to say that the

[1] Subsequently abbreviated to *E.N.*

psuche is angry is like saying that the *psuche* weaves or builds houses. It is perhaps better not to say that the *psuche* feels pity, or learns or thinks, but that the man does so by means of his *psuche*; and this should not be interpreted as if the movement or change occurred in the *psuche*. No; sometimes movement extends as far as the *psuche*, at other times starts from the *psuche*: as perception starts from perceived objects, while recollection starts from the *psuche* and travels to the changes or traces of these in the organs of sensation.

If the *psuche* is the principle of organisation of the living creature, there is evidently a sense in which this does not undergo change, but represents the standard or frame of reference in terms of which the body moves and changes; but we have seen that Aristotle himself does not use language in the careful manner prescribed here.

E. *Phusis*

Aristotle engages in very sensitive analyses of words, but at the same time, and as a principle of his philosophy, particularly in his ethical and political works, uses words in their ordinary significance; so that it is not surprising to find him using *phusis* of 'age', 'time of life' (*Politics* 1259b14, 1340b14), a usage characteristic of 'ordinary Greek', but not of Plato.

Aristotle, however, also defines *phusis*. In the *Metaphysics* (1015a13) we are informed that *phusis* in the primary and accurate sense is the essence of things which have in themselves, as such, a source of movement; which (*Physics* 192b8) include the simple bodies – earth, air, fire and water – inanimate compounds, parts of animals and plants or whole animals and plants. Earth, air, fire and water, according to Aristotle, have each a natural disposition to move, whether up or down, as have compounds of these substances; while plants, themselves compounded of these, also have a principle of growth, decay, and reproduction; and animals have in addition perception and locomotion. *Phusis*, then, for Aristotle, directs the mind to the sensible world; and human *phusis*[1] has its place in this. On one occasion (*De Generatione Animalium* 740b36) Aristotle seems to identify *phusis* in plants and animals with the nutritive *psuche*: a usage which was to influence the Stoics, but is not characteristic of Aristotle himself.

[1] Different kinds of existent have a different *phusis*; but the *phusis* of each has its place in *phusis* as a whole, and in the teleology of the whole.

Aristotle's view of *phusis* as a whole is teleological. 'God and *phusis* do nothing in vain' (*De Caelo* 271a33); '*phusis* always follows the best course possible' (*De Caelo* 288a2); '*phusis* leaves nothing to chance, and would not, while caring for the animals, overlook things so precious (the stars)' (*De Caelo* 290a31). For Aristotle as for Plato, man is by no means the most important phenomenon in the universe.[1]

Though *phusis* always does the best it can, it does not always produce good specimens. Aristotle (*Politics* 1316a8) holds, while rejecting Plato's 'magic number' (*Republic* 546A) as the cause that *phusis* sometimes produces human beings so inferior as to be incapable of education, and so incapable of becoming 'good'; and this view of *phusis* is developed into a justification of slavery. Some thinkers in the fifth century had held that the categories of slave and free existed only by *nomos*, and that there was no difference in *phusis*. Aristotle would have granted that sometimes unsuitable persons were enslaved by war, or piracy; but (*Pol.* 1254b20) 'he who is able to be another's (and for that reason is another's)[2] and has a share of reason sufficient to enable him to comprehend, but not to have reason himself, is by *phusis* a slave'.

Leaving slaves on one side, we may enquire whether Aristotle held that any other individuals were debarred by their *phusis* from *arete*. (The nature of Aristotle's view of *arete* will be discussed below.) In the *Politics* (1332a38) we find

There are three things which render men *agathoi* and worthy: *phusis*, habituation and rational principle. In the first place, one must be born (*phunai*) a human being and not some other animal, and then one must have a certain character of *soma* and *psuche*. And in respect of some qualities it is no good to be born (*phunai*) this or that, for habits cause them to change: for some qualities are so constituted by *phusis* as to be capable of change under the influence of habituation in two directions, both towards what is worse and towards what is better. Animals live by *phusis* for the most part, though some are influenced also by habituation. Man lives by rational principle, which he alone possesses, as well. And so these three – *phusis*, habituation, and rational principle – must be in harmony with one another; for men do

---

[1] On the other hand, living creatures are ranked from a human standpoint. Those animals which can be tamed have a better *phusis* than those which cannot, *Pol.* 1254b11.

[2] *Arete* is the quality or qualities which enables one to maintain oneself as independent and self-sufficient.

many things in despite of habituation and *phusis*, if they are persuaded that another course of action is better for them.

This is not altogether clear. It is clear that, for Aristotle, some of the endowments of *phusis* are *dunameis tōn enantiōn*, capacities or potentialities which may be developed in either of two directions. As he says (*E.N.* 1103a18), the ethical *aretai* spring up in us neither by *phusis* (for in that case they could not be changed by habituation) nor contrary to *phusis* (since we do acquire them). By *phusis*, we have the capacity to acquire them (or the vices opposed to them,) but they are perfected by habituation.[1] *Phusis* and habituation, then, furnish us with ethical *aretai* – or perhaps only some of us; for it would appear that certain characters of *soma* and *psuche* would debar one from being *agathos*, and these are part of our *phusis*. Again, one may act in despite of habituation and *phusis*, at the behest of reason. Possibly reason misused might cause one to fall short of the highest potentialities of one's *phusis*: it seems less likely that it could help one to act in a manner better than one's *phusis* would permit. (It is possible that one may fail to realise the full potentialities of one's *phusis*, which is an end in the sense of being a goal; it seems unlikely that one could exceed its potentialities, for it is an end also in the sense of being a limit.) At all events, Aristotle rarely grants such powers to the reason in practical matters, as will become apparent in the discussion of his view of human behaviour.

It is unclear how large a proportion of the human race Aristotle deemed to be debarred by *phusis* from *arete*; for some of his statements, set in the wider context of his thought, prove to be misleading. Slaves, certainly; and most non-Greeks and some Greeks were by *phusis* slaves, it would appear. Aristotle says (*E.N.* 1099b19) that *eudaimonia* is attainable by all who are not 'maimed in respect of *arete*'; but it would be rash to assume that Aristotle supposed that the majority even of Greeks were not so maimed. He himself insists that his requirements are less austere than Plato's. In *Politics* 1295a25 he says that he – in contrast with Plato, to whose views he is clearly referring, though he does not name him – is seeking to discover

---

[1] See below, pp. 182 ff.

What is the best form of state and what is the best life for the majority of cities and the majority of mankind, not those who are chosen out as having an *arete* which is beyond that of the common run of men, nor an education which requires a *phusis* and an 'equipment' which results merely from chance, nor a form of government which is a mere dream. No; there should be a kind of life in which the majority can share, and a form of government of which most cities can partake.

Aristotle is speaking of city-states, and hence of Greeks; and he believed (*Pol.* 1327b29,[1] 1252b9) that the Greeks were singularly blessed in their *phusis*. However, 'majority of mankind' should not be accepted even in this restricted sense: as will appear below, Aristotle did not consistently suppose that the majority even of Greeks were capable of *arete*, and hence of *eudaimonia*.

F. Aristotle's View of Human Behaviour

In discussing the Aristotelian view of human behaviour, it will be best to start from the child. In Aristotle's eyes, not merely the child but the young man is still prone to follow his passions (*pathē*, *E.N.* 1095a4); and this renders the young an unsuitable audience for instruction in ethics and politics, for the end is not knowledge (which might be acquired) but action, *prāxis*; and Aristotle does not believe that the young would act on what they had learned, since they would be swept away by their passions. Again (*E.N.* 1179b26), he holds that the person who lives by passion or emotion would neither hear the dissuading voice of reason nor understand it: passion does not yield to reason, but only to force. Persons in this condition do not respond to moral suasion, but to punishment alone. 'Persons in this condition' are somewhat redefined in this passage: Aristotle now says that words may have a protreptic effect on the 'liberal-minded' of the young (*E.N.* 1179b7), and render a noble character and one that is truly 'fond of the *kalon*' capable of being possessed by *arete*, but that words have no power to stimulate the majority of mankind towards *kalokagathia*, a word commending one of Aristotle's ideals of behaviour. For their *phusis* is not such (*pephukenai*) as to yield to shame, but only to fear, nor such as to refrain from base acts because of the

---

[1] Aristotle here attributes Greek superiority to Greek climate; cf. Herodotus IX, 122, for the relationship between climate and human characteristics.

aischron, but only because of the punishment they would incur. 'The liberal-minded young' in this passage are presumably somewhat older than the young persons mentioned in the former passage; and clearly they are only a few of the young. Their identity will be discussed below.[1]

The method of dealing with these passions and emotions is to habituate or condition them to proper responses. 'Conditioning' in Greek is *ĕthos* or *ĕthismos*, a word whose close resemblance to *ēthos*, from which *ēthikē arete* and *ēthika*, Aristotle's term for 'ethics', are derived, is noted by Aristotle (*E.N.* 1103a17). This conditioning is a necessary requisite of Aristotle's ethics; and from its possibility Aristotle concludes that the ethical *aretai* come to us neither by *phusis* – for we can change them by habituation, and no characteristics that anything possesses by *phusis* can be changed: one cannot habituate a stone to fly upwards – nor yet in a manner contrary to *phusis*, since we do acquire them. We are by *phusis* able to receive them, but they are perfected by habituation. In the case of those things which we have by *phusis*, we first of all have the capacity and then later manifest it: we have the capacity of sight and then use it, without need of training. But we acquire the *aretai* as craftsmen acquire crafts: one becomes a builder by building houses, and one becomes a man of a certain ethical character by performing acts of certain ethical characteristics. Just as one becomes a good housebuilder by building houses well, a bad housebuilder by building houses badly, so one becomes just by performing just acts in one's relationships with other men, unjust by performing unjust acts in those relationships. The subject matter is in each case the same: it is the manner in which one handles it that makes the difference. From an activity, many times repeated, of a particular ethical kind one acquires an ethical disposition, which Aristotle terms a *hexis*, of the same kind: by performing just acts one acquires a just *hexis* and is then, in the full sense, just. And this habituation, in Aristotle's view, produces a very reliable result: though he acknowledges that it is easier to change the product of habituation than to change *phusis*, he holds that this too is very difficult, for it resembles *phusis* (*E.N.* 1152a30).[2]

[1] See p. 211.
[2] And cf. *Rhetoric* 1370a7, *De Memoria* 452a27.

This analysis is evidently much superior to that of Plato who, as we have seen, did not clearly distinguish the roles of *phusis* and habituation. Yet Aristotle also speaks of *phusikē arete*, *arete* as given to us by *phusis*. He compares the relationship of *phusike arete* to perfect *arete* with that between cleverness and practical wisdom; and adds that in a sense we have each of the ethical attributes by *phusis* (*E.N.* 1144b1 ff.); 'for all men think that we are just, self-controlled, brave and have the other attributes from the time of our birth'. Even animals and children have the *hexeis*, dispositions, which come to them from their *phusis*. It is the addition of intelligence that is significant: till then, one is like a strong, blind man who stumbles because he cannot see where he is going. When intelligence is added, the actions performed are different; and the *hexis*, which is similar to what it was before, will then be *arete* in the full sense.

Editors sometimes treat these two passages as if they were entirely in harmony; but this is not so. In the former passage the infant, and indeed the youth, is regarded as entirely plastic, capable of being endowed with 'ethical *arete*' by appropriate habituation: the contrast is between a plasticity capable of becoming *arete* and that 'ethical *arete*' itself. In the second passage, we are said to possess certain *hexeis* by *phusis*: the crucial difference is the development of practical wisdom, which converts *phusike arete* into 'perfect *arete*'.

Aristotle frequently fails to harmonise discussions of the same topic, where these have different purposes. In the former of these passages, he is concerned to define the relationship of *arete* to *phusis*, in the latter to distinguish certain virtuous tendencies in us from perfect virtue, *arete*, in the sense in which Aristotle understands it. However, the confusion is not merely one of language – serious as this is in itself in a philosopher – but betrays two different views of the human being. The former, in which habituation is emphasised to the exclusion of thought, treats the human being as a creature that must be conditioned to respond; a view with which, so far as concerns all but a tiny fraction of humanity, Plato would have agreed. The second treats the human being as a creature whose desires are sound, but who is liable to make mistakes until his practical wisdom is developed. It is not surprising to find Aristotle mentioning Socrates almost immediately afterwards (*E.N.* 1144b18): though Socrates was mistaken to suppose that the *aretai* are practical wisdom, he was right in that they cannot occur without practical wisdom.

There is a real tension here; and it is a tension that runs through the whole of Aristotle's discussion of human behaviour. As a corollary, he sometimes speaks as though pleasure were necessarily the end of every human action, so that all influencing of human action must be achieved through the medium of pleasure and pain; sometimes he treats pleasure as the final completion of perfection of an activity choiceworthy – and capable of being chosen – on other grounds.[1]

In a similar manner, there seem to be two pictures or models of human behaviour in Aristotle's doctrine of the Mean, or *meson*. He states (*E.N.* 1106b36):

> *Arete* is a *hexis* or disposition, associated with deliberate choice, residing in a mean that has reference to ourselves, defined by reason or proportion, and by that by means of which the man of practical wisdom would define it.

Here the analysis prominently includes reason and deliberate choice; and earlier in his discussion (1106b5 ff.) Aristotle compares *arete* with knowledge and craft, *techne*, insisting that *arete* is more accurate and better than any *techne*, and hence more successful at aiming at the *meson* or mean. He uses as an analogy with the good moral action (1106b9) a good product of art or craft, to which one could add nothing, and from which one could take away nothing, without spoiling it. Again, Aristotle emphasises the skill required in moral action (1109a26 ff.):

> Anyone can become angry, or give money away, or spend it: for that is easy; but the question to whom, how much, when, why and how one should do this is not an easy one, and not everyone can act correctly.

One cannot calculate the answer, any more than one can calculate how to produce a good work of art, though this too is an intelligent activity: one can only aim at the Mean.

[1] Cf. *Merit and Responsibility*, pp. 317, 320 f., 323, 329(3), 329(9). The discussion of pleasure in *E.N.* VII (1152b1 ff.) may be contrasted as a whole with that of *E N.* X (1172a19 ff.). But the tension is always present. The discussion in Book X, which taken as a whole represents pleasure as the completion or perfection of an activity, begins (1172a19 ff.) with a passage which suggests the other view.

We can certainly recognise this picture of moral decision, which is one of Aristotle's models; but already certain features seem to require explanation. *Meson*, Aristotle's word here rendered by 'mean', is a quantitative rather than qualitative word; and even in offering his analogy with the products of craft, by speaking of additions and subtractions as such he emphasises the quantitative, rather than the qualitative, decisions taken in the light of the overall conception of the work by the artist. In his initial account of the Mean, however, he distinguishes it from an arithmetical mean between two extremes, which anyone can immediately calculate, and for which anyone should obtain the same answer (1106a28 ff.). Aristotle's Mean is related 'to ourselves', and must be determined in some way by the individual's characteristics; and the individual concerned, one would suppose on the basis of *E.N.* 1106b36 ff., must be the agent himself acting with reason and deliberate choice. As an illustration of what he means, Aristotle compares training for athletics (1106a36 ff.):

We cannot determine the Mean with relation to ourselves in this manner. For it is not the case that if ten minae of food is a great deal, and two a little, that the trainer will prescribe six minae; for perhaps six minae of food is a great deal, or a little, for the person that is to receive it: it would be a little for Milo, but a great deal for one who was just beginning to practise gymnastics. The case of running and wrestling is similar.

This 'illustration' throws more darkness than light on what Aristotle is trying to say. Either the gymnast or the trainer should be the analogue of the moral agent here, and should make a deliberate choice in association with his *hexis* residing in a Mean that 'has reference to ourselves', and presumably to himself: it is difficult to see how such a *hexis* or disposition could be determined with reference to anyone else (*E.N.* 1106b36). However, the individual whose characteristics determine the appropriate action to be taken is here the gymnast who is being trained (in order to build up a sound physical *hexis* in him, though Aristotle does not use the word); but it is the trainer who takes the decision, and 'aims at the Mean', and *his* characteristics should not affect the decision here at all. Hence the trainer is not a good analogue here for the moral agent. Nor yet is the gymnast: his 'Mean with relation to the individual' is in question, and this determines *arete*; but he should be making the choice, and he is not. It may appear strange that Aristotle, in seeking an illustration to explain moral decision, should have produced one which calls to mind ethical habituation by an expert; yet this seems to have occurred.

In fact, the more attentively one examines Aristotle's account of the Mean, the odder it appears. One might perhaps have expected him to contrast arithmetical calculation, impossible in matters of ethics, with aiming at the right thing to do in a given situation; and 'the right thing to do' might well appear to depend on 'hitting the target' in the situation, not on the agent's hitting 'some target' of response in himself.[1] If the moral agent under consideration in this example were the trainer, we might suppose that this was Aristotle's view, for the gymnast is then 'the situation' in which a *meson* is being sought; but then the *meson* is not in relation to the agent and his *hexis*, for the right amount of diet depends on the characteristics not of the trainer, but of the gymnast.

Aristotle, in fact, despite his comparison with skilled decisions, has in the doctrine of the *meson* an alternative and incompatible picture. *Arete* may be a *hexis* linked with deliberate choice, and the mean condition with which it is related may be defined by reason; but the Mean itself has quantitative implications. If we ask 'quantities of what?' the answer is again unclear. Aristotle says of *andreiā*, courage (*E.N.* 1107a33), 'in respect of instances of fear and rashness, courage is a mean'; of truth-telling or candour, 'in respect of truth-telling . . . pretence on the side of exaggeration is boasting . . . while that on the side of minimising oneself is mock-modesty'. In the case of courage, since culpable fear and rashness consist in running away or charging the enemy when reason would counsel otherwise, we might think of fear and rashness as drives uncontrolled by reason, and hence as quantitatively the wrong amount of response to a given situation; but it is more difficult to think of telling the truth, boasting and mock-modesty in this light. Are we concerned with a mean in respect of passion and emotion, or a mean in respect of action? Aristotle says that '*arete* is concerned both with passion and emotion and with action (e.g. *E.N.* 1106b24), in respect of which (both categories)

[1] The metaphor is Aristotle's, *E.N.* 1109a30.

excess and deficiency are errors, while the mean is praised and is correct'; and he says more fully (*E.N.* 1106b18 ff.):

> For example, one may experience fear, confidence, desire, anger, pity, and in general pleasure and pain[1] both more and less than one should, and both of these conditions are undesirable; but to experience them when one should, and on the occasions, with reference to the persons, for the reason and in the manner in which one should, this is the mean and the best, and this is the mark of *arete*. And similarly in respect of actions there is excess, deficiency and mean.

Here too the language suggests a quantitative picture. It is easier to understand what is meant by a quantitative emotional response which partakes of excess or deficiency than to understand the manner in which actions can be similarly classified.[2] Yet Aristotle explicitly uses the same language of actions here. In this passage he speaks of emotions and actions separately; but elsewhere he speaks of *arete* as concerned with emotions and actions together, and we have seen that some of his examples of the Mean seem to lay more emphasis on emotion or passion, some on action. Aristotle either fails to notice this, or regards it as unimportant for his purposes; and the reason may be that for him and for the Greeks of the period generally, accustomed to a calculative, not a volitional psychology, and to the total picture of human behaviour that accompanied it, the view that a certain degree of emotional response led directly to a certain type – or, one might be induced to suppose, degree – of action might well be most in harmony with their actual experience. (We have seen already that to speak of a 'calculative' psychology is not to exclude the presence of emotion; but the relevance of this point to Aristotle will be discussed below.) One of Aristotle's triads of virtues and vices may point in the same direction: the vices on either side of *sophrosune*, self-control

[1] In the light of what has already been said (p. 184, above) about the view, frequent in Aristotle, of the attainment of pleasure and the avoidance of pain as the necessary end of all action, it is interesting to note Aristotle's apparent readiness to reduce all emotions and desires to pleasure and pain in this passage.

[2] His first example that emphasises action is liberality, the giving and receiving of money, a mean between squandering and miserliness (*E.N.* 1107b8). Here a quantitative picture is plausible; and this may have rendered the exposition easier for Aristotle.

(*E.N.* 1109a4), are *akolasiā*, licence – literally 'lack of punishment' – and *anaisthēsiā*, literally 'want of sensation'. A different psychological picture would represent the extreme Puritan as savagely repressing his desires and emotions: the Greek word chosen here suggests that he has none, and so does not act on them;[1] and this suggests that the *sophron* has a mean emotional response.[2]

One element in Aristotle's doctrine of the Mean, then, suggests a picture of a response conditioned to be quantitatively correct, and produce a correct 'amount' of action, however this last is to be interpreted: the other suggests a skilled aiming at a mark, or an artist creating a work of art. We must consider whether the two can be harmonised, whether it is possible to argue that the correct amount of response created a situation in which the skilled aiming at the target can take place. Aristotle's definition, already quoted, of an *arete* as a '*hexis* or disposition, associated with deliberate choice, residing in a mean that has reference to the individual himself, defined by reason or proportion, and by that means of which the man of practical wisdom would define it' suggests that he holds his position to be an harmonious whole. 'Residing in a mean' is ambiguous; the Greek is 'being in a mean', which is equally so; but the Greek as a whole could be read in such a way as to suggest that the emotional response permitted the deliberate choice to be correct; though we have seen much in Aristotle's detailed discussion of the Mean that is incompatible with this theory.

For further light, we must turn to Aristotle's discussion of moral action in Book VI of the *Nicomachean Ethics* (1138b35 ff.). Here the characteristics of *praxis*, moral action, of which animals are incapable,

[1] The individual who controls himself only with an effort is the *enkratēs*, who is not placed by Aristotle in his triads of *aretai* and *kakiai*, for he has not a *hexis* or settled disposition. The *enkrates* is not the extreme Puritan: he is one who behaves in the manner of the *sophron*, but only with a great effort, whereas the *sophron* finds action on the basis of his *sophron hexis* (cf. *E.N.* 1099a18) pleasant and easy.

[2] This may be the reason why Aristotle finds it necessary to say that there can be no mean condition of vices of disposition such as envy, or of action, such as adultery, *E.N.* 1107a8 ff. One might infer from the doctrine of a mean response of passion leading to a mean quantity of action that any passion or emotion had its mean, so that there was an appropriate amount of envy, or that any action had its mean, so that there might be a proper quantity of adultery.

are set out. Its requirements are intelligence and *orexis*, psychological drive; and (*E.N.* 1139a21)

> Assent and dissent in the intellect are analogous to pursuit and avoidance in the field of psychological drives; accordingly, since ethical *arete* is a *hexis* or disposition associated with deliberate choice, *prohairesis*, and *prohairesis* is psychological drive associated with deliberation, for these reasons the *logos*, propositions presented to the intellect, must be true and the psychological drive correct, if the deliberate choice is to be good; and the intellect must assert and the psychological drives pursue the same things. . . . Accordingly (a33) deliberate choice cannot occur either without intellect or without an ethical *hexis* or disposition. . . . Deliberate choice (b4) is either intellect associated with psychological drive or psychological drive associated with intellect, and such a source of action is the human being.

The first necessity is to decide whether the analysis is logical or psychological. Aristotle may not have drawn a clear distinction; but part at least must be psychological. A logical analysis of the necessary elements of a deliberate choice might conclude that one must have a clearly defined goal before one's mind, and a drive sufficient to set one in motion towards it, on that particular occasion; but to require (1139a33) that there must be a *hexis*, a settled disposition, to pursue this type of goal, is more than logic requires, and must be a psychological element in the analysis. (For the requirement is not rendered necessary by the earlier stages of the argument, 1139a21 ff., where agreement between intellect and drive on a particular occasion would suffice.) Accordingly, the separation of intellect and drive in the argument is a psychological, 'real' one, not merely a logical distinction: to ensure good moral action, the drives must be habituated to be reliably correct and in agreement with the intellect which, as we have already seen,[1] Aristotle elsewhere holds to be incapable of controlling the drives by itself. The phrases in my translation above in which 'associated with' appears represent adjective-noun phrases in Greek, and might be rendered 'desiderative reason' and 'ratiocinative desire'; but Aristotle's Greek, in thus suggesting a unity of function in desire and reason here, goes beyond his psychological picture: the two may run in harness together if the desires are properly conditioned, but no greater unity is possible. ('Harness' –

[1] Above, pp. 181 ff.

though the word is mine, not Aristotle's – suggests the myth of the *Phaedrus*;[1] and this may not be irrelevant.)

Once again, habituation of passions and emotions is necessary before true moral action can occur. It is difficult to determine whether Aristotle in his ethical writings thinks of the passions and desires as differing in no way from those of an animal. He should not do so: as we have seen, the human *psuche* subsumes within itself the animal and plant *psuchai*, and is not an aggregate of the three; yet elsewhere he likens the young of the human race to other wild animals (*Probl.* 895b30). His views here must be inferred. On the one hand, the *hexis* or disposition to be (say) just is produced by performing just acts, under instruction but with the consciousness that they are held to be just acts, though one may not know why: as Aristotle says (*E.N.* 1095b6 ff.), in ethics the 'that' precedes the 'why', and if one has the 'that' the 'why' is really unnecessary. Having attained a good *hexis*, one will then certainly do what one ought to do, and one will be capable of *prohairesis*, deliberate choice, for one will also know what one ought to do, a knowledge which one will have been acquiring throughout the process of one's habituation. However, it is unclear so far whether the intellect has been acquiring knowledge while the passions and emotions have been merely conditioned by the application of suitable pleasures and pains as rewards and punishments, or whether the *psuche* as a whole has been 'educated' by its performance of just acts.

Aristotle's discussion of *enkrateia* and *akrasiā*, continence and incontinence, may throw some light on his basic position: the analysis above is only partial. Each of these conditions poses some problems for Greek philosophy. Much that Aristotle says elsewhere makes the possibility of the reason controlling the passions – the definition of *enkrateia* – difficult to understand; while Socrates had held that *akrasia*, acting against what one knew to be right, was impossible. If one knows what is right, one does it, in his view: all wrong action is the result of ignorance.[2] Aristotle, rather surprisingly, devotes little attention to the problem

---

[1] Above, pp. 133 ff.

[2] Aristotle, as in so many points related to this aspect of his philosophy, uses language in different places which suggests both views. To speak of becoming just by performing just acts suggests voluntarily choosing to learn, by doing,

of *enkrateia*, merely assuming it for his present purpose to exist. Most of his discussion concerns *akrasia*, and he introduces it rather defensively (*E.N.* 1145b6): 'if the objections are refuted and the common opinions are left undisturbed, this would be an adequate proof'. Furthermore, his discussion of *akrasia* is intended primarily to prove that such a condition is possible; but his solutions throw light on his view of human action. Solutions, not solution: *akrasia* is acting against what one knows to be right, and there may be more than one condition in which one can do this. His first two attempts have little plausibility (*E.N.* 1146b31 ff.). One may have knowledge and not be using it; but the incontinent man knows even when he acts that what he is doing is wrong, so that this throws no light on *akrasia*. Secondly, Aristotle introduces the practical syllogism, his analysis of the mental process involved in resolving to do something (or in doing it: a question which will be discussed below). He gives this example (1147a5): 'dry food is good for all men' is the major premiss, and there are two minor premisses, 'I am a human being' and 'such-and-such food is dry'; and he argues that the incontinent man either does not know, or is not using the knowledge, that 'this food is such-and-such'. But action of this kind, on Aristotle's terms or anyone else's, is not the result of incontinence but of a mistake: one does not possess at the moment of action the vital piece of information as a result of which one might be said to have knowledge of the nature of one's action. Neither of these 'solutions' illuminates *akrasia* at all. Aristotle's next solution (1147a10 ff.) is to liken the incontinent individual to one who is asleep, mad, or drunk. He observes that extremes of passion and desire can engender madness; and that those who are mad or drunk may be able to repeat scientific and other general propositions. He adds (1147a21):

---

what one did not know before, while e.g. *E.N.* 1104b11 ff. suggests that correct ethical education consists in habituating the learner, through the medium of pleasures and pains, to find pleasure and pain in what he should. One might attempt to harmonise these on grounds of mere difference of emphasis or perhaps suggest that the major, ethical, premiss of the practical syllogism 'all just acts are choiceworthy' results from habituation, while the minor 'this is a just act' results from learning; but both models of the *psuche* appear to be endemic in Aristotle's thought. The end-product in either case is *ethismos*; and the end, for Aristotle, is more important, and more clearly described, than the means.

And those who have just learnt something string together the words, but do not yet have knowledge; for it has to become ingrained in us (*sumphuēnai*), and that takes time.

His last explanation runs as follows (1147a25 ff.):

> The one opinion is universal, whereas the other is concerned with particulars, and here perception has authority; and when one opinion results from them (i.e. when a practical syllogism is formed from them) it is necessary that the *psuche* should in one kind of case affirm the conclusion, while in the case of opinions concerned with action or production, the *psuche* must act at once: for example, if one should taste everything sweet, and this is sweet in the sense of being one of the particular sweet things, then it is necessary that the person who can do so *and is not prevented* should do this at once. Accordingly, when there is one general premiss preventing one from tasting, and another maintaining that all sweet things are pleasant, and that this is a sweet thing (and it is this opinion that is active), and desire happens to be in us, the one opinion bids us avoid the object, but the desire leads us towards it; for it can move each of the bodily parts.

Of these last three examples, the first, likening *akrasia* to drunkenness or madness, does not illuminate *akrasia* as defined, for the sense in which someone who is drunk or mad knows what he is doing is very different from that in the crucial case of incontinence, in which an individual really knows that what he is doing is wrong and yet does it; nevertheless, similar states to drunkenness and madness are found in individuals of certain psychological types when neither drunk nor, in any normal sense of the word, insane; so that this is an account of a psychological condition which occurs, and which may be classified by Aristotle with *akrasia*; for such a person is not like the man with an ingrained vice, a bad *hexis*, who chooses to do what is wrong of set policy. The second example alludes to the necessity for habituation: only when we are accustomed to an idea has it any chance of affecting our actions.[1]

In both cases, the power of the desires and passions to sweep reason

---

[1] The example also suggests that Aristotle regarded rote-learning as the norm in education. Plato, in the more optimistic period of the composition of the *Republic* at all events, would not have favoured such a process for those in whose education he took an interest; and he would at no time have termed the result 'knowledge' (*eidenai*), as Aristotle does here.

aside is emphasised; but we have still not reached the crucial case, which Aristotle must, if anywhere, be discussing in the third example. Here it is stated quite clearly that if both premisses of a *practical* syllogism are present to the mind, the affirmation of the conclusion takes the form of immediate action. 'And is not prevented' must refer to prevention by external circumstances: otherwise this clause nullifies the rest of the sentence. This being so, there can be no conclusion to the practical syllogism in the second part of the quotation prior to the action taking place. Aristotle's statement of the premisses here changes in an interesting manner: we have not 'one should taste everything sweet' but 'all sweet things are pleasant'. The conclusion to be drawn from this premiss and 'this is a sweet thing' is 'this thing is pleasant': a proposition, not an action. It is the presence of desire, as Aristotle says, that supplies the motive for action; for desire is for what is pleasant. But what of the other major premiss, 'one ought not to taste (any)[1] sweet things'? On Aristotle's own principles, if this were ever employed with the minor premiss 'this is a sweet thing', the conclusion should be immediate action or rather aversion, experienced in taking action to avoid the thing; for this is a practical syllogism. Accordingly, the conclusion cannot have been drawn, and the minor premiss has never been used with this major, but only with the other major premiss. The presence of desire has prevented the moral practical syllogism from being used at all. Clearly *akrasia* only occurs when desire is present; and one would not judge anything to be pleasant at a particular moment if one in fact did not desire it:[2] 'X is pleasant but I feel no desire for it' is a strange proposition. Accordingly, desire is present throughout, and this syllogism is really a practical syllogism too, since 'all sweet things are pleasant' implies that all sweet things

---

[1] Aristotle merely says 'preventing one from tasting': he does not state this premiss in full: the presence or absence of 'any' is clearly important in cases where, so to speak, this premiss is victorious; but Aristotle is not precise in this instance, where the premiss is ineffective. The argument he offers implies that 'any' is present.

[2] The sequence of events naturally begins with the particular: the agent sees a sweet thing; aroused desire causes the proposition 'all sweet things are pleasant' to present itself to him; and the conclusion-and-action, this–thing–is–pleasant–and–I–act–to–gain–possession–of–it, follows when the *akratēs* yields to his *akrasia*. If the minor premiss is, by some means, used with the moral major premiss, the action does not occur.

arouse desire. The major premiss is supplied by the desires, and is a rationalisation of them; and this desire prevents the conclusion of the other practical syllogism – an action, or a refraining from action – from being drawn at all. There are two ways in which it might prevent this: desire might cause the suppression of the major moral premiss, so that the individual was not actively aware of it at the time. Aristotle's words might be so interpreted ('and it is this opinion that is active' might distinguish the effective major premiss from the ineffective one); but anyone in this condition would not know at the time that the action was wrong, and so would not be acting incontinently. Secondly, desire might so (as it were) drag the minor premiss over to its favoured major premiss that it was not available for use with the moral major premiss; an interpretation which does more credit to Aristotle, though it still does not analyse the crucial case, for anyone in this last condition would not know that *this* action was wrong, since the minor particular premiss has not been used with the moral major premiss.

We should not, however, conclude that this analysis is necessarily at variance with the facts of psychology present to Aristotle. In Homer's characters we have, it is true, an unusually fragmented personality type; but even in Plato, especially after he has freed himself from the influence of Socrates, we have seen much fragmentation, and an insistence that individuals must be habituated as in the *Laws*-state, to believe that the 'truly' pleasant, 'truly' beneficial and 'truly' honourable coincide; for observation leads Plato to suppose that the man who is capable of long resisting his passions in the interests of reason is very rare indeed (*Laws* 875A ff., 918C). We may be tempted to ascribe these views simply to the pessimism of an aristocratic perfectionist rationalising his dislike of democracy; and some doubtless should be written off to this account; but we have seen reason to believe that the shame- and results-culture in which the Greeks of this period lived still inhibited the development of personality structure to a considerable extent; and Plato's own solution to the problem of values would not have encouraged development.[1] Aristotle's own solution, as we shall see, would not have done so to any great extent; and his emphasis on the need for habituation to bring under control the otherwise unruly and virtually uncontrollable passions and

[1] See above, p. 167 f.

desires, felt as being 'over against' the rational aspect of the individual and capable of functioning, at best, in double harness with the reason, testifies to the inhibition of personality development by the society.[1] In fact, Aristotle's analysis seems somewhat more pessimistic than Plato's, for even in the *Laws* (645A) there was an 'I' to co-operate with the golden cord in its struggle with the others: Aristotle's final analysis of *akrasia* leaves no more than a spectral balance or tug-of-war, and, as in Homer, the inclination of the balance or the victory in the tug-of-war determines action. Indeed, the situation is in one sense less 'personal' than it was in Homer: there the democratic polity of psychological functions shared the consciousness among themselves, and were in effect so many little persons within the person, which had relationships with the personal pronoun, not with each other. The little 'personalities' did not cohere one with another; but all to some extent had attributes belonging to a complete personality. Now in Aristotle's analysis of action, the personality manifests itself simply as its warring functions; and in the analysis, at all events, it appears that the irrational aspect will not 'listen to reason', and responds only to reward of pleasure and the punishment of pain.

In the analysis only, of course: Aristotle is aware that self-controlled persons exist, and he insists (*E.N.* 1102b25) elsewhere that this aspect of the personality

> Seems to partake of reason, as we have said; at all events that aspect of the *enkrates*, the man who controls himself with an effort, obeys reason – but perhaps that aspect of the *sophron*, temperate, and *andreios*, brave, individual is more obedient; for all things in their case harmonise with reason. So it appears that the irrational element in us is twofold. The 'plant-aspect' in no way shares in reason, whereas the aspect concerned with desires and drives partakes of reason in a sense, in that it hearkens to it and obeys it. . . .

[1] Aristotle is usually understood (*Poetics* 1449b27 f.) to hold that the experience of a tragic performance should 'through the medium of pity and fear, purge us of similar emotions in ourselves'; a recommendation of tragedy, I suggest, unlikely to have occurred independently to a modern critic. If this is broadly correct, it would be possible, and indeed serve to explain the form of the expression, to interpret 'similar emotions' (*ta toiauta pathēmata*) as including more than pity and fear, in fact emotions in general; in which case the nature of Aristotle's theory of the effect of tragedy may well be related to the prevalence of the kind of psychological turbulence discussed in the text, and the longing for inner calm. Even if 'similar emotions' is restricted to pity and fear, the point seems valid.

That the irrational aspect is persuaded in a sense by reason . . . is indicated
by the existence of reproof, punishment and exhortation of all kinds.

This is 'common-sense' philosophy, where the former was analysis;
and it is clear that a society in which no self-control was possible
would not be a society of human beings, while a society which did not
engage at all in reproof, punishment and exhortation, in trying to
affect the behaviour of its members, is inconceivable. Even in Homer,
as we have seen, self-control is possible. It may, however, be more
difficult for certain types of personality; and Greek society may encourage these types of personality. Where self-control proves difficult
or impossible in this society, the psychological situation may well
present itself as in Aristotle's analysis of *akrasia*.[1] Indeed, elsewhere
(*E.N.* 1179b28) Aristotle says that passion and emotion (*pathos*) do
not yield to reason, but only to force: that is to say, that only punishment, not reproof or exhortation, is really effective. This is not analysis,
but practical advice to the politician: states need penal laws. The purpose of this statement is different from that of *E.N.* 1102b25 above,
which draws attention to the fact that self-controlled individuals
exist; but it makes their existence difficult to understand, since such
by definition[2] restrain their passions and emotions by reason.

At this point it may be relevant to discuss an apparent anomaly,
present from Homer onwards. The fragmentation, or rather, failure
to develop, of the personality, which resulted in great autonomy for
the desires and emotions, has been illustrated many times; yet the
pattern of decision has been seen to be calculative, not volitional.
Homer's 'and this course appeared the better (more advantageous) to
me', Plato's (or Socrates') 'no-one errs on purpose', which occurs

[1] No problem of personal responsibility is created. An action of which the
'first cause' is in the individual is the individual's action, for which he is responsible. See *Eudemian Ethics* 1224b21 ff., *E.N.* 1111b1 ff., and *Merit and Responsibility*,
chapter XV, pp. 319 ff.

[2] The definition of *E.N.* 1102b25 ff., at all events. In *Eudemian Ethics* 1224a7 ff.,
on the other hand, Aristotle speaks of the continent man (a34) as dragging
himself 'by force' from what he desires, while the incontinent man drags himself
'by force' from what his reason tells him to be *agathon*. The picture is comprehensible; but Aristotle's analysis leaves unclear what aspect of the personality
is available to perform such dragging. This passage is non-analytical and indeed
('they say', a34) a record of 'ordinary Greek'.

even in the *Laws*, Plato's last major work, and Aristotle's practical syllogism, all display this pattern. 'Calculative' suggests dispassionate mathematical reasoning; and this seems completely unsuited to other aspects of the Greek personality. The answer can perhaps be now given more clearly than before, in terms of the practical syllogism. The 'good' which the Greek pursues is what is good for himself, the pleasure, naturally enough, pleasure for himself. He should rationally desire what is good for himself, which will be sometimes pleasant, sometimes unpleasant: his irrational nature will desire the pleasant at all times. Both, however, are desires; and the conflict is inevitably seen as one between rational and irrational desire. Plato and Aristotle wish so to condition their citizens that the 'truly' pleasant is identified with what is 'truly' good for them, so that there is no conflict; but conflict or no, the major premisses relating to the good and the pleasant both concern desirables; and this is true in other circumstances, where the problem may be to discern which of two pleasant or beneficial courses is the more pleasant or beneficial. A man's relationship to major premisses capable of appearing in a practical syllogism is accordingly one of desire, rational or irrational; and he may then calculate the means to his desired end. But this is not dispassionate calculation: the situation is instinct with emotion throughout; and in Aristotle's view, as in Homer's, the conclusion of the practical syllogism is an action.

The extent to which Aristotle's own values would discourage the development of a stable personality structure will be discussed below.

G. Aristotle's Ideal of Human Behaviour

We may now consider Aristotle's ideal, or rather ideals, of human behaviour, attainable when the passions and desires have been satisfactorily habituated. In Book VI of the *Nicomachean Ethics* he discusses *phronēsis*, practical wisdom, and enquires what its usefulness may be (1143b21 ff.). For Aristotle as for all Greeks the end of life is denoted and commended by *eudaimonia*; and granting that action on the basis of *arete* is conducive to *eudaimonia*, it must be shown that *phronesis* renders us more capable of action on the basis of *arete*. Now

Let us grant that *phronesis* is concerned with things that are just and *kala*, honourable, and *agatha*, beneficial, for a man, and that these are the things

197

which it is the mark of the *agathos* to do; nevertheless we are no more able to act as a result of knowing these things, since the *aretai* are fixed dispositions, *hexeis*, than as a result of knowing things concerned with health and good physical condition, in the sense not of bringing about a healthy condition but of being a manifestation of it;[1] for our capacity for action is not increased as a result of our possessing a knowledge of medicine and gymnastics.

Again, if *phronesis* were valuable in bringing about *arete* in the first place, it would be of no use to those who were already *agathoi*; and indeed it would be of no use to those who were not already *agathoi*; for it would make no difference whether they had *phronesis* or obeyed others who had, and we could behave in the same manner as we do in matters of health: we do not learn medicine in order to become healthy.

Aristotle's solutions to this problem are interesting. In the first place (*E.N.* 1144a1) *phronesis* is an *arete*, an excellence, of a part or aspect of us, and so must be choiceworthy, since all excellences evidently enable us to function better, to be more *agathoi*; and so help us to attain *eudaimonia*. (Anything acknowledged to be an *arete* inevitably takes on the attributes of the traditional *aretai*. We have seen Plato using this earlier[2] in argument.) Secondly (*E.N.* 1144a6), for a full discharge of his function man needs both ethical *arete* and *phronesis*: *arete* makes the goal correct, *phronesis* the means to the goal. Further, just as we say that many people who perform just acts are not yet just, such as those who carry out the prescriptions of the laws either unwillingly, or on account of ignorance or for some other reason than that they are prescribed by law – despite the fact that such people do the things that the good man should do – similarly in order to be *agathos* one must not merely perform certain acts, one must perform them while in a certain condition: one must act as a result of deliberate choice, *prohairesis*, and for the sake of the acts themselves. Now *arete* makes the choice correct, but the discovery of what should be done to put the choice into effect belongs not to *arete* but to another faculty, *phronesis*.

Ethical *arete*, then, results from a proper habituation of desires and

---

[1] That is to say, simply knowing the temperature of the healthy human body does not help one to regulate one's temperature.

[2] Above, pp. 145 f., 167; and cf. *Merit and Responsibility*, chapter XIII.

passions so that they run in harness with reason, to enable *prohaeresis*, a deliberate choice of action in particular circumstances, to occur. *Phronesis*, practical wisdom, however, understands the general pattern of the good life, and is able to determine in particular circumstances which action will be most conducive to the maintenance of that pattern. Aristotle maintains (for in ethics he is always concerned to show that he is merely systematising and rendering more explicit the common opinion of men) that everyone, in defining *arete*, includes the requirement that it should be a disposition 'in accordance with the right rule' (*E.N.* 1144b23); and, says Aristotle, the right rule is that which is in accordance with *phronesis*. In his eyes, however, *arete* must be a disposition not merely in accordance with the right rule, which might occur as a result of ignorance or accident, but a disposition actually accompanied by the right rule: he requires that action be undertaken in knowledge of that rule (*E.N.* 1144b27). *Phronesis* is impossible without full ethical *arete*, and full ethical *arete* without *phronesis*; and Aristotle further concludes on this basis that the *phronimos* must have all the ethical *aretai*: it is impossible for him to have some, not others.

Once again we may enquire whether the analysis is logical or psychological. It has evident logical elements; but psychological analysis cannot be excluded. Aristotle maintains that *phronesis* is impossible without ethical *arete*: without it, *phronesis* would be mere cleverness (*E.N.* 1144a23 ff.), for *arete* must supply the correct goal, which transmutes cleverness into practical wisdom. One might have thought that an intelligent individual who had no stable good disposition, and hence lacked *arete* in Aristotle's sense, might have been able to *comprehend* the ethical goal, and the 'right rule', and so be able to determine what actions were consonant with it. His own desires and passions might prevent him from acting always in accordance with it, even though he fully understood it; but he might give practically wise advice to others, and even act on it himself in favourable circumstances, when not swept away by desire and passion. Aristotle does not consider this possibility; presumably because his concern is with the actual functioning of ethical *arete* and *phronesis* in the *psuche* of an individual who has to take moral decisions.

This concern is not surprising. Aristotle's ideal man, like Plato's and all earlier Greeks', is designed to fit a particular social and political context – a *polis* or city-state, for no Greek thinker had considered the possibility of a satisfactory life in any other context. It will be recalled that Aristotle defined man as a *polītikon zōŏn* (*Politics* 1253a3); and this does not mean 'a political animal', but 'an animal who lives in a *polis*'. Historical *poleis*, however, varied very widely; and Plato, as we have seen, designed two, differing widely from each other and from historical *poleis*. Aristotle's is different from either of Plato's, though closer to the *Laws*-state, and more nearly resembles historical *poleis*; and this affects the characteristics of his ideal citizen.[1] For Plato in the *Republic*, only a few in his *polis* have real ethical knowledge, and these are to communicate 'right opinion' to the rest. The philosopher-king, returned to the Cave, is to be compelled to 'practise implanting in the behaviour of human beings, in public and in private, the patterns he sees in the world of the Forms' (*Republic* 500D). How he is to achieve this is hardly clear; but Plato in the *Republic* is little interested in ordinary men. In the *Laws*, there are no philosopher-kings, and the laws are paramount. In this dialogue, Plato's system of education and conditioning throughout attempts to ensure that reason and passion, rational and irrational desire, pull in the same direction, that of the 'golden cord'.[2] The child will be taught from earliest days that the 'truly' pleasant, the 'truly' *kalon*, honourable and the 'truly' *agathon*, beneficial (for himself) coincide, so that, Plato hopes, his desires will coincide with the dictates of reason. Accordingly, ends are fixed by his conception of *agatha*, what is beneficial for him; and of this he will have indelible right opinion. The means to these ends will be laid down in the laws, which are to be extremely comprehensive and complete. Accordingly, though the inhabitants of the *Laws*-state will know what they are doing and, unless they are too

---

[1] His ideal is a citizen, a citizen in his own ideal state. When (*Pol.* 1276b16) he discusses whether the *agathos* citizen is the same as the *agathos* man, '*agathos* citizen' is relative to the constitution in which he lives (b30); and in any state '*agathos* citizen' will commend the appropriate discharge of one's functions in that state, whatever they are. The *agathos ruler* is the same as the *agathos* man, however (*Pol.* 1277a13); and in Aristotle's ideal *polis* all the citizens are to be rulers, so that these can be *agathoi* citizens and *agathoi* men. From Homer onwards, *arete* commends qualities on the basis of which men claim to rule.

[2] Above, p. 160.

stupid to understand their own laws, why they are doing it, they will never have to make a moral choice, ends being fixed and the means laid down. So long as these citizens behave – to take Aristotle's phrase – 'in accordance with the right rule' – they will enjoy *eudaimonia*; and this suffices Plato.

Aristotle, however, wished, as we have seen[1] (*Pol.* 1295a25), for a kind of constitution for his *polis* in which the majority could share. He may well have realised that, no matter how comprehensive a code of laws, it could not cover every situation: he certainly was averse from the idea of anything so rigid as either of Plato's states. His citizens, however, are not to be the whole of the inhabitants of the *polis* (*Pol.* 1329a17 ff.):

> Besides, the ruling class should be the owners of property, for they are the citizens, and the rulers of a state should be in good circumstances; whereas mechanics, or any other class which is not a producer of *arete*, have no share in the state. This follows from our first principle, for *eudaimonia* cannot exist without *arete*, and a city is not to be termed *eudaimon* in regard to a proportion of its citizens, but in regard to them all.

Aristotle, as has already been said, makes the ordinary usage of words his starting point in ethics. *Arete* in 'ordinary Greek' commended wealth and social position, and *eudaimonia* was held to consist largely in the possession of these. Aristotle argues (*E.N.* 1098b9 ff.) that these are not of primary importance, and insists on the importance of the ethical *aretai*;[2] but all of the usual overtones of *arete* are present, for Aristotle acknowledges as *aretai* all those recognised by the Greeks of his own day. Accordingly, not merely ethical and intellectual excellences appear in his list, but also social excellences, some of which could not be exercised at all without the possession of money and leisure. He included all these qualities in complete *arete*; and in his ideal state only those inhabitants who possessed them would be citizens, and would constitute the government of the *polis*. To these, however, would fall far more occasions for deliberation and planning, both in public and in private life, than Plato would have accorded to them; and accordingly, they must not only be able to behave 'in

[1] Above, p. 180 f.
[2] But see below, p. 207 f.

accordance with the right rule', but must have this and be conscious of it, and be able to plan and deliberate in ethical and political matters. Aristotle's *agathos*, ideal man, is designed to fit into Aristotle's *polis*.

At all events, one of his ideal men is so designed. There is, however, a tension in the *Nicomachean Ethics*, broadly between Books I plus X and Books II to IX. Aristotle's ethics, like other Greeks', is concerned with *eudaimonia*. His reasons for discussing the *aretai* at all is that his view of *eudaimonia* (E.N. 1098a16) is 'an activity of the *psuche* in accordance with *arete*, or if the *aretai* are numerous, in accordance with the best and most perfect'. A survey of the *aretai* is needed to establish which is the best and most perfect; but it may appear surprising that Aristotle should have added this requirement. If a human being has many possible excellences, it would seem best, and most conducive to *eudaimonia*, that he should possess and exercise them all. In the sixth book of the *Nicomachean Ethics* (1145a2) Aristotle says of *phronesis* that even if it were not necessary for action, we should need it since it is the excellence of our deliberative faculty (and each faculty should function as well as possible); and this would justify our acquisition of all the *aretai*, not merely the best and most perfect. *Aristotle* wishes all the *aretai* to be acquired, no doubt; but *eudaimonia* consists in the *activity* of the *psuche* in accordance with *arete* (E.N. 1098a5 ff.); and one cannot exercise all the *aretai* at once. In *Nicomachean Ethics* X Aristotle reverts to the question of the best *arete* (1177a12 ff.):

> If *eudaimonia* is an activity in accordance with *arete*, it is reasonable that it should be in accordance with the best; and this would be the *arete* of the best part of ourselves. Whether it is reason or something else, whose rule seems to be in accordance with *phusis*, and which guides us and takes thought of things honourable and divine, whether it be divine itself or merely the most divine element within us, it is the activity of this element in accordance with its own *arete* that would constitute perfect *eudaimonia*.

The activity turns out to be *theōriā*, intellectual contemplation, activity in accordance with *sophia*, wisdom, the *arete* of that aspect of the intellect concerned with subject-matter not susceptible to change. Aristotle holds that this is the most pleasurable activity (E.N. 1177a23); and it is concerned with the best objects. Plato and Aristotle both hold that theology, astronomy, mathematics and pure thought in general are pursuits far nobler than the study of man, for the objects studied are nobler: Aristotle had said earlier in the *Nicomachean Ethics* (1141a20):

> It is absurd if anyone supposes political action or *phronesis* to be the most important activities, unless it be true that man is the best of the contents of the cosmos.

Furthermore (*E.N.* 1177a27):

> Self-sufficiency, so much discussed, would be an attribute of 'theoretic' activity more than of any other; for a wise man engaged in intellectual contemplation will need the necessaries of life, in the same way as the just man and the rest, but when they are adequately equipped with things of this kind, the just man needs people to whom and with whom he will act justly, as will the self-controlled, the brave and all the others, whereas the wise man can engage in intellectual contemplation by himself, and the wiser he is, the more readily he will be able to do it. It is better perhaps to have colleagues, but nevertheless the wise man is the most self-sufficient.

Again (*E.N.* 1177b1), *theoria* alone seems to be chosen for its own sake, and not for any further results; whereas we gain other things as a result of practical activities. *Eudaimonia*, furthermore, is supposed to reside in the possession of leisure; for we are busy in order that we may gain for ourselves opportunities of leisure. But the life of the man engaged on the affairs of the city is lacking in leisure.

On every count, the life of *theoria* wins. In fact (*E.N.* 1177b26)

> Such a life would be higher than human; for one will not live in this manner in virtue of being a man, but in virtue of the presence within of some divine principle; and its activity will surpass that of activity in respect of the rest of *arete* by as much as that divine principle surpasses the composite nature of the rest of our being. If the reason, compared with man, is divine, the life in accordance with reason is divine in comparison with human life. Accordingly, we should not follow those who counsel us, being men, to think thoughts befitting men, nor being mortal to think mortal thoughts,[1]

---

[1] As did Pindar and other early writers (above, p. 87); but in a very different sense. In such writers, men were being dissuaded from the pursuit of earthly grandeur and glory, the kind of *arete* from excess of which one Greek view held that a man might become a god. Pindar counsels caution lest the Olympian gods should be wroth at such presumption: Aristotle counsels exercise of the divine within oneself, an exercise of which Aristotle's Unmoved Mover will be unaware, for he is unaware of all save himself.

but should live an immortal life so far as in us lies and do everything to
enable ourselves to live in accordance with the best element in us; for even
if this is small in mass, much more does it surpass all the rest in power and
worth. Indeed, each of us would appear to *be* this element in us, since it
is the authoritative and better element.

The last point is a fallacy in terms of Aristotle's own philosophy:
anything should be defined *per genus et differentiam*, and both are
constitutive of that thing. Man is not only his divine spark, but all
his other elements also. Aristotle, in this protreptic encomium of the
life of intellectual contemplation, has allowed himself to be carried
away. He does grant (*E.N.* 1178a9) that life in accordance with the
rest of *arete* is *eudaimonia* in a secondary sense; but much in his philosophy would have permitted him to argue that *eudaimonia* was the
exercise of all the *aretai*, each in its appropriate time and place.[1]
As it is, since *eudaimonia* is the end and *theoria* furnishes the highest
type of *eudaimonia*, then, even though one cannot, being human,
engage in *theoria* continually, *theoria* is always to be preferred to any
other kind of activity whatsoever: if one at any moment has the
choice between *theoria* and a good practical moral action, one should
always choose *theoria*. There is a real tension between *Nicomachean
Ethics* I and X and the remaining books.

It remains to try to determine the sources of this view of the ideal,
and the reasons for its appearance in this form. We saw earlier that
the active intellect disrupts, as a divine or divine-resembling element,
the scheme of *psuche* in Aristotle's account; and it is now apparent
that it disrupts Aristotle's ethics. It may be a legacy from Plato; but
Aristotle must have himself believed profoundly in it, in that he did
include an element so disruptive. Secondly, Aristotle is participating
with the sophists, 'moralist' and 'immoralist', Socrates and Plato in a
movement that is intellectual, and whose intellectual nature takes
priority over its other characteristics, moral or immoral. It is not
surprising that, in the view of all the participants, intellectual qualities
should have precedence. (Plato insists that the philosopher-kings
should return to the cave, *Republic* 519D ff.; but since he acknowledges

[1] See such expressions as 'when one should and in what conditions one should
and to whom one should and for the sake of what one should and as one should
. . . which is the mark of *arete*', *E.N.* 1106b21.

that they will then be less *eudaimon* than if they continued to philosophise, he can offer no adequate reason why they should do so.)

However, the commendation of *theoria* is not conducted solely in terms of philosophical religion and the preferences of an intellectual. *Theoria* renders one self-sufficient, and is carried on in leisure. From Homer onwards, the *agathos* has striven to render his household, so far as is possible, self-sufficient, and his wealth and position have furnished him with leisure, or at least with more leisure than has been available to the other members of society. In the pursuit of self-sufficiency, Greek values are self-centred and self-interested. Friends, *philoi*, are required for their usefulness: a character in Euripides remarks 'when heaven grants good fortune, what need of *philoi*?'; and Aristotle has the utmost difficulty in showing why *agathoi*, in his 'practical' usage, who are sufficiently well-supplied with this world's goods, should have *philoi* at all.[1] The pattern of Greek values had been set by Homeric society, a society of virtually autonomous households, each under its local *agathos*, which needed to be as self-sufficient as possible, and even in the fifth and fourth century B.C. in Athens the primary loyalty was to the household with its *philoi* (which might in some cases constitute a political faction), not to the city, as we have seen. Even in practical life, there was an uneasy tension: *polis*-values were not really suited to *polis*-life. The household under stress became more 'real' than the *polis*, and virtually detached from it. When *theoria*, philosophical activity, appeared to possess all the characteristics so long ascribed to *arete* – and furthermore was legal, and did not involve the risks in the 'immoralists'' route to greater self-sufficiency – small wonder that it was difficult to demonstrate that the philosopher should ever prefer practical activity to *theoria*.

H. Aristotelian Values and Psychological Development

In Greek life in general in the fourth century B.C., the competitive excellences retained an importance similar to that which they had enjoyed in earlier centuries: it should not be supposed that the philosophers affected greatly the values of the mass of Greeks, or even of Athenians. The stresses of such a value-system, accordingly, remained.

[1] See my ' "Friendship" and "Self-sufficiency" in Homer and Aristotle', C.Q. N.S. XIII (1963), pp. 30 ff.

Now Aristotle,[1] in *Problems* 953a10 ff.,[2] links eminence in various fields – philosophy, politics, poetry, the arts – with the possession of the *melancholikos* temperament; and he names Heracles, Ajax, Bellerophon, Plato and Socrates, adding that most of the poets and numerous other *gnōrimoi*, well-known persons, possessed such a temperament. Aristotle supposes that possession of the temperament leads to eminence;[3] but the attempt to attain and preserve one's eminence in a society whose values as a whole discourage the development of a stable personality might well induce irritability, markedly erratic behaviour and even insanity, all of which are treated by Aristotle as characteristic of the *melancholikos* temperament. The stresses, and the externalisation of the criteria of the approved action, place most strain on the *agathos*, the eminent, practitioner in any competitive field; this, it appears, is further evidence that the stresses indeed had such an effect on the personality, for the phenomena as described seem to go beyond anything generally observable in our culture.

We may now enquire whether Aristotle's own values encourage or discourage the development of a more stable personality structure. The end remains *eudaimonia*, the means *arete*; does Aristotle's use of these terms have a different effect from that found in his predecessors and most non-philosophical contemporaries?

Eudaimonia based on practical activity might at first sight appear to do so: 'an activity of the *psuche* in accordance with *arete*' seems to internalise the requirements of *eudaimonia* completely. It is true that it

[1] It is usually held that the *Problems* contains much post-Aristotelian material. This passage may be later than Aristotle in date. From the standpoint of my argument, however, this is of little importance; save that the later the observation could be made of contemporaries (here unnamed, but possibly some of the poets and *gnorimoi* were contemporaries of the writer), the more striking it becomes. (Whatever the date, the view of Plato and Socrates may well depend on anecdotal material.)

[2] I was reminded of this passage in a conversation with my colleague Mr A. E. Wardman, at a time when the Aristotle chapter, and indeed the book as a whole, were almost completed. I was naturally tempted to regard the passage almost as independent confirmation of the thesis advanced in this work; but though I had not realised what I now believe to be the significance of the passage, I was previously aware of its existence, and it may well be part of the unanalysed data which formed the initial stimulus to the work.

[3] 'All *melancholikoi* have remarkable gifts, not on account of disease, but on account of *phusis*' (955a39).

internalises them far more than did the non-philosophical Greek, for whom in general *eudaimonia* still primarily denoted and commended prosperity. However, we have seen that Aristotle includes social *aretai* among his *ēthikai aretai*, and that both *arete* and *eudaimonia* (*Pol.* 1329a19 ff.) are necessarily linked to the possession of property and leisure. It follows that the ability to lead the 'good life' and be *agathos* and *eudaimon* remains linked to matters which are in the last resort out of one's control. Aristotle's discussion in the first book of the *Nicomachean Ethics* illustrates the tensions of his position. In opposition to the common view (*E.N.* 1100b4) he says:

> For it is clear that if we were to make fortune our criterion, we shall call the same person *eudaimon* and again *athlios*, wretched, many times. . . . Or is it in no way correct to make changes of fortune the criterion? For faring well or badly does not reside in these. No; human life requires these in addition, as we have said, but it is activities in accordance with *arete* that are decisive in producing our *eudaimonia*.

Nevertheless, human life does require these things; and some actions in accordance with *arete* require considerable property. A few lines later we find (*E.N.* 1100b22):

> Now many things happen by chance, and these differ in importance. It is clear that small pieces of good or ill fortune do not make a decisive difference to our lives; but the occurrence of many important events will, if they turn out well, render our life more 'blessed' (*makarios*, a stronger word even than *eudaimon*, most frequently used of the gods) . . . while if they turn out unfortunately they crush and harm the *makarion*; for they bring pains upon us and hinder many activities. Yet even in these circumstances the *kalon* shines forth, whenever anyone bears with equanimity many great misfortunes, not through insensitivity to pain, but through nobility and greatness of *psuche*. If the activities are decisive in determining the character of our life, as we have said, none of the *makarioi* would become *athlios*; for he will never do things that are mean and hateful.

Aristotle is here doing his utmost to internalise *eudaimonia*; and goes on to say that the truly *agathos* individual will always make the best use he can of his circumstances, just as the good shoemaker will make the best pair of shoes he can out of the leather available; and he repeats that if this is so (*E.N.* 1101a6) the *eudaimon* would never become *athlios*, but would never be *makarios* either if he met with fortune like Priam's. Aristotle seems at this point to be trying to oppose an internalised *eudaimon* and *athlios* to a *makarios* which includes external *agatha*; but he continues immediately (*E.N.* 1101a8):

> Nor yet is he variable and very liable to change; for he will neither be displaced from his *eudaimonia* readily, nor by any ordinary misfortunes, but by many great ones, nor yet, if he has suffered such misfortunes, would he become *eudaimon* again in a short time. No; if he does so at all, this will occur in a long and complete time when he has become possessed of many great and *kala* things.

Aristotle has not fully internalised *eudaimonia*, from which loss of external *agatha* can still displace one, however well one behaves; and he concludes (*E.N.* 1101a14):

> Why then should we not say that the *eudaimon* is he who engages in activity in accordance with perfect *arete*, and is adequately supplied with external *agatha* not for some chance period of time but throughout a complete life?

Try as he will, Aristotle cannot oppose an internalised *eudaimon* to the *makarios*, for this *eudaimonia* is to be realised in active life in a *polis* by a leisured citizen; and *eudaimonia* and *arete* denote and commend this way of life, which would be impossible in default of external *agatha*. Were he completely to internalise *eudaimonia*, it would become unimportant in this ethics as a whole, and its role would be taken over by *makarios*. This move would be philosophically pointless, and in conflict with ordinary language (on which Aristotle sets a high value in his ethics); for no-one (*E.N.* 1100a8) accounts *eudaimon* anyone who meets with the lot of Priam and dies *athliōs*, in a wretched manner.

The *eudaimonia* and *arete* of the practical life, then, depend in part on circumstances beyond one's control. As Aristotle himself says (*E.N.* 1177a27), he who engages in *theoria* is more self-sufficient, and does not require the resources for a social and political career; so that the theoretic life, it appears, requires fewer external resources. However, he who pursues the theoretic life needs leisure, and some resources to enable him to live a leisured life; and even if Aristotle cannot show why he should ever perform a particular moral act, he is presumably, living in a *polis* as he does, to possess all the Aristotelian *aretai*: he is not to be a hermit in the desert, but an *agathos* in a *polis*. If so, the problem remains.

We may set on the other side that all the co-operative excellences are now *aretai*, and Aristotle represents the performance or non-performance of acts in accordance with these as being under the control of the individual. His *eudaimonia* may be destroyed by external circumstances over which he has no control; but it may also be destroyed by his performance of morally bad acts, which renders the attainment of *eudaimonia* at all events more within one's control than is the case in 'ordinary Greek'. Thus far, but only thus far, Aristotle's view of *eudaimonia* and *arete* encourages the development of a more stable personality structure; and it should not be forgotten that one can only manifest even such *arete* in the context of *arete* as a whole, which requires external *agatha*.

I. Basic Human Nature

The question whether Aristotle had a basic view of human nature, common to all members of the species, requires discussion. We have seen that slaves are by *phusis* endowed merely with sufficient reason to comprehend, but not to reason for themselves (*Pol.* 1254b20); and barbarians (*Pol.* 1252b7) are a community of slaves, male and female, for there is no-one among them who is by *phusis* a ruler. Aristotle (*Pol.* 1327b20 ff.) regarded the Greeks as being especially favoured in their endowment by *phusis*. Plato (*Politicus* 262D) had realised that 'barbarian' simply meant 'not Greek':[1] Aristotle assumes that the difference of word must be accompanied by a real difference. He does assign *aretai* to slaves, however, as well as to women and children, each of which groups differs from the others (*Pol.* 1260a10):

> Although the parts of the *psuche* are present in all of them, they are present in different ways. For the slave has not the power of planning; the woman has it, but it is without authority; the child has it, but it is immature.

[1] He is, however, merely making a *logical* point, which might be accompanied by the view that all non-Greeks, though they differed widely among themselves and should be differently classified, were inferior to Greeks.

As a result (*Pol.* 1260a14), though they must all have the ethical *aretai*, they necessarily have them in different ways. Accordingly, the ruler should have it in perfection (that is to say, he should have it with *phronesis*); the subjects, however, require only so much as is needful for the discharge of their proper function. The moral *aretai* of a man are displayed in commanding, those of a woman in obeying. All classes have their special attributes: one should not maintain with Socrates that *arete* is the same for all persons, but enumerate the *aretai* in the manner of Gorgias. A slave is useful for satisfying our wants, and will need only so much *arete* as will prevent him from failing to carry out his tasks through lack of self-control, or cowardice. Aristotle seems to deny to the artisan (*Pol.* 1260a36) any *arete* at all.

In comparing the *Politics* with the *Nicomachean Ethics*, we must bear in mind that, though the *Ethics* is in a sense the first part of the *Politics*, Aristotle's preoccupations are very different in the two works. In the first he is concerned to analyse the *aretai* in the interest of discovering *eudaimonia*, which must be possessed by the best individual manifesting activity in accordance with the best *arete* or *aretai*. In the *Politics* he is concerned with the functioning of individuals in a state. Now anything that is said to be *agathos* in Greek may be said to have an *arete*. If '*agathos* slave' has a meaning, so has 'the *arete* of a slave'. Now a 'good slave' is one who functions in the manner most convenient to the master of the house; and the roles of the other members of the household may be similarly treated. '*Agathos* citizen', where not all the citizens are concerned in the government, is one who functions in a manner convenient to the rulers: in any state (*Pol.* 1276b30) 'good citizen', and 'the *arete* of the citizen', will commend the discharge of one's functions in that state, whatever they are. It is the *agathos* ruler who coincides with the *agathos* of the *Nicomachean Ethics* (where *theoria* is not in question); and in Aristotle's ideal *polis* all the citizens are to be rulers, so that these men can be – and need to be – *agathoi* citizens and *agathoi* men. I have already mentioned Aristotle's view (*E.N.* 1179b26) that the majority of mankind cannot be stimulated by moral suasion to the pursuit of *kalokagathia*, but must be controlled by punishment. They are of course not assimilating from birth onwards the presuppositions and attitudes of the ruling group, and so are not conditioned to manifest all the Aristotelian *aretai*, from which they are indeed debarred by lack of wealth and social status. The young of the ruling group, indeed, may under favourable circumstances[1] (*E.N.* 1179b7) be capable of ethics and ethical behaviour while still young. Their habituation has worked quickly; but only within this group will the appropriate habituation occur at all.

Now the *values* of this account are those of a member of a leisured class in a patriarchal, slave-owning society, able to impose its own evaluations, for its own convenience, on that society. Aristotle, indeed, is either clearheaded enough to realise this, or inadvertently betrays by his use of language what he has not explicitly formulated. The subjects, and the slaves, *need* only so much *arete* to carry out their functions (*Pol.* 1260a15); and a good subject, or a good woman, or a good slave, will be one who has just so much *arete* as will enable him to do so, neither more nor less. Aristotle need not trouble himself unduly about the *arete* of the artisan: the slave (*Pol.* 1260a40) shares in his master's life, while the artisan is more remote, and causes less convenience or inconvenience by his activities.

However, Aristotle, as we have seen, tries to rationalise these values or prejudices in terms of the analysis of the *Nicomachean Ethics*; and we are justified in asking whether he has any unified concept of human nature at all. *Arete* has a divisive influence, as is usual in Greek writers: perfection seems attainable only by a few leisured Greeks living in well-constituted *poleis*. The conditions are not so rigorous as in Plato's *Laws*, nor the intellectual requirements so rare as in the *Republic*; but the favoured group remains very small when compared with the human race as a whole. And this restriction is based, according to Aristotle, on real differences. When rationalising his prejudices, Aristotle does not say 'these are the *aretai* for the following groups, since it is convenient for the ruler that they should be so', but that these differences exist by *phusis*. Now if slaves and barbarians by *phusis* totally lack the *bouleutikon*, the power of planning, their *psuchai* differ in an important respect from those of the *agathos*, the Greek

---

[1] See above, pp. 181 f. Aristotle does not necessarily imply that the young of the ruling group will always develop so quickly: to be 'liberal' in the sense of *E.N.* 1179b7 ff. it is not sufficient to belong to the ruling group; but is it necessary.

fitted to rule. Indeed, they are incapable of moral action in the full sense of the analysis in the *Nicomachean Ethics*, for this requires *prohairesis*, deliberate choice; and (*E.N.* 1139b4) '*prohairesis* is intellect associated with psychological drive, or psychological drive associated with intellect; and such a source of action is the human being'. It is also (*E.N.* 1139a23) 'psychological drive associated with planning, *bouleutikē*'; and of the faculty of planning, the *bouleutikon*, the slave and the barbarian have none. If Aristotle were always a rigorous systematic thinker – and he is not – he could deny on these grounds that slaves and barbarians were human beings at all.

8. The Stoics

A. Introductory

The Stoic school of philosophy was founded by Zeno of Citium in about 300 B.C. Zeno is said to have come to Athens about fifteen years earlier, to have read works by Plato and Xenophon which gave him an admiration for the character of Socrates, and thus to have been inspired with an enthusiasm for philosophy. His own philosophy and outlook on life, and that of the Greek Stoics in general, certainly *prima facie* resembles that of Socrates, poor and indifferent to money and position, rather than that of Plato or Aristotle; and inspiration could also have been derived from Antisthenes, who had been a pupil of Socrates, imitated the latter's austere life, and taught that *arete* was the sole requirement necessary for the good life;[1] and that *arete* consisted in complete *autarkeia*, independence of one's surroundings and absence of needs. Zeno might have been influenced by the literary record, whether of Plato, Xenophon, or Antisthenes himself; but it is an open question whether the resemblance should be attributed to the influence of Socrates, however exerted, or to social and political changes in the Greek world. Possibly both had their part to play: the philosophy might well be attractive as a starting-point for Zeno because it suited the new situation.

By this time Alexander the Great had lived and died, and his successors, to the accompaniment of large-scale warfare, had divided his empire into large segments, over which they ruled. The day of the city-state as a fully autonomous unit was over. Hindsight inevitably gives us a clearer realisation of this fact than can have been available to the Greeks of the period; but even a Greek of little perspicacity must have been aware that his life could now be affected by decisions,

---

[1] Aristotle knows, and opposes, certain tenets that were later characteristic of the Stoics: 'the *agathos* is *eudaimon* even in misfortune', *E.N.* 1096a1, 'the *agathos* is *eudaimon* even on the rack', 1153b19. He is also aware of a definition of the *aretai* as *apatheiai* and *ēremiai*, calms, *E.N.* 1104b24.

taken far from his own *polis*, over which his own *polis* had no control; and when wars swept over the Greek world these were on a much larger scale than in the days of the *polis*. Now an inhabitant of a much larger political unit, the Greek must have felt his stature diminished by comparison, and himself threatened by forces utterly beyond his control. Some kind of consolation and orientation was urgently needed; and one of the roles of both Stoicism and of Epicureanism is to satisfy this need. Plato was concerned to solve a pressing problem of values in the *polis* as he knew it, whether by means of logic and *elenchus* or by the creation of ideal *poleis* in the *Republic* and *Laws*. Aristotle, in the *Ethics* and *Politics*, analysed and delineated the characteristics of the best kind of man in the best kind of *polis*. Each agreed, as had their predecessors, that the *polis* alone furnished the necessary environment for the full development and perfection of man, whom Aristotle defined as 'the creature that lives in a *polis*'. Now the importance of the *polis* was, quite suddenly, reduced: the Stoics and Epicureans had to create a new frame of reference.

However, the difference should not be over-emphasised; as it is over-emphasised if one opposes the new situation to an idealised past in which Greeks lived in *poleis* of co-operating citizens all acknowledging the claims of law and justice as paramount; for, as we have seen, Athens, the only *polis* of which we have detailed knowledge, was quite different from this. In Athens, provided that the interests of his own household did not conflict with those of the *polis*, the *agathos* did indeed confer benefits on his *polis*, a unit of moderate size in which one person's contribution could be noticed, and one whose well-being he might hope to affect by his own efforts; but insofar as he did so, and contributed to the successful defence of the *polis* in war and to its finances in peace or war, he was doing a favour to a larger unit than that to which he owed his primary loyalty, his own household and its *philoi* (which might, if he were active in politics, constitute a political faction). Such contributions to the *polis* furnished the *agathos* with the grounds for his claim to be termed *agathos* by his fellow-citizens, to enjoy, with his household and friends, superior status in the *polis* and, should he be brought into court, to be acquitted on the grounds of his *arete* even if he had behaved unjustly.[1] His *arete* was more important than his *dikaiosune*;[2] the function of *arete* was primarily to ensure the security, prosperity and stability of the household, only secondarily – and as a favour – that of the *polis*; and the *agathos* and his household expected benefits and privileges in return for the favour. For, from Homer to Aristotle, Greek ideals were essentially self-centred and self-interested. When the *polis* developed, its claims existed in an uneasy tension with those of the individual, his family and his *philoi*; and the latter, in a crisis, when a choice had to be made between the two, were likely to be allotted first place. The household and its *philoi* constituted a more 'real' unit than the *polis*.

There was, nevertheless, a reciprocity in the relationship of the *agathos* to his *polis*. He bestowed favours and received privileges; and it was also true that the combined military forces of the city – the *agathoi* as a group – served to protect the individual *agathos* and his household. Now, with the coming of Alexander, the status of the *polis* had been diminished: political and military forces could be seen to be at work on a much larger scale. The individual *agathos* had small chance of preserving the prosperity and stability of his household, the *agathoi* as a group small chance of preserving that of the *polis*, should some great political or military wave sweep across the new larger unit in which they were now living. (Complete disaster might have overwhelmed the city before; but the likelihood was now more evident.) Now *arete*, in commending human nature and behaviour at their best, had always commended the ability of the *agathos* to secure the prosperity and stability first of his own household, then of

[1] See *Merit and Responsibility*, chapter X.

[2] By the fourth century, a number of writers were engaged in trying to persuade (as distinct from trying to convince by philosophic argument, in the manner of Plato) the 'ordinary Athenian' that the co–operative excellences were *aretai*, that *dikaiosune* is part of *arete*. For reasons I have set forth elsewhere (cf. *Merit and Responsibility*, pp. 336 ff.) it was easier to argue that those who were already *agathos* on other grounds should include *dikaiosune* in their *arete* than that the possession of *dikaiosune* in itself rendered one *agathos*. The extent to which the 'ordinary Athenian' held this view is difficult to determine: those whom we meet in private forensic speeches seem unconvinced; and the Athenian orator seems not to suppose that his audiences will consistently take this view (cf. *Merit and Responsibility*, pp. 213 f.). The tensions between the claims of the household and the *polis* were unresolved in the fourth century, even if some development had taken place since the fifth century.

the *polis*, and still had these overtones and raised these expectations; but the expectations might well appear impossible of fulfilment in the new scheme of things; and the day of the *polis* as an autonomous unit of a comprehensible size, with which one might emotionally identify oneself even if one's primary loyalties were to a smaller unit, was over. The individual and his family were very much thrown back on their own resources, emotionally and in every other way. Men urgently needed some standard, some guide, some consolation, and were likely to seek one which, so far as possible, satisfied the expectations of traditional *arete*: could *arete* be rehandled in such a way as to fulfil these expectations in a manner which suited the new conditions of life?

B. The Problem of the Sources

The Stoic school of philosophy – called 'Stoic' after the *Stŏā Poikilē*, or Painted Portico, the hall in Athens in which Zeno and his successors used to teach – contains many names famous in the ancient world; but their writings exist, if at all, only in fragments. Among the early Stoics were Cleanthes of Assos and Chrysippus of Soli, who was a copious writer and systematised the doctrines of the school; Ariston of Chios; Herillus of Carthage; and Dionysius of Heraclea. Diogenes of Seleucia, head of the Stoic school in succession to Zeno, Cleanthes, Chrysippus, and Zeno of Tarsus, went to Rome as an ambassador in 156–5 B.C., and lectured while there, thus introducing Stoic doctrines into Rome. These doctrines, suitably adapted by the later Greek Stoics Panaetius of Rhodes and Posidonius of Apamea, became the ethic of the more enlightened members of the Roman governing class; but this lies beyond the scope of the present book.

Where sources are so fragmentary, it is impossible to attempt to distinguish the doctrines of the above-named philosophers without much more argument than space permits: what follows is, on the whole, an account of the views of the earlier Stoa,[1] rather than a presentation of the views of any individual Stoic.[2]

[1] Some of the differences in doctrine of the Stoics named above are mentioned in the list of ancient authors at the end of this book.

[2] Source material for the Stoics is collected in Von Arnim, *Stoicorum Veterum Fragmenta*, 4 vols. (Teubner, 1905–1924). Quotations will be referred to this work, abbreviated to *S.V.F.*, with volume, page and line number.

C. *Phusis*

Phusis has a multiple usage in Stoic writers, one related to the cosmos as a whole, and two to human beings, in different senses. One sense is given by Philo, and related to other Stoic concepts, as follows (*S.V.F.* II, 149, 36):

> *Hexis* is shared also by objects without *psuche*, such as stones and logs of wood; and those aspects of ourselves which resemble stones, namely our bones, partake of *hexis*. *Phusis* extends as far as plants, and there are in ourselves aspects which resemble plants, namely nails and hair: *phusis* is *hexis* which is already capable of motion (or change). *Psuche* is *phusis* with the addition of imagination and desire or impulse; and this is shared by animals without reason. Our mind has something analogous to the *psuche* of the irrational animal. Again, the power of thought is peculiar to mind, and the power of reasoning is perhaps shared with more divine *phuseis*, but among mortal creatures peculiar to man.

In another passage appended to this in *S.V.F.*, Philo assigns to *phusis* the capacity for nurture, change and growth. It is evident that *phusis* in this usage has the same role as nutritive *psuche* in the Aristotelian analysis of the human being, animals and plants (and also that *hexis* has a different usage from Aristotle's). *Phusis* is transparently from the same root as *phunai*, to grow; and earlier chapters have shown that this fact was present to the mind of fifth-century writers. It is a very appropriate word to use for that aspect of plants, animals and human beings which attends to the functions of growth, nutriment, digestion, breathing, adjustments of body temperature, and so on. The Stoics may well have felt that these functions differed so radically both from imagination and impulse and from thought that they should not be included in *psuche*; and it will be observed that this passage also distinguishes thought and intelligence from *psuche*.

This usage is characteristic of Stoic writers: Galen (*S.V.F.* II, 212, 5) speaks of

> the *psuche* in the semen, which was called nutritive (*phutikē*) by the Aristotelians, appetitive (*epithūmētikē*) by Plato, and by the Stoics not *psuche* at all, but *phusis*, since they thought that it formed the embryo, but was not only not wise but altogether irrational.

However, the Stoics had a wider use of *phusis* (Philo has a wider use in the last line of the passage above; but Philo is an eclectic, and this may affect his use of language here). Alexander of Aphrodisias, an Aristotelian philosopher and commentator of the third century A.D., records (*S.V.F.* II, 272, 38) that

> The Stoics hold that this cosmos, which is one and contains all existent things within itself, and is governed by *phusis*, which is alive and has reason and intelligence, has the eternal governance of all things that are, proceeding along a certain chain and ordering of causes, the first of these functioning as causes for those that come afterwards. . . .

Phusis, then, pervades the whole cosmos, has life and intelligence, and controls all things, these being linked to one another by an ineluctable chain of causes. We are informed (*S.V.F.* I, 44, 35) that Zeno in his work on *phusis* identified *heimarmenē*, the Stoic word for this chain of causes, with *phusis* and *pronoia*, forethought and foreknowledge; and elsewhere (*S.V.F.* II, 269, 14) Zeus, the chief god of the Greeks, is added to the list. Alexander of Aphrodisias (*S.V.F.* II, 273, 25) adds the following:

> They say that *heimarmene* itself and *phusis* and the *logos*, reason or rule, in terms of which the whole cosmos is administered, is God; and this is in all things which are and come to be, and makes use of the individual *phusis* of all things that are with a view to the organisation of the whole.

Chrysippus (*S.V.F.* II, 292, 15) is said to have identified *heimarmene* with Atropos, Adrasteia, Ananke and Pepromene, all earlier names for necessity or goddesses dispensing to man 'what is to happen to him'; but whereas earlier Greeks did not believe that everything was subject to these deities or forces,[1] the Stoics did hold this view. (How they attempted to reconcile it with free will will be discussed below.) The change may be in part due to contact with more rigidly deterministic views arriving in Greece from further east; but the belief in a necessity controlling all actions and events could as readily be reached simply by drawing out the logical conclusions of beliefs and philosophical or scientific presuppositions already present in Greece. From Homer onwards, the gods are said to know everything; but the

---

[1] See *Merit and Responsibility*, pp. 11 ff., 17 f., 20 f., 116 ff., 324.

consequences of this generalisation are not drawn out. Oracles flourish from early times; but oracles depend on the belief that the future can be known combined with the belief that, at least in some cases, if it is known something can be done about it. The gods, or some power, are believed to strew calthrops in one's path; but with due fore-warning one may succeed in avoiding most of them. Anxiety about the future produces the oracle as an institution; and if the belief contains illogicalities, the anxiety is powerful enough to prevent dispassionate analysis of the situation; and, in pre-philosophical days, no-one is likely to have the intellectual resources to analyse it.[1] For the Presocratics, *phusis* is a cycle of material changes following certain fixed rules; but they seem not to have drawn conclusions about human behaviour from their cosmological speculations. Aeschylus (*Prometheus Bound* 518) says that not even Zeus can escape *peprōmenē*; but this is only one attitude, and others occur even within the same play. All these beliefs and attitudes occur already in Greece; but they are not systematised, and the implications are not considered.

Whatever the stimulus,[2] the Stoics now proceeded to draw out the implications. Like the Presocratics, they were materialists; and in this they differ from Plato and Aristotle. Plato may sometimes have used language of the *psuche* which implied materiality: in the *Phaedo* (81C) he explains the existence of ghosts by the theory that the *psuche* of non-philosophers is still interpenetrated with the corporeal; a condition, one might have supposed, only possible for something itself material.[3] In general, however, Plato clearly draws the sharpest of distinctions between the realm of *psuche* and the Forms and that of the material world. Aristotle's *psuchai*, being principles of arrangement, are evidently not material; and the immortal *nous*, which comes in 'from outside' to the human being, 'is in its essential nature an activity' (*De Anima* 430a18). But the Stoics are materialists throughout: indeed, they are more materialists than were the Presocratics, whose influence on both Stoics and Epicureans is apparent, for the Presocratics were

---

[1] The Stoics themselves favoured the belief in oracles. See *S.V.F.* II, 342–4 ff.

[2] The possible social and environmental reasons for the adoption of such a view of life are discussed at the end of this chapter, pp. 230 ff.

[3] And thus far an attitude at least related to earlier Greek ideas, e.g. corpse-feeding, above, p. 68.

writing when the distinction between material and non-material had not yet been drawn. For them, *phusis* is fire (*S.V.F.* I, 44, 1); but since everything in the cosmos is material, fire may be endowed with reason. It is divine and, spread through the universe, orders everything; and the Stoics interpret this with rigour, at least in intention: the chain of causes is eternal, and includes everything within its influence. Such fire (*S.V.F.* I, 34, 22) is not ordinary fire, but 'technic' or creative fire: ordinary fire consumes, converts into itself what it feeds on, whereas creative fire, which is *phusis* (in both the narrower and the wider usage) and *psuche*, increases and conserves, and does not consume. The reason why these two kinds of fire behave so differently is left obscure, like much else in Stoic physics: the attention of the Stoics is really directed elsewhere.

The 'technic' fire that is *phusis*, being God and Providence, acts purposively, in an manner far surpassing that of the human craftsman (*S.V.F.* II, 308, 12):

> The products of *phusis* are not merely finished on the surface, but are given form and moulded throughout their whole being: their inner complexities are finished with attentive skill. The products of *techne*, craft, are given exterior form, as in the case of statues; but their inner parts are not moulded. Accordingly, they say that in the case of things produced by *techne* the maker is separate and works from outside, whereas in the case of those things that are produced by *phusis* the power that shapes and produces them is present in the *hule*, matter.

For Aristotle's teleology, *phusis* works as final cause: it is the goal of perfection at which each thing aims. The Stoics, equally impressed by the complexity of the world about them, treat their *phusis* rather as an immanent efficient cause, working intelligently and with purpose and providence: a picture which gives greater emphasis to the continuity and unity of the chain of causes throughout the cosmos.

This is made very explicit. Chrysippus (*S.V.F.* II, 269, 22) held that

> Since the common *phusis* extends through all things, it will be necessary for everything that happens in any way, whether in the whole or any of its parts, to happen in accordance with it and its rational principle (*logos*) in respect of the sequence of causes, without any possibility of its being

prevented. For neither is there anything from without that can prevent its governance, nor has any of the parts any means whereby it may be moved or situated otherwise than in accordance with the common *phusis*.

'The common *phusis*' is the fire, the godhead, the divine reason, the providence, the *heimarmene*, that extends throughout the whole universe; and this controls to the last detail every aspect of the particular *phusis* in each individual thing (as we are justified in terming it from such passages as *S.V.F.* II, 273, 25 above): all are linked by an ineluctable chain of causation. Now 'every aspect of every thing' includes human beings: in this usage of *phusis*, which is the important usage for human behaviour, the controlling *phusis* governs and directs every action: it is not merely concerned with heart-beat, breathing, growth and those aspects of human existence and development which are evidently the result of natural processes. Every human action is, through the chain of causes, controlled by *phusis*, which is at the same time divine providence and *heimarmene*, and possesses all the other qualities listed above; and the *phusis* is diffused through the entire chain, for 'God is the *psuche* of the cosmos' (*S.V.F.* I, 120, 37); and that *psuche* is everywhere.

The Stoics believed that God who is also fire had produced the entire cosmos from himself by processes of change reminiscent of those in Presocratic nature-philosophy; and that at the end of a world-aeon he took the whole cosmos into himself again, by a process called *ekpurōsis*, all things becoming fire once more.

The effects of the Stoic doctrine of *phusis* on their view of human nature and behaviour will be considered below.

D. Psuche

For the Stoics, as we have seen, the cosmos has *psuche*. We are informed by Diogenes Laertius (*S.V.F.* II, 191, 34) that Chrysippus, Apollodorus and Posidonius all held that the cosmos is a living creature, with reason, *psuche* and *nous*; for (37)

> What is alive is better than what is dead; now nothing is better than the cosmos; therefore the cosmos is a living creature; and it has *psuche*; as is clear from the fact that our *psuche*, which comes from there, is a fragment of it.

Insofar as the step from 'living creature' to 'possessed of *psuche*' is necessary, it is so because plants, though alive, have no *psuche* in Stoic terminology: 'being alive' and 'having *psuche*' are no longer coextensive. Since the Stoic God, as we have seen, is fire and intelligence, and the intelligence naturally resides in *psuche*, it will come as no surprise to learn that the world-*psuche* is fiery, as are our *psuchai*, which are derived from it. The Stoics (*S.V.F.* II, 223, 11) held that *psuche* was immortal, but material (*soma*), and resulted from the cooling (*peripsuxis*) of the surrounding air, as a result of which it is called *psuche*. This seems an odd account of a fiery substance; but there is something more basic than *psuche*, to which *phusis* and *hexis* also may be referred: *pneuma*. This, the ordinary Greek word for 'breath', is used by the Stoics of God in their sense: so (*S.V.F.* II, 299, 11) God is 'intelligent and fiery *pneuma*, with no form or shape, but able to change into whatever he wishes'. This *pneuma* is spread throughout the whole cosmos, and is indeed God or *phusis* in the wider sense, appearing in stones as *hexis*, in plants as *phusis* in the narrower sense, in human beings and animals as *psuche* (*S.V.F.* II, 205, 17); and the *pneuma* of *phusis* is damper and cooler, that of *psuche* drier and warmer (*S.V.F.* II, 205, 13). That such a *psuche* was produced by cooling was found quaint already in the ancient world (*S.V.F.* II, 222, 18). The influence of Heraclitus is present in this aspect of Stoic thought.

The *psuche* is that which gives us life, and all the functions of perception and sensation that accompany being alive. Zeno and Chrysippus offered the kind of argument found in the Presocratics for the identification of breath[1] with *psuche* (*S.V.F.* II, 235, 20):

The Stoics say that the heart is the seat of the principal part of the *anima* (the Latin translation for *psuche*; our authority here is Chalcidius). . . . Zeno's argument for identifying *anima* with breath runs as follows: that assuredly is *anima* at whose departure the animal dies; when the 'natural breath' departs the animal dies; therefore 'natural breath' is *anima*.

Chrysippus' argument is similar. The various senses are explained as follows (*S.V.F.* II, 238, 32):

[1] The Greek word is *pneuma*; but the usage is distinct from the technical use discussed here.

Psuche is *pneuma* which comes to be along with us, and is diffused through the entire body, so long as the ability to breathe which accompanies life is present in the body. The parts of the *psuche* are assigned to each part of us: that which goes into the windpipe we call voice; that which goes into the eyes, sight; that which goes into the nostrils, smell; that which goes into the tongue, taste; and that which goes into our flesh in general, touch....

This, and the other Stoic accounts discussed so far in this chapter, resemble Presocratic nature-philosophy not only in the building bricks of which they construct the cosmos, but in their general indifference to the phenomena which they purport to explain: there is no resemblance whatsoever between voice and taste, or between *pneuma* as it is manifested in human beings and *pneuma* as it is manifested in stones. The whole Stoic cosmology and physics are *a priori*, and have some purpose other than explaining the phenomena; a point which will be of importance later in the discussion.

An important novelty in the Stoic view of *psuche* concerns the role and nature of the passions and desires. Plutarch informs us (*S.V.F.* III, 111, 13):

All these writers (the Stoics, Ariston, Zeno, Chrysippus) . . . think that the affective and irrational part of the *psuche* is not distinguished from the rational part by some difference residing in *phusis*, but that it is the same part of the *psuche* as the rational part, which they call intelligence and 'the directing, leading function' (*hēgemonikon*).

and again (*S.V.F.* III, 111, 27):

Some say that emotion is not different from reason . . . but that there is a direction of the one element of ourselves, reason, in each direction, which escapes our notice because of the quickness and rapidity of the changes. . . . Desire, anger, fear and everything else of this kind are bad opinions and judgments, which do not occur with reference to one aspect of the *psuche* alone, but are swingings, yieldings, assents and drives, and, in short, activities which soon change, pertaining to the whole directing function (*hegemonikon*). . . .

Emotions and passions are (not 'result from') bad opinions and judgments: the affective and rational parts of the *psuche* are one, namely reason. It would seem possible to assert the unity of these aspects of the *psuche* without reducing both to reason: how the Stoics came to do so will be discussed below.

The early Stoics say little of the eschatology of the *psuche*; but *psuchai* of those who were wise, and therefore *agathoi*, were believed to persist intact until the next *ekpurosis*, while those of the foolish persisted for a much shorter period (*S.V.F.* II, 223, 18); an advantage to the *agathos* undoubtedly, but not one that could be usefully employed in a theodicy, to balance the evil apparent in a cosmos supposed to be controlled by a benevolent power. (The Stoics, as we shall see, had a different solution.)

E. Human Excellence and the Human Goal

The goal of human existence is, not surprisingly, denoted and commended by *eudaimonia*; for all Greeks, as Aristotle says in the *Nicomachean Ethics* (1095a17), are agreed on the word, though their interpretations may differ. (The word raises certain expectations throughout, as will appear.) Stobaeus (*S.V.F.* III, 6, 7) informs us:

> They say that the end is *eudaimonein* (to have *eudaimonia*), for the sake of which all things are done, while it is itself done with no further goal in view; and that this is found in living in accordance with *arete*, in living conformably, *homologoumenōs*, and again, this being the same thing, in living in accordance with *phusis*. Zeno defined *eudaimonia* thus: *eudaimonia* is a smooth flowing of life. They say that *eudaimonia* is set up as a goal, the end being to attain *eudaimonia*, to do which is the same as *eudaimonein*.

Elsewhere Stobaeus (*S.V.F.* III, 5, 16) adds the information that Zeno held that the goal was 'living conformably, *homologoumenōs*'; that Cleanthes extended the definition to 'living conformably to *phusis*'; while for Chrysippus it became 'living according to one's experience of the things which happen by *phusis*'. Diogenes Laertius (*S.V.F.* I, 126, 28) informs us that Chrysippus understood the *phusis* in accordance with which one ought to live, as both the common *phusis* (of the cosmos in general) and in particular human *phusis*, while Cleanthes only allowed that one should follow the common *phusis*, not the particular one. (Since *phusis* in this usage clearly refers to 'human nature' as a whole, not simply its nutritive aspect, and human beings are bound into the same chain of causation as everything else, it

The Stoics

would appear that to live in accordance with any aspect of *phusis* would be to live in accordance with the whole; the distinction seems unimportant.)

The linking of *eudaimonia* with living in accordance with *arete* recalls Aristotle and Plato. However, there are striking differences, when the complete Stoic position is taken into account. Aristotle (*E.N.* 1101a14) says:

> What then prevents us from terming *eudaimon* the man who engages in activity in respect of perfect *arete* and is adequately supplied with, *choregeisthai*, external *agatha*, good things, not for some chance period but during a complete life?

Arete is necessary, but so are external *agatha*: Aristotle's *agathos*, as we have seen, is to be a leisured member of the governing class of a *polis*. The Stoics take a very different view. Philo seems to reflect Stoic attitudes[1] when he says (*S.V.F.* III, 177, 29):

> No-one is in want at all who has as the supplier of his needs (*choregos*) the riches of *phusis* that cannot be taken away: first, the air, the first and most necessary and continuous nourishment, breathed uninterruptedly by night and by day; then springs of water in abundance . . . to use for drinking; then for food the produce of all kinds of plants and trees which always bear their harvests in due season.

Nature supplies all the needs of the simple life; and Philo is explicitly contrasting the certainty of such wealth with the hazards of the life of the wealthy man, whom a sudden disaster may render poor. Evidently no-one can exist without a modicum of food and water; but the Stoics treat the minimum as all that is necessary. *Eudaimonia*, however, depends not on these, but on *arete* alone. Stobaeus (*S.V.F.* I, 47, 19) reports that

[1] The attribution is not certain: Philo is an eclectic, and does not here mention the Stoics; but the reflection suits the Stoic outlook in general, and in particular the passages in *S.V.F.* III, 177–180. Chrysippus is there stated to have quoted with approval lines of Euripides maintaining that a diet of bread and water is all that one needs. I cite the Philo passage for the use of *choregos*, which serves to point the difference between this view and Aristotle's.

Zeno says that . . . of existents some are *agatha*, some are *kaka*, some indifferent. *Agatha* are such as the following: practical wisdom, self-control, justice, courage and everything that is *arete* or partakes of *arete*. *Kaka* are such as the following: folly, license, injustice, cowardice, and everything that is *kakia* or partakes of *kakia*. Indifferent are the following: life, death, fame, obscurity, pain, pleasure, wealth, poverty, disease, health, and things of this nature.

Nothing is *agathon* but to be *agathos*, nothing *kakon* but to be *kakos*;[1] and to be *agathos* is to live in accordance with *phusis*, to be *kakos* to live not in accordance with *phusis*. The Stoic was not, however, enjoined necessarily to eat only bread, drink only water, and possess only such garments as would keep him warm. (Even these would not be *agatha*.) Provided that he clove to the belief that only *arete* is *agathon*, he might have possessions such as were in accordance with *phusis*; but these were not *agatha*, merely 'promoted' (*prŏēgmena*), in opposition to things held to be against *phusis*, which were 'demoted' (*apoprŏēgmena*); and these two categories are merely categories of the indifferent, which in no way affect one's *eudaimonia*. Life itself, and death, are listed among the indifferent: if the Stoic found it impossible to live life in accordance with *arete*, he might commit suicide; and many famous Roman Stoics did so. Now those things which are in accordance with *phusis* are, for example, health, strength, and soundness of one's organs of perception (*S.V.F.* III, 34, 15), those against *phusis*, disease, weakness and a maimed condition. Health and such qualities are indifferent so far as regards living 'becomingly' (in which resides living *eudaimonōs*, with *eudaimonia*); but they are not indifferent so far as regards their being in accordance with *phusis*.

The Stoic will naturally choose the *proegmena*, reject the *apoproegmena*, so far as he has the chance; though most of those mentioned above are not matters in which one is given free choice; but his *eudaimonia* depends on his *arete*, and on his *arete* alone. There appears to be a certain inconsistency here, in the matter of living 'in accordance with *phusis*', which some of our sources assert to be synonymous with

---

[1] The justification of such an assertion remains what it was in Plato and Aristotle (above, pp. 145 ff., 167, 197 f.): an *arete* is a human excellence, and *arete* as a whole renders the individual a good specimen of human being. See below, pp. 233 ff.

'living in accordance with *arete*', and both to be synonymous with *eudaimonia*; for it is just as much in accordance with *phusis* to be a healthy human being as to be a brave one. The answer in Stoic terms, terms quite familiar from Socrates, Plato, and Aristotle, is that the *psuche* (and *nous*) is more important than the body; but where earlier thinkers might have relegated health, strength and other bodily *agatha* to a lower plane of *agatha*, Stoic rigour denies that they are *agatha* at all.

The question of 'living in accordance with *phusis*' poses serious problems for the Stoic, as will be apparent from the discussion so far: if the whole of the cosmos is linked by a nexus of causes from which there is no escape, and *phusis*, God, providence, *heimarmene*, all names for the same phenomenon, sustain and are responsible for this chain of causes, surely one cannot live otherwise than in accordance with *phusis*? And if one must do so, if there is no free will, where are virtue and vice? The Stoic answer (*S.V.F.* I, 118, 24 and cf. II, 282, 20 and subsequent fragments) is that *heimarmene* will cause one to act in just the same manner, willy-nilly; but that it is ethically important whether one, so to speak, co-operates with *heimarmene* or not:

> Lead me, O Zeus, and you, *pepromene*,[1] to the place to which I am assigned by you; for I will follow without hanging back. And if I am not willing and show myself to be *kakos*, I shall follow just the same.

One's *arete* is demonstrated by willing co-operation with *heimarmene*, which is also *phusis*: *arete*, it might appear better to say, is living *voluntarily* according to *phusis*, since one will live according to *phusis* whether one likes it or not. The position is radically unsound from a logical point of view, as opponents of the Stoics in the ancient world were quick to point out; for if the chain of causes runs throughout the whole cosmos, and all is material and subject to that chain of causes, the individual's attitude to the knowledge is presumably, for good or ill, just as much the resultant of a physical chain of causation as are his actions.

Setting this illogicality aside, one might have thought that an

---

[1] Both Zeus and *pepromene* are synonyms for *heimarmene* in Stoic thought.

appropriate attitude to whatever one found oneself to have done would be held to suffice; that the Stoic would be advised to spend his life simply putting his seal of approval on sequences of actions over which he had no control. Of course, whatever one's view of causation, one's subjective experience of life is not at all like this: if one spent one's life waiting to see what the ineluctable processes of causation would cause one to do next, one would do little, though physiological events would continue. In fact, the Stoic goal is to live in accordance with reason, and *arete* and the several *aretai* are defined accordingly: Diogenes Laertius (*S.V.F.* III, 65, 5) says:

> Of the *aretai*, some are primary, others subordinate to these: the primary are the following: practical wisdom, courage, justice, self-control. . . . Practical wisdom is the knowledge of things which are *agatha*, *kaka* and indifferent, justice knowledge of what things are to be chosen, what to be avoided, and what neither. . . .

The emphasis is on knowledge and choice; and this suits the cosmological doctrine of *phusis* extremely badly. However, from this aspect of Stoic thought there follows the doctrine of the wise man, the *sophos* (Latin, *sapiens*) who possesses all the *aretai*, or rather *arete* as a whole, on the basis of his knowledge.[1] Since *arete* is knowledge, the separate *aretai* being merely knowledge exercised in particular fields, it follows that the truly wise individual will have *arete*, and he alone, for the Stoics would not have termed knowledge anything which fell short of the complete knowledge required for ethical behaviour. Accordingly, Zeno (*S.V.F.* I, 49, 21) held that the *aretai* were inseparable in practice, though logically distinguishable from each other; and Plutarch (*S.V.F.* III, 73, 29) records that Chrysippus said:

> The *aretai* accompany one another not merely in the sense that anyone who possesses one of them possesses all, but also that anyone who does anything in accordance with one *arete* acts in accordance with them all; for he denies both that a man can be perfect who does not possess all the *aretai* and that an action can be perfect that is not performed in accordance with all the *aretai*.

[1] It follows that the *arete* of all human beings is the same; and this is shared with gods too, *S.V.F.* I, 129, 9.

In every aspect of their system, even where these do not cohere with one another, the Stoics' quest is for complete harmony and perfection. One result here is to deny *arete* to all save a very few human beings, and grant it to those only towards the end of their lives: a conclusion not so surprising to the ancient world as it perhaps is to us, for *arete* had always been a prerogative of the few, and granted to them in virtue of circumstances over which they had no control. Stoicism – this aspect of Stoicism – not only swept away external *agatha* from the concept of *arete*, but also emphasised personal choice, however illogically. If *arete* was still denied to the majority of mankind, it was denied not in respect of externals that they did not possess, nor of a leisured life that their lack of external *agatha* prevented them from leading, nor yet of a knowledge so remote as to be accessible only to a few, as a result of some experience that had happened to them before coming into this world: this *arete* was lacking through failure to achieve knowledge of a much less esoteric kind; a failure to understand *phusis* and what was in accordance with it, what not; and this knowledge was by no means ineffable, but could be communicated by the Stoic wise man; though precisely how knowledge of this kind helped an individual to act appropriately in a particular situation, how he decided what *arete* demanded, was as unclear to critics of Stoicism in the ancient world as it has been to modern writers on the subject. To know that one should act in accordance with *phusis*, and that the *aretai* are the only true *agatha*, furnishes a firm ethical framework; but how does it help one to determine which action of those possible at any point is an expression of *arete*, and so conducive to one's *eudaimonia*? An answer will be attempted below, in the light of Stoicism as a whole.

The nature of our sources renders it unclear how far the early, Hellenistic Stoa – and it is with this, not with the Graeco-Roman Stoa, that we are concerned – troubled itself about the majority of mankind, who did not possess *arete* in the full Stoic sense, and so, in Stoic eyes, possessed no *arete* at all. When Stoicism was Romanised, the idea of progress towards the goal of *arete* received great emphasis. Panaetius, for example, gave prominence to the improvability of man; and later, in the first century A.D., the Roman Seneca wrote (*Epistulae Morales* 73, 15):

The gods are not disdainful: they hold out a helping hand to those who are climbing.

The fragments of the early Stoics, however, concern themselves little with those who are not already perfect; and some scholars have concluded that these writers cared nothing for the mass of mankind. Others have denied this, for the fragmentary sources – which are far less extensive than their bulk would suggest, for later Greek writers tend to cite, or comment on, passages relating to the same points, and the lost Stoic writers were voluminous – do not necessarily present a complete picture. We are left with inference and conjecture, which must be based on our view of the purpose of Stoic doctrine as a whole; and this will be discussed at the end of the chapter.

Unlike the ideals of Plato and Aristotle, the ideal of the Stoics is not set in the context of the *polis*: the *polis* no longer played a role that would have rendered this possible. The individual was thrown back upon his own resources; and many thinkers might have left the matter there. However, we find in Philo (*S.V.F.* III, 79, 38)

This cosmos is a *megalopolis*, a great city, and uses one constitution and one law. The *logos* (reason or principle) of *phusis* enjoins what must be done, and forbids what must not be done.

One should be a citizen of this great city rather than of the cities of men[1] and follow the laws laid down by *phusis*. Men, accordingly, are fellow-citizens with all the intelligent inhabitants of the universe: they not only live under the law of the whole, which is the reason or principle of *phusis*, but, since that principle is also Zeus and providence, they are fellow-citizens of the most high God.

F. Conclusion

It now remains to sum up, and if possible to account for, the Stoic tenets concerning man and his position in the cosmos of which a brief survey has been given. We have seen that the Stoics advanced a theory of total determinism which went far beyond anything demanded, or apparently demanded, by their scientific knowledge;

[1] For a discussion of the further implications of this doctrine in Stoic thought, see H. C. Baldry, *The Unity of Mankind in Greek Thought* (Cambridge 1965), pp. 151 ff.

and that it was based on physical premisses, though logical conundrums known to them also seemed to favour total determinism. Yet at the same time they advanced an austere ethic which was logically incompatible with their cosmological views. Again, they asserted that *arete* was living in accordance with *phusis*; but nevertheless excluded health and strength from the *agatha* whose choice was a mark of *arete*, though health was certainly in accordance with the *phusis* of the organism as a whole. We have observed also their complex equation of *phusis* with *pronoia* with Zeus with *heimarmene*, their revival of nature-philosophy in a rather crude and rudimentary form, and of the *simpliste* Socratic view of *arete* as knowledge, despite the much more complicated psychologies of Plato and Aristotle, which, so far as extant fragments permit us to judge, the Stoics did nothing to refute.

The position is in a variety of ways intellectually unsatisfactory; but to say this is completely inadequate, for such a judgment fails to understand the reason for the appearance of Stoicism and for its continued popularity with intelligent Greeks (and, later, Romans) despite these difficulties which, even if they could not see them for themselves, other intelligent Greeks were eager to point out to them. We should rather try to discover the purpose that Stoicism was designed to serve, or – putting the matter more cautiously – the elements in the total environment that encouraged the Stoics to adopt such a world-view. (The degree to which the problem was clearly formulated, and the solution deliberately related to it, is, and must necessarily remain, obscure.)

The Stoic wished to believe, and convince others, that he was living in a world subject to immutable causal laws. He may well have had access to systems of total determinism from further east, and he was also drawing out the logical implications of statements long made in Greece; but what was his inducement to accept these unfamiliar systems, or to draw out the logical implications? Why did he find them intellectually, or emotionally, attractive? Traditionally, the Greek was capable, from Homer onwards, of ascribing an action to divine causation, or to *moira*, and at the same time holding the individual responsible for it.[1] A warrior-society, a society, *oikos* or *polis*, whose very existence depended on the *arete* of its fighting

[1] See *Merit and Responsibility*, chapter II and pp. 116 ff., 324.

men could allow no such excuses for cowardice. The need for vigorous and courageous action prevented, with rare exceptions, any conclusion of non-responsibility from being drawn; and there was no attempt made to produce a deterministic system. Furthermore, the individual *agathos* must have felt that he could influence his city's fortunes, for good or ill, by his actions, whether in war or in democratic politics. Now we need not say that a particular state of affairs *causes* a particular world-view: it suffices to say, and keeps strictly within the evidence, that a particular world-view seems well suited to a particular state of affairs. The early Stoics, as has already been said, found themselves in a political world in which the scale of events had suddenly increased, with the result that the stature of the individual had been correspondingly diminished. At any time he might be affected by political decisions, or military events, whose source was far away and not subject to his control, and whose scope was such that he had no hope of affecting them decisively. To anyone placed in such a position – and all save the few who could take the important decisions were in such a position – the doctrine that everything was immutably settled by the order of nature, by *phusis*, must have been intellectually and emotionally attractive.

All-embracing immutable *phusis* would absolve the individual from the feeling of failure and guilt likely to result from his inability to influence events, in a society in which the ability to defend one's household and one's *polis* had been the mark of *arete*: events are not to be influenced anyway. Nor yet are actions. In the fifth century, Sophocles' Neoptolemus had said (*Philoctetes* 1316 ff.):

> Men needs must bear the misfortunes sent to them by the gods; but men who wallow in self-chosen misfortunes have no right to compassion or pity.

The contrast is between Philoctetes' disease, which was sent by the gods, and must be borne, and the possibility now given to him of leaving the island on which he had been marooned. In this case, the decision is his; and if he stays on the island, he has no right to be pitied, for he could enjoy a better lot. In Stoic eyes, the chain of causes will also determine whether Philoctetes leaves the island or not: wisdom and *arete* consist in a cheerful acquiescence with *phusis*, the chain of causes. One is no longer responsible for success or failure, or for the actions which lead to either result: if one's city or household is overwhelmed by a military disaster, caused by an army incomparably larger than one could resist, it was to be, as a result of *phusis*, and one's *arete* is not affected.

Yet *arete* there must be, for *arete* commends the individual at his best, and there must be a condition of the individual which is the best condition, and *eudaimonia* there must be, for at *eudaimonia*, a fully satisfactory life with no regrets, all aim; and a goal must be set up. The Stoics, at all events, did not propose that one should bob like a cork on the waves of *phusis*. Again, traditional *arete* raised certain expectations, and had certain overtones: the *agathos*, for example, should be, so far as possible, self-sufficient, stable and prosperous, qualities which were denoted and commended by *eudaimonia*, to which the moral philosophy of the preceding century had added certain internal, ethical qualities. In the new circumstances created by the Hellenistic monarchies, with new stresses and strains, the individual needed to feel himself stable and proof against the buffets of fortune more than ever before, in proportion as the buffets might be more severe: *arete* and *eudaimonia* must be so interpreted as to fulfil the expectations raised by the words, without postulating qualities and conditions exposed to the vicissitudes of life. The Stoic turned to the *arete* or *aretai* of the moral agent, internal and inherent in the individual, and exhorted him to be just, brave, self-controlled and practically wise. Traditional *arete* would have exhorted him to be successful, and valued as *aretai* such qualities as could be demonstrated to lead to success. But external success is too evidently not now to be commanded; and moral philosophy has made it a commonplace that the ethical *aretai* are *aretai*. To have these *aretai* is to be *agathos*; and to be *agathos* is to be a good specimen of human being. In the quest for certain stability, even bodily excellences had to be jettisoned: an index, particularly in the society of Greece, where health had always ranked high among *agatha*, of the urgency of the quest. Only what was entirely within the control of the individual was reliable, and would produce a stable way of life; and only the *aretai* of the reason, logical and ethical, fitted these criteria. One's health, prosperity, the result of one's actions: none of these are completely under the control of the individual, and the Stoic was living in an environment which emphasised this fact. However, at a common-sense level one's attitude to one's state of health, prosperity and the result of one's actions is under one's own control, and it is possible to differentiate human beings by their responses to such events. The Stoic, as we have seen, had one motive for emphasising the absolute rigour and inevitability of the chain of causation; but he had another, equally strong motive for continuing to employ *arete* and *eudaimonia*, with all of their over-tones that it proved possible to retain, in a manner which suited the new circumstances of Greek life. Plato, too, had emphasised that the excellences of the *psuche* are *agatha* in themselves; but he insisted that their practice would bring all the other good things in their train (*Republic* 612C ff.), as, in a stable *polis*, might well happen. Aristotle in his ethical works took it for granted that the ethical virtues are *aretai*, and so 'good for' their possessor; and he tacitly assumed[1] that material success in this life would be one of the ways in which they would prove to be 'good for' the *agathos*, who, for Aristotle, had to be adequately provided with this world's goods before he could be *agathos*. The Stoic, it should be noted, is still relying on the picture of an *arete* as an excellence of a human being that causes him to be in his optimum condition: it is for this reason that he is able to argue that the *aretai* are *agatha*, and indeed the only true *agatha*; and he is relying on this picture even more thoroughly than Plato, for in his changed circumstances he is not so sure as Plato that other *agatha* will follow from being just. It is clearly good for the individual to be an excellent specimen of his kind; and to say that he possesses *arete* is to say that he is an excellent specimen of his kind; and this being the only certain *agathon*, it must be held to be the only *agathon*, the only *eudaimonia*. The bricks are traditional Greek bricks; but a new kind of house has to be constructed to face severer storms.

However, though disaster may come, and one may not be able to control it, it may not come at all; and though the city-state as an effective autonomous political unit faced by other city-states of similar size had passed away, the city-state as a complex of buildings in which human beings live, move, and engage in business and local politics had not. There was a role to play in this context, even if it

---

[1] This led to certain problems. See my 'Aristotle and the best kind of tragedy', *C.Q.* N.S. XVI (1966), pp. 78 ff. and especially pp. 97 ff.

was more difficult to believe in its importance, and it might at any time be disrupted from without. The Stoic did not wish to deter mankind, or himself, from the practical life. The simple life contains all that is necessary for *eudaimonia*: indeed, more than is necessary, for life itself is not an *agathon*. But the Stoic did not conclude that he should withdraw from practical life, equip himself with a single garment, and consume only bread and water. His knowledge that the *aretai* were the only true *agatha* fortified him against the loss of all else, including life; but provided that other things were not used in such a way as to prevent the life of *arete*, provided, as he put it, that he chose things which, though indifferent, were in accordance with *phusis*, he was living as he ought, and suitably fortified against the vicissitudes of an uncertain world. If fortified in this manner, he might indeed – and some Stoic teachers would have encouraged him to do so – lead an active political life on the largest possible stage and attain to the highest positions of power, if such were within his grasp.[1]

[1] As a result, it was possible for Stoicism later to supply the ethic of the more worthy members of the Roman governing classes under the later Republic, and also under the Empire. Some modifications were necessary: Panaetius and Posidonius, the two Greeks primarily responsible for introducing Stoicism to Rome, are supposed (one cannot be more definite where the evidence is so fragmentary) to have given greater emphasis to the idea of duty, or *officium*, than seems to be present in earlier Greek Stoicism. However, the basis of the Stoic ethic remained the same. This may at first sight appear less appropriate to the situation of a member of the Roman governing classes: such Stoics were at the centre, where decisions were taken; and under the later Republic an individual politician might wield great power, military and civil. However, if the prizes were great, they were also few, and competition was fierce; and Stoicism, appearing in Rome as it did in the second half of the second century B.C., coincided fairly closely with the beginning of the break-up of orderly Republican government, and the rise of individuals who attained – sometimes legally, sometimes illegally – positions of great power very rapidly, from which they sometimes fell with equal rapidity. Conditions at the centre of the Roman world were not stable nor peaceful during this time. Even in peaceful periods, only a few even of the comparatively small number who had any likelihood of gaining high office could in fact do so; and the elements of shame-culture in Rome of the period should not be underestimated. Some escape from its tensions was still needed; and this is furnished by the Stoic ethic as a whole. Under the Empire, effective power was in the hands of one man, though a public career was naturally still possible for others; but at times, under certain emperors, the hazards of taking part in public life, or even of being a prominent private citizen, were very great. The Romans too, whether under Republic or Empire, needed the consolations and reassurances offered by Stoicism.

But further reassurance was desirable, if it could be furnished; and the Stoic could furnish it. The chain of causes which from one point of view was *phusis* and *heimarmene* was also Zeus and *pronoia*, providence. Everything was for the best in this best of all possible worlds; and of that world he was a fellow-citizen along with the gods. The Stoic God, like those of earlier philosophers, is all-benevolent, so that everything that happens is not only out of one's control, it is also the best that could possibly happen to one. The Stoics, like other thinkers, had certain difficulties in accounting for some aspects of the world in terms of this view; but a rigid adherence to the view that only *arete* is an *agathon* renders such optimism difficult to confute logically, even if it lacks psychological conviction to a non-Stoic.

The assertion of the identity of *phusis* with *heimarmene*, Zeus and *pronoia* to produce a universe at once quasi-mechanistic, teleological and benevolent might well generate problems of philosophical theory; but enough has been said to indicate that the Stoics were not primarily, if at all, engaged in dispassionate philosophical theory, so far as their view of man in the cosmos is concerned. The long-accustomed Greek view of the ideal life as one lived in an autonomous *polis*, where an individual had some significance, had been rendered obsolete by events: a new outlook on life, which would render the individual able to face the problems and vicissitudes of a new kind of existence with adequate psychological support, was urgently needed. This the Stoic thinkers endeavoured to supply, with considerable psychological success; and this success was more important than mere theoretical difficulties. It is doubtless for this reason that the early Stoics, at all events,[1] seem to have devoted little time to casuistry, to enabling the Stoic pupil to discern what was the just course in particular circumstances. It has been objected that the statements that it is reasonable to live in accordance with *phusis* and natural to live in accordance with reason do not give much help in determining the

---

[1] We may contrast Cicero in the *De Officiis*, and Seneca in his moral works. Each writer abounds in casuistry and examples. Our evidence from the early Stoa is fragmentary, and it is hazardous to argue from silence; but certainly the extant remains indicate a much greater emphasis on casuistry in later, and particularly in Roman, Stoicism.

content of *arete*. A sound philosophical objection; but perhaps not in point here. Society of the day, like other societies, held definite views on the characteristics of just, self-controlled, brave and wise action. These views will sometimes have posed practical problems, as occurs in any society; and the Stoic, with his tenet that all save *arete* was relatively unimportant, and with some kind of a grading among the 'indifferent', may well have been better able than most Greeks to solve such problems. But we are mistaken to suppose that in this system it is the *objective* justness of a just action that is most important, as it is for Plato, in whose work the objectively just act will help to sustain the *polis*, the objectively unjust act to destroy it. When the Stoic says that justice is an *agathon*, one of the few real *agatha*, for the agent, it is subjective reassurance in a baffling world that is being offered; and for consolation it suffices that one supposes oneself to have acted justly.

The Stoics' picture of man in the cosmos is comprehensible in terms of the problem with which they were faced. The Stoic psychology seems similarly linked to this problem. As we have seen, the Stoics reached over the heads of Plato and Aristotle to the simpler view of Socrates that *arete* is knowledge, with the concomitant that all vice is (*not* 'results from') a mistaken judgment. Now the Stoics were emphasising that an individual who is *agathos* is in the best possible state, and hence that an individual who is *kakos* is in a bad state: *kakos* and *kakia* have overtones not only of vice but of wretchedness and misery, and no-one would choose wretchedness and misery in preference to a good condition for himself: it is rational to choose *arete*. The argument is not new, and Plato and Aristotle are far more subtle. Furthermore, desire, anger and fear did not present themselves to the Stoics purely in the guise of bad judgments. To repeat a passage quoted above (*S.V.F.* III, III, 27):

> Some say that emotion is not different from reason . . . but that there is a direction of the one element of ourselves, reason, in each direction, which escapes our notice because of the quickness and rapidity of the changes. . . . Desire, anger, fear and everything else of this kind are bad opinions and judgments, which do not occur with reference to one aspect of the *psuche* alone, but are swingings, yieldings, assents and drives and, in short, activities which soon change, of the whole directing function, *hegemonikon*.

'Swingings, yieldings, assents and drives' has the ring of introspection; and does not resemble in the least a description of a bad judgment. Once again we have a Stoic assertion that one thing is another thing, with little theoretical cogency, but perhaps with practical effect. The Stoic is aware of the tumultuous surge of passion and desire, and we have seen reason to suppose that a low degree of personality structure was characteristic of the Greeks, and that this phenomenon may be related to their living in a results-culture, in which the evaluation of actions is not related to intentions, or efforts; for when the result is all-important, and intentions unimportant, the action is judged in terms of what is exterior to the personality, and the development of a stable core of personality is not encouraged. Hellenistic society was still essentially a results-culture; and in proportion as success and failure were even less within the control of the individual than before, the stresses suffered by the personality must have been even more violent than before. The passage quoted (*S.V.F.* III, 111, 27) testifies that the ordinary man, and the Stoic before he reached the Stoic goal, were well aware of the internal seething of an inadequately structured personality.

A major purpose of the Stoic philosophy was to relieve these stresses. I have already suggested that both the Stoics' view of the cosmos as subject to a *heimarmene* which was also benevolent providence and their fully internalised account of *arete* should have had this effect; and the latter, the sharp contrast of an *arete* dependent on right attitude and right choice with the uncontrollable vicissitudes of fortune, which for the Stoic affect neither *arete* nor *eudaimonia*, gives encouragement to the development of a more structured personality at the same time as it lulls the turmoil within. Where Homeric man, who at any moment might be faced with a demand that he should do what is impossible, and who had the least structured personality of all, will *ochthein*, *meneainein*, or *choesthai*,[1] and later generations, whose actions are similarly reckoned by results, testify to tumult within, the Stoic, convinced of the irrelevance of fortune to the achievement of his goal, could achieve *apatheia*, a condition in which desires and passions are at rest, leaving the Stoic sage master of himself, even in a situation where the achievement of 'competitive' success

[1] Cf. chapter 2, pp. 39 ff.

238

might be more evidently out of the individual's power than in Homer. To define the goal in this negative manner testifies to the oppressive presence of the storm within, and the longing for a calm.

Attainment of the goal depends on having the right intellectual judgments and consequently the right attitudes. In terms of his own philosophy, the Stoic is illogical in maintaining that these are entirely – or at all – within the individual's control; but the individual's experience suggests that this is so, with the result that the Stoic's control of his own *psuche* is sharply opposed to his lack of control, or possible lack of control, over everything else; and this must help to produce a more stable personality structure, which will present itself primarily as *apatheia*, for reasons already stated.

The right intellectual judgments concern *agatha* and *kaka*: *arete* is knowledge of *agatha* and *kaka*. I have already said that there seems to be little casuistry in early Stoicism, and attempted to suggest reasons for this. There also appears to be an inability, or a refusal, to distinguish between a sound judgment or knowledge and an action performed in virtue of a sound judgment or knowledge; and on the other side, between a bad judgment or ignorance and an action performed in virtue of a bad judgment, or ignorance, or not effectively bringing one's intellect into play at all. Furthermore, we have seen that introspection does not present wrong action to the Stoic in the light simply of intellectual error. In the first place, we have observed in Aristotle's doctrine of the practical syllogism the tendency to treat the conclusion of such a syllogism as being an action rather than a proposition; and when *apatheia* had supervened the Stoic might presumably hope for such an outcome immediately, without any tug-of-war such as is experienced by Aristotle's *akrates*. We have observed a number of indications that this type of account of what we term decision may be an accurate report of Greek psychological experience. However, such an account of virtuous action does not entail that vicious action is or even depends on a mistake or ignorance: one may act *in* ignorance, granted, but not *because of* ignorance, but because of greed, or lust or some other drive. Greek philosophy had proved capable of drawing the distinction: Aristotle draws it in *Nicomachean Ethics* 1110b25 ff. However, the protreptic and hortatory value of 'all *kakia* is ignorance' was already apparent to Socrates;

and Plato retained 'no-one is voluntarily *kakos*' long after his psychological analysis of action would have enabled him to abandon it.[1] The Stoics too clearly have a protreptic purpose.

If the interpretation offered in this chapter is correct, the purpose of the Stoic cosmology and psychology is practical; and the early Stoics are not to be viewed as a small band of self-congratulatory perfectionists, but as men endeavouring to find a solution for an urgent practical problem. In this light, it seems likely that the early Stoics, like the later ones, encouraged those who were still on the way to perfection, and that their insistence that only the wise man is *agathos*, while all others are *kakoi*, should be interpreted as a spur to greater effort rather than the condemnation of mankind *de haut en bas*.

[1] Above, pp. 160 ff., and *Merit and Responsibility*, pp. 304 ff.

9. The Epicureans

A. Introductory

Epicurus, the founder of the Epicurean school of philosophy, lived from B.C. 342/1 to 271/70. An Athenian by descent, he may have been born in Samos, to which his parents migrated as colonists. In 311/10 he opened a philosophical school of his own at Mytilene, the chief city of Lesbos. He later moved to Lampsacus, a prosperous city in the Troad. Meeting with success as a philosophical teacher, he moved in 306 B.C. to Athens, the philosophical centre of the Greek world. He purchased a house and garden, which attained to such fame that the school was known as 'The Garden' (*kēpos*), just as the Stoic school was known as 'The Porch' (*stŏā*). He lived in Athens almost continuously for thirty-six years; his way of life, and that of his pupils, was simple, quiet, and removed from public affairs.

Epicurus was a voluminous writer, but the majority of his works are lost, or survive only in scattered fragments, either quoted by other ancient writers or on papyrus. The extant works are the *Letter to Herodotus*, the *Letter to Pythocles*, the *Letter to Menoeceus*, the *Kūriai Doxai*, and the *Sententiae Vaticanae*. The letters are all to pupils, and were presumably meant for circulation to others in addition to those to whom they were addressed. The *Letter to Herodotus*[1] contains a survey of Epicurus' physical doctrines, the *Letter to Pythocles* is concerned with Epicurus' meteorology, while the *Letter to Menoeceus*[2] treats of his ethics. The *Kūriai Doxai*,[3] or *Authoritative Doctrines*, is a collection of forty ethical maxims, well suited for memorising. The *Sententiae Vaticanae*, or *Vatican Maxims* (so called because they were discovered in a manuscript in the Vatican in 1888) is a collection of eighty maxims, almost all ethical. Our longest and fullest document of Epicureanism is not by Epicurus, nor yet in Greek: the didactic poem *De Rerum Natura*, in six books, by the Roman poet Lucretius.

---

[1] Abbreviated to *Ep. Hdt.*
[2] Abbreviated to *Ep. Men.*
[3] Abbreviated to *K.D.*

B. *Phusis* and *Psuche*

The overt purpose of the Epicurean philosophy is to liberate men from their anxieties; but this purpose is achieved through the medium of the doctrine of the cosmos, which must be discussed first. Epicurus, like Zeno, reaches back beyond Socrates, Plato and Aristotle to the Presocratics; but where Zeno's primary source was Heraclitus, Epicurus turned to the atomism of Democritus. His *On Phusis*, a work of thirty-seven books, and Lucretius' *De Rerum Natura*, take their rise from the view that the cosmos consists entirely of atoms and void. The Epicureans are empiricists, and found all judgments on the evidence of the senses; so that arguments for the existence of atoms based on sense-experience must be supplied.

Epicurus[1] held that the contents of the cosmos were always the same: nothing could be created from nothing, and nothing could pass away into nothing. If it were possible for anything to be created from nothing, there would be in the universe effects without antecedent causes (which experience teaches us is not the case), and there would be no order in nature. If anything that perishes really passed away into nothingness, the whole cosmos would be used up. The universe is also infinite, both in respect of void and in respect of the number of the atoms. That bodies exist is evident to our senses; and if there were no 'place' or void, the bodies would have nowhere in which to move. Now sensible bodies are destroyed and dissolved; but they cannot be utterly destroyed into nothingness, for reasons already given. There must, then, be some bodies which are incapable of dissolution; accordingly, the basic bodies in nature must be individual corporeal existences, atoms. To account for the wide variety of sensible objects, the atoms must have incomprehensibly numerous (though not infinite) different shapes; and different kinds of atom must be different in size, though there cannot be an infinity of different sizes, or some would be visible; and our senses inform us that this is not the case. In these circumstances, the infinite supply of atoms produces an infinity of types of cosmos, both like and unlike ours. The atoms are in perpetual motion, and move 'as quickly as thought'. Their weight causes them to fall straight down in the void;

[1] The following account is derived principally from the *Letter to Herodotus*.

but Epicurus also postulates a 'swerve' (*parenklīnein*) to account for collisions between the atoms, and their eternal motion in all directions. Atoms in gases are widely spread apart; those in solid objects close-packed.

Sense-perception must now be linked with these imperceptible atoms. Epicurus asserts that images similar in shape to solid bodies are perpetually given forth by solid bodies; and that these, consisting of a very tenuous pattern of atoms, constitute the data of sight. The atoms are individually imperceptible, of course: we only perceive their results when they are present in large numbers; but Epicurus argues – as he always does when discussing matters not perceptible by sense – that nothing in our perceptual experience contradicts this theory. Hearing and the sense of smell are similarly accounted for. Epicurus treats images as being also the object of thought. For Epicurus, the *psuche* too is composed of atoms. It is body, *soma*, composed of very fine particles distributed throughout the whole structure of the organism, for the whole is alive and capable of sensation; and it is most like wind or breath (*pneuma*: but with no reference to the technical Stoic usage of the term) with a certain mixture of heat in it. These are material substances in Epicurus' eyes; and he adds a third, un-nameable substance, much finer than these in its composition, 'and for this reason more capable of sensation in harmony with the rest of the structure of the organism'. It is from the *psuche* that we derive the power of sensation; but to possess this the *psuche* must be enclosed in a body and must be extended throughout that body. So long as it is enclosed in a body, even if a part of the body – and so, presumably, of the *psuche* – be lost, the *psuche* continues to feel; but if the *psuche* be lost, the body ceases to have sensation; as does the *psuche* itself, for it is dissipated when the body perishes, and reverts to its constituent atoms.

For Epicurus, as for all other Greeks, to debate the existence of *psuche* would be pointless: *psuche* is simply that whose presence distinguishes a living organism from a dead one. As Epicurus says of his account (*Ep. Hdt.* 63):

All this is made clear by the capacities of the *psuche*, and its sensations, readiness of movement, its thoughts, and by what we lose when we die.

Lucretius gives a more complex account of *psuche*, distinguishing *anima*, *psuche*-atoms spread out over the body, as vital principle and principle of sensation, from *animus*, the mind, a collection of pure *psuche*-atoms assembled in the breast. He also adds air or mist (*āēr*) to breath, or wind (*pneuma*), and heat as one of the constituents of *psuche*, so that the 'third unnameable substance' becomes for him the '*quarta natura*' (III, 241). Epicurus' letters are brief summaries, which may account for omissions.

Breath or wind, warmth and air or mist: all these are aspects of a living human being, and of many animals, which are lacking to a dead one. (We need not expect of Epicurus the subtlety of Aristotle's observation that many living creatures do not breathe, or that some are not warm: Epicurus' physical doctrine is a means to an end.) The Epicurean approach, and that of the Stoics, resembles the Presocratic empirical search for the characteristics of *psuche*; but they, like the Stoics, and some Presocratics before them, are somewhat embarrassed by the realisation that the qualities exhibited by *psuche* are not possessed by ordinary specimens of breath, warmth, air or fire. The Stoics, as we have seen, make creative or technic fire into a special kind of fire, qualified in some way; the Epicureans resort to an indescribable and indefinable 'third substance' or *quarta natura*. Definition or further description is unnecessary to Epicurus' purposes: it suffices that it is material, composed of atoms, and dissipated at the death of the individual.

An account in atomic terms of celestial phenomena is also important to Epicurus' purpose. Plato, Aristotle and the Stoics had all accorded divine status to the heavenly bodies,[1] and this was also the belief of the unphilosophical Greek, though his views were naturally more inchoate and less co-ordinated: one of the charges against Socrates (*Apology* 26D) was that he had taught that the sun was a stone, thereby shocking Athenian beliefs. On the other hand, the Presocratic nature-philosophers had held views which entailed that the sun, moon and stars were not divine: Socrates replied that his prosecutors should really be accusing Anaxagoras. For Epicurus, the heavenly bodies are not deities, but merely agglomerations of fire. (He does not deny

[1] For example, Plato, *Republic* 508A, Aristotle, *E.N.* 1141a34, *Metaphysics* 1026a18, *Physics* 196a33, *S.V.F.* II, 30, 19; 187, 9; 306, 24; 315, 23; 316, 3.

that there are gods; but these live lives of undisturbed bliss beyond the confines of the world, about which they trouble themselves not at all.) He has no very satisfactory theory to offer of the regularity of celestial phenomena; but his view is that the concern of the science of *phusis* is to discover the most important facts about the cosmos: we should not be disturbed if we have a choice of theories to explain celestial phenomena. This attitude of Epicurus is sometimes compared with that of modern science: rival theories must be entertained together until a crucial experiment can be devised to decide between them. In reality, Epicurus' attitude is quite different: provided one has clear in one's mind the important facts relating to the science of *phusis* (*Ep. Hdt.* 79), *it does not matter* what the correct explanation for a given phenomenon may be; for the explanation must then be carried out in terms of the basic tenets of Epicureanism, and this guarantees only limited variation in the types of explanation available. Provided all is atoms and void, no explanations of a kind that Epicurus would consider unfortunate can be devised (*Ep. Hdt.* 80):

> If therefore we think that it is possible for a phenomenon to occur both in this way and in other ways, in circumstances in which it is equally possible for us to be in a state of peace, *ataraxiā*, then we shall be in a state of *ataraxia*, while recognising that it may occur in different ways, just as much as if we know that it occurs in some particular way.

The end of cosmological and all other speculation is to furnish *ataraxia*, a state of peace, or *eudaimonia* (*Ep. Men.* 122) or to render one *makarios*, blessed (*Ep. Hdt.* 78), a word more powerful even than *eudaimonia*, and used frequently in Greek of the gods. The further implications of this will be discussed below.

C. *Eudaimonia*

The *Letter to Menoeceus* begins as follows:

> Let no-one when he is young hesitate to begin the study of philosophy, nor let him grow weary of philosophising when he is old. For no-one can be too early or too late to attain to the health of his *psuche*. The man who says that the proper time of life for philosophy has not yet come, or has gone by,[1] is just like the man who says that the proper time of life for *eudaimonia* has not yet come, or has gone by. And so young and old should study

[1] A likely attitude for a non-philosophical Greek, cf. Callicles in *Gorgias* 485A.

philosophy, the old so that as he grows older he may be young in *agatha*, good things, as a result of the grateful recollection of what has been, the young so that in his youth he may be old at the same time, as a result of his lack of fear of what is to come. We must accordingly study the things that bring about our *eudaimonia*, since when we possess that we have everything, and when it is absent we do everything to obtain it.

This is a new note in Greek philosophy. Stoicism may be a system whose effect is to sustain the believer throughout the turmoil of life; but this seems not to be its entire conscious purpose. Some activities have value in their own right. Here, *eudaimonia* remains the goal, as it must, and knowledge is related to it; but whereas Plato and Aristotle held that *eudaimonia* consisted in the contemplation of truth, an intellectual activity, for Epicurus *eudaimonia*, as will appear, is an absence of painful sensations, guaranteed to an important extent by certain knowledge about the cosmos, which is worth pursuing just so far as it will ensure that *eudaimonia*.

The *Letter to Menoeceus* as a whole sketches in the method of attaining such *eudaimonia*, and the manner in which the Epicurean ethic is related to this. The first principle to be borne in mind is that the gods care nothing for us, and neither reward nor punish, nor indeed take any account of the cosmos at all. Secondly, death is nothing to us (124):

> For all *agathon* and *kakon* for us resides in sensation; and death is deprivation of sensation. As a result, a correct understanding that death is nothing to us makes the mortality of our life enjoyable, not by adding an infinity of time to it, but by taking away the longing for immortality. For there is nothing terrible in not being alive. And so the person who says that he fears death not because it will cause him pain when it comes, but because its anticipation causes pain to him, is a fool. For what causes no trouble when it comes is an empty pain in anticipation. So death, the most terrifying of *kaka*, is nothing to us, since so long as we exist, death is not present; and when death is present, we do not exist. Death then concerns neither the living nor the dead since, for the living it is not, and the dead are no more.

Other Greeks had reflected that it is better not to be born, but that if born it is best to die and go down to Hades as quickly as possible.[1]

[1] Epicurus quotes Theognis 427; we may compare Sophocles, *Oedipus at Colonus* 1224 and the Middle Comedy writer Alexis, *Mandragorizomenē* frag. 141, 14 ff. Kock: the sentiment must have been a commonplace.

Epicurus thinks this to be foolish: anyone who holds such views should commit suicide; and he clearly supposes, as our much more scanty knowledge of Greek behaviour would also lead us to conclude, that few Greeks acted on the belief. One should not, however, aim at a life as long as possible, but one as pleasant as possible.

Epicurus has now to his own satisfaction removed the two principal fears of Greek life: death is not to be feared in itself, nor yet as a gateway to a Last Judgment, for after death we are nothing; and the gods care nothing for reward and punishment in this life either, for they take no heed of the world. He has also sawed through the two chief planks on which traditional Greek moralists erected their systems; and must now construct a way of life without them, and evidently without some of the material drawn upon by Plato, Aristotle and the Stoics.

He begins thus (*Ep. Men.* 127):

> We must consider that of the desires some are *phusikai*, pertain to *phusis*, and that some are empty and vain; and that of the *phusikai* some are necessary, while some are merely *phusikai*; and that of the necessary ones some are necessary for *eudaimonia*, others to bring about a lack of disturbance in the body, others for life itself. An 'unwandering contemplation' of these facts enables us to know how to refer all choice and avoidance to the criteria of the health of the body and the *ataraxia*, lack of disturbance, of the *psuche*, since this is the aim of the life of blessedness (*to makariōs zen*). For it is to this end that we always act: to avoid pain and fear. When once we attain to this, all the storm of our *psuche* is abated, since the living creature has not to go about as if it were searching for something lacking, nor to seek for something else by means of which it can fill up deficiencies in the *agathon* of the *psuche* and of the body. For it is then that we need pleasure, when we are in pain from the absence of pleasure; [and when we are not in pain] we no longer need pleasure. It is for this reason that we say that pleasure is the beginning and end of living blessedly (*makariōs*). For we recognize pleasure as the first *agathon* and one innate in us; and from pleasure we begin every act of choice and avoidance, and return again to pleasure, and judge every *agathon* by the criterion of pleasant sensation.

This division of the desires occurs before Epicurus, for example in the *Nicomachean Ethics* (1118b8 ff.), where an ancient commentator adds the explanatory note that the desire for food and clothing is necessary (and *phusikē*); the desire for sex is *phusike* but not necessary;

while the desire for *particular* food, clothing or sexual partner is neither *phusike* nor necessary. This is found in earlier philosphy; but Epicurus' direction of arguments is new, for the goal of his philosophy is new. All should aim at health of the body and *ataraxia* of the *psuche*; and the analysis of the desires enables us to attain these goals, and to avoid the pain and fear that accompany our failure to attain them. Until we reach the goal, our *psuche* is tossed by a storm of pain and fear.

Epicurus continues (129) by constructing a hedonistic calculus, of the kind that has already appeared in Plato's *Protagoras*.[1] Simply because pleasure is the chief *agathon*, we should not choose every pleasure, for in this way we may readily suffer more pain than pleasure:

> Every pleasure, then, in that it possesses a *phusis* akin to ours[2] is an *agathon*; but not all pleasure is to be chosen; just as all pain is *kakon*, but not all to be avoided on all occasions. We should decide all these things by a comparison (*summetrēsis*, a measuring of one thing against another) and inspection of advantages and disadvantages. On certain occasions we treat the *agathon* as *kakon*, and conversely the *kakon* as *agathon*.

Epicurus, like all earlier Greeks, treats *autarkeia*, self-sufficiency, as a great *agathon* (*Ep. Men.* 130). This is to be attained by limiting needs:[3]

> Not in order that we may make use of only a few things under any circumstances, but that if we do not possess abundance, we may make use of the few, in the genuine conviction that those who least need it enjoy luxury most, and that everything *phusikon*, that pertains to *phusis*,[4] is easy to be obtained, whereas that which is superfluous is hard to obtain. Accordingly, inexpensive savours bring us a pleasure equal to an expensive diet, when all the pain that results from want is removed; and bread and water give the highest pleasure, when someone who needs them partakes of them. To

---

[1] Above, p. 132.

[2] The argument presumably being that, in default of this relationship, it would not be a pleasure for us, though it might be a pleasure for some other living creature.

[3] Cf. Democritus above, p. 110.

[4] Epicurus treats *phusis* as the same in all individuals, whereas Democritus (pp. 111 f. above) uses the word to denote qualities which appear to a different extent in different individuals.

accustom himself to simple and inexpensive diet both gives a man health to the full and makes him unslothful in his approach to the necessary employments of life; and it also disposes us better towards expensive foods when we occasionally after long intervals meet with them; and it renders us fearless against all that chance can do to us.[1]

Pleasure, in the Epicurean sense, is the goal, the *agathon*; a simple, frugal diet will enable us to attain it; and this will also furnish us with self-sufficiency, *autarkeia*, the traditional Greek goal. Accordingly, we shall then possess *eudaimonia* (or, in Epicurus' words, be *makarioi*, blessed, which is even higher commendation) and *autarkeia*.

It follows that for Epicurus to say that pleasure is the goal is not to commend sensuality or excess of any kind, but freedom from pain in the body and from trouble (*tarattesthai*) in the *psuche* (*Ep. Men.* 132):

> For it is not continuous drinking and revelling, nor the sexual enjoyment of women and boys, nor the enjoyment of fish and the other luxuries that an expensive table furnishes, that produce the pleasant life, but a sober calculation that seeks out the reasons for all choice and avoidance, and banishes mere opinions, which are the cause of the most disturbance to the *psuche*.

Anyone holding such views will be likely to set a high value on *phronesis*, practical wisdom; and Epicurus indeed values it more highly than philosophy (*Ep. Men.* 132). From it by *phusis* (*pephukenai*) spring all the other *aretai*, causing us to understand that we cannot live pleasantly without living prudently (*phronimōs*) honourably (*kalōs*) and justly (*dikaiōs*), nor prudently, honourably and justly without living pleasantly. For the *aretai* are by *phusis* bound up with (*sumpephūkenai*) the pleasant life, and the pleasant life is inseparable from them. The Epicurean is reverent towards the gods, has no fear of death, and has reasoned out the end for man ordained by *phusis*.

He also – and now Epicurus embarks upon polemic – laughs at *heimarmene*, or destiny. He knows that some things happen by necessity

---

[1] It should be noted that Epicurus does not here state that luxurious living is bad for one, though he does say that a simple diet is both healthy and pleasant. In fact, he appears rather wistful at the prospect of meeting with occasional luxury. Contrast e.g. Democritus B234, p. 107 above, and Plato, *Republic* 372A ff., who set their faces sternly against luxurious diet.

and some by chance, while some are within our control. What is within our control is subject to no master (*adespoton*), and to it by *phusis* (*pephukenai*) are attached praise and blame. Better to believe myths about gods who take an interest in the world (unlike the Epicurean gods) and can be placated; for *heimarmene* is incapable of placation. The prudent man will exercise his free will in prudent choices, and will prefer to be unfortunate in reasonable action rather than fortunate in unreasonable action.

The *Letter to Menoeceus* closes with the following exhortation (135):

> Rehearse these thoughts and thoughts like them to yourself and to someone like yourself by night and by day; and you shall never be disturbed (*diatarattesthai*) whether waking or asleep, but you shall live like a god among men. For a man who lives among immortal *agatha* is in no way like a mortal being.

The words are as heartfelt as the closing words of the *Republic*; however deep their differences in other respects, Epicurus, like Plato, is pointing the way to salvation as he sees it.

D. The Rise of Man

Epicureans gave an account in terms of the atomic theory of the development of plant, animal and human life. Little of this survives in the extant remains of Epicurus: in the *Letter to Herodotus* 75, we find

> Moreover we must suppose that their [human beings'] *phusis* too was taught and compelled to do many things of all kinds by circumstances themselves; and that later on reasoning made more accurate the things that had been handed over to it by *phusis* and made further discoveries, in some cases quickly, in others slowly. . . .

The picture is of progress; but Prometheus, being a god, is of course eliminated. Lucretius (V, 783 ff.), after speaking of the earth as having put forth grass and trees as animals grow feathers and hair, supposes that the earth developed wombs at its surface from which the first animals and men were produced. These (925 ff.) were originally much hardier and more resistant to disease. They lived like wild beasts, and had no fire, agriculture or crafts: they were vegetarian and drank water. They had no laws and no idea of the common good. When they had got themselves huts, skins for clothing, and fire (which was made available when lightning struck trees, or when two trees rubbed their branches together), and had learned how to cook (taught by observing the ripening effect of the warmth of the sun), and had wives and children, 1019 ff.,

> Then neighbours began to make pacts of friendship desiring neither to harm nor be harmed by each other, and commended children and women to mercy, indicating in broken speech by voice and gesture that it is right for all to pity the weak. And though harmony could not come about altogether, yet a large part kept the agreements honourably, otherwise straightway then would the human race have been destroyed, nor would breeding have continued their generations till now.

Friendship and justice arose out of the requirements of the situation. Justice was neither implanted in men by Zeus (as the *Protagoras*-myth had it), nor are men by *phusis* impelled to communal life (as Aristotle and the Stoics had it), but make a compact on the basis of mutual utility.

All things were discovered by men themselves. Kings built towns and fortifications and (1110)

> divided cattle and lands and gave to each man in proportion to his beauty, strength and intellect; for beauty and strength were highly valued. Later, wealth was discovered and gold found, and this readily took honour away from the strong and beautiful; for men, however brave and handsome of body, for the most part follow in the train of the richer man.

This is an hypothesis: Lucretius had no documents – and we have none – of a period in early Greek or Roman history when wealth was the reward for beauty, strength and intellect, wherever they might be found. The Homeric world, as we have seen, was different. Nevertheless, Lucretius' hypothesis is much more rational than earlier attempts. He continues with a narration of an outline of history up to his own day, drawing only on human intelligence and needs to account for progress, or rather change; for an Epicurean does not believe that all change is progress. For example (1161 ff.) men invented the gods, drawing on a variety of sources: visual images seen by the imagination or in dreams, and a need to account for the regular circling of the heavens and other celestial and meteorological phenomena. Again, the growth of power and luxury is treated with disapproval by the Epicurean. The quotation given above continues (1117 ff.):

> Yet if a man were to guide his life by true reasoning, to live frugally with a mind free from care is great riches; for there is never any lack of a little. But men wished to be renowned and powerful, so that their fortune might rest on a firm foundation and that they might be able to lead a tranquil life in wealth. In vain; since as they strove to reach the height of honours they made their road full of danger; and from the top, should they reach it, envy like a lightning-stroke sometimes smites and casts them down in scorn to foul Tartarus; since for the most part it is the topmost parts and those which rise above others that are blasted by envy as by a lightning-stroke; so that it is far better to obey in peace and quiet than to wish to rule and possess kingdoms.

Earlier thinkers and writers had sought to dissuade the powerful man from over-reaching himself by such reflections as these; Lucretius – and he speaks for Epicurus – here attempts to dissuade his readers from reaching at all.[1]

This naturalistic account resembles the view of life associated with the culture-hero Prometheus insofar as it represents human life as development; but differs from it in rejecting all supernatural causation, and also in its critical attitude to many aspects of human 'progress'. Many aspects of life are useless or hurtful; but by rational choices we can make the best of life, and enjoy life at its best here and now.

Epicurus, then, is promising to all who follow the way of life

[1] Here Epicurus and Lucretius differ from Democritus. Democritus (B3, above p. 110) counsels restraint, and cautions that one should not go beyond the capabilities of one's *phusis*, whatever these may be. However (B267, above p. 111 n. 1) 'by *phusis* ruling belongs to the *kressōn*, better or stronger'. In a *polis*, the *agathoi* might have an influence on events, and it was reasonable for those whose *phusis* was equal to it to endeavour to do so: in the situation in which Epicurus and Lucretius lived, the number who could hope to influence events was so small, and the world so large, confused and confusing, that such ambition appeared to them to be extreme folly. (Democritus himself valued research more highly than power, B118; but did not seek to dissuade from power those whose *phusis* thereby found appropriate expression.)

he commends an existence whose characteristics are *eudaimonia* (or which even renders one *makarios*, which is a condition more than human), the possession of *agatha*, and *autarkeia*; and these are the goals for which the Greek has striven throughout the entire period discussed in this book, though the Greek words employed may have been different in the earliest times. Previously *eudaimonia* and *autarkeia* in practical life, evaluated whether by the ordinary man or by Aristotle in terms of the values of a prosperous class, have been for the few; and when evaluated by Plato with the philosopher-king, or by Aristotle with *theoria*, in mind, the true *eudaimonia* of the philosopher contemplating the Forms or engaged in *theoria* is only available to a limited number, on the basis of their aptitudes. Epicurus' *eudaimonia* and *autarkeia* are for anyone prepared to follow through and assent to his arguments about the *phusis* of the cosmos; and he who does so is promised an end to fear, and pleasure in the sense of removal of pain.

E. Problems of Epicureanism

In the Epicurean, as in the Stoic, picture of the world and man's place in it there are manifest contradictions left unresolved, and difficulties left unexplained. The swerve of the atoms which results in collisions, and hence in the existence of material objects at all, is mere dogma, quite inexplicable in terms of the forces postulated by Epicurus as governing the cosmos; and the 'third substance' or '*quarta natura*' with its peculiar properties cries out for explanation, and receives none. Again, free will, on which Epicurus lays such emphasis, contrasting his position scornfully with Stoic *heimarmene*, should have no place in this system: the swerve of the atoms, in itself unaccountable, would contribute an element of randomness to the cosmos, but not of free will, for which the collisions of the billiard-ball atoms leave no room at all. Again, the *agathon*, the real *agathon* which we pursue by *phusis*, is said to be pleasure; but this 'pleasure' proves to be simply the condition in which desires are satisfied, healthy equilibrium for the body and *ataraxia* for the *psuche*. Plato (*Philebus* 44A) termed this state neither pleasure nor pain, and held that only those who knew nothing of true pleasures would be content with this; why is the philosopher of pleasure content with it? Plato and Aristotle speak not only of the *eudaimonia* of philosophical activity, but also of its pleasures (*Republic* 581C ff., *E.N.* 1177a23 ff.); but Epicurus' position is different. For him, philosophy, carried to the point at which the true *phusis* of the cosmos is understood, leads to *ataraxia*: it is not commended as furnishing a particularly pure pleasure in itself, but as a means to an end. Everything else, even *aretai*, must be judged by the same criterion (frag. 23):

> But I summon you to continuous pleasures, and not to vain and empty *aretai*, which have hopes of results that are disturbing (*tarachōdeis*, from the same root as *tarattesthai*, absence of which is *ataraxia*).

As we have seen, Epicurus also holds (*Ep. Men.* 132) that all the other *aretai* spring from *phronesis*, and that we cannot live pleasantly without living *phronimōs*, *kalōs* and *dikaiōs*, so that the *aretai* (or some of them) are necessary to the Epicurean life. Yet they are merely means to the end of pleasure, or rather *ataraxia*. There is something strange here:[1] Epicurus may regard the *aretai* as necessary means, but he can also speak of them as vain and empty. Earlier generations treated it as a necessary criterion of an *arete* that it should conduce to *eudaimonia*, and would not have termed an *arete* anything that they did not hold to be so conducive; so that anything termed an *arete* was highly valued, and the human being endowed with it possessed an excellence linked with the desired end. We have seen Thrasymachus[2] denying *dikaiosune* to be an *arete* precisely because, in his opinion, it did not conduce to this end. If anyone accepted that any quality was an *arete* he had to accept also the conclusions which followed: Aristotle[3] (*E.N.* 1144a1) could offer as one reason for the need to have *phronesis* that it is an *arete*, excellence, of one aspect of the human being, so that it must be choiceworthy as conducing to *eudaimonia*. These associations of *arete*, however, seem not to be present to Epicurus' mind: while terming a quality an *arete*, he nevertheless can speak of it as vain and empty; and also finds himself constrained to demonstrate

---

[1] Aristotle (*E.N.* 1102a5 ff.) gives as his reason for discussing *arete* at all in the *Nicomachean Ethics* that it is conducive to *eudaimonia*; but his demonstration that *arete* is linked with *eudaimonia* depends (*E.N.* 1098a7 ff.) on the idea of *arete* as the most effective functioning of the human being.

[2] Above, p. 146.

[3] Above, p. 198.

that the *aretai* are means to the desired end, rather than discovering the means, and subsequently terming them *aretai*. There seems to be some confusion here: or at all events a situation that has not so far appeared in Greece.

F. Conclusion

These are all real problems. The reason for their existence is probably to be sought, as in the case of Stoicism, in the conditions of the time and the function which Epicureanism was intended to perform in this context. There are no grounds for supposing that Epicurus did not believe in the truth of the atomic theory which, with some modifications, he took over from Democritus, any more than there are grounds for supposing that Zeno did not believe in the Heraclitean fire which he adopted as one of the building-bricks of his cosmos. But it was a hypothesis, and a hypothesis which posed immediately apparent difficulties, as we have seen; and we may seek for reasons to account for Epicurus' selection of this hypothesis out of the many conflicting ones available, and his adherence to it in the face of the theoretical difficulties. The atomic hypothesis as presented by Epicurus fails, since the 'swerve' is a postulate utterly unjustifiable in the light of the forces in terms of which he has undertaken to explain the cosmos, to account for the phenomena; fails indeed to account for the existence of any physical objects at all. But it does eliminate any possibility of the survival after death of the *psuche* and, if Epicurus' arguments are accepted in detail, of the concern of the gods with the cosmos in which we live. Epicureans are thus freed from fear of death and fear of the gods; and this is the function of the cosmology. The cosmology also eliminates free will: all that Epicurus can logically deduce from it is either determinism (since the billiard-ball atoms might be expected to function mechanistically) or, from our point of view, a random unpredictability, since we cannot know or foresee the behaviour of the atoms, however, mechanistic this may in fact be. Nevertheless, Epicurus insists on the reality of free will and pours scorn on the Stoic *heimarmene*. He is in the same position as the Stoics: he needs his cosmology for one purpose, free will for another; and so includes both in his system. He has no grounds for this, or for any of the distinctions on which he builds his ethic: *phusis* is merely the dance of the atoms in the void, and any individual's *phusis* is the resultant of the dance of *his* atoms: if he expresses a desire for anchovies and marmalade topped with cream, that desire is just as much from his *phusis* as a desire for bread and water would be. Useless to speak of 'false opinion': one's opinions too are merely the resultant of the atomic dance. In his ethics, in fact, Epicurus uses *phusis* with quite different overtones. His position derives partly from earlier medical thought and conclusions drawn from that thought by earlier philosophers, such as his atomist predecessor Democritus, partly from the *phusis* doctrine of the sophists. Drawing on these resources, Epicurus states that pleasure is the *agathon*, the goal we pursue by *phusis*; and yet health of the body and *ataraxia* – little, if anything, more than the absence of pain – of the *psuche* is all that he offers as a goal that can be reached. Surely it would be less confusing to propound health of the body and an analogous condition of the *psuche* as the goal? The proposition would be familiar to Greeks by the time of Epicurus. The answer is perhaps to be sought in Epicurus' purpose. We have observed Plato in an earlier chapter searching for suitable protreptic means of inducing the Athenians in his day to pursue philosophy, and among these means Plato himself, in the *Protagoras*, experimented with the hedonistic calculus. That pleasure is what human beings by *phusis* pursue is familiar in the sophistic movement, and is present, not merely in the foreground in the *Protagoras*, but in the background throughout the ethical writings of Plato and Aristotle. It is, to say the least, neither an esoteric nor an implausible position: Plato and Aristotle themselves hold that, whatever *ought* to be the case, the majority of mankind are motivated by the desire to gain pleasure and avoid pain; and on the theoretical side, the writings of Plato and Aristotle had neither abolished the books of the sophists nor the diffused effects of their teaching in society. It is easy to suppose, since we know little of the sophists' work – precisely because the Academy and the Peripatetics were so influential as organised philosophical schools – that their teaching very soon ceased to have any effect; but this supposition, particularly where it concerns their more popular and readily transmitted views, is not self-evidently true; and indeed Plato supplies evidence to the contrary: in *Laws* 890A, 891B the antithesis between *phusis* and *nomos* is mentioned as having a great influence on the young, and (891B) it is stated that these views are widely spread throughout all mankind. That pleasure is what men pursue by *phusis*, and accordingly the *agathon*, is a doctrine likely to be attractive in any society; and in Greece it had considerable support from earlier thinkers. It is, strictly, an equation to which Epicurus has no right: that what we pursue by *phusis* is our *agathon*, what is beneficial for us, has teleological implications that are out of place in Epicurus' cosmos; but its protreptic power, when the *agathon* is identified with pleasure, is undeniable. Accordingly, Epicurus has powerful reasons, as a philosopher who wishes to affect the behaviour of others, for promising pleasure, even if the utmost he can in fact fulfil is an absence of pain and fear. It is this, *ataraxia*, that is the real fruit of his philosophical position; but even if his prospective adherents desired both pleasure and *ataraxia*, it is evident that the promise of the former has the greater protreptic effect. This is not to deny that Epicurus and his followers believed these tenets, with their contradictions; it is to point out that the tenets and the contradictions in fact have a function to perform.

Epicurus' use of the word *arete* seems similarly linked to the situation in which he found himself. We have seen him decrying *aretai* as vain and empty, and as raising disturbing hopes of results; and also commending *aretai* as necessary to the life of *ataraxia*. There can be only one solution: these are different kinds of *aretai*, differently evaluated. He is rejecting one *arete*-standard, in which one's performance is reckoned by results, in favour of another: the *aretai* which he explicitly mentions with favour (*Ep. Men.* 132) are living prudently (*phronimōs*), honourably (*kalōs*) and justly (*dikaiōs*). Of these, *phronimōs* and *dikaiōs* are certainly co-operative rather than competitive; *kalōs* by this time may span both, but the whole tenor of Epicurean philosophy renders it most likely that co-operative excellences are in Epicurus' mind here. This is an indication, which will be made more explicit below, that Epicurus is freeing himself and his followers from the competitive results-culture: it is *aretai* that raise disturbing hopes of results, in other words competitive *aretai*, that are vain and empty. (Epicurus is not attacking Stoic values, which have also disengaged themselves from the results-culture, but the persisting traditional competitive values.)

It is to be noted that Epicurus does not deny that the competitive *aretai* are *aretai*: he simply says that they are vain and empty. Greek society is on its way to, or may have already reached, a situation in which there is plurality of values to a higher degree than can be discerned in the extant records of earlier Greece: earlier generations for the most part attempt to add new qualities to *arete*, or the list of *aretai*, rather than rejecting those already held to be *aretai*; and earlier generations certainly did not reject a quality while continuing to term it an *arete*. One result of this is to reduce the emotive power of the word *arete*, now applied to qualities which the speaker does not himself value: Epicurus found it necessary to construct an argument to demonstrate that his favoured *aretai* were choiceworthy, though most people by this time probably termed the co-operative excellences *aretai*.

Stoics, who treated the *aretai* – which for them included the traditional Greek *aretai*, but freed from the tyranny of results – as human excellences *per se*, and indeed made this one of the cornerstones of their view of life, might well be scornful of the Epicurean demonstration that they were merely external means to a desired end, just as they, in their belief that human communities of all kinds resulted from the *phusis* of mankind, which drew human beings to associate with one another, might be scornful of the Epicurean doctrine of social contract and utility. (The Stoic belief resembles Aristotle's view of man as *zōŏn politikon* by *phusis*, though the primacy of the *polis* as a community could no longer be maintained in changed political circumstances.) In Cicero's *De Finibus* (II, 78–9) we find the following attack on the Epicurean position: the Epicurean is imagined as saying that he pursues the useful in human relationships; and the reply is:

> Then your *amicitia*, friendship, will remain as long as usefulness accompanies it; and if usefulness is to establish *amicitia*, then it will destroy it too. What will you do if, as often happens, usefulness departs from *amicitia*? Will you abandon it? What kind of an *amicitia* is that? Will you preserve it? How is that to your advantage? . . . 'I fear I may be hated, if I cease to support my friend.' But why is such action worthy of hatred, unless because it is base?

Amicitia is wider than 'friendship' in English, and covers many other kinds of association; and the argument is relevant to any kind of co-operative relationship. We need not consider the philosophical merits and demerits of the attack here. My point is that if Epicureanism is considered as philosophical analysis, it is open to assault from many directions; but that if it is viewed as an attempt to produce a world-view to meet a new, and difficult, practical situation, the reasons for its contradictions become clearer. (Despite his explanation that social relationships arise from utility, Epicurus, as we have seen, uses language which suggests that the *aretai* are connected by *phusis* with the pleasant life. This powerfully commends the *aretai*; but is incompatible with the assertion that utility is the source of social relationships; for the exercise of the ethical *aretai* presupposes social relationships, and if the *aretai* are connected by *phusis* with the pleasant life, then logically social relationships should also be thus connected.) There need of course be no contradiction between 'pleasure' and 'utility' as criteria: 'useful' can be interpreted as 'serving to maximise pleasure'.

This, in broad outline, is the Epicurean view of man, his nature and his position in the cosmos. Like the Stoic view, it is put forward in the new and disturbing position in which the Greeks found themselves after the change in the scale of the effective political units resulting from the empire of Alexander and the kingdoms of his successors. It is in many ways a very different view from that of the Stoics; but in its choice of goal, *ataraxia*, freedom from disturbance of the *psuche* as compared with *apatheia*, freedom from emotions and passions in the *psuche*, it has a strong resemblance, however different the means to the similar end. I have repeatedly argued that the competitive nature of Greek society, with its emphasis on results, not intentions, was responsible for a low degree of personality structure in Greece, which resulted in the individual's feeling his emotions and passions as something 'over against' his reason, over which his reason had little or no control. Epicurus, as we have seen, speaks (*Ep. Men.* 128) of the tempest of the *psuche*, and holds that this will abate firstly (127–8) if we recognise that only a limited number of desires are *phusikai* and necessary.

This already restricts the need for competition and success; for the objects of such desires are modest (*K.D.* XXI):

> The man who has learned the limits of life knows that it is easy to obtain that which removes the pain resulting from want and makes the whole of life complete; so that there is no need of actions which involve competition.

To obtain the requirements of life, properly understood, competition is unnecessary; and Epicurus also holds (*Ep. Men.* 135) that the prudent man, the *phronimos*, thinks it better to be unfortunate while acting reasonably than to prosper in unreason. Its rationality, not its success, is for him the criterion by which an action is to be judged. It would have been very difficult for an *agathos*, or indeed for any inhabitant, in an independent *polis* to take such an attitude and consistently live by it: the link between successes and the prosperity and stability of both the *polis* and the wealthy household was too evident. Hence a results-culture, reckoning actions in terms of their success and failure, was to be expected in the *polis*; and this entails all the psychological stresses noted in earlier chapters, with their effects. Epicurus, however, is writing neither for the traditional *agathos* nor for the *polis*; and anyone who, in the new situation, lives by the standard set up by Epicurus has escaped from the tensions of a results-culture and has gone far to quiet the tempests of his *psuche*. The criterion of his actions is related to his reason, not to their success; and, however difficult it may be to justify it in terms of Epicurean physics, the reason is given autonomy.

This criterion is within the personality, not external, and should favour the development of a more stable personality structure. This will not appear overnight; but, particularly if he accepts the other Epicurean tenets, the Greek follower of Epicurus should have what Epicurus promised him. I argued in my discussion of the Stoics that the change of scale of Greek life had rendered intolerable the stresses of the results-culture: if *arete* was interpreted as the human excellence that would enable an individual to defend his own, and at least stem the tide of hostile events, the impossible was being demanded, more evidently than in earlier periods considered in this book. The Stoics offered one answer: in the writings of Epicurus we have another.

A further resemblance between Epicureanism and Stoicism lies in the kind of function they assign to the intellect in ensuring the attainment of the goal of calm in the *psuche*, which is related to appropriate behaviour. Plato and Aristotle had both emphasised the need for habituating the individual to act correctly, so that on the basis of this habituation rational ethical action[1] might become possible.

---

[1] Though Plato and Aristotle differed in their account of the situation, above, pp. 162 ff. and 197 ff.

Stoics and Epicureans immediately offer him certain propositions about the nature of the cosmos and himself. Wrong action, for the Stoic, is wrong judgment; right judgment brings *apatheia* and right action. Similarly, for the Epicurean, the correct view of the nature of the cosmos and of man, his desires and true *agatha*, will bring *ataraxia*; and this, it seems, is to be accomplished at least on some occasions by the repetition of maxims to oneself. The *Letter to Menoeceus* ends with the injunction to rehearse these doctrines night and day, both to oneself and with a companion; and the existence of two sets of Epicurean doctrines in maxim form points to the same conclusion.

The reasons for this difference between Stoicism and Epicureanism on the one hand, and the philosophies of Plato and Aristotle on the other, are likely to lie in the different functions and social context of the former. Plato and Aristotle were concerned to delineate a way of life for *agathoi*, a limited class of people in the enclosed environment of a *polis*. In this environment, similarity of 'background', of attitudes and presuppositions in social and cultural as well as strictly ethical matters, was held to be desirable: a number of the Aristoletian *aretai* – and in this Aristotle reflects the usage of his day – are social and cultural rather than ethical. Habituation of the growing *agathos* from childhood upwards in the *polis* would, it was hoped, produce this similarity of attitudes and behaviour, so that, 'when reason was added', Aristotle's[1] mature *agathos* would be able to take an active part in the government of his *polis*, and could act intelligently within the presuppositions of that *polis*,[2] living a life most of whose material circumstances were predictable and definable, along with others of his kind. Stoics and Epicureans, on the other hand, are not concerned

---

[1] Plato is more pessimistic in the *Laws*-state, so that the need for habituation is even more emphasised: the citizens are to be habituated to have the same ethical presuppositions, in order that they may be harmonious members of society. In the *Republic*, earlier, though the philosopher-king will ultimately *know* objective truths of fact, during his training he is only habituated whether into an appropriate emotional response (e.g. *Republic* 376E ff.) or into a 'right opinion' on ethical matters (e.g. *Republic* 466E ff.). Note the importance of learning the right lessons from childhood even in the very physiological account of *Timaeus* 87B (above, p. 142).

[2] Provided he shares the presuppositions, he is capable of intelligent ethical behaviour: he does not need justification for them, in Aristotle's view, *E.N.* 1095b6.

primarily with action, nor specifically with particular classes in society, though I shall suggest that they were likely to appeal broadly to different groups in society. In saying this I am not denying that there is a Stoic or an Epicurean ethic, nor yet that these were important aspects of the philosophies. However, the immediate urgent purpose was to furnish an anchor and a guideline to those tossed by either the actual storms of war without, or the consciousness that events were, even if calm, out of their control, and by the answering storms and stresses within, which were an intensification of those which had always been present. *Eudaimonia* and *autarkeia*, self-sufficiency, had always been the goal, it is true; and we have seen in both Plato and Aristotle that it was in the last resort not possible to demonstrate why one should engage in ethical, or political, activity if intellectual activity rendered one more *eudaimon*.[1] However, in either case the emphasis was upon activity. Now the emphasis is upon release from stress and tension, and the furnishing of a condition which will withstand external buffeting, come what may; and such goals are to be achieved by the entertainment of certain propositions. Now the Stoic proposition that all is at best 'indifferent' save *arete* differs from the Epicurean proposition that pleasure is the *agathon*, and the necessities of life are few and easily obtained; but the disregard which each instils for the traditional external *agatha* is similar. Further, there is a much wider difference between the Stoic doctrine that all is under the control of an *heimarmene* which is at once ineluctable, intelligent and benevolent, and that all that is needed is one's willing co-operation with *heimarmene*, and the Epicurean doctrine that the cosmos is neutral and non-sentient; but they share the same goals.

Again, the Stoic and Epicurean philosophies resemble each other, and differ from Platonism, Aristotelianism and traditional Greek philosophies, in that they are available to all seekers for the goal who can understand the position held; and the broad outlines of the positions are not difficult to understand, though the details of certain aspects of Stoicism are complex in the extreme.

Traditional *arete* was for the few; and those few needed a certain social position to be *agathoi*, to reach the ideal of human existence. The Epicurean goal was open to all; *attainment* of the Stoic ideal was

[1] See above, p. 149 and pp. 202 ff.

for the few, but the way was open to all. Once again there is an extension of the audience in mind, as there was in the age of the first sophists; but whereas then the goal was to render the pupil to whom *arete* had been imparted able to take an active and effective part in his *polis*, now the primary goal is to arm the pupil against the storms without and the storms within.

To this goal Stoic and Epicurean take very different paths. Any attempt to explain this must of course be speculative; but it is of interest to consider the persons likely to be attracted by the two systems. Broadly, the Epicurean is quietist, the Stoic resigned but more active. (*Andreiā*, courage, appears prominently in the Stoic canon of *aretai*, not in the Epicurean.) Each acknowledges that this world's goods come and go: one may not have the resources wherewith to carry on an active life like that of the old *agathos*. But while the Stoic acknowledges this, and treats wealth as an 'indifferent', it is clear that he need not refuse to live an active public life so long as this lay within his power, while not terming this – or indeed life itself – as anything more than an 'indifferent'. The public life of a Greek in his *polis* was now much less important, and might be disrupted by events over which he had no control; but public service was still needed, and a Stoic could justify his taking part in it, whether in his *polis* or, if opportunity offered itself, in a wider sphere, while remaining unmoved by disaster and unelated by success: all was *heimarmene*, and it was his attitude and voluntary co-operation that counted. (He, too, had mitigated the stresses of a results-culture.) An Epicurean, on the other hand, sought his peace by reducing his needs (*K.D.* XV):

> The wealth required by *phusis* is limited and easily obtained; whereas that demanded by empty imaginings reaches to infinity.

This is a philosophy of withdrawal (*K.D.* XIV):

> The purest source of protection from men comes about to some extent by a power of distancing oneself from them,[1] and it is the security which results from a quiet life and departure from (the ways of) the majority of mankind.

The Stoic and Epicurean standpoints are two solutions to the same

[1] Reading *exoristikē*, 'setting over the boundary'.

problem. The choice between them depended doubtless partly on temperament; but possibly in part also on social position. The Stoic philosophy enabled an individual to pursue a political career in circumstances only partly within his control, and indeed, suitably adapted, became the accepted philosophy of the more enlightened members of the governing class at Rome, who had more control over events: it is a philosophy suited to one who regards himself as fit to govern, though it equally suits a private individual. The Epicurean philosophy is for the private individual whose response to the tempests of life is to seek a safe harbour out of the wind, repeating his consolatory maxims to himself, and who, whether from temperament, status or both, would have been unlikely to influence events in any political system. In Epicureanism we have a philosophy, in the sense of a reasoned way of life, suitable for the Greek who was not *agathos* in the traditional sense, and who did not aspire to be.[1]

This raises the last question of this chapter. Epicurus, like Democritus earlier, and the Epicurean Lucretius later, treats fear of the gods and of punishment after death as one of the chief terrors of human existence. However, the articulate Greeks whose ideas are preserved in literature show little fear, in the fifth century or later, of punishment after death; and the articulate Romans are no more afraid on this score. If we confine our attention to these classes and to this topic, it is difficult to understand the prophetic zeal of these writers. We have however little direct evidence of the beliefs of the less articulate Greeks, or of any Greeks whatsoever in the vast majority of Greek *poleis*. We must presumably accept the attitudes of Democritus and Epicurus as being an appropriate response to widespread belief in punishment after death;[2] though it is hard to imagine the *Roman* non-articulate classes picking their way through Lucretius' gnarled hexameters. However, setting aside punishment after death, most Greeks, at least

[1] Compare and contrast Democritus above, p. 111, and p. 252, n. 1.

[2] Plato (*Republic* 330D) represents fear of punishment after death as one that affects only the old; in *Laws* 904D, however, it is treated as being more widespread. Plato, unlike Democritus, Epicurus and Lucretius, has nothing to gain by exaggeration, and presumably is a trustworthy witness; but the absence of the belief from funeral speeches made to mass audiences – where the possibility of reward, at least, might be expected to appear if a considerable proportion of the audience held such a belief – is striking (cf. p. 66, n. 1 above).

in the forms of words they used, ascribed successes and failures in this life to the gods, or gave heaven a share in them; and we must enquire why Epicurus regarded this belief as causing more anxiety than ascription of such events to chance: after all, moderating one's desires in the face of a capricious heaven[1] might seem as effective as moderating one's desires in the face of a capricious chance. (Lucretius' attack makes the point that, in seeking to placate heaven, men have performed wicked acts such as the sacrifice of Iphigenia; but this seems not to be in Epicurus' mind.) A possible answer seems to be that the effort to persuade and placate the gods, personal beings with personal motives,[2] may draw one away from paying proper attention to the circumstances of one's life, and the best way in which one could dispose them in order to ensure one's *ataraxia*: belief in the gods externalises one of the factors on which one's *ataraxia* depends. Chance, not being placable, does not to the same extent divert one's attention from matters which are under one's control; and thus a belief in chance leads the Epicurean more surely to his goal.

---

[1] Even this, as we have seen (above, p. 249) was better than believing in *heimarmene*.

[2] Compare and contrast Plato's ethical objections to the belief that the gods may be persuaded and placated by prayer and sacrifice, *Laws* 905D–907D.

10. Conclusions

It will long have been evident that there is no one Greek view of human nature. Yet the range of variation should not be overstated. Even if the data exhibited little structure, it would be desirable to piece together, so far as possible, the picture that has emerged; but in fact, despite the degree of variability in the views of human nature discussed in the preceding chapters, there is at their heart a common core which seems to hold in relationship the Greek social and political situation, Greek values and Greek psychology; and these, at all events until the coming of Alexander, display only limited variation during the period discussed. It may be helpful to recapitulate the data briefly, drawing no conclusions until all the material is set out.

In Homer, man appears as a dweller in small competitive *oikoi*, in a stratified society in which all, from god to homeless wanderer, have their place, reckoned in terms of *arete* and their share of *time* (status and possessions). The *oikos* needs the *arete* of the *agathos*, his strength, fighting ability and wealth, successfully employed to ensure its prosperity, stability and continued existence. If he is successful, society will commend him as *agathos* and his qualities and way of life as *arete*: if he fails, society will decry him as *kakos* and his qualities as *kakotes*; and these are the most powerful value terms; for it is by results, not intentions, that the *oikos* continues to exist or fails to do so. The *agathos*, accordingly, may at any moment be faced with a categoric demand that he shall successfully achieve what is beyond his powers. No matter what his personal qualities, no matter what his intentions, no matter what his efforts, if they do not lead to success, they, and he, are valueless: he is *kakos*, his situation is *aischron* and entails *elencheie*. The criteria in terms of which his actions are judged are entirely exterior to himself. Above the *agathos* are the gods, more powerful than he, but not omnipotent, nor even much more powerful, to judge by their expressed fears of what men may achieve without the gods' aid; and jealous, malicious, and capricious, at any time likely to interfere in his affairs. Some men have one human, one divine parent, which furnishes a claim to favoured treatment in life. After death, however, even such 'heroes' go down to Hades to twitter among the other *psuchai*: with high status, indeed, in the shame-culture of the dead; but even this lot is inferior to that of the meanest living man. Only Menelaus is offered a better lot after death, as an acknowledgement of his status as son-in-law of Zeus. Even where there is no overt competition, no striving for success or fear of failure, *agathos* and *arete*, the most powerful words in Homeric Greek available to commend human beings, denote and commend status, high birth, and a prosperous way of life, the achievement of which does not rest with the intentions of the individual, particularly in a society so rigidly stratified as that portrayed by Homer. Again, the Homeric poems – and for the moment I simply set down the data side by side – use language which suggests that Homeric man has a highly fragmented psychological, and also physiological, experience. Such words as *thumos*, *kradie* and *etor* are much more in evidence than the personality as a whole, and enjoy a considerable degree of autonomy. Similarly, there is little mention of the body as a whole, much of its parts; and these may be spoken of as initiating action in the same manner as *thumos* and similar psychological phenomena. (Indeed, the distinction between psychological and physiological phenomena is not relevant to the Homeric poems, as has been demonstrated.) Again, the 'spectral balance' is frequently present as a psychological model of the passage from thought to action: the Homeric Greek says 'it seemed better to me. . . .', not 'I decided . . . .'. Furthermore, the gods are often portrayed as initiating human action by 'putting into a man' a drive (or an idea), which again suggests that Homeric man was highly aware of the spontaneous element in his psychological experience; and he is very emotional, and distinguishes between his emotional responses in a manner unfamiliar to us. In fact, it might be said that Homeric man experiences himself as a plurality, rather than a unity, with an indistinct boundary.

The Greeks discussed in chapter 3 have a time-dimension, and a choice of views of human development, aspects of which may have been present to the society in which the Homeric poems developed, but which are nowhere apparent, except insofar as the bards of the tradition treat the heroic period in which the poems were set as one of mightier warriors than now exist (e.g. *Iliad* V, 304). The pessimistic picture of Hesiod's five *gene* contrasts sharply with the optimistic picture of progress, albeit in the face of a hostile Zeus, stated by Aeschylus' Prometheus (despite the fact that Hesiod contrives to fit Prometheus into his view of the world). The separate creation of the different *gene*, and the belief found in other myths that most of mankind were sprung from stones, renders unlikely the development of any concept of human nature in general; and during this period the idea of Greeks and barbarians as groups with sharply opposed qualities is at its strongest. Eschatologically, there are now three views of the lot of man after death: the Homeric belief, the belief that the dead are nearby in their graves, and that of the mystery-cults. The nearby dead, at his most powerful, might be a 'hero'; but the rewards of the mystery-cults, whether for initiation or a just life, promise a far more attractive existence after death to a much larger group of the dead. *Arete* now commends behaviour in a *polis*; but this too is a competing unit among other competing units, more evidently needing the competitive excellences which were held to ensure the prosperity, security, and continued existence of the unit than the co-operative excellences, whose importance was less recognised; and, as becomes even clearer in subsequent chapters, the household in the last resort remains more important than any larger unit, and the need that its head should maintain its prosperity, security and continued existence in a *polis* containing many similar competing units, is still most urgent: *arete*, whether exerted in the interests of *polis* or household, is still competitive, and makes continuous demands that the *agathos* may be unable to satisfy and that, in the wider context of the *polis* at all events, only the *agathos* can satisfy: all others are debarred from the most valued type of action by circumstances beyond their control. *Phusis*, normally rendered by 'nature', becomes important in the fifth century; but human *phusis* differs markedly from what we denote by 'human nature'. *Phusis* denotes the qualities with which an individual is endowed by his birth; but at this period it is unusual to distinguish the genetic inheritance from the social circumstances into which one has been born. All are, in favourable circumstances, commended by *arete*; and *phusis* for the most part reinforces the effects of the use of *arete* and *kakia*. Not necessarily, however, in relationships between men and gods: *arete* draws one on to ever greater efforts, since super-abundance of *arete* might render one divine; but Sophocles, at all events, can contrast our mortal *phusis* with that of the gods, and counsels that one should 'think mortal thoughts'. The effect is likely to have been small. *Arete* is the most powerful word of commendation in the society, and its pull is ever-present; and *phusis* in most contexts has quite different overtones. Sophocles is preaching in this passage, casting his words against the prevailing flow of Greek competitive values, which *phusis* at this period helps to reinforce. *Psuche* now begins to be the core and carrier of personality. (The choice of this word may have been encouraged precisely by its previous colourlessness.) There is more core than in Homer; but there are indications that it is not yet very far developed.

The Presocratic philosophers are concerned with the reality of the cosmos which lies behind appearances. The earlier writers are reported to have used *phusis* of this reality; the later Presocratics certainly did so. Such reality exhibits sequences of necessary causation. The Presocratics analyse human beings in terms of the basic building-blocks of their theories, but seem not to draw any conclusions which affect human free will. When they speak of human *phusis*, it seems always possible to act against its requirements where action is concerned: its inevitabilities are concerned with growth, change, death and decay. Human *phusis* now begins to be distinguished from nurture and environment, but frequently in a manner unfamiliar to us: some individuals have abilities which are innate in the sense that they would reach full development without training; but other people could be trained to have these abilities; and it is the person who does not possess these qualities by *phusis* that must learn. *Arete* is still affecting *phusis*. The goal of learning is to become *agathos*; and in this society *agathoi* are traditionally *agathoi* by birth. Such have their *arete* (a concept as yet unanalysed) by birth, by *phusis*: *phusis*, though frequently rendered 'nature', does not in these writers denote natural qualities by whose exercise one might rise in a socially stratified *polis*, but the qualities as a whole of those who are by birth *agathoi* (or *kakoi*). Nor is there any other Greek word for human 'nature': *phusis*, with all its overtones and associations, was the only word available to the society. *Psuche*, whose presence distinguishes a living specimen from a dead one, however the distinction is analysed and explained, receives explanations in terms of the general cosmologies of these thinkers. The explanations are 'materialist', but in this resemble non-philosophic thought: the distinction between material and non-material has not yet been drawn. The distinction between *soma* (body) and *psuche*, however, now receives great emphasis. This is most evident in Pythagoreans and others who believe in the trans-migration of the *psuche*, but is important even to the atomists, who believe in the dispersal of the *psuche* at death. The *psuche* is the more highly valued by all: it is the carrier of the intellect, and this is an intellectual movement.

The early doctors, too, are concerned with *phusis* and *psuche*. They disagree on the extent to which the general *phusis* of the cosmos, as opposed to the *phusis* of the individual patient, should be studied. They agree in treating the *psuche* as material, and are professionally interested in the manner in which its, and the body's, well-being is related to diet and regimen. They are inevitably aware that patients differ in their response to treatment; and even doctors who lay empha-sis on the importance of understanding the general *phusis* of the cosmos ascribe this difference of response to the differing *phusis* of particular individuals. Doctors as a profession have more inducement than any other group to distinguish the inherent characteristics of the patient, or of all patients, from what is merely extrinsic; and the doctors' use of *phusis* relates to the physiological characteristics of the patient, both those which he shares with all other human beings and those which are peculiar to himself.

Among the early moral philosophers and sophists, Democritus agrees with the doctors in emphasising differences between the *phusis* of different individuals, and also in linking *euthumia*, which is or depends on the well-being of the *psuche*, with prudent behaviour, in not attempting to exceed the limitations imposed by one's *phusis*. For Antiphon and other sophists, however, *phusis* knows no limitations, and is opposed to the limits of *nomos*. *Phusis* demands the fullest satisfaction of all 'natural' desires for gratification and power. Only an exceptional individual can achieve this without suffering reprisals; hence only an exceptional individual can live according to *phusis*. This *phusis* is assumed to be the same in all, and to be what truly exists, as opposed to the mere conventions of men: one may ignore the demands of *phusis*, but to do so will be to one's detriment, even if other men approve, whereas ignoring the decrees of *nomos* will do one no harm, if one can avoid retribution from other men. The opposition of truth to convention seems derived from the Presocratic opposition of *phusis*, the reality of the cosmos, to what we perceive with our senses. The view of human *phusis* as the same for all may be derived from, or encouraged by, medical thought no less than the view of *phusis* as differing from one individual to the next: medical investigations reveal not only differences between patients, but also what is common to all. Such emphasis might have stimulated – there are signs of it in Antiphon – the development of a view of human nature that transcends race. The usual result is to emphasise differences of status; for the social and political situation, and the implications of Greek values, still had their part to play. *Phusis* draws attention to the basic needs and drives of men; but no doctor, naturally enough, deduces from man's possession of a stomach by *phusis* that *phusis* demands that the stomach's gratification must be maximised at all times, as some sophists do. It is *arete*, commending 'human nature at its best', that urges the individual to succeed in his enterprises and maximise his gratifications; and *arete* colours the use of *phusis* by the 'immoralist' sophists and their pupils. The sophists' view of human *phusis*, accordingly, is affected not only by medical and philosophical thought, but by the value-structure of Greek society. Such sophists do not suggest that one cannot act against *phusis*, merely that anyone who had the opportunity to express his *phusis* would do so, and indeed would be ill-advised not to do so. Athenian society remains a shame- (or results-) culture essentially; and the same tensions are present as in earlier periods. The picture of human decision remains calculative as it has been since Homer; with the proviso that, as in Homer, it is a calculation of desirables, and the situation is instinct with emotion. Where desires are inhibited, it is the unity represented by the personal pronoun that inhibits them. However, there are indications that such inhibition might be notably difficult. A persistent analysis sets the ebb and flow of emotion and desire in the foreground, with little sign of any well-developed core of personality: the spectral balance, which has also been present since Homer, is much in evidence.

This suggests that a firmly structured personality has still not developed.

Plato intensifies the opposition of *soma* to *psuche* by making the immortality of the latter one of the cornerstones of his philosophy. (To take this view need not in Plato, any more than in earlier writers, give cohesion to the *psuche* in itself; and Plato's analysis of action emphasises the contending 'parts' of the *psuche*.) All *psuche* enjoys a higher order of reality than the sensible world: there is now a contrast between material and non-material; but human *psuche* is now distinguished from *psuche* in general by the requirement that the human *psuche* must have glimpsed the Forms. Plato emphasises the variety of human *phusis* more than any earlier extant writer. Like earlier thinkers, he continues to ascribe to *phusis* much that we should ascribe to nurture and environment: in his view, as in that of some Presocratics and sophists, certain attributes, good or bad, may be the result either of *phusis* or of training; and he even appears to hold that one may acquire by training a better *phusis* which one may transmit genetically to one's descendants. (Here the aristocratic Plato may be drawing on contemporary theories of stockbreeding.) Plato's ethical revaluation enrols the co-operative excellences among the *aretai*; and this might have been expected to mitigate the strains of competition. However, Plato could only justify their enrolment by demonstrating that they were as necessary to the prosperity, stability and continued existence of the unit as the traditional competitive *aretai*. It does not suffice to have good intentions based on one's ethical presuppositions: the action must succeed in being objectively just and so beneficial to the unit, and to oneself. The criteria of the good co-operative moral act are now set completely 'outside' the agent's intentions, as those of competitive *arete* have always been. An expert, a kind of *psuche*-doctor, is needed to ensure the well-being of the *psuche*. Again, the Platonic mythology explicitly sets beyond the individual's control many aspects of his life: the extent to which he has glimpsed the Forms, for example, seems to set an irremovable ceiling on his aspirations. Plato's philosophy leaves the determinants of human action certainly no more within human control than did the views of the 'ordinary Greek' of the period; and he evaluates human action in terms of them. In his earlier dialogues, the ability of the reason to control the passions and desires is emphasised; but even in the *Republic* this seems to be doubted, and its prominence earlier may have a protreptic aim: in the *Laws*, Plato is concerned to condition what is little more than a bundle of discrepant and conflicting desires.

Aristotle's view of *psuche* is more complex and detailed than Plato's. The *psuche* is the form of the creature, and only 'fits' that creature. Human *psuche* only 'fits' human beings, and indeed its own particular human being: it subsumes animal and plant *psuche* within itself. Transmigration of *psuchai* is thus impossible, and indeed *psuche* in general perishes with the creature of which it is the form; but Aristotle regards the active reason as immortal, though it has no personal immortality, having no memory. Aristotle's account of *psuche* does not, any more than Plato's, give unity to the human *psuche* in analysis of ethical decisions and behaviour, in which the *psuche* frequently appears less 'real' than its conflicting 'parts'. *Phusis*, for Aristotle, is teleological, so that its condition by *phusis* is the best state of a creature, of which statements may be true which are not true until that state is reached. (Aristotle's view of human *phusis*, that man is 'by *phusis* a creature who lives in a *polis*', is evidently culturally determined, and related to the traditional – post-Homeric – Greek, and to his own, view of *arete*, human nature at its best, each of which is inextricably linked with life in a *polis*.) There are tensions and discrepancies in Aristotle's account of human action. He sometimes writes in such a way as to suggest the unity of the *psuche* in action, in which the desires obey the reason, this being possible even for those who have not yet attained to a good ethical *hexis*; but in many analyses, and those some of his most radical, the *psuche* seems to dissolve into its 'parts', and the spectral balance appears, even more starkly than in Homer. Aristotle has two views of *eudaimonia*, the life of 'theoretic' and the life of practical *arete*, the latter being inferior, and choiceworthy only insofar as *theoria* is unattainable for a particular individual, either altogether or at a particular time. For Aristotle, the co-operative excellences are *aretai*, and have not the 'logic' of the competitive excellences; but the *agathos* must possess all the Aristotelian *aretai*, and could not do so unless he had considerable possessions. *Eudaimonia* does not now consist in external *agatha*, as had been the case in the fifth century[1] and remained the case for those who were not philosophers or influenced by them: external *agatha* are not sufficient; but for anyone who is to live an active life in a *polis* they are a necessary condition of *eudaimonia*. *Eudaimonia* is the goal, and Aristotle, try as he will, cannot render it independent of the buffets of fortune. Some of one's *eudaimonia* depends on one's ethical *hexis*, and on one's consequent choices and intentions in ethical matters; and Aristotle holds that these are within the power of the individual to control, or at least that he is responsible for his ethical behaviour. That such behaviour at its best is a manifestation of *arete* must diminish tensions to some extent; but the tensions associated with the dependence of *eudaimonia* and *arete* as a whole on external *agatha* remain.

The Stoics and Epicureans are faced with a new situation, in which the importance of the *polis* is much reduced.

The Stoics use *phusis* in a variety of ways: they are concerned with the *phusis* of the cosmos and that of the individual, and also term *phusis* what Aristotle termed the 'plant' or 'nutritive' *psuche* of the individual plant, animal or human being. Since the *phusis* of the cosmos interpenetrates everything, the *phusis* of the individual is merely an aspect of the *phusis* of the cosmos; but *phusis* as 'plant' *psuche* is a highly specialised usage. The Stoic *psuche* is Aristotle's 'animal' *psuche*, *phusis* with the addition of imagination and desire or impulse; while the human being has intelligence in addition. The *phusis* of the cosmos and that of the individual in the wider sense are at the same time *heimarmene*, fate, and also *pronoia*, providence, God and fire. (The Stoics are materialists, and by choice, since Plato's and Aristotle's *psuchai* are non-material.) Determinism is thus combined with benevolent providence; and *arete* consists in voluntary co-operation with providence, which would drag one along willy-nilly anyway. *Eudaimonia* is still the goal, *arete* essential thereto, as in Aristotle, Plato, and 'ordinary Greek', however the interpretations might differ; but *eudaimonia* is completely internalised, and consists altogether in

---

[1] As an indication of the predominance of the overtones of material prosperity in the usage, see *Medea* 598 f., where Medea says 'May I never have a *eudaimon bios* – i.e. prosperity – which is painful to me, nor an *olbos* – a synonym for *eudaimonia* – which grieves my mind.' These lines are at once an implied criticism of the purely materialistic standard of *eudaimonia* and an acknowledgment that this is the normal usage of the word.

arete. If one is *agathos*, then, come what may, success or disaster, one is *eudaimon*: nothing else, even life itself, is more than 'indifferent'. Tensions arising from emphasis on the successful result of an action thus vanish; and the Stoic is explicitly promised *apatheia*, an end to the tumults of his *psuche*, as a result of his beliefs and attitudes.

The Epicurean has a very different view of the cosmos. For him, *phusis* is the dance of the atoms in the void. There are gods, but they care nothing for human beings. The *psuche* is an agglomeration of very small atoms, dispersed at death; which is not to be feared, for we do not experience it until it comes, and when it does come we experience neither it nor anything else. The needs that we have by *phusis* are few and easily satisfied. (This view of *phusis* is derived from earlier medical and philosophical thought: it cannot be deduced from the dance of the atoms in the void.) If we know these things, we can readily attain to *eudaimonia*, and indeed become *makarioi*, blessed. There is no need for competition, for the few *agatha* we need are not such as to require competition to secure them; and furthermore, the prudent man thinks it better to be unfortunate while acting reasonably than to prosper in unreason. Anyone who holds such views has escaped from the results-culture and its stresses and strains; and Epicurus promises *ataraxia*, freedom from tumult and disturbance, to those who follow the way of life, and hold the beliefs, that he recommends.

The foregoing paragraphs are the merest outline of some of the contents of this book, and are naturally not meant to stand or fall by themselves. I have merely set down some of the data side by side, as a reminder to the reader before a conclusion is drawn. To me, at least, the conclusion seems clear. It is the conclusion that I have set down in the several chapters: from Homer to Aristotle the characteristic portrayal of Greek personality which we find in surviving documents appears to be far more fragmented than that which we regard as normal; or rather, the characteristic Greek personality seems not to have developed so firm and stable a structure as that which we regard as normal, for the egocentred personality develops during the individual's life in an environment that favours such development: it is not the case that Greek culture, or any other culture that has similar characteristics and tendencies, has disrupted a previously existing and harmonious whole. Furthermore, this failure to develop an ego-centred personality seems closely linked with the structure and values of Greek society, which necessarily externalise the criteria of action and render intentions of little account. If this is so, not only was the Athenian *polis*, as I attempted to show in an earlier work, even in the late fifth century a democracy only in the most curious sense, since, despite its extreme democratic institutions, its values were highly undemocratic and it judged and acted on the basis of those values: it was also a type of society which of its very nature exposed the individual to such stresses and strains as to inhibit the development of a firm personality structure, and to render likely, particularly in prominent *agathoi*, erratic instability and even sudden onsets of madness. The achievements of the Greek *polis*, and of Athens in particular, were outstanding; but it appears likely that they were bought at a high price. Paradoxically, it is only with the loss of importance of the *polis*, regarded by the earlier Greeks as being the only milieu in which *eu zen*, *eudaimonia*, the *agathos bios*, the good life, was possible, that any solution appears. The strains of traditional values in an unfamiliar and larger context become so evidently impossible to endure that in their different ways the Stoics and Epicureans are drawn to construct views of the world and systems of values which remove their adherents from the results-culture and, as Stoics and Epicureans themselves contend, render possible *apatheia* and *ataraxia*, an end of the storm and tumult of the *psuche*: a condition in which the development of a more stable personality should be rendered possible.

Appendix

Brief notes on the ancient authors who appear in this work

(This list is intended merely to locate the authors in space and time, for the benefit of the reader who has not previously studied the period. For further information such readers should consult next the various Dictionaries of Antiquities, Classical Dictionaries and Handbooks.)

Aeschylus (525/4–456 B.C.) The first of the three great Attic tragedians. Of about eighty plays known to us by their titles, seven are extant: *Suppliants, Persae, Seven against Thebes, Prometheus Bound*, and the *Oresteia* trilogy, *Agamemnon, Choephori* and *Eumenides*. The order of composition is disputed, but raises no questions relevant to the present work.

Aëtius (first or second century A.D.) His summary of the views of the Greek philosophers on natural philosphy survives only in the epitomes of others, but is one of our most important sources for the views of the Presocratic philosophers.

Alcaeus (born *c.* 620 B.C.) Lyric poet of Mytilene in the Aegean island of Lesbos. His works survive only in fragments.

Alexander of Aphrodisias (*floruit* early third century A.D.) The ablest and most famous of the Greek commentators on Aristotle. (Aphrodisias was a town in Caria, in the south-western corner of Asia Minor.)

Alexis (*c.* 372–270 B.C.) Though born at Thurii, a Greek city in Lucania in southern Italy, he became a comic dramatist of the Middle Comedy at Athens. His work survives only in fragments.

Anaxagoras (*c.* 500–*c.* 428 B.C.) Presocratic philosopher of Clazomenae, an important Greek city on the coast of Asia Minor. He is said to have been the first philosopher to reside in Athens, having arrived in 480 B.C., possibly in the train of the Persian army of invasion, and to have remained there for about thirty years.

Anaximander (born 610 B.C.) Presocratic philosopher of Miletus, a prosperous Greek city on the coast of Asia Minor. He is said to have written the first Greek treatise in prose, about 546 B.C.

Anaximenes (*floruit c.* 546 B.C.) Presocratic philosopher of Miletus. He was possibly a pupil of Anaximander.

Antiphon the Sophist (*floruit* in the later fifth century B.C.) Sophist, of Athens. He is termed Antiphon the Sophist to distinguish him from Antiphon the Orator, though some scholars hold that the two are in fact the same person.

Antisthenes (*c.* 455–*c.* 360 B.C.) Pupil of Socrates, whose austerity of life he imitated. See the introduction to chapter 8 for his possible influence on Zeno of Citium and subsequent Stoics.

Appendix

Apollodorus of Athens (born *c.* 180 B.C.) The Bibliotheca, or Library, an uncritical compendium of Greek mythology, is traditionally ascribed to Apollodorus of Athens, but in fact belongs to the first or second century A.D., and is of unknown authorship.

Apollodorus of Seleucia (second century B.C.) Stoic philosopher, author of an *Ethics* and *Physics*. (Seleucia was an important city on the Tigris, founded as the capital of his empire by Seleucus I about 312 B.C.)

Archelaus (fifth century B.C.) Presocratic philosopher, probably an Athenian. A pupil of Anaxagoras, he is said to have had Socrates as a pupil at one period.

Archilochus (eighth or seventh century B.C.) Iambic and elegiac poet, of the Aegean island of Paros. The extant fragments of his work vividly reveal an individual personality, one of the earliest accessible to us in Greek literature.

Ariston (third century B.C.) Stoic philosopher from the Aegean island of Chios, pupil of Zeno of Citium, from whom he differed in making no distinction, in the realm of the indifferent, between *prŏēgmena* and *apoprŏēgmena*, holding that one should be completely indifferent to them all.

Aristophanes (*c.* 450–*c.* 385 B.C.) The most famous writer of Attic Old Comedy, and the only one of whose plays some (eleven) have survived complete. His extant works (in order of production) are *Acharnians, Knights, Clouds, Wasps, Peace, Birds, Lysistrata, Thesmophoriazusae, Frogs, Ecclesiazusae,* and *Plutus.*

Aristotle (384–322 B.C.) Philosopher, born at Stagirus in Chalcidice. His early dialogues survive only in fragments: all his extant work, apart from the *Constitution of Athens* (if this is genuine) belongs not to his published writings, but to what appear to be memoranda in some way related to his lectures.

Chrysippus (*c.* 280–207 B.C.) Stoic philosopher from Soli, a city on the coast of Cilicia, in the south-east of Asia Minor, who succeeded Cleanthes as head of the Stoa. He greatly elaborated the doctrines of Stoicism, and his philosophy, which differed in some respects from that of his predecessors, was regarded subsequently as Stoic orthodoxy.

Cicero (106–43 B.C.) Marcus Tullius Cicero, Roman statesman, barrister, orator and theorist of oratory. His chief claim to importance in the history of philosophy rests on his having preserved the thoughts of others which are not preserved elsewhere; but his experience as lawyer and statesman may have furnished him with data from which he enriched the casuistry of the Greek ethics on which he draws.

Cleanthes (331–232 B.C.) Stoic philosopher from Assos, a city in the Troad, opposite to the island of Lesbos, pupil of Zeno of Citium and his successor as head of the Stoic school from 263 to 232 B.C. He infused religious fervour into Stoicism: his hymn to Zeus is the best known of his works.

Critias (*c.* 460–403 B.C.) Athenian aristocrat, one of the thirty tyrants at Athens at the end of the Peloponnesian War, related to Plato on Plato's mother's side. He was associated with Socrates and the sophists, and his writings show marked sophistic influence.

Appendix

Democritus (*c.* 460–*c.* 370 B.C.) Presocratic philosopher of Abdera, a Greek town in Thrace, and an atomist like his master Leucippus. He was a voluminous writer, and differed from many of the Presocratics in that he interested himself in ethical questions.

Demosthenes (384–322 B.C.) The greatest of the Athenian orators. In his public speeches he attempted to spur the Athenians to a more effective and active policy against Philip of Macedon.

Diogenes of Apollonia (*floruit c.* 440 or *c.* 430 B.C.), a Presocratic philosopher. Apollonia in Crete or Apollonia in Phrygia may have been his birthplace.

Diogenes Laertius, a writer of about the first half of the third century A.D. The title of his work is 'History of Philosophy; or on the lives, opinions and apophthegms of famous philosophers'. It is in itself a work of indifferent quality: its importance lies in the fact that most of our knowledge of the lives of the ancient philosophers is derived from it.

Diogenes of Seleucia (*c.* 240–152 B.C.) Stoic philosopher, pupil of Chrysippus, succeeded Zeno of Tarsus as head of the Stoic school. He visited Rome in 156/5 B.C., and excited interest in Stoicism there. Panaetius was his most famous pupil. (For Seleucia, see Apollodorus of Seleucia.)

Dionysius of Heraclea (*c.* 328–248 B.C.) Stoic writer, little of whose extensive works now survives. (Heraclea was a city on the Pontus, in northern Asia Minor.)

Empedocles (*c.* 493–*c.* 433 B.C.) Presocratic philosopher of Acragas in Sicily. The fragments of his works show him to have combined in himself elements of nature-philosopher, poet and miracle-worker.

Epicharmus (fifth century B.C.) A writer of comedy from Syracuse in Sicily.

Epicurus (342/1–271/70 B.C.) Athenian atomist philosopher in the tradition of Democritus, and founder of the Epicurean school.

Euenus (fifth century B.C.) Poet and sophist from the Aegean island of Paros. He gave metrical expression to the rules of rhetoric.

Euripides (485?–406? B.C.) The youngest of the three great Attic tragedians. Of his plays nineteen (if the *Rhesus* is genuine) are extant. They are thus arranged in the Oxford Classical Texts edition (there is some dispute about the chronological order of their production): vol. I, *Cyclops, Alcestis, Medea, Heraclidae, Hippolytus, Andromache, Hecuba*; vol. II, *Suppliants, Heracles, Ion, Troades, Electra, Iphigenia in Tauris*; vol. III, *Helen, Phoenissae, Orestes, Bacchae, Iphigenia at Aulis, Rhesus*. Euripides was an intellectual sponge: his plays reflect the intellectual and ethical discussions and conflicts of his own day, for which they are a valuable source.

Gorgias (*c.* 483–376 B.C.) Sophist and rhetorician of Leontini in Sicily. He founded, and taught, artistic prose style, and his visit to Athens in 427 B.C. had a profound effect on the development of Attic prose.

Heraclitus (*floruit c.* 500 B.C.) Presocratic philosopher of Ephesus, an important Greek city in Asia Minor, renowned for his obscurity. His epistemology influenced Plato, while his cosmology was the basis for that of the Stoics.

Appendix

Herillus (third century B.C.) Stoic philosopher from Carthage, pupil of Zeno of Citium. He seems to have regarded knowledge as more important than the life of moral *arete*.

Herodotus (born *c.* 485 B.C.) 'The Father of History.' Born in Halicarnassus, an important city in Asia Minor. His history of the Persian Wars ranges widely over the history, geography and customs of the then known world, in addition to treating of the Ionian Revolt and the campaigns of Marathon, Thermopylae, Salamis and Plataea. Herodotus' own framework of value and belief is traditional, but he incorporates 'sophistic' material (for example, the debate on the best form of constitution, III, 80 ff.) into his work.

Hesiod (eighth century B.C.) Didactic poet from the foothills of Helicon, in Boeotia. His *Works and Days* contains practical advice on farming, an agricultural calendar, and moral precepts. His *Theogony* is an attempt to give order and coherence to the anarchic confusion of Greek mythology.

Hippasus (fifth century B.C.) Presocratic philosopher, an early Pythagorean, from Metapontum, a famous Greek city in Lucania, on the gulf of Taranto.

Hippocratic Corpus. A body of medical writings traditionally attributed to Hippocrates of Cos. It is possible that none is by Hippocrates himself, and certain that not only more than one author, but more than one school of medicine, is represented. The Corpus appears to be a collection of the best medical writing of the fifth and fourth centuries B.C.

Hippon (fifth century B.C.) Also called Hipponax. A Presocratic philosopher of the Periclean period, probably from the Aegean island of Samos.

Hipponax (*Hornit* 540–537 B.C.) Iambic poet of Ephesus from which he was banished and went to Clazomenae. (Both cities are on the coast of Asia Minor.)

'Homer'. It is now generally agreed, at all events by English-speaking and French scholars, that the Homeric poems stand at the end of a long development of oral poetry employing a formulaic technique. 'The Homeric poems' are now confined to the *Iliad* and *Odyssey*. The phrase leaves open questions of authorship, whether of the whole or the parts, all of which have in any case to be restated in the light of the discoveries of Milman Parry and his followers concerning oral composition. The poems preserve material of very different dates, but in the picture they give of Homeric ethics and psychology they are on the whole homogeneous.

Leucippus (*floruit c.* 440 B.C.) Presocratic philosopher from Miletus, an important Greek city on the coast of Asia Minor. He was the originator of the atomic theory, of which he is said to have laid down the broad outlines, while the details were worked out by Democritus.

Lucretius (94?–55? B.C.) Titus Lucretius Carus, Roman poet and follower of Epicurus, whose doctrines he expounded in his didactic poem *De Rerum Natura*, a work which gains its philosophical importance from the fragmentary nature of Epicurus' extant works.

Mimnermus (*floruit* 632–629 B.C.) Elegiac poet of Colophon, a Greek city in Asia Minor, north-west of Ephesus. He is best known for the extant fragments of poems on the fleeting pleasures of youth and the horrors of old age.

Panaetius (c. 185–109 B.C.) Stoic philosopher, born in Rhodes. From Athens, where he received his education, he visited Rome in about 144 B.C., became a member of the 'Scipionic Circle' (a group of philhellene Romans who gathered round P. Cornelius Scipio Aemilianus), and played an important part in introducing Stoicism to Rome.

Parmenides (fifth century B.C.) Presocratic philosopher of Elea, a Greek town in Lucania on the west coast of southern Italy, who had a considerable influence on Plato.

Philolaus (fifth century B.C.) Presocratic philosopher, a Pythagorean. He was a contemporary of Socrates.

Pindar (518–438 B.C.) Lyric poet from Cynoscephalae in Boeotia. The most famous Greek lyric poet, represented in his surviving work largely by *Epinīkia*, or victory-odes. These odes contain not only narration and praise of the victor's achievements but also, and frequently at much greater length, myths, moral maxims and praise of the gods. Some of Pindar's *Thrēnoi*, or Laments for the Dead, survive in fragments. The fragments appear in different orders in different editions: the numbering used in this work is that of the Oxford Classical Text.

Plato (c. 429–347 B.C.) Athenian philosopher. His published works, some twenty-five dialogues, and the *Apology of Socrates*, are extant, together with thirteen letters, concerning whose authenticity – and that of a few minor dialogues – there has been much argument. The earliest dialogues are 'aporetic', and lead to no solution. Plato's two longest works are the *Republic*, the major dialogue of his middle period, and the *Laws*, possibly his last work. Plato does not appear as a participant in the dialogues, the chief role in the majority of them being taken by Socrates, with the result that it is very difficult to distinguish the contribution of Socrates to philosophy from that of Plato in the early dialogues. Plato is certainly a philosopher in his own right before the composition of the works of his middle period, but it is not until the latest works that the convention that Plato is merely setting down the words of his master Socrates is dropped, Socrates' place being taken by the Athenian Stranger.

Plutarch (c. 46–after 120 A.D.) Philosopher and biographer, of Chaeronea in Boeotia. He was primarily an Academic in philosophy, though his – far from carefully integrated – position is eclectic. In his attacks on the Stoics he preserves much material which throws light on Stoic doctrines.

Posidonius (c. 135–c. 51/50 B.C.) Stoic philosopher of Apamea in Syria. He studied at Athens under Panaetius, and later settled in Rhodes. The inhabitants of Rhodes sent him as an ambassador to Rome in 87 B.C. In 78 B.C. Cicero attended Posidonius' school in Rhodes.

Protagoras (fifth century B.C.) Sophist, of Abdera, a Greek city in Thrace, best remembered for his dictum 'Man is the measure of all things'.

Sappho (born c. 612 B.C.) Poetess, of the Aegean island of Lesbos.

Appendix

Seneca (Lucius Annaeus Seneca), Seneca the Younger, born at Corduba (Cordova) in Spain, but taken to Rome as a child. He had a prominent public career, marked by abrupt vicissitudes, which he did not bear with the Stoicism which he professed, and in his moral works expounded.

Simonides (*c.* 556–468 B.C.) Lyric and elegiac poet, born at Iulis in the Aegean island of Ceos.

Sophocles (*c.* 496–406 B.C.) Second of the three great Attic tragedians. Of the 123 plays he is said to have written, seven are extant: *Ajax, Electra, Oedipus Tyrannus, Antigone, Trachiniae, Philoctetes* and *Oedipus at Colonus.* Of these the last two show most signs of the 'New Thought', which commands Sophocles' overt disapproval, though the mental ferment associated with it evidently directed Sophocles' attention to new themes, and enabled him in the *Oedipus at Colonus* to solve a pressing ethical problem.

Stobaeus (probably fifth century A.D.) Anthologist. His works are useful in that they contain many citations from earlier literature.

Thales (sixth century B.C.) The first of the Presocratic philosophers, from Miletus, an important Greek town on the coast of Asia Minor.

Theognis, or the Theognid Corpus. Theognis' *floruit* is 544–541 B.C., but l. 894 of his work refers to the Cypselids, whose rule ended in about 580 B.C., as still in power, while 773–82, a prayer to Apollo to keep the Medes away from Megara, cannot have been written much before 490 B.C., at which date the Persian threat became apparent. Furthermore, the poems attributed to Theognis as we have them contain a number of lines also attributed to other authors. 'Theognis' seems to be a collection of poems, on ethical, political, social and amatory themes, in elegiac couplets, mostly of the sixth century B.C.

Thrasymachus (*floruit c.* 430–400 B.C.) Sophist and rhetorician of Chalcedon, at the entrance to the Bosphorus. Fragments of his work survive. His fame now rests primarily on Plato's portrait of him in the first book of the *Republic.*

Thucydides (born probably between 460 and 455 B.C., died about 400 B.C.) Athenian historian of the Peloponnesian War. He is deeply influenced by the 'New Thought' of the sophists, and also by medical thought; and in general rejects mythological elements and divine causation from his work.

Tyrtaeus (seventh century B.C.) Elegiac poet, of Sparta. Most of the extant fragments are warlike exhortations. He led the Spartans as general in the Second Messenian War, and helped to capture Messene.

Xenophanes (born *c.* 570 B.C.) Presocratic philosopher and poet, of Colophon, a Greek city in Asia Minor, north-west of Ephesus. Only fragments of his poems survive: these criticise traditional belief in the Olympian gods and traditional social values; and advance physical theories, and a belief in a non-anthropomorphic deity.

Xenophon (*c.* 430–*c.* 354 B.C.) of Athens, soldier, historian and pupil of Socrates, whose views, as he understood them, or as he wished them to be understood, he set forth in his *Memorabilia, Apology, Oeconomicus* and *Symposium.*

Zeno of Citium (335–263 B.C.) Philosopher, founder of the Stoic school. (Citium was a town in Cyprus.)

Zeno of Elea (born *c.* 490 B.C.) Pupil and friend of Parmenides. He is best known for his paradoxes concerning motion, including 'Achilles and the tortoise' and 'the flying arrow'. (For Elea, see Parmenides.)

Zeno of Tarsus (third and second centuries B.C.) Stoic philosopher, successor of Chrysippus as head of the Stoic school in 204 B.C. (Tarsus was the chief city of Cilicia, in south-eastern Asia Minor.)

Select Bibliography

(The following is not intended to be a comprehensive bibliography of any aspect of the subject. It contains no learned articles, and only a selection of the available books, chosen, so far as I have been able, to furnish a variety of views and approaches to the topics discussed. It is my hope that it may be of some service to students and to non-specialist readers. I have included no translations, save in the case of the Presocratics (F.7) and Epicurus (K.1), where the non-specialist might otherwise experience great difficulty in finding an English translation. Translations of most of the authors discussed in this book are readily available, frequently in paperback. The Greekless reader desirous of pursuing further for himself the questions raised here would be well advised to learn at least the Greek alphabet – a task whose difficulty is frequently exaggerated by those who have not attempted it – and then consult the translations of the Loeb or Budé series, where a page of English or French respectively is faced by the original Greek, so that he may ascertain whether a particular Greek word was or was not used by the author he is studying.)

A. *Anthropology and Psychology*

Adler, A., *Understanding Human Nature*, tr. by Wolfe, W. B., New York 1927.
—— *The Practice and Theory of Individual Psychology*, tr. by Radin, P., 2nd edn., London 1950.
Barbu, Z., *Problems of Historical Psychology*, London 1960.
Benedict, R., *The Chrysanthemum and the Sword; Patterns of Japanese Culture*, Boston 1946.
—— *Patterns of Culture*, 2nd edn., Boston 1959.
Blum, G. S., *Psycho-analytic Theories of Personality*, New York 1953.
Boas, F., *General Anthropology*, Boston 1938.
Boer, W. de, *Das Problem des Menschen und die Kultur: neue Wege der Anthropologie*, Bonn 1958.
Bonaparte, M. (*Princesse*), *Psychanalyse et Anthropologie*, Paris 1952.
Brand, H. (*ed.*), *The Study of Personality*, New York and London 1954.
Caplan, B. (*ed.*), *Studying Personality Cross-culturally*, Evanston, Ill., 1961.
Chapple, E. D., and Coon, C. S., *Principles of Anthropology*, New York 1942.
Chase, S., *The Proper Study of Mankind*, rev. edn., New York 1956.
Cohen, Y. A., *Social Structure and Personality; a Casebook*, New York 1961.
Coon, C. S., *A Reader in General Anthropology*, New York 1948.
Evans-Pritchard, E. E., *Social Anthropology and Other Essays*, New York 1964.
Fortes, M. (*ed.*), *Social Structure: Studies presented to A. R. Radcliffe-Brown*, Oxford 1949.

Bibliography

Freud, S., *The Complete Introductory Lectures on Psycho-analysis*, tr. and ed. by Strachey, J., New York 1966.
—— *Civilization and its Discontents*, tr. by Riviere, J., London 1949.
—— *Totem and Taboo*, tr. by Strachey, J., New York 1950.
—— *The Ego and the Id*, tr. by Strachey, J., New York 1960.
Gernet, L., *Anthropologie de la Grèce Antique*, Paris 1968.
Guntrip, H. J. S., *Personality Structure and Human Interaction: the Developing Synthesis of Psycho-Dynamic Theory*, New York 1961.
Healy, W., *The Structure and Meaning of Psychoanalysis as related to Personality and Behaviour*, New York 1930.
Herskovits, M. J., *Man and his Work: the Science of Cultural Anthropology*, New York 1948.
Honigmann, J. J., *Culture and Personality*, New York 1954.
Hsu, F. L. K. (*ed.*), *Aspects of Culture and Personality: a Symposium*, New York 1954.
Jung, C. G., *The Undiscovered Self*, tr. by Hull, R. F. C., Boston 1908.
—— *Psychology of the Unconscious*, tr. by Hinkle, B. M., New York 1916.
—— *Collected Papers on Analytical Psychology*, ed. by Long, C. E., London 1916.
—— *Psychological Types; or, The Psychology of Individuation*, tr. by Baynes, H. G., London and New York 1923.
—— *Man in search of a Soul*, tr. by Dell, W. S., and Baynes, C. F., New York 1933.
—— *The Integration of Personality*, tr. by Dell, S. M., New York and Toronto, 1939.
—— *The Interpretation of Nature and the Psyche*, New York 1955.
Kluckhohn, C., and Murray, H. A. (*ed.*), *Personality in Nature, Society and Culture*, 2nd edn., New York 1953.
Kroeber, A. L., *Anthropology: Race, Language, Culture, Psychology, Prehistory*, New York 1948.
Levi-Strauss, C., *Structural Anthropology*, tr. by Jacobson, C., and Schoepf, B. G., New York 1963.
—— *Le Cru et le Cuit: Mythologies*, Paris 1964.
—— *The Savage Mind*, Eng. trans., London 1966.
Lewin, K., *A Dynamic Theory of Personality; Selected Papers*, tr. by Adams, D. K., and Zener, K. E., New York and London 1935.
Lienhardt, G., *Social Anthropology*, 2nd edn., London and New York 1966.
Linton, R., *The Cultural Background of Personality*, New York 1945.
McCary, J. L. (*ed.*), *Psychology of Personality; Six Modern Approaches*, New York 1959.
Malinowski, B., *A Scientific Theory of Culture and Other Essays*, Chapel Hill 1944.
—— *Sex and Repression in Savage Society*, London 1927.
Mead, M. (*ed.*), *Cooperation and Competition among Primitive Peoples*, enlarged edn., Boston 1961.

Murphy, G., *Personality; a Biosocial Approach to Origins and Structure*, New York 1947.

Sanford, N., *Self and Society: Social Change and Individual Development*, New York 1966.

Shapiro, H. L., *Man, Culture and Society*, 2nd edn., New York 1960.

Smelser, N. J., and Smelser, W. T. (*edd.*), *Personality and Social Systems*, New York 1963.

Sontag, L. W., and others, *Personality Formation*, New York 1951.

Stavenhagen, K., *Person und Personlichkeit: Untersuchungen zur Anthropologie und Ethik*, Göttingen 1957.

Venable, V., *Human Nature: the Marxian View*, London 1946.

Wallace, A. F., *Culture and Personality*, New York 1961.

B. *Philosophy and Semantics*

Anscombe, G. E. M., *An Introduction to Wittgenstein's Tractatus*, 2nd edn., London 1963.

Black, M., *Language and Philosophy: Studies in Method*, Ithaca 1949.

—— *A Companion to Wittgenstein's Tractatus*, Ithaca 1964.

—— *The Labyrinth of Language*, New York 1968.

Carnap, R., *Introduction to Semantics and Formalization of Logic*, Harvard 1959.

Christensen, N. E., *On the Nature of Meanings; A Philosophical Analysis*, Copenhagen 1965.

Cohen, L. J., *The Diversity of Meaning*, 2nd edn., London 1966.

Emmet, D. M., *Function, Purpose and Powers*, London 1958.

Fogelin, R. J., *Evidence and Meaning*, London 1967.

Hallett, G., *Wittgenstein's Definition of Meaning as Use*, New York 1967.

Morris, C. W., *Signification and Significance*, Massachusetts Institute of Technology 1964.

—— *Signs, Language and Behaviour*, New York 1946.

Nesbit, F. F., *Language, Meaning and Reality; a Study of Symbolism*, New York 1955.

Ogden, C. K., and Richards, I. A., *The Meaning of Meaning; a Study of the Influence of Language upon Thought and of the Science of Symbolism*, London and New York 1923.

Quine, W. V. O., *Word and Object*, Massachusetts Institute of Technology 1960.

Reiss, S., *The Universe of Meaning*, New York 1953.

Sherwood, J. C., *Discourse of Reason: a Brief Handbook of Semantics and Logic*, New York 1960.

Sondel, B. S., *The Humanity of Words; a Primer of Semantics*, Cleveland 1958.

Vendler, Z., *Linguistics in Philosophy*, Ithaca 1967.

Wittgenstein, L., *Tractatus Logico-Philosophicus*, in German with English translation by Pears, D. F., and McGuinness, B. F., London and New York 1961.

—— *Philosophical Investigations*, tr. by Anscombe, G. E. M., 2nd edn., New York 1958.

Bibliography

C.

(This section contains a selection of works, whose themes range beyond those of the individual chapters of this book, chosen to furnish more vantage-points from which to survey Greek views of human nature.)

Adkins, A. W. H., *Merit and Responsibility: a Study in Greek Values*, Oxford 1960. (In this work I offer fuller discussions of the basic concepts of Greek values than space permits in the present work.)

Andrewes, A., *The Greeks*, London 1967.

Baldry, H. C., *The Unity of Mankind in Greek Thought*, Cambridge 1965.

Dodds, E. R., *The Greeks and the Irrational*, Berkeley 1951.

Gouldner, A. W., *Enter Plato*, New York 1965. (The first part of this work is devoted to Greek thought and attitudes before Plato.)

Jaeger, W., *Paideia*, tr. by Highet, G., 3 vols., New York 1949.

Kitto, H. D. F., *The Greeks*, Harmondsworth 1951.

Snell, B., *The Discovery of the Mind*, tr. by Rosenmeyer, T. G., Oxford 1953.

Vernant, J.-P., *Mythe et Pensée chez les Grecs; Études de Psychologie Historique*, Paris 1965.

D. Chapter 2

Allen, T. W., *Homer; the Origins and Transmission*, Oxford 1924.

Böhme, J., *Die Seele und das Ich im homerischen Epos*, Leipzig 1929.

Bowra, C. M., *Tradition and Design in the Iliad*, Oxford 1930.

Chadwick, H. M., *The Heroic Age*, Cambridge 1912.

Finley, M. I., *The World of Odysseus*, London 1956, New York 1965.

Hainsworth, J. B., *The Flexibility of the Homeric Formula*, Oxford 1968.

Kirk, G. S., *The Songs of Homer*, Cambridge 1962.

—— *Homer and the Epic* (shortened version of the above), Cambridge 1965.

Lesky, A., *Göttliche und menschliche Motivation im homerischen Epos*, Heidelberg 1961.

Lord, A. B., *The Singer of Tales*, Harvard 1960.

Lorimer, H. L., *Homer and the Monuments*, London 1950.

Onians, R. B., *The Origins of European Thought about the Body, the Mind, the Soul, The World, Time & Fate*, Cambridge 1951.

Page, D. L., *History and the Homeric Iliad*, Berkeley 1959.

—— *The Homeric Odyssey*, Oxford 1955.

Parry, M., *L'Epithète Traditionelle chez Homère*, Paris 1928.

Wace, A. J. B., and Stubbings, F. H., *A Companion to Homer*, London and New York 1962.

Webster, T. B. L., *From Mycenae to Homer*, 2nd edn., London 1964.

E. Chapter 3

Abbott, G. F., *Thucydides, a Study in Historical Reality*, London 1925.

Bibliography

Andrewes, A., *The Greek Tyrants*, London 1956.

Bowra, C. M., *Early Greek Elegists*, Harvard 1938.

—— *Sophoclean Tragedy*, Oxford 1944.

—— *Greek Lyric Poetry from Alcman to Simonides*, 2nd rev. edn., Oxford 1961.

Burn, A. R., *The Lyric Age of Greece*, New York 1960.

Conacher, D., *Euripidean Drama; Myth, Theme and Structure*, Toronto 1967.

Cornford, F. M., *Thucydides Mythistoricus*, London 1907.

Deubner, L., *Attische Feste*, Berlin 1952, reissued with corrections and bibliography 1966.

Finley, J. H., Jr., *Thucydides*, Harvard 1942.

—— *Pindar and Aeschylus*, Harvard 1955.

Flacelière, R., *La Vie Quotidienne en Grèce au Siècle de Périclès*, Paris 1959.

Freeman, K., *The Life Work of Solon; with a Translation of his Poems*, Cardiff and London 1926.

Greenwood, L. H., *Aspects of Euripidean Tragedy*, Cambridge 1953.

Grube, G. M. A., *Drama of Euripides*, London 1941.

Grundy, G. B., *Thucydides and the History of his Age*, 2nd edn., Oxford 1948.

Guthrie, W. K. C., *Orpheus and Greek Religion*, London 1935.

—— *The Greeks and their Gods*, London 1950.

Harrison, J. E., *Themis; a Study of the Social Origins of Greek Religion*, Cambridge 1912.

—— *Prolegomena to the Study of Greek Religion*, Cambridge 1908.

—— *Epilegomena to the Study of Greek Religion*, Cambridge 1921, New York 1962.

Kern, O., *Die Religion der Griechen*, 3 vols., Berlin 1926.

Kirkwood, G. M., *A Study of Sophoclean Drama*, Ithaca 1958.

Kitto, H. D. F., *Greek Tragedy*, London 1939.

—— *Form and Meaning in Drama*, London 1956.

—— *Sophocles, Dramatist and Philosopher*, London 1958.

Linforth, I. M., *Solon the Athenian*, Berkeley 1919.

—— *The Arts of Orpheus*, Berkeley and Los Angeles 1941.

Long, A. A., *Language and Thought in Sophocles*, London 1968.

Moore, J. A., *Sophocles and Arete*, Harvard 1938.

Moulinier, L., *Le Pur et l'Impur dans la Pensée des Grecs*, Paris 1952.

Myres, Sir John, *Herodotus, Father of History*, Oxford 1953.

Nilsson, M. P., *Griechische Feste*, tr. by Rose, H. J., Oxford 1948.

Norwood, G., *Pindar*, Berkeley 1945.

Opstelten, J. C., *Sophocles and Greek Pessimism*, tr. by Ross, J. A., Amsterdam 1952.

Powell, J. E., *The History of Herodotus*, Cambridge 1939.

Rivier, A., *Essai sur le Tragique d'Euripide*, Lausanne 1944.

Rohde, E., *Psyche; the Cult of Souls and the Belief in Immortality among the Greeks*, London and New York 1925.

288

Bibliography

Romilly, J. de, *Thucydide et l'Impérialisme Athénien*, Paris 1947.
—— *L'évolution du Pathétique d'Eschyle à Euripide*, Paris 1961.
Solmsen, F., *Hesiod and Aeschylus*, Ithaca 1949.
Thomson, G. D., *Aeschylus and Athens; a Study in the Social Origins of Greek Drama*, 2nd edn., London 1946.
Ure, P. N., *The Origin of Tyranny*, Cambridge 1922.
Vandvik, E., *The Prometheus of Hesiod and Aeschylus*, Oslo 1943.
Walcot, P., *Hesiod and the Near East*, Cardiff 1966.
Waldock, A. J. A., *Sophocles the Dramatist*, Cambridge 1951.
Webster, T. B. L., *An Introduction to Sophocles*, Oxford 1936.
—— *Greek Interpretations*, Manchester 1942.
—— *The Tragedies of Euripides*, London 1967.
Whitman, C. H., *Sophocles; a Study of Heroic Humanism*, Harvard 1955.
Wilamowitz-Moellendorf, U. von, *Sappho und Simonides*, Berlin 1913.
—— *Pindaros*, Berlin 1922.
—— *Der Glaube der Hellenen*, Berlin 1931–32.
Woodhouse, W. J., *Solon the Liberator*, London 1938.

F. *Chapter 4*

Burnet, J., *Early Greek Philosophy*, 4th edn., London 1930 (in paper, New York 1960).
Cleve, F. M., *The Giants of Pre-sophistic Greek Philosophy, An Attempt to reconstruct their Thoughts*, The Hague 1965.
Cornford, F. M., *From Religion to Philosophy*, London 1912.
—— *Before and after Socrates*, Cambridge 1932.
—— *Principium Sapientiae*, Cambridge 1952.
Diels, H., and Kranz, W., *Fragmente der Vorsokratiker*, 10th edn., Berlin 1952.
Freeman, K., *Ancilla to Diels*, Oxford 1948 (English translation with notes of all extant fragments of the Presocratics, which constitute Section B of each part of Diels).
—— *The Presocratic Philosophers*, a companion to Diels, *Fragmente der Vorsokratiker*, 3rd edn., Oxford 1953.
Guthrie, W. K. C., *A History of Greek Philosophy*, Vols. I–III, Cambridge 1962–69.
—— *In the Beginning; some Greek Views on the Origins of Life and the Early State of Man*, Ithaca 1957.
Jones, W. H. S., *Philosophy and Medicine in Ancient Greece*, Baltimore 1946.
Kirk, G. S., and Raven, J. E., *The Presocratic Philosophers, a Critical History with a Selection of Texts*, 2nd edn., Cambridge 1960.
Martiny, M., *Hippocrate et la Médecine*, Paris 1964.
Parker, G. F., *A Short Account of Greek Philosophy from Thales to Epicurus*, London 1967.

Bibliography

Pohlenz, M., *Hippokrates und die Begründung der wissenschaftlichen Medizin*, Berlin 1938.

Regnéll, H., *Ancient Greek Views on the Nature of Life*, Lund 1967.

Weidauer, K., *Thukydides und die Hippokratischen Schriften, Der Einfluss der Medizin auf Zielsetzung und Darstellungsweise des Geschichtwerks*, Heidelberg 1954.

Zeller, E., *Presocratic Philosophy*, tr. by Alleyne, S. F., 2 vols., London 1881.

G. *Chapter 5*

Dupréel, E., *Les Sophistes, Protagoras, Gorgias, Prodicus, Hippias*, Neuchâtel 1948.

Gomperz, H., *Sophistik und Rhetorik*, Leipzig 1912.

Gomperz, Th., *Greek Thinkers*, Vol. I, tr. by Magnus, L., London and New York 1901.

Heinimann, F., *Nomos und Physis*, Basel 1945.

Hirzel, R., *Agraphos Nomos*, Leipzig 1903.

Thimme, O., *Physis, Tropos, Ethos*, Quakenbrück 1935.

Untersteiner, M., *The Sophists*, tr. by Freeman, K., New York 1954.

H. *Chapter 6*

Bluck, R. S., *Plato's Life and Thought*, London 1949.

Brumbaugh, R. S., *Plato for the Modern Age*, Crowell-Collier 1962.

Chaignet, A.-Ed., *De la Psychologie de Platon*, Paris 1862.

Crombie, I. M., *An Examination of Plato's Doctrines*, 2 vols., New York 1962.

Festugière, A. J., *Contemplation et Vie Contemplative chez Platon*, Paris 1936.

Field, G. C., *The Philosophy of Plato*, Oxford 1949.

Friedländer, P., *Plato*, 3 vols., tr. by Meyerhoff, H., New York 1958–69.

Frutiger, P., *Les Mythes de Platon*, Paris 1930.

Gould, J., *The Development of Plato's Ethics*, Cambridge 1955.

Grube, G. M. A., *Plato's Thought*, London 1935.

Hager, F.-P., *Die Vernunft und das Problem des Bösen im Rahmen der Platonischen Ethik und Metaphysik*, Bern and Stuttgart 1963.

Hall, R. W., *Plato and the Individual*, The Hague 1963.

Hardie, W. F. R., *A Study in Plato*, Oxford 1936.

Lodge, R. C., *Plato's Theory of Ethics*, New York 1928.

—— *Plato's Theory of Education*, London 1947.

Mugler, C., *La Physique de Platon*, Paris 1960.

O'Brien, M. J., *The Socrates Paradoxes and the Greek Mind*, Chapel Hill 1967.

Reinhardt, K., *Platons Mythen*, Bonn 1927.

Robinson, R., *Plato's Earlier Dialectic*, 2nd edn., Oxford 1962.

Ross, Sir D., *Plato's Theory of Ideas*, Oxford 1957.

Ryle, G., *Plato's Progress*, Cambridge 1966.

Solmsen, F. E., *Plato's Theology*, Ithaca 1942.

Bibliography

Stewart, J. A., *The Myths of Plato*, London 1905.
Taylor, A. E., *Plato: the Man and his Work*, New York 1936.
Wild, J., *Plato's Theory of Man*, Harvard 1948.

I. Chapter 7

Allan, D. J., *The Philosophy of Aristotle*, London 1952.
Bambrough, R. (*ed.*), *New Essays on Plato and Aristotle*, New York 1965.
Barker, Sir Ernest, *Political Thought of Plato and Aristotle*, London 1906.
Charlesworth, M. J., *Aristotle on Art and Nature*, Auckland 1957.
Cherniss, H., *Aristotle's Criticism of Plato and the Academy*, Vol. I, Baltimore 1944.
Grene, M., *A Portrait of Aristotle*, London 1963.
Hamburger, M. E., *Morals and Law; the Growth of Aristotle's Legal Theory*, New Haven 1951.
Hantz, D., *The Biological Motivation in Aristotle*, New York 1939.
Jaeger, W., *Aristotle*, 2nd English edn., Oxford 1948.
Mure, G. R. G., *Aristotle*, London 1932.
Randall, J. H., Jr., *Aristotle*, New York 1960.
Robin, L., *Aristote*, Paris 1944.
Ross, Sir David, *Aristotle*, 5th edn., London 1956.
Rüsche, F., *Blut, Leben und Seele*, Paderborn 1930.
Solmsen, F., *Aristotle's System of the Physical World*, Ithaca 1960.
Stigen, A., *The Structure of Aristotle's Thought. An Introduction to the Study of Aristotle's Writings*, Oslo 1966.
Stocks, J. L., *Aristotelianism*, London 1925.
Taylor, A. E., *Aristotle*, London 1943.
Veatch, H. B., *Rational Man. A Modern Interpretation of Aristotle's Ethics*, Bloomington 1962.
Walsh, J. J., *Aristotle's Conception of Moral Weakness*, New York 1963.
Woodbridge, F. J. E., *Aristotle's Vision of Nature*, New York 1965.

J. Chapter 8

Arnim, H. von, *Stoicorum Veterum Fragmenta*, 4 vols., Leipzig 1903–14.
Bevan, R., *Stoics and Sceptics*, Oxford 1913.
Bréhier, E., *The History of Philosophy, The Hellenistic and Roman Age*, tr. by Baskin, W., Chicago 1965.
Dyroff, A., *Die Ethik der alten Stoa*, Berlin 1890.
Edelstein, L., *The Meaning of Stoicism*, Harvard 1966.
Grumach, E., *Physis und Agathon in der alten Stoa*, Berlin 1932.
Guillermit, L., and Vuillemin, J., *Le Sens du Destin*, Neuchâtel 1948.
Hicks, R. D., *Stoic and Epicurean*, New York and London 1910.
More, P. H. E., *Hellenistic Philosophies*, Princeton 1923.

Bibliography

Moreau, J., *L'âme du Monde de Platon aux Stoiciens*, Paris 1939.

Pohlenz, M., *Die Stoa*, Göttingen 1948–55.

Rieth, O., *Grundbegriffe der stoischen Ethik*, Berlin 1933.

Rodier, G., *Histoire extérieure et intérieure du Stoicisme*, in *Études de Philosophie grecque*, Paris 1926.

Simon, H., and Simon, M., *Die alte Stoa und ihr Naturbegriff*, Berlin 1956.

Stein, L., *Psychologie der Stoa*, Berlin 1886–88.

Virieux-Reymond, A., *La Logique et l'Épistemologie des Stoiciens*, Chambéry 1950.

Vogel, C. J. de, *Greek Philosophy*, Vol. III, Leiden 1959.

Watson, G., *The Stoic Theory of Knowledge*, Belfast 1966.

K. *Chapter 9*

Bailey, C., *Epicurus, the Extant Remains*, with Short Critical Apparatus, Translation and Notes, Oxford 1926.

—— *The Greek Atomists and Epicurus*, Oxford 1928.

Bignone, E., *L'Aristotele Perduto e la Formazione Filosofica di Epicuro*, Florence 1936.

Farrington, B., *The Faith of Epicurus*, Amsterdam 1966.

Festugière, A. J., *Épicure et ses Dieux*, Paris 1946.

Furley, D. J., *Two Studies in the Greek Atomists*, Princeton 1967.

Grilli, A., *Il Probleme della Vita Contemplativa nel Mondo Greco-Romano*, Milan and Rome 1953.

Guyau, M., *La Morale d'Épicure*, 2nd edn., Paris 1881.

Joyau, E., *Épicure*, Paris 1910.

Merlan, P., *Studies in Epicurus and Aristotle*, Wiesbaden 1960.

Oates, W. J. (ed.), *The Stoic and Epicurean Philosophers*, New York 1940.

Stradach, G. K., *The Philosophy of Epicurus*, Evanston, Ill., 1963.

Witt, N. W. de, *Epicurus and his Philosophy*, London 1954.

Zeller, E., *The Stoics, Epicureans and Sceptics*, tr. by Reichel, O. J., London 1892.

Index Locorum

Figures in brackets refer to footnotes

293

Index Locorum

ANTIPHON THE SOPHIST (Diels-Kranz)

Index Locorum

General Index

Figures in brackets refer to footnotes

305

Index

Rebuking, in Homer, see *Neikeiein*.
Reincarnation, 65 f., 99, 133 ff.
Religion, Greek, 49, 73 f., 218, 264 f.
Responsibility, 26 f., 121 ff., 163,
    167, 190 ff., 218 f., 227 ff., 230 ff.,
    249 f., 253 f., 255 f.
Results *versus* intentions, 11 f.; in
    Homer, 28 ff., 40 ff.; in traditional
    writers, 78 f., 89 f., 213 ff.; in
    sophists, 126; in Plato, 158 ff.,
    167 f.; in Aristotle, 206 ff.; in the
    Stoics, 225 ff., 228 ff., 233 ff.; in
    the Epicureans, 259 ff.
Results-culture, in Homer, 29 ff.,
    42 ff.; in traditional writers, 74 ff.,
    89 f.; in Plato, 166 f.; in Aristotle,
    206 ff.; in Stoics, 238 f., 263; in
    Epicurus, 257 ff.

Sapiens, and the Stoics, 228.
Science, Greek, 49 f., 91 ff.
Science, modern, and Epicurus, 245.
Self-sufficiency, 28 ff., 74 ff., 95, 110,
    203 ff., 248 f.; see also *Autarkeia*.
Seneca, 229 f.
Sensation, and the four elements, 99.
Sense-experience, 135, 243.
Shame, see *Aideisthai*, *Aischron*,
    Aischūnē, *Elencheiē*.
Shame-culture, in Homer, 31 f.,
    42 ff.; in fifth-century Athens,
    138 (1); in Plato, 166 f.; among
    the dead, in Homer, 35; in
    fifth-century Athens, 66 ff.
Slaves, and Aristotle, 179 f., 209 ff.
Sleep, and *akrasiā*, 191.
Snell, B., ix, 21, 23.
Society, and the individual, 1 f.; in
    Homer, 28 ff., 40 ff.; in traditional
    writers, 74 ff., 83 ff.; in sophists,
    110 ff., 113 ff., 117 f.; in Plato,
    143 ff., 148 ff., 151 ff., 155 ff.,
    158 ff.; in Aristotle, 170 f., 181 ff.,
    199 ff., 202 ff., 205 ff., 209 ff.; in
    the Stoics, 213 ff., 224 ff., 230,
    231 ff., 236 f.; in Epicurus, 250 ff.,
    258 f., 261 f., 263 f.

Sōma, in Homer, 21; in Thucydides,
    64; in atomists, 100, 243; in
    doctors, 106 ff.; in Plato, 129 ff.,
    137 ff., 139 ff., 158 (1).
Sophiā, and Xenophanes, 74 ff.; in
    Bacchae, 88; in Plato, 149; in
    Aristotle, 202; in the Stoics, 228.
Sophists, 91, 110 ff., 137 f., 138, 143,
    270 f.
Sōphrōn, 115, 188 (1), 195.
Sōphrosunē, 115, 120; not an *aretē*
    during most of fifth century, 124;
    and Aristotle, 187 f.
'Soul', see *psūchē*.
Specialisation, in Plato, 151.
Spectral balance, 271; in Homer, 24,
    46 f.; in traditional writers, 126;
    in Aristotle, 195.
'Spirit', in Homer, see *Menos*,
    Thūmos.
'Spontaneity', and Homeric
    psychology, 26, 46; and the
    Homeric bard, 60 f.
Structure, psychological, 275 f.; in
    Homer, 46 ff.; in traditional
    writers, 61 ff., 89 f.; in sophists,
    126; in Plato, 167 f.; in Aristotle,
    206 ff.; in Stoics, 237 f.; in
    Epicurus, 260 f.
Success, see Results.
Suicide, and Stoics, 226; and
    Epicurus, 247.
Swerve, of atoms, 243, 255.

Target, and Aristotelian ethics,
    186.
Technē, 138, 159 f.; and the Stoics,
    220.
Theology, Greek, 49, 202 f.
Theōriā, 202 ff., 208 f., 253.
Thrasymachus, 111 (1), 117, 143,
    149, 254.
Threats, in Homer, see *Apeilein*.
Thūmoeides, 133, 152.
Thūmos, 5, 7; in Homer, 14 ff., 22 ff.,
    44 ff., 267; and Medea, 124; in
    Aristotle, 175 f.

311

Index